CUBA

MICHELIN
Travel Publications

Cub. ang. 1

Note to readers

To understand how the guide is organised, turn to the contents list on page 4.

Just one point here about the practical information. The chapter entitled "Practical Information" gives general information to help you prepare your trip and get along once there. In the chapter "Exploring Cuba", after each description of a town or tour itinerary there is a practical section (eg page 145 "Making the most of Havana") giving all the information about the place in question: access, useful addresses, accommodation, eating out, other things to do, shopping guide, etc.

The tour itineraries described and shown on the maps give ideas for excursions off the beaten track; ■ indicates possible overnight halts.

Cuba's tourist currency has become the US dollar (US$). Hotels and restaurants are classed by price category (in US dollars) to help you plan your budget. However, we are obliged to point out that living costs vary constantly and opening hours are subject to modification, so that prices and practical information may have changed since publication.

Michelin Travel Publications
Published in 2000

◄ N E ⊙ S ►

N ew – In the NEOS guides emphasis is placed on the discovery and enjoyment of a new destination through meeting the people, tasting the food and absorbing the exotic atmosphere. In addition to recommendations on which sights to see, we give details on the most suitable places to stay and eat, on what to look out for in traditional markets and where to go in search of the hidden character of the region, its crafts and its dancing rhythms. For those keen to explore places on foot, we provide guidelines and useful addresses in order to help organise walks to suit all tastes.

E xpert – The NEOS guides are written by people who have travelled in the country and researched the sites before recommending them by the allocation of stars. Accommodation and restaurants are similarly recommended by a ☕ on the grounds of quality and value for money. Cartographers have drawn easy-to-use maps with clearly marked itineraries, as well as detailed plans of towns, archeological sites and large museums.

⊙ pen to all cultures, the NEOS guides provide an insight into the daily lives of the local people. In a world that is becoming ever more accessible, it is vital that religious practices, regional etiquette, traditional customs and languages be understood and respected by all travellers. Equipped with this knowledge, visitors can seek to share and enjoy with confidence the best of the local cuisine, musical harmonies and the skills involved in the production of arts and crafts.

S ensitive to the atmosphere and heritage of a foreign land, the NEOS guides encourage travellers to see, hear, smell and feel a country, through words and images. Take inspiration from the enthusiasm of our experienced travel writers and make this a journey full of discovery and enchantment.

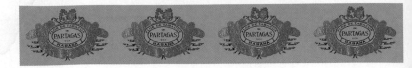

CUBA

Official name: Republic of Cuba
Area: 110 922 sqkm
Population: about 11 000 000
Capital: Havana
Currency: the Cuban peso; but
the US dollar is in general use

Setting the scene

A mogote in the
Viñales Valley

A LONG GREEN LIZARD

"In the sea of the Antilles
Also called Caribbean,
Beaten by waves
And polished by foam,
Burnished by the sun
And embossed by the wind,
Eyes filled with tears, but singing,
Cuba straddles the map:
A long green lizard,
Eyes of water, eyes of stone."

Nicolás Guillén *(A Long Green Lizard)*

Cuba is by far the largest of the Caribbean islands. A neighbour of Haiti (77km away) and Jamaica (140km), Cuba projects westward into the Gulf of Mexico, halfway between Florida to the north (180km) and Mexico itself (210km). This strategic location led the Spanish conquistadors to call the country "the key to the Gulf", and Cuba's fate has long been tied to its sensitive geographical position.

Excluding the 1 600 keys and islands strung along its long coastline, Cuba has a total area of 110 922sqkm, about half that of Great Britain. Its great length – some 1 250km from east to west – compared with its width – 190km at its widest point and a mere 31km at its narrowest – earned it Nicolás Guillén's epithet *"long green lizard"*.

A land of plains and mountains

Cuba is basically a lowland country with some two thirds of its area consisting of extensive plains. But there are mountain ranges too, in the centre of the island, in the west, and at its easternmost point. Together with the Camagüey plain, these *sierras* make up the country's four main natural regions.

Geological foundations

Cuba's geological history seems to have begun in early Jurassic times. These ancient metamorphic rocks were subsequently overlaid by calcareous deposits to the north and volcanic sediments to the south. The island was subjected to continual tectonic movements followed by periods of erosion right up to Pliocene times, when the dramatic uplift affecting the whole of Latin America took place. Subsequent erosion left few traces apart from the famous **Yunque** (anvil), the table mountain overlooking Baracoa in the easternmost part of the country. When the climate warmed up in the Quaternary period about a million years ago, Cuba began to take on its present outline. Sea level rose, submerging much of the lowland area, the outer limits of which are marked by today's islands, keys and reefs. Splendid natural harbours, like those at Havana and Santiago, were formed when valleys were drowned by the rising waters.

One of the country's most remarkable features are **"mogotes"**, the strangely shaped limestone mountains in the Pinar del Río area, karstic formations resulting from the action of underground rivers.

Western Cuba

See map p. 158

Cuba's western extremity is formed by the long, thin **Guanahacabibes peninsula**, a marshy and virtually uninhabited area protruding into the Yucatan Channel. Its magnificent array of lagoons and caves are a UNESCO designated Biosphere Reserve.

To the east, the **Guaniguanico cordillera** straddling the provinces of Pinar del Rio and Havana consists of two mountain ranges of contrasting character. The **Sierra de los Órganos** is a landscape of rounded hills separated by fertile plains. In the beautiful **Viñales valley**, the rugged limestone cones known as *mogotes* in Spanish and haystack hills in English rise dramatically from the dead flat floor of the plain, while the surrounding area is threaded with caverns and underground rivers.

Beyond San Diego de los Baños the hills give way to a parallel range of real mountains, the **Sierra del Rosario**, which reach their highest point in the Pan de Guajaibón (699m) to the northeast of the Güira Natural Park.

The northern coast is bordered by the unspoiled beaches and mangrove swamps of the *cayos* (keys or islets) which make up the **Colorados Archipelago**.

To the south of the mountains is a vast plain, crossed by the muddy courses of several sluggish rivers. Rice is cultivated here, but the best known part of the area is the **Vuelta Abajo** to the southwest of Pinar del Rio since it is here that the island's finest tobacco plantations are found, producing the raw material for famous Havana cigars.

The plain extends eastwards as far as the boot-shaped **Zapata peninsula** *(see map p. 206)*, a vast area of wetlands in the southern part of Matanzas province. In the past, the peaty soil of the region provided a living for charcoal-burners, but since the Revolution, much of the area has been drained and converted into citrus plantations.

Central Cuba

See map p. 206

Consisting more or less of the former Las Villas province, this region comprises the *municipios* (districts) of Cienfuegos, Villa Clara, Sancti Spíritus and Ciego de Ávila. To the east of the Zapata peninsula rises the Guamuhaya range, more commonly known as the **Sierra del Escambray**. About 80km in length, the range is dominated by the peak of San Juan (1 140m). Sugar plantations and tobacco fields occupy the valley floors, while coffee is grown on the mostly calcareous soils of the lower slopes. Artificial lakes *(embalses)* at Zaza and Hanabanilla offer excellent trout fishing.

To the north, low-lying hills give way to coastal plains. A few miles offshore, the **Sabana archipelago** is made up of countless *cayos*, keys or islands.

The Camagüey area

The area covered by the *municipios* of Camagüey, Las Tunas and Holguín is the flattest in the country, a vast plain with savannah-like vegetation and very few watercourses. This arid landscape, extending as far as the eye can see, is largely given over to cattle-raising, particularly in the area around Camagüey, which is known for its dairy products. To the north, the Sierra de Cubitas rarely rises above 300m. Clay soils provide the raw material for *tinajones*, the water jars which are the symbol of Camagüey. The northern shoreline is bordered by the islands of the **Camagüey archipelago** and by a 400km long coral reef, the second longest in the world after the Great Barrier Reef.

A land of plains and mountains

13

Eastern Cuba
See map p. 262

The mountainous eastern part of the country consists of the provinces of Granma, Santiago de Cuba and Guantánamo. Lowlands are limited in extent, consisting of an area around Guantánamo on the south coast and along the course of the Cauto, Cuba's longest river (343km), north of Bayamo.

Straddling the provinces of Granma and Santiago de Cuba, the **Sierra Maestra** runs for 250km along the southern coastline, rising to 1 972m at **Pico Turquino**, the highest point in Cuba. The southern flank of the sierra drops almost vertically into the Caribbean into the 7 000m deep Cayman Trench.

Further mountain ranges like the **Sierra del Cristal** and the Sagua-Baracoa highlands occupy the north of the region. Part of the latter massif, the **Sierra del Purial** has an exceptionally diverse landscape, varying from the arid, cactus-clad countryside of its southern slopes to the coconut groves of the north which thrive in the abundant tropical rainfall.

The eastern extremity of the island is marked at **Punta de Maisi** by high cliffs of porous rock. This remote and arid area has become even more inaccessible since the bridge over the Yumurí river was destroyed.

Climate

Cuba's subtropical climate is hot and humid with a limited annual temperature range – an average 22°C in winter and 27°C in summer. Because the island is so narrow there is little temperature variation between the coast and the interior. However, diversity of relief creates **distinct local climates** in a number of places; in Oriente winters are milder and summers hotter, the Baracoa area has a high rainfall, and nights are cooler in the mountains.

What is known as the **"dry" season** occurs in winter (November to April), while the **"wet" season** (May to October) is characterised by frequent, short storms. **Hurricanes** may occur in September and October. The coolest and driest months are January and February. Though the temperature rarely falls below 20°C, this is the time when Cubans complain about *frentes fríos* (cold fronts), and watch with amazement as foreign tourists splash around happily in the sea, the temperature of which has dropped to 24°C (compared with 28°C in summer). But as the thermometer rises in July and August, no Cuban is able to resist the lure of the beach.

A long green lizard

ABUNDANT NATURE

Over the centuries, human activity has had a dramatic effect on the forests which once covered most of Cuba. A number of native animals have either been hunted out of existence or, like many plant species, have disappeared as a result of deforestation. Only in 1990 did any sort of coherent conservation policy begin to emerge, when the country adopted a series of environmental protection measures on signing up to the International Convention on Trading in Protected Species Threatened with Extinction.

Wildlife and conservation

Unlike its neighbours in South America, Cuba has hardly any animal species which pose a danger to human beings. Because the country is an island it has relatively few large mammals. However, there is a very large number of endemic species; among the 19 600 animals native to Cuba there are about 600 vertebrates of which almost a third are unique to the island.

Animal life

Apart from a few exotic animals, like the zebras and antelopes imported into Cayo Saetía, Cuba has few large carnivorous or herbivorous mammals. Those native species which do exist have mostly retreated to the remoter parts of the country, the mountains or the cayos. Prominent among them are the various types of **jutías**, large rat-like rodents related to the agoutis of South America. They are still trapped and eaten by country people.

Compared with the small number of mammals the country is home to a great variety of reptiles, among them around 100 species of lizard or iguana. Pride of place must go to the **crocodiles** of the marshlands of the Zapata peninsula and the Island of Youth. Once present in huge numbers, they have only been saved from extinction by the setting up of breeding farms. Cuban snakes may not be poisonous, but the sheer size of some of them is impressive; the biggest is the *majá de Santa María*, a type of python which can reach a length of four metres. Not in quite the same league is the *ranita*, the smallest frog in the world, all of a centimetre in size.

For every Cuban terrestrial vertebrate there are around twenty invertebrates, most of them insects. More attention-worthy than the inevitable mosquitoes are the clouds of butterflies which fill the countryside, or the **polymitas**, the prettily coloured snails which occur mostly in the east.

Birdwatchers' paradise

Cuba is famous for its extraordinarily varied bird life. Of the 354 species that have been recorded here, 232 are permanent residents and 25 are endemic. The island is also a haven for migratory birds during the winter months (November to April).

H. Choimet

Polymitas

Outstanding among the native species is the country's national bird, the **tocororo**, its colourful plumage the same as the red, white and blue of the country's flag. Other natives include the **fermina**, a member of the passerine family, with a wonderfully melodious song, and the little hummingbird known as the **zunzuncito**, the smallest (6cm) bird in the world, able to hover in front of flowers while extracting their nectar with its long thin beak.

H. Choimet

Endangered species are now protected in various ways. Among them are the parrots (*cotorras*) of the Island of Youth, once on the verge of dying out but now benefiting from conservation measures which also safeguard *grullas* (cranes).

A common sight are white egrets, a wading bird which keeps company with cattle, while the flocks of pink flamingos which flourish in the north of Camagüey province and in the Zapata peninsula are one of the country's great wildlife spectacles.

Life in the water

The shallow seas around Cuba are home to a wonderfully diverse marine life, with around 900 kinds of fish and 4 000 types of mollusc living in the seas around its shores. Swordfish, marlin, and barracuda are among the species tempting the deep-water fisherman. Sharks rarely approach the coast, but have occasionally been seen in the waters around Santiago de Cuba. Corals, sponges, molluscs and an array of shellfish including the country's celebrated lobsters complete this exceptionally colourful picture.

Hummingbird

Endangered marine creatures include the *carey* and the *tinglado*, members of the turtle family now to be found more as exhibits in local museums than in the wild. Swimming languidly in river mouths is the **manatí** or sea-cow, a marine mammal with a fish-shaped body, sightings of which have given rise to many a mermaid story.

Fresh water lakes are home to only a limited number of creatures, but not to be forgotten is the living fossil known as the *manjuarí*, an extraordinary prehistoric survivor half-way between fish and reptile.

The richest plant life in the West Indies

Around 6 700 plant species grow in Cuba. Half of them are endemic, an exceptionally high proportion which is due not only to the fact that Cuba is an island but also to its varied relief and diversity of soil types and microclimates.

Centuries of clearance

Cuba's mantle of vegetation has undergone dramatic change since the arrival of Christopher Columbus and the observation made at the time by Bartolomé de las Casas that "a man can travel the three hundred leagues from one end of the island to the other beneath a canopy of trees". But by the middle of the 20C this almost continuous cover had been reduced to a mere 14% of the total land surface, a loss attributable to urbanisation, conversion into farmland, and the felling of choice hardwood trees for cabinet-making and other decorative purposes. In more recent times, conservation measures and reafforestation programmes have pushed the area covered by woodland back up to around 20%.

Every shade of green

Cuba's plant life is best understood in terms of vegetation zones. The **alluvial soils of the coastline** and the *cayos* provide excellent conditions for the **mangrove**, a tree able to thrive in swamps or in the sea thanks to the aerial roots hanging from its branches. Beaches are frequently fringed by **coconut groves** or less often by the spiky outline of **uvas caletas**, known for the sweetness of their fruit. In places, the dry climate of the coast is also favourable to the growth of **cacti**, of which Cuba boasts about a hundred different species. The island's **plains** are generally given over to farming: pastures, fields of sugarcane, rice and tobacco, and groves of bananas and (in the Zapata peninsula and the Island of Youth) citrus fruits.

The greatest diversity in vegetation occurs in the forests and **mountains**. In winter the landscape is enlivened by the spectacular red flowers of the **royal poinciana**, while in summer, riverbanks are the setting for the flowering of the **mariposa** (literally: butterfly); its delicate, butterfly-like blooms are Cuba's national flower, the symbol of the independence movements during the 19C wars of liberation.

Low-lying areas are characterised by trees whose wood is highly valued for decorative purposes. They include cedar, mahogany and ebony, all of which have contributed to the fame of Cuban-made furniture. Sadly, they have been over-exploited, and when replanting has taken place the favoured species has usually been eucalyptus.

Mariposa

H. Choimet

One tree that cannot pass unnoticed is the **jagüey**, a member of the *ficus* family. With its chubby body and aerial roots it almost upstages the **ceiba**, the kapok or cotton tree, which is also easily identifiable because of its imposing trunk and horizontal branch pattern.

Much prized for their resin as well as for their timber, **pine trees** flourish at the island's eastern and western extremities and have given their name to the Island of Pines (nowadays Island of Youth) and Pinar del Río (literally: pine-grove by

A rich plant life

the river). Around 10 % of the land surface is covered by pine forests of one kind or another, some of them consisting of endemic species like the *pinus maestrensis* of the Sierra Maestra or the *pinus cubensis* of the Mayarí area. At high altitudes the abundant rainfall encourages the growth of numerous varieties of **tree ferns** and **orchids**; more than 250 varieties of orchid are endemic to the island, many of them on show at the orquideario at Soroa.

The prodigious palm

Cuban countryfolk make use of almost every part of the palm tree. Fibres from its trunk are dried and then woven to make the walls of the "bohío" (cabin) and the fence around it. From the top of the tree comes "yagua", the tough, insect-resistant bark which makes a useful wall cladding. Then the broad leaves of the palm are used to weatherproof the cabin with a thatched roof. But in addition to being a building material, the palm yields fodder for pigs, wood for rustic furniture, and material for cord, rope, basketwork and cigar boxes, not forgetting the traditional headgear known as the "guajiro".

The national tree

It is difficult to imagine a Cuba without its **palm trees**. As well as featuring on the country's coat of arms, the royal palm has become a symbol of the dignity and determination of the Cuban people. With its slender, pale grey trunk and its great plume of foliage, it is part of every Cuban landscape, in town as much as in the countryside. seventy million palms grow in Cuba, more per square mile than anywhere else on earth.

In addition to the royal palm about a hundred other species of palm have been recorded on the island, 70 of them endemic. Around Pinar del Río there are fascinating examples of the *palma corcho*, the cork palm, a living fossil originating 100 million years ago, as well as the *palma barrigona* the pot-bellied palm, with its characteristically swollen trunk.

A rich and varied natural heritage

Coconut palms near Baracoa

"CUBA LIBRE"

Dates	Events
1492	**Columbus** lands in Cuba
1511	Founding of Baracoa, the island's first *town*
1519	The city of **Havana** laid out on its present site
1607	The capital moved from Santiago to Havana
1762	Havana captured by the British
1868	The **Ten Years War** against Spanish colonial rule begins when **Carlos Manuel de Céspedes** frees his slaves
1878	End of the first war of independence with the signing of the Convention of Zanjón
1886	Abolition of slavery
1895	Outbreak of the **second war of independence**; return from exile of **José Martí** and **Antonio Maceo**
1898	Explosion aboard the **USS Maine** in Havana harbour Treaty of Paris (10 December)
1901	The **Platt Amendment** adopted by the US Congress
1902	Proclamation of the **Republic of Cuba**
1925	Founding of the Communist Party of Cuba
1934	Annulment of the Platt Amendment
1952	Coup d'etat led by Fulgencio Batista
1953	Attack on the **Moncada** Barracks in Santiago by a group of rebels led by **Fidel Castro**
1956	Rebels land from the *Granma* in Oriente Province **Che Guevara** leads guerilla fighting in the **Sierra Maestra**
1959	**Triumph of the Revolution** – Castro's followers enter Havana on 2 January
1961	Diplomatic relations broken off with Washington Failure of the invasion at the **Bay of Pigs** The United States begins its **blockade** (*bloqueo*) of Cuba
1962	The **Cuban Missile Crisis**
1967	**Che Guevara** executed in Bolivia
1975	Cuban troops intervene in Angola
1976	Adoption of the Constitution of the Republic of Cuba
1980	Large-scale emigration from the port of **Mariel**
1989	The Ochoa Affair
1990	Start of the "Special Period in Time of Peace"
1992	Final ending of Soviet aid
1993	Legalisation of possession of dollars
1994	The **Balseros Crisis**
1996	The **Helms-Burton Law** adopted by the US Congress
1998	Visit by **Pope John-Paul II**

The Colonial Era

The Conquest

At the moment of **Columbus'** landfall on 28 October 1492, Cuba's indigenous population consisted of around 100 000 people, members of the Arawak group. The great Genoese navigator disembarked on the Bay of Bariay, to the east of Gibara, though the exact spot is still subject to dispute. He carried with him a message from Ferdinand and Isabella of Spain addressed to the Emperor of China and at first thought his voyage in search of a new route to the Indies had brought him to the coast of Japan. The fact that Cuba was an island was only established several years later, when the explorer Sebastián de Ocampo succeeded in sailing right round it in 1508.

Ordered by the Spanish crown to colonise the island, **Diego Velázquez de Cuellar** arrived in Cuba in 1511, accompanied by an army of 300 men. Isolated attempts at resistance by the indigenous population were soon overcome, including the revolt led by the heroic *cacique* (chief) Hatuey, and the invaders' tactics of pillaging and massacring left the native people with no alternative but submission. Within four years the conquistadores had founded seven *villas* or settlements either close to mine workings or on the coast.

Cuba's first national hero

No visitor to Cuba can fail to notice the defiant-looking native chieftan depicted on the beer bottles from the Hatuey brewery. A cacique who originally came from Santo Domingo, Hatuey took the lead in organising resistance to the advance of the Spanish invaders. He and his followers sustained a siege of several months in the Baracoa area before retreating into the mountains, where he was eventually captured. The story goes that shortly before being burnt at the stake, Hatuey was given the opportunity to be baptised as a Christian. On learning that he would meet Spaniards in the after-life, he declined the offer. But he achieved immortality nevertheless, becoming a symbol of Cuban fortitude, and the first of a long line of heroes who fought for the country's independence.

Havana harbour in the 18C

A. Hodalic/EXPLORER

The Spanish colonists established a society founded on slavery, a system denounced by **Bartolomé de las Casas** *(see p. 233)*. Mass killings and inhuman treatment, together with newly introduced European diseases like smallpox led in the space of a few decades to the virtual disappearance of the native population and their replacement by slaves brought from Africa. Quite soon, the gold deposits which had attracted the attention of the conquistadores were worked out; new and more promising horizons beckoned, and as early as 1519 expeditions like the one led by Hernán Cortés were being organised to explore Florida and Mexico.

The Threshold of the New World

By the end of the 16C the Cuban population started to grow again, and the country acquired a new role as a commercial staging post. Strategically located between the Old World and the New, the island became an important port of call for merchant vessels trading between Spain and its colonies.

Captains-general
The Spaniards divided up their colonial empire into vice-royalties, each covering a vast area, as well as into so-called captaincies-general. The latter were four in number; each ruled by a captain-general, they included Guatemala (1544), Venezuela (1773), Chile (1778) and Cuba (1778).

The introduction of sugar cane in the very early days of colonial rule gave rise to a **sugar industry** which has undergone continuous modernisation ever since. Towards the end of the 16C the first *trapiches* were installed, little sugar mills activated by the muscle-power of men or beasts. Lacking a sizeable native workforce, the colonial regime began to depend on slaves shipped over from Africa. The **slave trade** only finally came to an end in the last decades of the 19C, at a time when Blacks already outnumbered Whites. Along with sugar-cane, tobacco-growing and cattle-rearing were staple activities. However, all such activity was subjected to the commercial monopoly of the mother country, and the taxes and regulations imposed by Spain weighed ever more heavily on the *criollos* (Spaniards born in Cuba, in contrast to the *peninsulares* from Spain itself). At the beginning of the 18C a series of revolts were precipitated by the tobacco monopoly imposed in 1717. This climate of defiance against the colonial power coincided with increasing competition among the countries of Europe for new markets, and right up until the end of the 18C Cuba was subjected to frequent raids by **pirates** and corsairs in the pay of the enemies of Spain. Preyed on in this way, the population often came to terms with the buccaneers, and in any case it made more sense to deal in smuggled goods than toiling to pay Spanish taxes.

The 10-month British occupation of Havana from August 1762 *(see p. 114)* marked a decisive turning point in the Cuban economy. It taught the city important lessons about free trade and about new markets, in particular those offered by Britain's American colonies. Even after the departure of the **British** Havana remained firmly locked into the international trading system, which American independence did nothing to diminish. In the course of the following century, the United States increased its trade with Cuba to such an extent that it became the main customer for many of the island's products. In 1791, the slave rebellion led by Toussaint-Louverture in Haiti gave the Cuban economy an unexpected boost. The destruction of the French-owned plantations on the neighbouring island caused the price of Cuban sugar to rise dramatically; in response to international demand, the country modernised its infrastructure, installing up-to-date *ingenios* (sugar-mills) and opening its first railway line at the early date of 1837.

"Cuba libre"

The Wars of Independence

At the end of the 18C the whole of the American continent was gripped by the desire for independence, from the British colonies in the north to the Spanish possessions in Latin America. By 1825, only Puerto Rico and Cuba remained under Spanish rule.

Universal unrest

At the beginning of the 19C the whole of Cuban society was simmering with discontent. Revolts by *cimarrones* (fugitive slaves) were put down and the *palenques* (fortified encampments) in which they had sought refuge were destroyed. Slavery continued to be a mainstay of colonial society, and final emancipation was only to come in 1886 following the end of the first of the two wars of independence.

By the middle years of the century, mechanisation had begun to drive workers into unemployment, particularly in the tobacco industry, and the decade between 1850 and 1860 saw the beginnings of an organised workers' movement.

The interests of Spain and those of local landowners began to diverge ever more sharply. Faced with the growth of independence movements from 1820 onwards, Spain embarked on a policy of repression and terror, and reinforced its military presence on the island. This period of instability also saw differences in outlook developing among the richer creoles; the **loyalists** favouring Spanish rule were opposed by the **annexationists** who looked to an ever more intimate relationship with the United States, whose interests they saw as identical to those of Cuba. In 1850, a futile attempt was made by the annexationists to force the issue. As on many subsequent occasions, when one group or another hoped to change the course of Cuban history, an invasion from outside the country was attempted. This one was led by General Narciso López, whose small force was repelled ignominiously after landing at Cárdenas (see p. 201). Subsequently, once the United States had abolished slavery in 1865, the idea of annexation lost its appeal to many of its former supporters. They looked instead to a gradual and peaceful solution to the country's deep-rooted problems, but Spain remained deaf to their appeals. In 1867, the imposition of even more burdensome financial measures marked the point of no return in the relationship between the mother country and its Caribbean colony.

Thirty years of struggle

On 10 October 1868, when the sugar-grower **Carlos Manuel de Céspedes** rang his plantation bell, it was not to summon his slaves to work, but to give them their freedom (see p. 278). It was also the signal for the beginning of a long period of armed conflict. Céspedes placed himself at the head of a tiny army, determined to liberate his country from the colonial yoke, thereby setting in motion the events which came to be known as the **Ten Years War**. On the 20 October the rebel force seized the town of Bayamo, where the Cuban national anthem was sung for the first time. A year later the Assembly of the Republic in Arms abolished slavery and elected Céspedes President. Armed with *machetes*, the *mambises* (a Congolese word used by the rebels to describe themselves) set off to drive the Spanish from Cuba. Uprisings took place in the central provinces, particularly at Camagüey, where the young patriot **Ignacio Agramonte** led a determined struggle. But the rebels failed to take the west of the country, where the landowners had remained loyal to Spain.

The fight for independence was weakened by internal disputes, and the rebels never succeeded in mounting the sort of unified offensive which might have made up for their inferiority in weapons and equipment. They also suffered the loss of several of their leaders, including Céspedes himself, shot by the Spanish in 1874.

The Ten Years War was brought to an end on 10 February 1878 with the signing of the **Convention of Zanjón** by the Spanish General Martinez Campos and rebel representatives. A group of of rebel generals, among them **Antonio Maceo**, refused to accept the terms of the convention, describing it as a "cut-price peace", which neither freed slaves nor gave the country independence. But despite their call to resume the struggle, known as the **Protesta de Baraguá** (23 March 1878), the treaty was pushed through and the protesting generals went into exile. From now on the independence movement would be organised from beyond Cuba's shores. The key figure in the renewed struggle for independence was **José Martí**, the driving force behind the Cuban Revolutionary Party which he founded in 1892. Spending most of his life in exile in Spain, South America and the United States, Martí worked tirelessly to prepare the armed uprising which would bring about

José Martí statue in Havana's Parque Central

The Apostle of Independence

Streets are named after him, the tiniest village has a statue of him, and his ideas and poems are dear to every Cuban heart. And is there anyone, anywhere, who hasn't hummed to the tune of Guantanamera "Yo soy un hombre sincero de donde crece la palma...", based on his Versos Sencillos? Yet José Martí (1853-95), thinker, poet, journalist, revolutionary and national hero spent most of his life outside Cuba. At the age of 16 he was deported to the Island of Pines because of his involvement in the struggle for independence, then exiled to Spain. From there he went to South America, then settled in the United States. Here, "in the belly of the monster", he learnt to distrust American imperialism just as much as Spanish colonial rule. Determined to show that he was not just a thinker but a man of action, he joined in the armed attempt to overthrow the colonial regime, and died a hero's death on 19 May 1895.

the freedom of his nation. The second war of independence broke out in February 1895, and two months later, Martí, accompanied by **Antonio Maceo** and Máximo Gómez landed in Cuba at the head of an army, intending to liberate the country from east to west. Martí was soon to die, felled by a bullet fired by a Spanish soldier, but the rebel advance towards the western provinces continued and by 22 March 1896 Maceo had taken the town of Mantua in the Pinar del Río area.

In an attempt to stem the onward march of the *mambises*, the Spaniards brought in General **Valeriano Weyler** as the island's Captain-General. In October 1896 Weyler initiated a policy of *reconcentración*, the resettlement of the peasant population in concentration camps in order to deprive the rebels of their support. In the insanitary conditions of the camps many innocent people paid with their lives for Weyler's ruthlessness.

Meanwhile the rebels pursued a scorched-earth policy, laying waste the crops and plantations of the rich colonial landowners. In the end the Spanish government recalled Weyler and opted for a more moderate approach, but by now events had gained their own momentum, taking the conflict beyond the confines of a quarrel between Spain and Cuba into a new, international dimension. The *mambises* refused to have any truck with ideas of autonomy, and the beginning of 1898 was marked by a series of troubles. By this time, US interests had invested heavily in Cuba, particularly in tobacco, mining and sugar, and to protect them in the face of all this unrest the American government decided to send a gunboat. When the **USS Maine** was blown up in Havana harbour on 15 February 1898, the United States needed no further pretext to enter the war. The cause of the explosion aboard the battleship remains a mystery: was it an accident or was it deliberately engineered by the Spanish, or even by the Americans themselves? Whatever the reason, public opinion in the USA was outraged and revenge was demanded. On 25 April war was declared on Spain, within three months the Spanish colonial army was defeated, surrendering at Santiago (*see p. 283*). (*see p. 283*) Signed by the United States and Spain on 10 December 1898, the Treaty of Paris gave Cuba its independence….but the country was immediately placed under American military occupation.

American hegemony

Cuba was now ruled by an American military government, backed by US troops. When the Constituent Assembly reconvened in 1901, the Americans made their withdrawal conditional upon the inclusion in the Cuban constitution of the **Platt Amendment**. The text of the amendment – named after the US Senator who drafted it – gave the United States the right to intervene at any time in the affairs of the island. Complete subservience of Cuba to American demands was necessary before the country was formally granted independence on 20 May 1902, the date when the conservative President Tomás Estrada Palma took office with US support. Dominated by American capital and bound by a reciprocal commercial treaty, the island's economy was almost entirely in US hands. When Palma was accused of electoral fraud, he appealed to the United States by quoting the Platt Amendment and demanding a second term in office. Once again an American military government was set up, lasting from 1906-1909 in an attempt to bring order into the island's chaotic internal affairs. The years which followed were characterised by a succession of puppet presidents, many of them corrupt, by fraudulent elections and dictatorships, and by American military interventions, all in the context of total American control of the country's political and economic life.

Pervasive corruption, together with increasing poverty and hardship, nourished the growth of working-class movements and stimulated radical action. In 1925 the **Cuban Communist Party** was founded by Julio Antonio Mella, a student leader. In the same year, President **Gerado Machado** was faced with a wave of strikes among railwaymen and sugar-workers, unrest which intensified with the onset of the world slump in 1929. Machado's answer was a programme of brutal repression, but in 1933 a general strike forced the dictator to resign and flee the country. On 4 September a group of students and military men overthrew Machado's successor, Grau San Martin. Among them was Sergeant **Fulgencio Batista** who became Commander-in-Chief of the armed forces and in effect ruler of the country until 1940, when he was formally elected President. One interesting development during this period was the removal of the Platt Amendment from the constitution in 1934. The two presidents who followed Batista after 1944 were in no position to combat the corruption which dominated the country's political life. A few months before the holding of a new presidential election, Batista took power again in the **coup d'etat of 10 March 1952**. His US-supported regime became a byword for corruption, the power of the mafia, the predominance of foreign interests and ruthless suppression of all opponents.

The Revolution

The end of the Batista dictatorship

Batista's coup d'etat was soon followed by a series of attempts to overthrow his dictatorship. These took place in the context of a deep-seated desire to rebuild Cuban society on completely new foundations.

The first step towards revolution was taken when a group of young radicals led by **Fidel Castro Ruiz** – active politically since 1948 – decided to storm the **Moncada** barracks at Santiago and seize the weapons stored there. On 26 July 1953, at the height of carnival time, a hundred men attacked the fortified building (see p. 283). But they were beaten off, and in the course of the bloody coun-

Icon of the Revolution
Photography has contributed to the romantic appeal of the Cuban Revolution by immortalising Che Guevara in any number of striking images, most memorably as a bearded and beret wearing guerrilla fighter smoking his cigar with panache or as a Christ-like corpse after his execution. A doctor of Argentinian origin, Ernesto Guevara allied himself with Fidel Castro in the struggle for the liberation of Cuba and thereby set out on his road to mythic status. On being made Minister for Industry in 1961, he evolved his theory of the "New Man" who would be motivated by morality rather than materialism and thereby overcome the alienation of the modern world. "Che" was a passionate internationalist, and in 1966 he bade farewell to the Cuban people in order to carry his revolutionary message out into the world. Ambushed in Bolivia, he was executed on 9 October 1967 at the age of 39.

termeasures ordered by Batista half of them were murdered or tortured. Nevertheless, the failed attack left its mark on history as a result of the trial that followed; the speech that Castro made in his own defence – History Will Absolve Me – was less of a plea than a statement of his political programme. Republished, its text served subsequently as a kind of revolutionary manifesto. Together with his comrades, Castro was condemned to 15 years forced labour on the Island of Pines (now the Island of Youth). But in 1955 public pressure led Batista to amnesty the men of Moncada.

Released from prison, the rebels regrouped, setting up a movement called **M-26** (after the date of the attack on the Moncada Barracks). Its leadership was entrusted to **Frank Pais** in Santiago, while Castro moved to Mexico to raise funds and prepare for a future landing on Cuba. In Mexico he met a young Argentinian doctor, **Ernesto "Che" Guevara**, who was inspired to join in the preparations for the expedition.

On 2 December 1956, exhausted by a week aboard the **Granma**, 82 men landed (or in Che's words "were shipwrecked") at Las Coloradas in eastern Cuba. Their arrival had been timed to coincide with a series of uprisings organised by M-26, but they were delayed by bad weather and spotted by coastguards who had been on the look-out for some time. The alarm was soon sounded and within three days Batista's troops had surrounded the rebels at Alegría del Pío. Che was wounded and only a handful escaped into the wilderness of the **Sierra Maestra**. Now known as the *barbudos* (bearded ones), the rebels gradually won the support of the local inhabitants, and launched a war of nerves against the Batista regime. Every effort was made to gain publicity for the existence of what was described as "liberated territory". A journal was published, *Cubano Libre*, and in February 1957 Castro granted an interview to the New York Times journalist Herbert Matthews. A year later, *Radio Rebelde* began transmission.

On 5 May 1958, Batista ordered an offensive which would crush "this nest of agitators" once and for all. But his 12 000-strong army was unable to overcome the 300 or so *guerrillas*, familiar as they were with every nook and cranny of the sierra.

Success in repelling Batista's forces was an important psychological victory for the rebels, and the subsequent disarray of the government army completely reversed the balance of power. The time had come to leave the mountains. Che Guevara and Camilo Cienfuegos headed two columns which set out in the direction of Havana. By 28 December "Che" and his men were at the gates of Santa

The Revolution steps out: from the left, Fidel Castro, Osvaldo Dorticos and Che Guevara

GAMMA

Clara. On 31 December, after three days of siege (see p. 222), the town fell into their hands. Events moved towards their climax. Under cover of darkness, Batista and his entourage boarded a plane and sought refuge in the Dominican Republic, and on 2 January 1959 the barbudos entered Havana, followed five days later by Fidel Castro.

The Triumph of the Revolution

In 1959 Cuban living standards were extremely low, unemployment was rife, and economic life largely controlled by American monopolies. From its first days in office, the revolutionary government began to tackle these problems, the aim being nothing less than a complete transformation of the country's social, economic and political landscape.

The period of reforms – The post of President was filled by Manuel Urrutia, with Castro as Prime Minister. The first wave of reforms included an increase in wages, a reduction in the cost of rents and public services, the nationalisation of the telephone service, the development of education, and the improvement of medical services and public health. Harsh measures were taken against those who had served the Batista regime; as well as recovering some of the ill-gotten gains made during his dictatorship, the new government oversaw a series of arrests, trials, and executions and carried out a thorough purge of army, police and civil service.

On 17 May 1959 the first of a series of laws was passed promoting **agricultural reform**. From now on, no holding was to exceed 400ha in area. A number of large American owned estates were broken up and the land shared among some 100 000 smallholders. In July, deemed to have failed in pushing through these and other revolutionary measures, President Urrutia was dismissed and replaced by **Osvaldo Dorticos** who would remain in post until 1976.

Relations with the United States – The country soon found itself in difficulties as a result of the flight of capital, an exodus of technicians, and a drop in the price of sugar. Throughout 1960 Cuba and the United States indulged in a series of tit-for-tat measures each of which ratcheted up the tension between the two countries.

In January 1960 America announced a drastic reduction in its sugar quota from Cuba. A month later the **Soviet Union** committed itself to filling the gap by buying an equivalent amount of sugar, then, on 8 May resumed the diplomatic relations which had been broken off long before. The United States observed these developments with growing alarm, and, when Soviet crude oil began to arrive in Cuba, the American-owned refineries refused to process it. The Cuban reaction was swift; the plants owned by Texaco, Shell and Esso-Standard were **nationalised**. Washington replied with a further reduction in sugar imports of 700 000 tonnes, whereupon Cuba expropriated the owners of sugar-cane plantations without compensation and also nationalised the banks. Then, in October 1960, the United States decided to put an **embargo** on a number of goods destined for Cuba, a move which had serious effects on the island's economy. Abandoning its traditional trading partner, Cuba now began to cultivate economic ties not only with the Soviet Union but with other Communist countries like China and East Germany. On 24 October the remaining US-owned enterprises in Cuba were nationalised. On 19 December the US stopped all imports of Cuban sugar, then on 3 January 1961 severed all diplomatic ties with Havana. The Cold War context in which these events took place made it inevitable that Cuba should now range itself alongside the USSR.

These diplomatic manoeuvrings were accompanied by conspiracies aimed at overthrowing the Castro regime. The island entered a phase of near-paranoia, in which the possibility of an invasion seemed ever-present. On 15 April 1961, three airfields were bombed by American aircraft. Castro used his funeral oration for the victims of the attack to proclaim the definitively socialist character of the Revolution. On 17 April a group of Cuban exiles supported by the CIA landed at the **Bay of Pigs** (see p. 209). The attempted invasion was quickly defeated and more than a thousand mercenaries were taken prisoner. Humiliated by this reverse, in June 1961 the United States imposed a total economic **blockade** (bloqueo) on Cuba, a state of affairs which continues to this day.

But the most fraught episode in Cuban-American relations was still to come. In October 1962 there began the period of global tension known as the **Cuban Missile Crisis** which brought humanity close to the brink of nuclear war. For 13 days the eyes of the world were riveted on this tiny island and the seas around it.

On 14 October, American U2 spy planes discovered launching ramps for Soviet missiles being constructed in the west of the island, facing Florida. The US government immediately ordered a naval blockade to prevent the delivery of more missiles and demanded the dismantling of the launch sites. Without consulting the Cubans, Presidents Kennedy and Khrushchev agreed on 28 October that in return for an American promise not to invade the island the missiles would be removed.

Exporting revolution – Towards the middle of the 1960s Cuba turned its attention to the countries of **Latin America** (Venezuela, Colombia, Guatemala and Bolivia), giving aid to the revolutionary movements involved in guerrilla activities there. Then in the 1970s the country won a series of minor victories over the isolation which the United States had attempted to impose on it by excluding

Fidel speaks!

R. Cundy/EXPLORER

The Revolution

it from the Organization of American States. Castro paid state visits to Peru, Ecuador and Chile, and one by one a number of Caribbean and South American countries (Barbados, Guyana, Jamaica, Trinidad and Tobago, Panama, Venezuela and Colombia) recognised Cuba and re-established diplomatic relations.

This was also a period in which Cuba became involved in revolutionary activity in **Africa**. The regime sent 20 000 troops to **Angola** to fight for the MPLA leader Agostinho Neto in his struggle with nationalist rebels supported by America and South Africa. This involvement came to an end in 1989 when Cuba agreed to withdraw its forces and its 50 000 civilian advisors, in return for the granting of independence to Namibia, formerly South West Africa. In 1978, Cuban forces also intervened in **Ethiopia**, where they helped the Mengistu regime put down a nationalist revolt. Cuba's role in these and other struggles was recognised the following year when the country hosted the sixth **Summit Conference of the Non-Aligned Nations**.

In search of a new way forward

By 1990 no foreign country was intervening in Cuban affairs, but it was now that the country began to experience its gravest ever economic crisis.

The Revolution runs out of steam – The early 1980s were marked by a series of crises. In summer 1979, 100 000 exiled Cubans were allowed to return to the island to revisit their families. Both sides were shocked by the experience, most of all the islanders, inevitably cast in the role of poor relations. A year later, an ever-increasing number of Cubans wanting to leave the country sought refuge in Havana's foreign embassies. On 4 April 1980 Castro ordered the guard on the Peruvian Embassy to be removed, whereupon the compound was stormed by thousands of would-be émigrés. On 22 April a fleet manned by exiled Cubans gathered off the port of **Mariel** in order to pick up further contingents of people anxious to quit the country. Castro decided to let them go, handing over to the United States the problem of how to cope with the massive influx. After some hesitation, President Carter accepted the responsibility, while Castro took advantage of the opportunity to rid himself of numerous social undesirables as well as political opponents and dissidents. In the course of the following four months more than 125 000 *marielitos* made their way across the Florida Strait aboard improvised vessels of one kind or another.

1980 was not a good year for Cuba. First the sugar plantations and the tobacco fields were struck by a series of pests, then the island's pigs fell victim to an outbreak of disease. Three hundred thousand people were affected by an epidemic of tropical fever brought back from Angola by returning soldiers. And the country's position in the world was not enhanced by the election of the fiercely anti-Communist Ronald Reagan as President of the United States. In the course of his two terms of office Reagan showed himself to be an implacable foe of the Castro regime. Among other measures he authorised the setting up in Florida in 1982 of **Radio Martí** which kept up a continuous flow of anti-Castro propaganda. Then in 1983, the US invaded Grenada, killing a number of Cuban "advisers".

Within Cuba itself, the campaign of **Rectification of Errors** was launched in 1986 to combat the evils of absenteeism, theft, negligence and abuse of power brought about by excessive bureaucratisation and over-centralisation of the administration. The whole nation suffered a severe shock when, on 13 July 1989 the Angolan war hero General Arnaldo Ochoa was executed along with three other officers on charges of corruption and drug-dealing. **The Ochoa Affair** unleashed a period of arrests and purges as well as major changes in the political structure.

The "Special Period in Time of Peace" – Coming on top of political scandals the collapse of the Communist bloc only served to undermine further the power of the Castro regime, which was now deprived of its ideological and economic support. Between the fall of the Berlin Wall in November 1989 and the collapse of the USSR at the end of 1991 the Cuban economy was affected more and more by delays and shortfalls in Soviet supplies. Daily life suffered and living standards plummeted. In September 1990, the "Special Period in Time of Peace" was inaugurated. Still in force at the time of publication, it plunged Cuba into a survival economy; investment was cut or stopped altogether, factories were closed, power-cuts (*apagones*) became a feature of everyday life, and public transport was cut back in order to save energy. Queues lengthened outside the state-run shops which had little to stock their shelves with anyway. Housewives found it more and more difficult to find the basic supplies supposedly guaranteed by the ration-books (*libretas*) which every family had first been issued with in 1962. People learned to make do and mend, and the black market flourished, based largely on supplies pilfered from the workplace.

When Soviet aid finally came to an end in 1992, Cuba was forced to look to other countries for economic help. Joint ventures were promoted with foreign capital, notably in tourism, mining and oil. The regime reluctantly adopted more liberal policies, even permitting a degree of free market activity, albeit under rigorous government supervision. In August 1993, with possession of dollars no longer an offence, Cubans with hard currency were allowed to use it in the *diplotiendas* (hard currency shops). A law passed on 8 September 1993 allowed a limited amount of private enterprise and more than 200 000 **"cuentapropistas"** (entrepreneurs) took advantage of its provisions to set up private businesses of one kind or another. In 1994 *agromercados* were permitted, private markets where farmers were able to sell their products at prices well above those in state stores. In August 1994, despite this softening on the part of the regime, Castro was faced with a renewed wave of emigration. The **"balseros" crisis** (*balsa* – liferaft) saw attempts by up to 35 000 Cubans to cross to Florida. Refused entry by the US Coastguard, 20 000 of them languished until May 1995 in the Guantánamo base until the two governments came to an agreement about their fate (*see p. 305*).

It was now that the extreme anti-Castro faction in the United States chose to deliver what it hoped would be Castro's coup de grace. In February 1995 Senator Jesse Helms declared: "Whether Castro leaves Cuba vertically or horizontally is for him and his fellow-Cubans to decide, but one thing is for sure: he's got to go. The moment has come to tighten the vice". The notorious **Helms-Burton Act** intensified the embargo by denying access to US territory to any company trading with Cuba. In addition, anyone who had lost property in Cuba as a result of the Revolution could bring an action against a foreign company benefiting in any way from that property. Despite a majority UN resolution calling for the repeal of this law it was adopted by Congress in March 1996, though for the time being its implementation has been suspended by the Clinton administration.

Cuba today

Cuba today

For more than four decades **Fidel Castro** has been the living symbol of the Cuban Revolution. Though well into his seventies, his appearances still evoke the young guerrilla fighter from the Sierra Maestra, defying the march of time and a lifetime spent in confrontation. Still President of the State Council, Head of State and government, commander-in-chief of the armed forces and First Secretary of the Communist Party, he has dominated the Cuban scene since 1959.

In 1976 Cuba was subjected to an administrative reorganisation by being divided into **14 provinces**: Pinar del Río, Havana, Havana City, Matanzas, Villa Clara, Cienfuegos, Sancti Spiritus, Ciego de Ávila, Camagüey, Las Tunas, Holguín, Granma, Santiago de Cuba, and Guantánamo. In addition there is the Isla de la Juventud (Island of Youth), which enjoys a special status under direct government control. The provinces are divided into a total of 169 **"municipios"** (municipalities).

These administrative divisions form a framework for the political institutions foreseen by the Socialist style **Constitution** adopted in 1976, when Castro became President and the **Communist Party** held its first Congress. Despite being the sole party and dictating the country's political line, the PCC no longer has the right to interfere in detailed administration and management. This task now falls to the organs of the **"Poder popular"** (People's Power), which has some freedom of manoeuvre at the local level.

The country's political foundation rests on **mass organisations**, among them the CTC (Cuban Workers' Organisation), the FMC (Federation of Cuban Women), the UJC (Union of Communist Youth), the ANAP (National Association of Small Farmers), and the CDR (Revolutionary Defence Committees). Founded in 1960 to mobilise people in the event of an external threat, the CDRs are neighbourhood organisations responsible for watching over the population – in every sense of the term. They have 7 million members. The mass organisations send delegates to the municipal assemblies responsible for economic and social matters at the local level, which in their turn elect the members of the provincial assemblies. Legislative power is in the hands of the **National Assembly**, which is elected for a period of five years. Following an amendment to the constitution in 1992 the deputies are no longer elected by the municipal and provincial assemblies but by universal direct suffrage. The National Assembly meets twice yearly to promulgate laws and decrees, a power shared with the **Council of State**, a collegiate body. Executive power belongs to the **Council of Ministers** whose members are elected by the National Assembly. Since the adoption of the new constitution in 1976, the title of President of the Republic has disappeared, and the Head of State exercises the functions of President of the Council of State and Head of Government.

The first elections to the National Assembly and the provincial assemblies under universal suffrage were held in February 1993. The internal opposition remained without a voice, thanks to the system of single candidate lists. With a turn-out of 98.8 %, about 20 % of the votes cast were negative, because of blank or spoiled ballot papers. These elections, and the polls conducted in 1998, confirmed Castro in office.

MARKET SOCIALISM

Cuba is a net exporter of agricultural products but is almost totally dependent on imports for energy supplies and manufactured goods. Before the collapse of Communism, 80 % of the country's trade was with the Soviet Union and its allies, and the loss of these trading partners in the early 1990s plunged the island into an acute economic crisis, with GNP shrinking by 37 % over a 5 year period. The government has attempted to solve the problem by liberalising the economy, albeit to a very limited degree. The first signs of a turn-around came in 1994, when GNP grew by a modest 0.7 %, a trend which continued in the following years, rising to 1.2 % by 1998. While restricting expenditure as much as possible, the country is continuing to look for new trading partners and is encouraging the growth of tourism, a lucrative source of dollars.

The emergence of a private sector

Since the beginning of the 1990s the government has been forced bit by bit to move away from its absolute control of all sectors of the economy, and a series of reforms has been introduced with the aim of expanding the private sector and reviving the country's flagging economy with an injection of dollars.

In 1992 foreign companies were invited to enter into **joint ventures** with Cuban enterprises. The first sectors to benefit were mining, telecommunications, the oil industry and tourism, as capital began to flow in from Europe, Canada and Mexico.

In 1995 all sectors of the economy with the exception of defence, health and education were opened up to investment from abroad as well as to Cuban emigres working through the intermediary of a foreign company. This attempt to attract much-needed dollars has only met with limited success, not least because the country offers foreign investors little in the way of long-term guarantees. There have been problems with communications and supplies, to say nothing of the high rates of interest charged because of the uncertain political situation. In addition, the **Helms-Burton Act** (see p. 31) has discouraged otherwise willing investors by threatening them with the loss of their markets in the United States.

The country's economic problems have led to shortages of all kinds, and, inevitably, have given rise to a flourishing black market. Consumer goods have disappeared from state shops, while the high price of imported products in hard currency stores puts them far beyond the reach of most Cubans whose average monthly wage is around 180 pesos (about US$9).

Starting in August 1993, Cuban citizens were finally permitted to hold dollars, and a month later they were allowed to set up family businesses thanks to a new law on **"cuentapropistas"** (people working on their own account). The effect of these measures has been to reduce unemployment (8 % of the population according to official figures) and to make the US dollar the country's second currency.

Since 1996 dollar earnings by individuals have been subject to a special **tax** and life as a *cuentapropista* has become hazardous, with large numbers of bankruptcies; in 1997 about a quarter of all small businesses – (craft workshops, *paladares*, bed-and-breakfast establishments) – went out of existence. Others have continued without being registered officially despite the risks of a heavy fine. In total, registered *cuentapropistas* only account for about 3.5 % of the economically active population.

An important source of hard currency is the Cuban community living in Florida and elsewhere, who channel US$800 million a year to their compatriots on the island.

The existence of two parallel economies has created glaring inequalities. On the one hand, there is a minority of Cubans with access to dollars and consequently to consumer goods of all kinds, on the other the rest of their fellow-countrymen who have to content themselves with the meagre offerings on the sparsely-stocked shelves of state shops.

Sugar-cane supreme

The Cuban economy is dominated by agriculture, but the beginning of the "Special Period" was marked by what could be called a "great leap backward", when shortages of fuel and a lack of spare parts led to tractors being replaced by oxen and machinery by the *machete*.

The history of Cuba is inextricably entwined with the **sugar-cane**, a plant introduced by the Spanish early in their conquest of the New World. Local conditions are ideal for growing cane, in terms of both soil and climate. Settlers began to plant it as early as 1523, but it was not until the end of the 16C that a real sugar industry started to emerge. In the years that followed various factors came together to ensure its continued development, among them the growing sweetness of the European tooth, the demand created by a newly-independent United States, then the collapse of Haiti's sugar industry at the end of the 18C. In the 19C, in the face of competition from the new European sugar-beet industry, Cuban growers pushed through a successful modernisation programme. The damage done to the industry in the course of the First War of Independence gave American interests the opportunity to invest in Cuban sugar on a grand scale, and as the country came progressively under American control its agricultural landscape became more and more a **sugar monoculture**, and the island's fortunes depended more than ever on the success or failure of this single crop, its economy tied inexorably to every fluctuation in the world price of sugar.

Immediately after the Revolution, the new government looked for ways of escaping from this chronic over-dependence on sugar by promoting a greater variety of crops. By 1963 sugar production had been cut by half. But policy then underwent a dramatic reversal. A series of agreements were signed with the Soviet Union in which the country's new partner undertook to purchase guaranteed quantities of its sugar at a price well above world market level. Once again sugar production became a national priority, with every effort being made to increase production year on year. In 1970, a record target was set, and the whole nation was expected to buckle down to the task of bringing in a **"Gran Zafra"** (bumper harvest) of 10 million tons. Castro led the way, having himself photographed in the cane-fields, *machete* in hand. The resulting harvest was indeed the biggest (8.5 million tons) Cuba had ever brought in, even though it fell short of the target and was only achieved at the expense of every other sector of the economy.

The exceptional effort of the *Gran Zafra* was followed by a drop in production. But in the years that followed, thanks to mechanisation, output rose again, reaching an annual level of about 7 million tons, at least until the beginning of

Ph. Beuzen/SCOPE

Cutting cane in the "zafra", the sugar harvest

Ph. Beuzen/SCOPE

Tobacco drying shed

the "Special Period". Along with all other economic activities, sugar was severely affected by the crisis. After a dramatic drop in production to 3.3 million tons, yields rose in 1996, only to fall again in 1998 to 3.2 million tons. But despite these disappointing figures, Cuba is still one of the world's foremost producers of sugar, with the industry responsible for no less than 70% of its country's exports.
Tobacco is as big a source of pride to Cuba as sugar, and its cigars are of course second to none (*see p. 38*). The finest tobacco is grown in the **Vuelta Abajo**, the area around Pinar del Río. The average size of a tobacco plantation is around 6 or 7ha, the *vegueros* (plantation owners) being allowed a maximum holding of 5 *caballerías* (about 67ha). These private growers account for more than two-thirds of the country's tobacco, but the cigar industry is run by *Cubatabaco*, a state monopoly. Tobacco has suffered as much as any sector of the economy, with shortages of fertiliser and of energy inputs. But after several years of disappointing results, production has picked up, with around 100 million cigars being exported in 1997 (compared with 55 million in 1994).

Other important agricultural products include coffee and sweet potatoes, and the area devoted to **rice** has increased considerably since the 1970s in an attempt to make the country as self-sufficient as possible in this crop. Drainage programmes in areas like the Zapata peninsula and the Island of Youth have been undertaken in order to create plantations of **citrus fruits**. Great efforts have been made to develop **cattle raising**, but beef remains a luxury and the dairy industry is still insufficient for the country's needs.
Fishing has only really developed since 1959. As well as supplying the home market, the industry has had some export successes, notably with prawns and **lobsters**.

Industry in the shadow of agriculture

Until 1959 Cuban industry was underdeveloped because of the country's total reliance on the United States for all kinds of manufactured products. Post-Revolutionary attempts at diversification have met with only limited success, and agriculture has remained the mainstay of the economy. In recent years, foreign investment has been encouraged to promote manufacturing as well as developing the country's natural resources.

Nickel is the most important of Cuba's minerals. There are outcrops in the north of Holguín province, and there are important processing plants at Moa and Nicaro. The country is one of the world's biggest producers of the metal, with more than 27 000 tons of nickel ore being extracted in 1996. Other mineral resources, like manganese, chrome, cobalt and iron, are less developed. The reserves in the north of the Matanzas region provide the country with around a million tons of **crude oil** a year, and foreign companies have investigated offshore deposits in this area. But for the time being Cuba remains very dependent on imported supplies. Since the ending of Soviet aid, the government's energy policy has concentrated on reducing consumption, while the "Special Period" has meant that completion of the country's only nuclear power station near Cienfuegos has been postponed indefinitely.

Perhaps surprisingly, in view of a prevailing severe shortage of medicines, the country has a well-developed **pharmaceutical industry** with a considerable export trade to Africa and Latin America. Among the industry's products is a vaccine against a particular form of meningitis.

Turning to tourism

The figures speak for themselves; 600 000 tourists came to Cuba in 1993, 1.5 million in 1998, and 2.5 million are expected in the year 2000. In 1998 the tourism sector earned the country almost US$2 billion. The largest number of tourists come from Canada, followed by visitors from Italy, France, Spain and Germany.
Tourism has become the country's number one priority. Modern hotels built with foreign capital have risen from the ground, old colonial buildings have been painstakingly restored, international airports extended, and *pedraplanes* (causeways) laid out to connect the cayos with the mainland.
Despite a tradition of **package and group holidays**, Cuba is well-suited to the individual traveller, not least because of the recent growth of private activity in providing rooms and meals in exchange for dollars. It should be noted however that the government's tolerance is limited and the 1997 increase in taxes on such activities has put their future in some doubt, at least in the short term.
One of the most dramatic effects of the arrival of large numbers of foreign visitors has been on the country's social structure, with a wide gap opening up between people with dollars and those without. Visitors invariably come across lawyers, teachers, architects and engineers who have abandoned professional activity in order to open a *paladar* or act as chauffeur to foreign tourists.
Though there are now many contacts between foreigners and local people, an unpleasant kind of "tourist apartheid" still exists, with Cubans denied access to certain beaches and the majority of international hotels. The economic crisis has also given rise to what is known as **"jineterismo"** (from *jinetero*, literally squire or jockey). In areas frequented by tourists, visitors will be approached by people offering every kind of service imaginable in exchange for dollars. There are plenty of *jineteras* too, young females willing to exchange their favours for dollars, nice clothes, an evening at a restaurant, even – if exceptionally lucky – for a proposal of marriage and the prospect of a foreign passport.

"Market socialism"

TOBACCO

At the end of the 15C it was not only Cuba that was discovered by Columbus's crewmen but also the use to which the dried leaves of Nicotiana could be put. Tobacco was employed by the Indians in a variety of ways, in religious ceremonies, as a medicine, but above all as an accompaniment to social life. "The *caciques* (tribal chiefs) would use a Y-shaped tube, inserting the prongs of the Y into their nostrils and the tube itself into a smouldering bundle of leaves. Those unable to procure the right kind of wood for themselves would inhale the smoke through a hollow reed; it is this that the Indians are wont to call tobago, and not the plant or its effects as certain people do suppose" (*Historia general y natural de las Indias Occidentales* by Gonzalo Fernadez de Oviedo, 1526). In 1559 tobacco plants were brought to France by **Jean Nicot**. At first, tobacco was used as a medicinal herb, but Europe soon discovered the pleasures of taking snuff, and then of smoking the aromatic weed.

Growing tobacco
Between May and September the red-brown earth of the tobacco fields, the *vegas*, is left fallow, then meticulously weeded and cultivated. In the meantime a careful watch is kept on the growth of the young plants in the seedbeds. After about six weeks, when they have reached a height of around 20cm, they are planted out, 40 000 of them per hectare. Within a month the leaves have started to mature, turning the fields a brilliant green colour. The plants earmarked for forming the outer casing of cigars are often protected from sun and dew by field-sized sheets of cheesecloth netting. During the whole of the growing period, right up to harvest time, the tobacco plants are carefully checked for disease and insect damage.

The harvest
By the end of March the tobacco plants have reached a height of 1.80m. Each one has between eight and a dozen broad leaves, enough to make half-a-dozen cigars. The tobacco-fields are a fascinating sight at harvest time, with the dark green of the tobacco plants standing out against the lighter colours of the surrounding hills, and the ever-present palm trees contrasting with the cedars whose wood is ideal for making cigar boxes.

From March to May, the shady lanes dividing the fields are the scene of frenetic activity as the tobacco leaves are carefully gathered and placed in boxes. They are then threaded together and hung from the beams of the *casas de tabaco*, the barns which are such a feature of tobacco-growing areas, their roofs thatched with palm leaves or, more frequently nowadays, covered in corrugated iron (*See illustration page 36*). After a few weeks, the leaves are packed together and covered in palm leaves to encourage fermentation, the process which removes some of the tar and nicotine and results in a smoother flavour. When this phase had been completed it is time for the *escogeda* to begin, the sorting and classification of the leaves according to their quality and colour. They are wrapped in palm leaves again and formed into bales which are shipped to warehouses to await despatch to the factory.

Pinar del Río tobacco factory

The making of a fine cigar

The best cigars are made entirely by hand. Since the Revolution, women have joined the men who traditionally dominated this relatively well-paid occupation. Like the material with which they work, aspiring cigar makers are subjected to a careful selection process and undergo a three-year apprenticeship before being able to join the ranks of fully fledged *torcedores* (rollers). Visitors with fond memories of Carmen who come to Cuba expecting to find beautiful girls rolling cigars between their thighs will, alas! be disappointed.

The first stage in the creation of a cigar involves the rolling together of selected leaves to make up the **filler**. This is then enclosed in a **binder leaf** and placed in a press so that it keeps its **form**. The *torcedor* picks out a particularly fine leaf to serve as the wrapper leaf, removing its stalk and cutting the resulting half-leaf to shape with a curved blade, the *chapeta*. The wrapper is then skilfully wound around the filler, a circular piece of leaf is stuck to the head of the cigar and the other end trimmed to the right length. The cigars are checked for quality and appearance, the factory's label is wrapped round each one, and they are packed in cedarwood boxes of 50, ready for sale.

COLONIAL-ERA ARCHITECTURE

The typical Cuban **colonial town** was laid out on a grid pattern with streets intersecting at right angles. At its heart was the **parque central**, a spacious square usually with a formal garden in the middle. Often lined with splendid private palaces and official buildings, these town squares continue to be the focal point of town life today. The country has a magnificent heritage of buildings, but much of it is in acute danger; attrition by the elements and forty years of neglect has led not only to decay but in many cases to actual collapse. However, a recent influx of foreign capital has enabled a number of restoration programmes to be carried out, notably, under the auspices of UNESCO, in Old Havana and in the colonial-era jewel of Trinidad.

Spanish influence

Native architecture can hardly be said to have existed at the time of the Conquest and the first colonial buildings were direct borrowings from the Spanish architectural tradition. But while military architecture continued to follow European models, other structures such as churches and residential buildings soon began to incorporate specifically Cuban features, reflecting the local environment and the new socio-economic conditions.

The **colonial house** was built around its **patio**, a courtyard surrounded by arcaded galleries giving access to various rooms. The patio's function was twofold: it enabled sunlight to penetrate into the heart of the building – hence the name *solar* given to this type of dwelling – and allowed air to circulate freely. Entrance to the patio was normally via the *zaguán*, the vestibule. One particularly Cuban feature was the *traspatio*, a second, more modest courtyard at the rear of the building, used for various domestic tasks like drying laundry. Sometimes a dining room would be placed between the two patios, an arrangement described by the term *obra cruzada* (cross-construction).

Families would normally live on the first floor, while the ground floor would be used for commercial purposes. A fine example of a typical 17C house is the one now occupied by the Hanoi restaurant on the corner of Calle Bernaza and Calle Brasil in Havana (*See Making the most of Havana*). Early colonial-era dwellings frequently had a *curato mirador* on the first floor, a turret-like room at the corner of the building with a wooden balcony and a little tiled roof.

Colonial-era building is characterised by *"techos de alfarjes"* (timber ceilings) in the mudéjar style which Christian architects had copied from their Moorish counterparts during the Reconquest of Spain. Often painted green or bright blue, these ceilings consist of a series of beams, sometimes with cross-braces, and are frequently decorated with geometrical patterns. They feature in houses like the Palatino in Cienfuegos just as much as in religious buildings like the Convent of Santa Clara in Old Havana. Some are pointed, some keel-shaped, others form a cupola. Many give a wonderful feeling of spaciousness to the room. A sloping roof in mudéjar style helped keep interiors cool and also encouraged the rapid run-off of rain, factors which meant that this type of construction lasted well into the 19C.

In the 18C, the typical house acquired a mezzanine floor which served as the servants' quarters. The owner and his family lived on the upper floor, in a series of spacious, high-ceilinged rooms. The Hostal Valencia (*See Making the most of*

Havana) is a superb example of this kind of building. Architecture in Cuba reached a high level of sophistication in the second half of the 18C, when the style known as **Cuban Baroque** reigned supreme. Havana's Cathedral and the Palacio de los Capitanes Generales are among its greatest achievements. The Palace combines sober, almost Classical lines with rich **decorative elements** on windows, doors and arches, while the Cathedral displays the whole panoply of conventional Baroque features – pediments, volutes, niches – together with a highly individual, undulating facade and a sinuous cornice.

In the 19C building was dominated by the **neo-Classical** style, inspired by the forms and proportions of Greek and Roman architecture and best illustrated by the little edifice on Havana's Plaza de Armas known as the Templete. Sloping mudéjar roofs gave way to *azoteas*, the flat rooftops which are such a feature of Havana and other towns today. Wrought-iron was used for balconies and for *rejas*, the elongated grilles protecting windows. Windows also featured **"mediopuntos"**, wooden or stained-glass panels designed to filter the strong sunlight; Alejo Carpentier described them memorably as "intermediaries between sun and Man".

Towards the end of the century the scale of building increased, and massive structures made their appearance in the townscape, among them Havana's Manzana de Gómez, a shopping arcade occupying an entire city block.

By the end of the colonial era new middle-class residential areas were being developed, characterised by a new type of house. Surrounded by a garden, these detached dwellings had openings on all sides to allow light to penetrate and to encourage good ventilation. With the arrival of this type of building, the patio, which for centuries had been such an important feature of buildings in Cuba, finally disappeared.

The Convent of Santa Clara

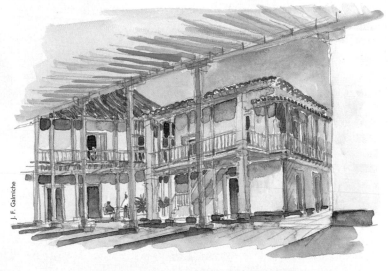

J.-F. Galmiche

Meeting the people

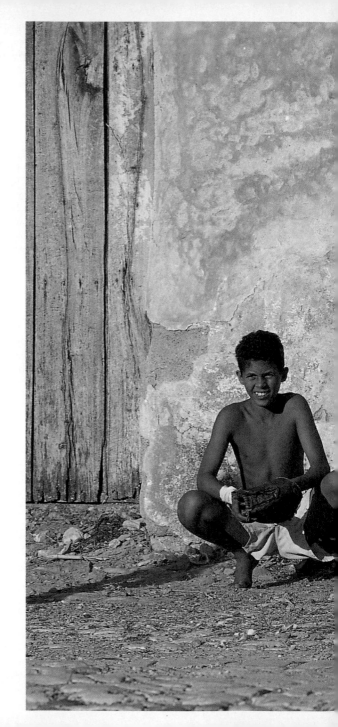

Tomorrow's
baseball stars

A CUBAN PORTRAIT GALLERY

Everyone agrees that Cubans are "special", vital, outgoing, uncomplaining, welcoming. They are also exceptionally good-looking. Could this be the result of what Nicolás Guillén, one of the country's most famous writers, described as the "mulatto spirit", the mingling of black and white which has now been going on for several hundred years?

Cubans all

Statistics and... statistics

There are few reliable population figures for today's Cuba, the most recent census having been carried out as long ago as 1981. The country has around 11 million inhabitants, giving a population density of about 100 to the square kilometre, very roughly the same as France and half as much as California. In spite of government policies designed to favour rural areas and promote the development of provincial towns, three quarters of the population live in towns. No less than one Cuban in five is a *habanero*, a citizen of Havana. The number of exiled Cubans living in Miami has been estimated at more than a million, making it the biggest Cuban city after Havana.

Unlike many of its neighbours in the Caribbean and Latin America, Cuba has the population profile of an advanced country; infant mortality is low (13 per 1000), life expectancy high (76), and fertility low (1.9 children per female). A third of the population is aged between 14 and 27, a figure which will not surprise anyone who has noticed the number of children and young people everywhere.

In contrast, the official figures for ethnic origin seem way out of line. The population is supposed to consist of 66 % Whites, 12 % Blacks, and 22 % people of mixed race or mulattos. The unofficial total of 50 % Whites seems less at odds with reality.

Ancestors from everywhere

Ever since Cuba was first colonised, successive waves of immigration have resulted in a mingling of different races.

Native Cubans – About 100 000 indigenous people lived on Cuba at the time of Columbus's landfall. They belonged to a number of different groups, and unlike the Caribs who formed the population of most of the other Caribbean islands, they were mainly **Arawaks**.

The **Guanahatabeyes** had been the first to settle on the island, around 2000 BC. They were hunter-gatherers, using tools fashioned from sea-shells. Traces of them are most abundant in caves in the area around Pinar del Río in the west of the country.

A second wave of immigration brought the **Siboney** to Cuba. They lived from hunting and fishing, and made tools from shells as well as from wood and stone. Their principal area of settlement was in the centre and south of the country. Some of their cave paintings have survived, notably the remarkable set adorning the walls of the Punta del Este cave on the Isle of Youth. Some of the Siboney suffered enslavement with the arrival of a third group of immigrants.

A settled people who grew *cassava*, maize and tobacco, the **Taino** came to Cuba about 200 years before the Spanish Conquest. They lived in villages consisting of *bohíos* (huts) grouped around the *caney*, the circular building lived in by the *cacique* (Indian chief) *(See page 211)*. Potters and weavers, it was the Taino who left the greatest mark on Cuban culture, particularly as far as language was concerned. But the native inhabitants were almost completely wiped out in the course of the Conquest. Today all that is left of the Taino population are a handful of descendants of those who fled into the remote mountain areas around Baracoa in the east of the country.

Europeans – Most of the Europeans who colonised Cuba were **Spaniards**, but there were also limited numbers of Italians, Portuguese and Germans. Many Spanish immigrants came from the poorer regions of that country like Galicia (among them Fidel Castro's father), Asturia, Estremadura and the Canary Islands. There were sharp distinctions between people who had come from Spain, who were called *peninsulares*, and those of Spanish origin but born in Cuba, who were referred to as *crillos* (creoles). At the end of the 18C there was a wave of **French** immigrants fleeing the slave revolt on Haiti. Most of these settled in the eastern part of the country. A century later Cuba attracted fortune-seekers from a variety of European countries, including France, Germany, Italy and Great Britain. Cuba's close links with the Soviet bloc meant that many Cubans made their way to Eastern Europe, and some of them have stayed there, just as a number of Russians, Czechs and Poles have remained in Cuba.

Africans – It is thought that something like a million Africans were shipped as slave labour to Cuba between the beginning of the 16C and the abolition of slavery in 1886. By the middle of the 19C, Blacks made up more than half of the country's population – 589 333 compared with 418 291 Whites, according to the census of 1841 which did not distinguish between slaves and freemen. Cuba's Black population came from a variety of ethnic backgrounds, but a number of groups stood out, particularly the **Yoruba**; their influence on Cuban culture has been considerable, particularly as far as religion is concerned. When a labour shortage developed in the early years of the 20C,

Another celebration!

Cubans all

a new element was introduced into the country's Black population; between 1913 and 1927 a total of a quarter of a million immigrants made their way to Cuba from Jamaica and Haiti.

Chinese – The Chinese presence in Cuba is at its most visible in Havana's *barrio chino* (Chinatown). The first ships bringing **Cantonese** labourers to the island landed here in 1847, and it is estimated that a total of around 120 000 Chinese immigrants came to Cuba during the second half of the 19C. Their number has shrunk until today they only comprise about 0.1% of the population.

Some of dictator Batista's good looks were attributed to his having Chinese blood in his veins.

Ethnic mixing

References to a person's ethnicity and colour are frequently made by Cubans and do not necessarily have pejorative overtones. A rich vocabulary is used to describe the spectrum of skin tones, ranging from *prieto* (meaning extremely swarthy) through *negro, mulatón, mulato, trigueño, rubio* (fair). Nicknames are common, and many of them are based on a person's apparent origin; thus someone with oriental features is more than likely to be referred to as *Chino*. Cubans are proud of pointing out that racism has no place in their country, and it is a fact that one of the first laws to be passed after the Revolution involved the abolition of all forms of racial discrimination. But segregation has a long history in Cuba; institutionalised during the colonial era, it metamorphosed into social segregation after slavery had been abolished. Picture books on Cuba published during the Batista years hardly show a Black face, and in 1959, on the eve of the Revolution, the Black population still found itself at the bottom of the heap, unequal and underprivileged in every way.

Though subsequent progress has been considerable, in education and in health and welfare, much remains to be done; 40 years of Revolution have not been enough to wipe out the legacy of five centuries of prejudice. Despite the emigration since 1959 of a substantial proportion of the (by definition White) middle-class, White people continue to occupy most of the top jobs, and it is obvious even to the most superficial observer that the Black population has the worst housing conditions.

National character

It is always difficult to pin down something like national character in words. But the author of a guidebook published in Cuba had this to say about the nature of his fellow-Cubans: "warm and light like the sea-breeze, noble like the palm-tree, sweet as sugar-cane and as robust as our plains and mountains!"

Such metaphors might not occur to everyone, but few visitors to Cuba leave without fond memories of their hosts. Trivial encounters like being asked for directions or given a lift give Cubans a chance to demonstrate their charm and kindness to strangers, even across the language barrier. Lasting friendships have been known to develop from such occasions, which will be immeasurably enriched if the visitor has taken the trouble to learn some basic Spanish.

Cubans are famous for their **hospitality** and have few inhibitions about inviting perfect strangers to come home with them. Despite the dire economic situation and the sacrifices this entails, visitors are likely to be sat in a place of honour, plied with rum and served copious quantities of food, possibly with the family retreating discreetly to another room.

L. Franey/RAPHO

Under the bonnet again

A tiny minority take advantage of the growing number of tourists and the openness of their fellow-Cubans to make dubious propositions of one kind or another. A modicum of street-wisdom is all that is necessary to avoid being exploited by such rip-off merchants.

Cubans are a basically **cheerful** people, always ready to smile or have a laugh. They have a well-developed **sense of humour** and conversations are studded with innumerable *chistes* (jokes). Few targets are spared, least of all the jokers themselves, to say nothing of Fidel or the privations which the "special period" has brought with it.

Cuban joie-de-vivre is at its most evident after nightfall. Once partying has started, it is likely to go on well into the small hours. No Cuban can resist the siren call of rhythm. Whether in a discotheque, the street, a bar or café, once the music strikes up and people of all ages begin to dance, they demonstrate an extraordinary mixture of vitality and unselfconscious **sensuality** that makes them the envy of most Europeans.

By day the picture is very different. Life is taken at a very relaxed pace, which is fine when no-one wants anything more than to escape from the heat of the sun into pleasurable torpor. But it can be a very different matter when something urgent needs doing, like retrieving a passport from a laid-back customs officer as the plane is about to take off. Most visitors encounter such situations. Keep calm, don't shout, and think about all the other wonderful people you have met in Cuba.

Cubans themselves have to face bureaucratic indifference, long queues at the shops and interminable waits at the bus stop every day of their lives and **patience** has become a necessary virtue. At the same time they have found ways of working the system and have pushed the art of **improvisation** to extraordinary lengths. Past masters at DIY, they throw very little away and can find a new use for virtually anything.

DAILY LIFE

Cuba's housing crisis, run-down public transport and the shortage of even the most basic goods forces people to spend large parts of their day standing in queues or walking from one place to another. Their resourcefulness, already considerable, has been pushed to the very limit.

Three generations under the same roof

Cuban families tend to be very close, in a literal as well as a sentimental sense. It is normal for grandparents, parents, and children to live together, though this is due more to the acute shortage of dwellings than to any other factor.

The way the household is managed on a day-to-day basis shows the extent to which *machismo* is alive and well in today's Cuba; virtually all domestic tasks are still carried out by **women**. When both parents are working children are usually looked after by the *abuela* (grandmother). Since the beginning of the "special period" the housewife's daily round has degenerated into something of an obstacle course; she has to hitch-hike or walk long distances to buy food on the black market or in farmers' markets, stand in line, sometimes in vain, to obtain rationed goods with her *libreta*, put together a family meal with a minimum of ingredients, then squeeze the very last drop of detergent out of the holder to do the washing up.

Love hotels

Every Cuban understood what it meant when Tomás Gutiérrez set the opening scene of his film "Fresa y chocolate" in a tatty little hotel. The accommodation provided in such state-run "posadas" (literally "shelters") is one response to the acute housing shortage, allowing married couples to share a few hours of privacy away from parents, children and other distractions. It has to be said that it's not only married couples who take advantage of these arrangements.

It is normal for young people to live with their parents up to the time of their **marriage**. Even after they have wed, the dearth of housing means that many young couples continue to live in one or other of the parental homes. The resulting overcrowding and lack of privacy is a contributory cause to the high rate of **divorce**, particularly among the urban population. Many people remarry, some more than once, and have further children, resulting in the phenomenon of enormously extended families.

Cubans at home

A lot of Cuban life is led out of doors. This can make for an extremely lively, not to say noisy urban scene, with children playing, home-made carts rattling along, people carrying on shouted conversations from one balcony to another, even the click of dominoes being slammed down on an outside table.

With a total of more than two million inhabitants, Havana is the prime example of an overcrowded Cuban **town**. In **inner-city areas** generally, multiple families are crammed into *solares*, the old colonial-era residences arranged around an internal courtyard. The term *solar* has become a negative one, and is now simply a label for a grossly overcrowded building of this type. As more and more people move in, rooms are either partitioned up or improvised *barbacoas* (mezzanine floors) are added, further reducing privacy and contributing to the instability of the building itself. In Old Havana, the throb of drums often means that a *guaguancó (See page 60)* is going on in the patio of one of the area's many old *solares*.

In the aftermath of the Revolution, many dwellings in the **residential suburbs** were taken over by new residents after their mainly middle-class owners had fled the country. Those that stayed put now usually share their homes with several generations of their family. Some of these grandiose villas seem trapped in an early 20C time-warp, their spacious interiors still filled with the furniture and fittings of the time. The decor of other dwellings shows the delight many Cubans take in accumulating all sorts of odds and ends. These might include an occasional table with a lace cover, an embroidered cushion, a brightly-coloured bed-spread, a plastic seat next to an old rocking chair. Shelves groan beneath their load of knick-knacks, framed photographs, dolls, perfume samples and bouquets of plastic flowers.

Beginning in the 1960s, the government tackled the country's severe housing shortage by building **estates of apartment blocks** on the urban fringe sites once occupied by shanty towns. "Micro-brigades" of volunteers made up for the lack of labour, their efforts supervised by state-employed architects and rewarded by being first in the queue when construction was completed and the flats assigned. The most striking and successful example of this approach to the housing problem can be seen in the Alamar area to the east of Havana, where a whole series of multi-storey concrete blocks of somewhat bleak appearance were erected in the 1970s *(See page 144)*. But since the beginning of the "special period" new construction has virtually ceased because of the acute shortage of materials.

A bohío in western Cuba

Ph. Hausheer/HOA QUI

Wherever people live, they suffer frequent power cuts (*apagones*), both of electricity and gas, and even the water supply is affected. Cuts can happen at any time because of the decayed state of the infrastructure, while others, possibly several in one day, are planned, and carried out on a district by district basis. Friends and acquaintances often organise themselves in order to avoid the worst effects of the cuts.

Conditions in the countryside are even more critical than in the towns, even though much effort has been expended since the Revolution in attempting to raise standards in **rural areas**. Schools and hospitals have been built, agricultural land has been reclaimed, as in the Zapata peninsula, and new **rural communities** have been created like the one at Las Terrazas in the Sierra del Rosario (*See page 161*). The amenities in places like this are far superior to those commonly found in the **bohíos** (cottages) which are such a feature of the Cuban countryside. Some of these timber huts with their roofs of thatch or corrugated iron are frighteningly substandard in modern terms, often with earth floors and no electricity or running water.

Cuban **villages** usually consist of wooden houses painted in pastel colours bleached by the sun. The dwellings lining the main street often have porticoes in which residents take their ease at the end of the day. One of the most picturesque examples of this type of village is Vinales in Pinar del Río province.

Education

The Revolution's number one priority

For many people the Cuban Revolution is synonymous with the universal provision of health care and education. When in 1959 the State was made responsible for all schooling, it guaranteed access to education for all, along with the principle of non-payment.

One of the new government's first great undertakings was the **literacy campaign** of 1961. In the course of this "Year of Education" thousands and thousands of teachers and students were sent into the most remote areas of the country, in order to teach people – 30% of whom were illiterate – to read and write. The campaign's success was marked at the end of the year by a great celebration which filled the streets of Havana. By 1970 the educational system had been restructured with the aim of grounding it firmly in the socio-economic realities of the country. In 1968, in an attempt to promote the development of backward rural areas a network of special "secondary schools in the countryside" (known by their initials – **ESBEC**) was created. As well as conventional studies, these boarding schools give their pupils a land-based education which includes the running of a 500-hectare farm to make the establishment self-sufficient.

Education today

Cuba's literacy rate of 94% places it ahead of all other developing countries. Compulsory schooling lasts for nine years. Everywhere in Cuba there seem to be swarms of children in their neat **uniforms**, red for primary schools, mustard yellow for secondary schools. The girls have short skirts with straps, the boys shorts or long trousers. All wear white shirts with a loosely knotted necktie.

The education system has not escaped the effects of the "special period". Schools are poorly equipped, with a severe shortage of textbooks and writing materials. Just as serious is an apparent lack of motivation on the part of many teachers,

Outside a school near Santiago

many of whom can earn the equivalent of a month's salary in a day by providing some sort of service for tourists. Once the *pre-universitario* (more or less the equivalent of a British sixth-form college) is over, more and more students are skipping university. Since traditional qualifications are no guarantee of a job, they prefer to look for well-tipped work in an international hotel rather than study for years only to end up with a meagre salary of a few pesos a month as a doctor, architect, lawyer or engineer.

Sport

The Revolution has made Cubans a nation of sportspeople. The country's sporting prowess is a source of national pride and sport is the subject of countless discussions and arguments. Reported in detail, the achievements of Cuban athletes in international competitions have won the country first place among the nations of the Third World and Latin America.

After the long period of previous neglect, the new regime made sport an important part of the educational curriculum. A National Institute of Sport, Physical Education and Leisure **(INDER)** was set up in 1961 and sports facilities were provided all over the country. Even in primary schools, children have good access to sportsgrounds and equipment. In a country where sport has been deprofessionalised – all teams are made up of amateurs – competitive sport in schools gives the talented a chance to prove themselves and to continue to develop their skills, first at secondary level, and then at special institutions known as Advanced Schools of Athletic Improvement (EPSA).

51

This policy has achieved astonishing results. Ever since the 1972 Olympics, Cuban **boxers** have regularly carried off gold medals for their country. But despite its glorious record, boxing is only Cuba's second sport. Pride of place is occupied by **baseball** (*béisbol* or *pelota*), the national sport. Every square and public park is used as a pitch for lively games, in which youngsters with bats and gloves much too big for them do their best to imitate the style of whoever happens to be the reigning champion. Cubans are superb players and regularly thrash teams from the United States in international games.

The country has encouraged progress in other sports too, with the result that it gained second place in the **Pan-American Games** which were held in Cuba in 1991. It was ranked fifth in the 1992 **Barcelona Olympics** and eighth at **Atlanta** in 1996. Cuba's top athletes, like the high jumper Javier Sotomayor and the runner Fidelia Quirot enjoy world-wide fame.

As the 1990s progressed and the "Special Period" showed no signs of coming to an end, the deterioration of sports facilities and lack of equipment meant that large numbers of Cuban athletes were tempted to join foreign teams. In 1995 the government allowed fifteen Cuban baseball players to take part in a Japanese championship. During the Atlanta Olympics a number of Cuban boxers quit the national team and asked for asylum in Mexico and the United States.

Leisure

Poor public transport and the drop in spending power has meant that public places are much less lively than they used to be. People tend to spend their free time at home or with friends and neighbours, preferably comfortably installed in a favourite rocking chair in front of the **television**. The small screen has become Cubans' window on the world. It tends to be permanently switched on, with or without the sound. It is extraordinarily popular; the streets empty whenever a favourite *telenovela* (soap opera) is being screened. The nation's favourite game, at least as far as men are concerned, is **dominoes**, played on the living room table, in the doorway or even on the street.

J. F. Galmiche

Getting an old record-player to work again can be the perfect excuse for a party, when the fun can go on till dawn.

Despite everything, certain places still attract a crowd. There is no missing the focal point of any provincial town – the *parque central*. It is here, or nearby, that two essential Cuban institutions are invariably to be found.

As its name implies, the **Casa de la Cultura** is the setting for all kinds of cultural activities (concerts, drama, exhibitions), often organised in the face of an almost total lack of resources.

The other great rendezvous is the **Casa de la Trova** (literally: house of the troubadour), the nursery nourishing local musicians. Virtually every town in Cuba has a Casa de la Trova, each with its own character and particular charm. A comparative study would bring out the contrasts between the Casas in different places, like the intellectual atmosphere of Havana's Casa, the delightful courtyard in Santiago, and the smoky dive in Baracoa. Most evenings see some sort of activity. Couples dance, others simply enjoy the music with a bottle of rum or rough *aguardente* to hand. Tourists are welcome, especially if they can be persuaded to join in.

In the larger towns or in places where there are large numbers of visitors from abroad, hotel **bars** are favoured by young people on the lookout for a dollar or two. **Discotheques** are popular, as are pop **concerts**.

Inside the Casa de la Trova at Baracoa

A FUSION OF RELIGIONS

Cuba is a secular country in which **freedom of worship** is guaranteed, though since the Revolution the various religions have been limited to a minor role in national life. In recent years there have been attempts to bring about a degree of reconciliation between Church and State. In 1991, the 4th Communist Party Congress decided that Party members should once again be free to practise the religion of their choice, and, in a time of acute economic difficulties, the government seems prepared to admit that religion can be a welcome help to people.

Roman Catholicism

Four centuries of Spanish colonial rule ensured that **Catholicism** became the country's dominant religion, but even before the Revolution only 10 % of Cubans were regular churchgoers.

In the early years of the Castro regime, a fiercely anti-Communist Church could only disapprove of the resumption of diplomatic relations with the Soviet Union. Some members of the clergy were involved in counter-revolutionary activity, and the Church's negative attitude towards the new government and its policies led to a wave of arrests, church closures and expulsions from the country. In addition many believers emigrated of their own accord. Although relations were never completely severed between Church and State, practising Catholics could not become members of the Communist Party and were automatically excluded from certain occupations.

The Church still has no access to the media, and religious education is still forbidden. Nevertheless, there have been numerous instances of a more relaxed attitude, beginning with the import of 30 000 Bibles in 1988. Churchmen from abroad have been allowed to enter the country, and in 1996 Castro was received in the Vatican by **Pope John-Paul II**. Catholic publications have increased in number and in June 1997 a grand mass was held in Havana's Cathedral Square. The Pope's visit to Cuba in January 1998 was a major event in Cuba's recent history.

In addition to its many Catholics, Cuba has around 100 000 **Protestants**, the result of strong North American influence in the early part of the 20C. And there is also a small **Jewish community**.

Santería

Akin to Haitian voodoo or the *changó* of Trinidad, Cuba's *Santería* conjures up an array of vivid images. They might include good luck offerings left at the foot of a *ceiba* tree, a picture of the *Virgen de Regla* atop a little shrine crowded with candles, dolls, flowers and statuettes of saints, or a figure clad in dazzling white emerging from a rapt and swaying crowd as a ceremony reaches its peak of intensity.

Origins

The term *Santería* covers a range of Afro-Cuban beliefs, most of which have their origin in the **Regla de Ocha**, the religion practised by the Yoruba people of southeastern Nigeria.

Though they were usually baptised on their arrival in Cuba, African slaves nevertheless managed to preserve some of their religious beliefs by giving their gods the names of Christian saints. Subtle exploitation of similarities between the two religions led to the fusion of the worship of African deities and Catholicism, and the emergence of *Santería*. The boundary between the two religions is often highly tenuous; it seems a matter of complete indifference to many worshippers whether they address their prayers to a Christian saint or an equivalent African deity.

Practised in semi-secret during the early years of Castro's regime, *Santería* has become much more visible since the end of the 1980s and the government has had to acknowledge the importance of a belief system which affects all levels of society. One instance of the increased official tolerance of *Santería* was when Castro formally welcomed the ruler of the Yoruba to Cuba in June 1987.

The economic crisis now gripping the country has led to a massive increase in the popularity of *Santería*. Closely connected to everyday life, it is looked to for support by people confronted by the daily problems of finding a job, warding off illness or keeping clear of the police. And there is widespread belief in its efficacy in keeping evil spirits at bay.

But even *Santería* has not escaped the effects of dollar worship. Special ceremonies are now held for the benefit of tourists as well as for the State, which rakes in the hard currency through the intermediary of *diplobabalaos* (a play on words meaning a Santería priest working for dollars).

Santería altar

Ph. Roy/HOA QUI

Santería

The Yoruba pantheon

About twenty of the 400 Yoruba *orishas* (gods) are worshipped in Cuba. Each of these African deities is identified with one or more Christian saints, and each is associated with particular colours, faculties, character traits or other attributes in line with Yoruba mythology.

A ceremony always begins by those present invoking **Elegguá** (St Anthony of Padua), the master of human destiny, appointed by the supreme deity Olofi as his intermediary. His colours are red and black. One of the most important divinities in Yoruba mythology is **Ochún** (the Virgin of Charity of El Cobre), Cuba's patron saint. She is the goddess of love, motherhood, fresh water and gold, and her colour is yellow. She was married to **Orula** (St Francis of Assisi), a diviner by trade whose powers depended on his *ékuele* (magic collar). Tiring of her old husband, she took many lovers, among them the frightening figure of **Changó** (St Barbara), the god of thunder and lightning, of drums and of war. Changó is often shown clad in red and white carrying a sceptre ending in a two-headed axe. His brother **Oggún** (St Peter), the god of metal, strength and virility, is another Yoruba deity given to warlike pursuits.

Yemaya (the Black Virgin of Regla), the patron saint of the city of Havana and a sort of female counterpart of Ochún, is the subject of a popular Cuban cult. Dressed in blue, she is the goddess of salt water and was present at the time of the Creation. Another high-ranking *orisha* is **Obbatalá** (Our Lady of Grace). In her white cloak she symbolises peace, intelligence and harmony. She is a thoughtful deity, able to keep order among her fellow divinities.

Babalaos and santeros

There are around 10 000 santería priests in Cuba, called **"babalaos"**. Assisted by male *babalochas* and female *iyalochas*, they are doctors of body and soul, using magic and divination to solve the problems people bring to them. Thanks to his initiation into the secrets of Orula, the *babalao* is able to interpret oracles by using *cauris* (shells), *obbis* (coconuts) or by casting an *Ékuele* (collar) on a *tablero de Ifa* (mat or wooden board).

The *babalao*'s powers of divination are also used to identify those of the faithful to whom a patron saint can be attributed, and who can become **"santeros"** by means of an elaborate initiation ceremony. For this, candidates must be spiritually aware and able to live according to the fundamental values of *santería*, based on the unity of humankind and Nature and the worship of deities and ancestors. They must also have a sponsor. Both men and women can become a *santero*, whereas the office of *babalao* is exclusively male.

Once the *babalao* has identified the *orisha* of the person to be initiated, they must **dress in white** from head to toe for a whole year. Allowance is made for people for whom this would be particularly difficult, like anyone who has to wear a uniform.

The ceremony

At the end of the waiting period an **initiation ceremony** is arranged, in the course of which the *orisha* takes possession of the candidate. Offerings of fruit, vegetables and herbs are made, and chickens, white doves or goats are sacrificed. The clothes worn during the ceremony are in the colours of the deity concerned. To the beat of drums, the sound of ritual chants in Yoruba, and the rhythmic movement of the dancers, the candidate gradually enters into a trance-like state, a sign that the *orisha* is now part of their being.

Once a year on the **anniversary** of their initiation, the *santero* organises a ceremony in honour of their *orisha*.

The religious calendar

Certain dates in the Christian calendar have a special significance for practitioners of *Santería*. On **8 September** (Birth of the Blessed Virgin Mary) huge gatherings take place at two places in the country. At Regla *(See page 142)*, on the far side of the harbour from Old Havana, there is a great procession in honour of **Yemaya**, while in the east pilgrims flock from all over the country to the shrine of El Cobre to pay tribute to **Ochún** *(See page 294)*.

On **17 December** a growing number of believers make a painful pilgrimage – on their knees, with ball and chain – to the church of San Lazaro at Rincón, a village close to Havana airport, in honour of **Babalú-Ayé** (St Lazarus), the god of healing.

Santería ceremony

Other cults exist in Cuba, among them the **Regla de Palo Monte**, an animistic religion imported by Bantu tribespeople from the south of what is now Angola. Another is *Ñañiguismo*, a cult originating in the delta of the River Niger and practised by a **secret society called the Abakuá**. Much remains obscure about this confraternity, whose *ñañigos* (initiates) are exclusively male, but it began as a mutual aid society for slaves, opening its doors to White members in the middle of the 19C. Many of its adherents were to be found in the port cities of Havana, Matanzas and Cárdenas. At one point it seems to have sunk into criminality, with different branches fighting each other like mafiosi for control of Havana's commerce, and initiates were obliged to go out into the street and kill the first person they encountered.

Once having passed through his initiation rites, the *ñañigo* is subject to an extremely strict code of honour, and must give moral and financial support to his *ekobios* (brothers), devote himself to the cult of ancestors and pay tribute to Ekue, the voice of the Supreme God Abasí.

A LAND OF MUSIC

Cuba is unthinkable without music and dance. Every Cuban seems born with an innate sense of rhythm and every second Cuban seems to be a musician. The modern world has grown up with the sounds of Cuban music in its ears, and it would be an unlucky visitor that did not rediscover something of themselves in the rhythms throbbing in the streets, bars and Casas de la Trova of this festive island.

Afro-Cuban music and dance

Salsa is the music most people associate with Cuba. But in fact salsa was born in New York in the 1960s among Cuban exiles and other members of the Hispanic community, and the term now covers many contemporary styles of Latin American popular music. Its international popularity is simply the latest manifestation of the riches Cuba's musical traditions have given the world.

Beginnings

It was only in the middle of the 19C that distinctive musical forms began to emerge in Cuba. In his *Music in Cuba*, Alejo Carpentier suggested that there was a lack of creative energy among the Spanish colonists, in architecture as much as in music, and that this could be explained by the "feeble resistance put up by the indigenous population". But though the Taino people failed to influence the subsequent evolution of Cuban music, the picture is very different as far as the African contribution is concerned. To begin with, the slaves brought to Cuba very soon learned to adapt the songs and dances brought with them to the Spanish instruments available. Social conditions helped African influences become widespread; for many years Cuba's middle-class Spanish population looked down on music-making as a career, favouring instead the more "respectable" professions. The country was only saved from an acute shortage of musicians because Blacks stepped into the gap, integrating the rhythms of their ritual ceremonies, exploiting the percussive potential of European instruments, and extracting music from a whole range of tools and everyday objects.

European melody, African rhythm

Cuba became a melting pot in which the heritage of Spain and France was fused with the pulsating rhythms of Africa to yield new and distinctive musical forms.

A contribution from France – The courtly **contredanse** or quadrille (*contradanza*) came with the French colonists to Saint-Domingue (what is now Haiti and the Dominican Republic) and then to Cuba, where it gave rise to a whole series of musical developments. The way in which the *contredanse* makes dancers come close then draw apart in a kind of flirtatious quarrel had so many parallels with African dances that it immediately caught on in Cuba, rapidly becoming the country's favourite musical style. From it there evolved the *danza*, the *habanera*, and above all the *danzón*. The **danzón** originated in 1877 in the town of Matanzas. Based on the classical *contredanse*, it was danced by couples rather than in a group. Right up until the 1920s, the *danzón* remained the most popular kind of dance music in Cuba, played by bands known as *charangas* which added a flute, violins and plenty of brass to the traditional line-up. By the 1940s it had

Street musicians

evolved into the **mambo**, which conquered the world in the 1950s largely thanks to Pérez Prado and his famous band. The no less popular **cha-cha-cha** was born at the same time, named for the sound made by the rhythmic scraping of the dancers' footwear.

A marriage of Spain and Africa – Another kind of music emerged from the mixing of Spanish and African traditions. Nearly all contemporary Cuban music – like salsa – is based on *son*, which originated in Oriente province in the east of the country in the late 19C. It combined the metre of the typical Spanish song with the solo/chorus structure characteristic of much African music. It is distinguished by the way in which the melody is provided by voices and the rhythm by instruments, with even the guitar being used for rhythm rather than melody. By the 1920s *son* was well established among the Black population of Havana. A number of variants developed from it, for example *son montuno*, which is also linked to the *guajira* (a type of Spanish country music popular among rural Whites).

The guitar-playing *trovadores* (troubadours) who were largely responsible for bringing *son* to the capital, popularised other types of music, of Spanish origin, like the cheerful *guaracha* or the sultry *bolero*. By the 1920s the normal line-up for *son* was the *sexteto* with two singers (one with *claves*, the other with *maracas*), a *tres* (small guitar with three double strings), a conventional guitar, a double-bass and a *bongó* drum. With the addition of a trumpet, this evolved into a *septeto*, and the line-up has been growing ever since.

Rumba – The rumba originated among the Black communities of Havana and Matanzas at the end of the 19C. It had deep roots in the ritual dances associated with the various Afro-Cuban cults which in some cases go back to the fertility rites of West Africa. A number of distinct forms exist. The **yambú** is relatively slow and is often referred to as the old folks' dance, in contrast to the **columbia**, a solo dance for men involving movements of almost acrobatic dexterity. Then there is the **guaguancó**, full of those suggestive pelvic movements – *vacunaos* – which give the rumba its inimitably erotic character.

A living tradition

Cuban music has not stood still but continues to develop, with new rhythms and dances continuing to emerge in recent years both in and outside Cuba.

In the 1970s the leading figures in what came to be called **Nueva Trova** were Silvio Rodríguez and Pablo Milanés, specialists in *canción protesta* (protest songs) sung to the accompaniment of a guitar and with a political content which sometimes got its practitioners into trouble.

Others became involved in **Latin Jazz** which as its name implies brought together jazz sounds and Latin rhythms. In 1973 Jesús "Chucho" Valdés formed his *Irakere* band, which subsequently became the model for this fusion of jazz, rock and traditional Cuban music.

The early 1970s also saw the birth of *Los Van Van*, the renowned group still fronted by Juan Formell, with its line-up of electric guitar, synthesiser and drums – so much for tradition! Van Van invented **songo**, described by Isabelle Leymarie in *Cuban Fire* as a "sort of *danzón* crossed with pop", and which had a major influence on the next generation of musicians. In recent years new bands have sprung up, many of them undertaking highly successful tours in Europe as well as in Cuba. Cuban music seems safe in the hands of groups like *La Charanga Habanera*, *NG La Banda* and *El Médico de la Salsa*.

With its substantial Hispanic community, **New York** has become one of the strongholds of Afro-Cuban influence. It was here at the end of the 1960s that **salsa** was created, that exciting music inspired by *son* but mostly performed by Puerto Rican singers. The dominant salsa label is *Fania*, which has spread its message throughout the United States and which brings together the *Fania All Stars* for the occasional block-busting compilation, featuring the talents of stars like Celia Cruz, Rubén Blades, Willie Colón, Ray Barretto, Hector Lavoe and Johnny Pacheco.

Cuban musical instruments

"The music of Cuba is in the smoke of its tobacco and in the sweetness of its sugar...

White in sugar and in the guitar, black in coffee and the drum. And today, in a mulato fusion, we have white coffee and the bongó."

Fernando Ortiz *La Africania de la música folklórica de Cuba.*

Afro-Cuban music is dominated by the sound of **drums**. Shaped like a tall barrel and normally held between the legs, the **conga** *(tumbadora)* lays down the basic rhythm. The **bongó** consists of two small round drums of unequal size, linked together and supported on the drummer's knees. The **timbales** consist of a pair

PERCUSSION INSTRUMENTS

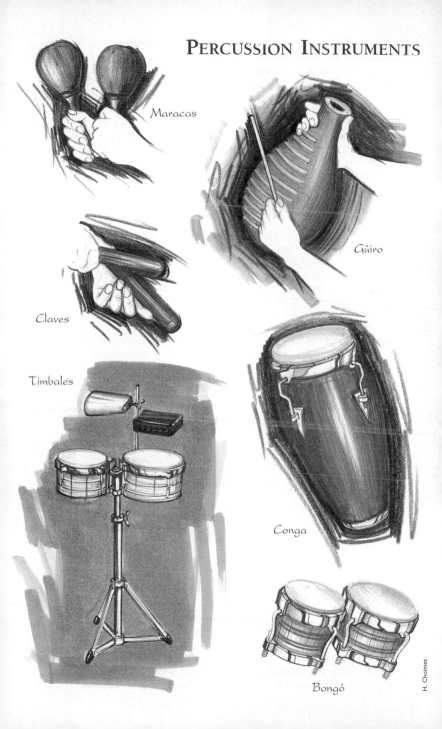

Maracas

Güiro

Claves

Timbales

Conga

Bongó

H. Choimet

of side drums mounted on a stand together with cowbells. On no account to be forgotten are the **claves**, the keystone of the Cuban musical edifice. One of these batons of hardened wood is tapped against the other to give the characteristic sharp metallic sound which lays down the basic rhythm of *son* and salsa. Almost as important are the **güiro**, a ribbed and elongated gourd scraped with a stick, and the **maracas** filled with seeds and used like a rattle. *Santería* ceremonies take place to the sound of three **batá drums**, each of a different size and each with its own name; from the smallest to the biggest they are the *okónkolo*, the *itótele*, and finally the *iyá*, is considered to be the "mother of all drums".

The trumpet, the saxophone, the piano, the double-bass, the violin, the flute all play their part in Cuban music, as does the **tres**, a guitar from Oriente province with three sets of double strings.

Ballet and dance

Alongside its popular dances, Cuba also has a world-famous **classical dance** company. Now more than 70 years old, **Alicia Alonso** is still in charge of the **Ballet Nacional de Cuba**, the blindness from which she has suffered since the age of 20 in no way hindering her from pursuing her career as a dancer and choreographer. The National Ballet's rehearsals in the Gran Teatro on Havana's Parque Central are open to the public. The country's second classical company is the Ballet of Camagüey.

The country's **Afro-Cuban dance** heritage is kept alive by a number of groups, notably by the **Conjunto Folklórico Nacional**. Based in Havana, they regularly put on shows and their rehearsals are open to the public every other Saturday (*See Making the most of Havana*).

LITERATURE AND CINEMA

As in many of the other countries of Latin America, it took time for Cuban literature to establish its own identity. But with independence a distinctive literary voice began to be heard, a rich and fascinating synthesis of the country's diverse cultural influences.

Cuban literature

See Bibliography page 102

A portrait of colonial society

The poem *El Espejo de Paciencia* (The Mirror of Patience, 1608) by **Silvestre de Balboa** is the first recorded Cuban work of literature. It depicts the society that had developed in the new colonial environment and includes some references to native flora and fauna. But the emergence of a real literary tradition had to wait until the 19C.

The first Cuban novel to be widely read was *Cecilia Valdés* by **Cirilo Villaverde** (1812-94). Published in 1882, it achieves a grand historical sweep, denouncing slavery while depicting the social structure of colonial society through a gallery of wonderfully perceptive character studies. Villaverde became famous, but the end of the 19C was nevertheless dominated by one of the greatest writers Cuba has ever produced, **José Martí** (1853-95), the "Apostle of Independence", and the most important Latin American literary figure of his era. Thinker, poet, journalist and revolutionary, he became an exile at the age of 16 and spent most of his life abroad. Most of his work was written in the United States and it was from that country that he engaged in the struggle for Cuban independence *(See page 24)*. Martí wrote novels, pamphlets, essays, newspaper articles and dramas, but his greatest achievement is his poetry, gathered in collections like *Ismaelillo* and *Versos sencillos* (Simple Verses, his last work, published posthumously). His boundless poetic talent, expressed in a straightforward, spontaneous and accessible style, made him the forerunner of Latin American modernism.

The search for roots

Towards the end of the 1920s the whole of the Caribbean area was gripped by the growing cult of negritude. Europe too was affected, but it was particularly here that many artists looked for inspiration in the region's African heritage. Among those who sought to understand Afro-Cuban culture – he may even have coined the term – was the prominent anthropologist and historian **Fernando Ortíz** (1881-1969), whose writings still carry weight today. The same Afro-Cuban themes permeate the work of **Lydia Cabrera** (1900-91). Her first book, *Negro tales of Cuba*, was an adaptation of tales inspired by African folklore and her ethnological study *El Monte* (The Forest) of 1954, has remained a standard reference in the area of Afro-Cuban culture.

Cuba's African background was a fruitful source of inspiration in the early works of **Nicolas Guillén** (1902-89). The central theme of his collections of poems entitled *Motivos de son* and *Sóngoro Cosongo* is that of the mixing of races and the development of a real mulatto culture. The language of the poems is colourful in the extreme and some of them can be recited to the rhythm of *son (See page 59)*; they celebrate Afro-Cuban culture and claim a place for Black people in society. Exiled during the Batista period, Guillén returned to Cuba and became one of the country's leading literary figures. He helped found UNEAC (Unión Nacional de Escritores y Artistas Cubanos – National Union of Cuban Writers and Artists) and served as its president. For the rest of his life Guillén's prolific output was largely devoted to promoting the cause of the Revolution.

Afro-Cuban culture is also at the heart of *Ecue-Yamba-O*, the first novel by **Alejo Carpentier** (1904-80). Following the example of **Wilfredo Lam** in painting, Carpentier drew on African sources in order to affirm a national, Caribbean identity. One of Cuba's finest writers, much influenced by the Surrealists he had associated with while in exile in France, he developed his highly original theory of "magic realism", which he saw as "the future fusion of two apparently incompatible states of being – dream and reality – in a sort of absolute reality, surreality". All through his works, particularly in *El Siglo de las Luces* (The Age of Enlightenment), the meeting of different worlds (Old and New) is used to explore the nature of reality in unusual ways. "Magic Realism" has had a strong influence on other writers, notably the Columbian Gabriel García Márquez and, in Britain, Salman Rushdie.

Book market on Havana's Plaza de Armas

A special place in the Cuban literary pantheon is occupied by **José Lezama Lima** (1910-76), editor until the 1950s of the literary journal *Origenes*. Published in 1956, his controversial masterpiece *Paradiso* is full of abstruse metaphors and written in a style which the author himself described as "baroque". Dealing intimately with themes of homosexuality and the mixing of races, the novel had a limited run of only 4 000 because of its supposedly "pornographic" character. A writer closely linked to Lima, despite their many differences, was **Virgilio Piñera** (1912-79), who, after working with Lima on *Origenes* founded his own review, *Ciclón*. As well as composing poetry and writing for the theatre, Pinera was known for his short stories, among them *New Cold Tales*, whose treatment of the fantastic and absurd found numerous imitators. Like Lima, Piñera suffered because of his non-conformism and his homosexuality and after 1970 publication of his work was forbidden. Both writers were condemned to a form of internal exile which lasted right up until their deaths.

Art in the service of the Revolution
In his 1961 speech, *Words to Intellectuals*, following the banning of the film PM, Fidel Castro made it clear what the new cultural policy was to be: "In the Revolution, everything; outside the Revolution, nothing".

This pronouncement was enough to make a number of Cuban intellectuals decide to leave the country, but the regime's real harshness only became apparent ten years later. In 1968, the publication of a prize-winning book of poems by **Herberto Padilla** (1932-) was accompanied by a denunciation of their ideological content by the Writers' Union UNEAC. The poet himself was arrested in 1971, but given his freedom in exchange for a public retraction. The "Padilla Affair" caused considerable controversy among intellectuals across the world, but led to the silencing of many Cuban writers suspected of "ideological diversionism". Ten years later many of them were to take advantage of the Mariel boatlift to quit the country.

The literature of exile
Cuba has remained the principal subject of many exiled writers, each expressing in his or her own way the intertwining of their own fate with that of their country. From his refuge in London, **Guillermo Cabrera Infante** (1929) evoked the Havana of the 1950s in his *Three Trapped Tigers* of 1967, with a wealth of puns, alliterations and plays on words.

Reinaldo Arenas (1943-1990) was to take his life in New York, having completed his stunning autobiography *Before Night Falls,* a work in which the persecution he suffered before leaving Cuba is recounted in a mixture of eroticism, burlesque, self-mockery and lyricism.

A not dissimilar spirit infuses the mordant work of **Zoé Valdés** (1959-), author of *Yocanda in the Paradise of Nada*. She is able to mix the sordid and the marvellous to create an unreal environment, which at the same time is well and truly – and horribly – anchored in the real Havana.

Constant references to the great Cuban writers of the past permeate the pages of *Dime algo sobre Cuba* by **Jesús Díaz** (1941-). Against the background of the "Special Period", his novel paints a bitter but comic picture of the four young founders of an intellectual magazine, attempting to free themselves from the heavy burden of their literary heritage.

A century of cinema

The first cinematograph was brought to Cuba in 1897 by a Frenchman, Gabriel Veyre, right in the middle of the Second War of Independence. The subsequent history of the cinema in Cuba closely paralleled that of the country itself. Going to the cinema soon became fashionable, particularly among the upper echelons of Havana society. Most of the early films came from Europe, but after the First World War the moving pictures filling Cuban screens came mostly from the United States and it was the all-powerful American movie industry that dominated local production and distribution.

New Cuban cinema

The Revolution brought about a radical transformation of Cuban cinema. As early as March 1959 the regime set up the **ICAIC** (Cuban Institute for the Art and Industry of Cinema). Headed by Alfredo Guevara (no relation of Che), the Institute decided to revive Cuban cinema and use it for propagating Revolutionary ideas and ideals. In 1961, the year of the great anti-illiteracy campaign, the **"cinemóvil"** was introduced, a mobile cinema which could be transported by lorry and boat, and even on the backs of mules, to bring the message of literacy to the remotest parts of the country.

Cinema proved to be an effective way of getting the government's message across, helping to develop strong feelings of national identity, especially when relations between Cuba and the United States began to deteriorate. But alternative points of view were not permitted. In May 1961, the short film entitled *PM* by Sabá Cabrera Infante and Orlando Jiménez Leal was banned. Its subject, night-life in the bars of the working-class districts of Havana, using the techniques of free cinema, was considered out of step with the spirit of Revolutionary mobilisation in the days following the Bay of Pigs invasion.

Dominance of the documentary

Influenced by Italian neo-Realism, the French New Wave, the independent American cinema and the classic productions from the Soviet Union, Cuban cinema nevertheless managed to develop a voice of its own. Under the leadership of **Santiago Alvarez**, the quality of documentaries was particularly high, but ordinary films too sometimes won international plaudits, among them Humberto Solás's *Lucia* of 1968.

Well into the 1980s, only about three fictional films were produced every year, compared with an average of 35 documentaries. In the 1990s the film industry was affected by the economic crisis, with lack of resources making it impossible to produce more than a very limited number of films. But even in the throes of the "special period" Cuban cinema has attracted world attention thanks to the two last films directed by **Tomás Guitiérrez Alea**. Alea, who died in April 1996, was one of the founders of the ICAIC. He had been responsible for a number of exceptionally fine films, among them *La Muerte de un burócrata* (Death of a bureaucrat) of 1968, *Memorias del subdesarollo* (Memories of Underdevelopment) of 1971 and *La Ultima cena* (Last Supper) of 1988. Co-directed with Juan Carlos Tabío, his two last films were hugely successful both at home and abroad. *Fresa y chocolate* (Strawberry and Chocolate) of 1994 depicts a friendship between a homosexual artist and a militant young

Literature and cinema

Les cahiers du Cinéma

Scene from "Fresa y Chocolate" (with Vladimir Cruz and Jorge Perrugoria)

Communist. Two years later came *Guantanamera*, in which a strange funeral procession makes its way across Cuba from Guantánamo to Havana. It has been interpreted as an allegory of the future that awaits the country, or alternatively as a premonition of the director's own death

Since 1979, Havana has been the venue every December for the **International Festival** of new Latin American film. For a whole fortnight, the city's hotels are crammed with film-makers and journalists from all over the world. It is a chance for local people to catch up with the latest productions from neighbouring countries and to rediscover those cinematic pleasures which have largely been replaced by television.

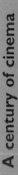

A century of cinema

Do's and dont's

Meeting local people

Human contact is easy in Cuba, especially if the visitor has mastered some basic Spanish. Cubans are intrinsically good-natured and spontaneous. It is easy to be irritated by constant approaches from passers-by, but apart from folk who live from selling to tourists, most people are fascinated by foreigners and are simply curious, their chances of foreign travel being practically nil.

The only places where it might prove difficult to make the acquaintance of Cubans are the so-called "green zones", the international enclaves which have been set aside for tourist development. Elsewhere it is difficult not to meet them; this is a country where even asking people the way can lead to all sorts of fascinating conversations.

One of the best ways of mixing with ordinary people is by patronising Cuba's tiny **private sector**. Taking lodgings in a private house and eating in *paladares* (private restaurants) can give a good insight into daily life as it is lived in Cuba. Hosts are normally keen to talk and answer any questions, and a visitor who stays for several days in the same place is likely to be introduced to an ever-widening circle of relatives and acquaintances. This is particularly true of the smaller towns and **villages** away from the main tourist trail. Traditional hospitality is alive and well in such places, and while it still makes sense not to let one's guard down completely, it would be a shame to be over-cautious and miss out on the good times your Cuban friends are hoping to share with you.

Patronising Cuba's **public transport** is not such a good idea. Trains and buses may look picturesque, but the "special period" has not improved comfort and reliability, and it makes more sense to have one's own transport. This also puts the visitor in the position of doing local people a favour by giving a lift to some of the many **hitch-hikers.** Depending on the degree to which a language is shared, this can be both useful (their directions can help make good the woeful lack of highway signposting) and entertaining (shared life histories etc).

Etiquette

Addresses – Swapping addresses seems second only to baseball and dominoes as a national obsession. Visitors' details will often be demanded so that they can be entered in a notebook already full of Canadian, German or Italian names. In return they are likely to build up an interesting souvenir of their journey in the form of a collection of odd bits of paper with the scribbled names and addresses of Cuban acquaintances, however brief they may have been.

No-one should be surprised if, a few weeks after their return home, they receive a letter from one of these new friends, probably given to another visitor to post abroad to get round the vagaries of the Cuban postal service. Cubans are very keen to compensate for their inability to travel by communicating in this way, and really appreciate getting mail in return, especially if it includes postcards or photos (particularly ones taken of them!)

F. Nichele / HOA QJI

Making friends on the Malecón

Gifts – When invited into a Cuban home, it is good manners to bring a small gift. A bottle of rum is always acceptable. Even better are foreign cigarettes, and mementoes of the visitor's own country, though even small items like cigarette lighters or bottles of perfume are also welcome.

Manners – With their unforced charm and natural behaviour, Cubans have no difficulties in putting their guests at ease. Even the uniform worn by various State employees is not enough to stop their wearers being typically "Cuban" on occasion (though visitors should not rely on this – Cuban officialdom can be formidably inflexible).

Cubans are very physical. Even slight acquaintance is no hindrance to exchanging kisses when meeting or parting, usually one or two on the same cheek. Men shake hands with each other or indulge in a hearty embrace *(abrazo)*.

Cubans like to get on familiar terms as quickly as possible. This means using the *"tu"* form in Spanish early on in an acquaintance, exceptions being when dealing with an official or when there is a great difference in age. Lots of people punctuate their conversation with endearments such as *mi amor, mi cielo, mi vida* or *mi corazón* (my love, sky, life, heart). These have no more significance than being called "love" by a London taxi-driver.

Style – Cubans take great care in their appearance and a tubby figure in baggy T-shirt, sagging shorts and flip-flops is almost certainly a foreign tourist. Such garb should be avoided by anyone invited by local people to any sort of occasion, since it could be interpreted as a lack of respect.

Dancing – Foreigners' attempts to imitate Cuban grace and sensuality on the dance floor can cause great hilarity. But it is not meant unkindly; any effort to join in is appreciated, and there will be plenty of volunteers eager to help improve a visitor's salsa technique.

On the beach – Perhaps surprisingly in view of the revealing attire worn by many shapely locals, toplessness and nudity is not acceptable on Cuban beaches, except on those used more or less exclusively by foreign visitors.

Politics – Local people rarely discuss politics and it is only polite not to push them to do so, least of all in public places. But airing opinions about the country's economic problems is a different matter.

Queuing – Inured to shortages of all kinds, Cubans are used to queuing and queues are generally well-disciplined affairs. Most visitors will find themselves queuing *(hacer la cola)* at some point during their stay, even if it is only to buy an ice-cream (though in Havana's famous Coppelia ice-cream parlour foreigners are whisked into a special section without the need to stand in line). The polite way to get into a queue is to position oneself behind the last person and ask *¿El ultimo?* (the last?) if it is a man, or *¿La ultima?* if it is a woman.

Appointments – Keeping an appointment *(tener una cita)* in Cuba can be a revelation. This is a country which takes its time to get things done, not just out of indolence but because of all the problems involved in getting from one place to another. It's best to keep calm and not put too much faith in expressions like *"vengo ahora"* (I'm on my way). A smile and a sense of humour will ease many a situation, particularly in encounters with officialdom. Losing one's temper is likely to be counter-productive.

Language

The official language of Cuba is of course **Spanish**. Cuban Spanish differs from the Castilian Spanish of Spain in a number of ways *(See the Glossary on page 104 and on the reverse of the cover)*. Over the centuries it has been enriched by the addition of words from the indigenous languages, from African tongues, and from English. It has also kept quite a few expressions which have fallen into disuse in Spain itself, as well as employing *cubanismos* (specifically Cuban words and expressions) and *americanismos* (words and expressions in use in Latin America generally).

Even for fluent Spanish speakers, Cuban Spanish takes a little getting used to. It is worth remembering that in colonial days the dominant influence was not the refined Spanish of Castile but the southern variant spoken in Andalucia, from whose ports the New World was explored and colonised. So, as elsewhere in Latin America, the "th" of Castilian does not exist, and "c" is pronounced as "s". In addition, the final "s" of a word is almost always dropped. Cubans talk rapidly, often running one word into another, and there are a number of distinct accents.

Cuban catchphrases

All Cubans, not just the young, pick up catchphrases from the media and use them freely. Some of the most widespread come from popular songs. Your local acquaintances will be mightily impressed if you are able to memorise a few and trot them out at an appropriate moment. Charanga Habanera were responsible for *"papiriqui con guaniquiqui"* (meaning "loaded"), while Médico de la Salsa coined *"estar arriba de la bola"* (to be on top form). And Médico's *"preparate pa'lo que viene"* (get ready for what's on the way) became a useful slogan when the Ministry of Tourism started to encourage people to take a positive attitude to the growing numbers of foreign visitors.

Dominoes in the street

F. Ancellet/RAPHO

English is the language of foreign tourism in Cuba and is widely spoken by people who have regular dealings with visitors from abroad. A few also speak some German, French or Italian. Quite a lot of young people are keen to use their English, often with an accent betraying the influence of American films shown on TV. Spanish comes into its own elsewhere and a Spanish-English dictionary or good phrase book is recommended for anyone venturing anywhere off the beaten track.

An interesting reminder of the days of 'eternal friendship' with the Soviet Union is the number of people who speak fluent **Russian** or some other Eastern European language.

CUBAN FOOD

Creole cooking

Few visitors come to Cuba for its cuisine. With a few exceptions, Cuban food tends to be bland, monotonous and unexciting, with few spices but plenty of fats and starch.

Most *paladares* (private restaurants) have a more or less identical menu, based on **pork** and **chicken**, grilled or fried, accompanied by **rice**, **bananas**, **manioc** (or *cassava*), and a tomato, cucumber and avocado **salad**.

Preparation of these ingredients hardly varies from one place to another. The ever-present rice *(arroz)* is served boiled or *congrí* (with red beans), a variant on *moros y cristianos* (literally "Moors and Christians", rice with black beans). Bananas are served in a number of different ways, as a purée *(fufú de plátano)*, fried *(plátanos fritos)*, as fritters *(tostones)*, and as delicious crisps *(mariquitas)*. Despite their enormously long coastline Cubans are not great eaters of fish, generally preferring the taste of meat. Most menus offer several variations on the theme of pork *(puerco* or *cerdo)* or chicken *(pollo)* but usually only one or two fish dishes. Beef *(res)* is normally reserved for State restaurants, but ways round this can usually be found. The same applies to Cuba's famous **lobster**, most of which is exported. When it does appear, it is accompanied by a lightly spiced but very salty tomato sauce *(langosta enchilada)*.

The fish from nowhere
The arrival of the August full moon is awaited every year with great impatience by the people of Baracoa in eastern Cuba. Seven days later, strange glutinous capsules begin to appear in the mouth of the Río Toa. Once they meet fresh water they begin to disintegrate, releasing countless tiny "tetí", minuscule translucent fish which then try to swim upstream. The phenomenon continues until December, during which time the tetí netted by local fishermen are consumed with great relish in and around the town.

A typical Cuban dessert consists of a piece of fruit accompanied by fromage frais or grated cheese. A Coppelia ice-cream is a possible alternative. Meals can be nicely rounded off with a dark and well-sugared *café cubano*.

Some parts of Cuba seem to be more interested in food than others. Baracoa, close to the country's eastern tip, is something of a gourmet's delight, and Havana does of course have a number of good restaurants. Baracoa boasts the best **ajiaco**, the national dish of casseroled meat, bacon and vegetables, as well as the famous local *tetí*.

Drinks galore

For a country where fruit grows in abundance, Cuba offers surprisingly little in the way of fresh fruit juice, though juices can be bought in cartons. Soft drinks *(refrescos)* are widely available, including *Tropicola*, the local cola, or *Cachito*, a sort of Seven-Up. Excellent *batidos* (milk-shakes) made from bananas or guavas cost only a few pesos at roadside stands, and in the countryside *guarapo* (fresh cane juice) is sold as well.

The queen of Cuban drinks is of course **rum** *(ron)*. There are many excellent brands, but the market leader, on sale everywhere, is *Havana Club*. Dark rums like the five year old *Carta de Oro* and the seven year old *Añejo* can be drunk neat or on the rocks, whereas three year old *Carta Blanca*, a white rum, is more suitable as a base for the hundred or so **cocktails** for which Cuba is famous. The best known internationally is **Cuba Libre** (rum and coke with a twist of lemon or lime and ice), but Cubans' favourite cocktail is the **mojito** (rum, lemon or lime, sugar, soda, ice, and a sprig of mint). Hemingway fans will want to alternate between a *mojito* and his much-loved **daiquirí** (rum, lemon or lime, sugar, crushed ice, stirred, maraschino cherry). After which there is Ron Collins, Papa's Special, Cuba Bella, Cubanito, Mulata, Piña Colado, punch, and many, many more.

Cuban wine, made from oranges and grapefruit as well as from grapes, is worth trying as a curiosity, but imported wines are expensive. To accompany a meal, it makes more sense to drink *agua mineral* (mineral water), *con gas* (sparkling) or *sin gas* (still), or **beer** (*cerveza*). Lager-type Cuban beers like *Hatuey, Mayabe, Bucanero, Lagarto* or *Cristal* are all worth trying, and international brands are usually available too.

Inside Havana's Bodeguita del Medio

Cuban food

Practical Information

Varadero
beach scene

BEFORE LEAVING

• **Local time**

Cuba lives and works to Eastern Standard Time, five hours behind Greenwich Mean Time. At midday in Britain it is 7am in Cuba.

• **Telephoning to Cuba**

To telephone to Cuba from the United Kingdom dial 00 53 followed by the city code and the subscriber's number.

• **When to go**

The timing of a visit to Cuba will depend on the kind of holiday wanted. Summer is best for a beach holiday and winter for sightseeing, but the two can be combined in **March** and **April** which have the additional advantage of being outside the main tourist season.

Anyone wishing to visit Cuba for some special event like Carnival at Santiago (26 June) should book their journey and hotel room well in advance.

Average maximum and minimum temperatures (Celsius)

	Jan	Feb	Mar	Apr	May	Jun	Jul	Aug	Sep	Oct	Nov	Dec
Max	27	28	29	30	31	31	32	33	32	32	30	28
Min	17	16	18	20	21	22	23	23	22	21	20	18

Throughout the year nightfall never occurs later than 7pm and it may make sense to get up early in order to make the most of daylight. Sunrise and sunset at Havana at different times of the year are shown below:

	sunrise	sunset
21 December	7.22am	6.10pm
21 March	6.34am	6.41pm
21 June	5.44am	7.18pm
21 September	6.18am	6.27pm

• **What to wear**

Only light clothing is necessary in Cuba. Clothes that wash easily and dry quickly are best as humidity levels are high; 82% during the wet season and not much less in the dry season. An umbrella or some sort of waterproof is essential in summer, particularly in the wetter parts of the country such as the area around Baracoa in the east. A pullover or light jacket will come into its own not only in upland areas but also in places with air conditioning (including overnight trains) which can sometimes be goose-pimplingly effective. Tough, waterproof footwear is necessary for walking in the countryside or in the mountains.

Formal clothes are not needed, but most Cubans take considerable pride in their appearance and visitors should do the same if invited home by anyone or when going out in the evening to a good restaurant or a cabaret. A smart casual look is all that is required.

• **Things to take**

A torch is useful for power cuts or when walking along dimly-lit streets. Cuba runs on 110 volts, and an adapter is essential for any electrical apparatus brought from abroad (*See also page 100*).

Before going

• Travellers all

Travelling with children

Staying in a beach resort like Varadero, Guardalavaca or Marea del Portillo is unlikely to present parents of young children with any special problems, and many such places even have creches. However, anyone touring the country will soon run into difficulties unless well prepared. Outside the main tourist areas the supply of essentials such as milk, baby foods, nappies and medicines is erratic to say the least, and finding them can easily become a full-time activity.

The tropical sun shines fiercely. Summer is best avoided and tender young skin should be protected at all times.

Single travellers

Lone travellers are unlikely to remain on their own for very long. Cubans have few inhibitions about making contact with strangers and single people will soon be engaged in conversation or bombarded with offers of help in finding their way or requests of one kind or another. This can be tiresome or very rewarding, the latter even more so if the visitor speaks at least a little Spanish.

Provided she takes the normal precautions, like keeping away from ill-lit streets at night and not flaunting valuables, a **female** visitor need have few fears. However, Cuba is a Latin country, with all that implies. A woman on her own will be the recipient of constant *piropos* (flirtatious compliments). These are made as a matter of course, and it is normally sufficient to make it quite clear that one is not interested for the *caballero* to turn his interest elsewhere.

Different problems face lone **men**. They are a natural target for the *jineteras* (prostitutes) who hang around areas frequented by tourists. Their somewhat direct approach has startled more than one sophisticated man of the world.

Couples

Travelling together tends to cut down on the number of chance encounters, both agreeable and disagreeable.

Gay couples are beginning to be tolerated but should be discreet in public.

Senior citizens

Older people should not come across any special problems in Cuba, though they should avoid summer heat and make sure they are in a fit condition to tackle mountain walks.

Disabled travellers

There is hardly any provision in Cuba for the special needs of disabled travellers, the only exception being Cayo Coco.

• Address Book

Tourist information

Canada – Cuban Tourist Board, 55 Queen Street East, suite 705, Toronto, Ontario M5C 1R6, ☎ (416) 362 07 00, Fax (416) 362 67 99.

Bureau du tourisme de Cuba, 440 boulevard René Levesque Ouest, bureau 1402, Montréal, Québec H2Z 1V7, ☎ (514) 857 80 04, Fax (514) 875 80 06.

United Kingdom – Cuban Tourist Office, 167 High Holborn, London WC1V 6PA, ☎ (020) 7240 6655.

Web sites

Cuba Solidarity Campaign www.poptel.org.uk/cuba-solidarity/

Embassies and consulates

Canada – Cuban Embassy, 388 Main Street, Ottawa K1S 1E3, ☎ (613) 563 0141.
United Kingdom – Cuban Embassy, 167 High Holborn, London WC1V 6PA,
☎ (020) 7240 2488. Cuban Consulate, 15 Grape Street, London WC1V 6PA,
☎ (020) 7240 2488, open 9.30am to 12.30pm Monday to Friday.

• Documents required

ID, visas

All foreign visitors to Cuba must have a **passport** valid for a minimum of
6 months after the date of their return journey, plus a **tourist card** *(tarjeta del
turista)* which must be handed back to passport control on leaving the country.
Tourist cards cost around £15 and are issued by Cuban consulates (see above)
though it is normally more convenient to obtain them through a travel agent.
You will need to fill in a simple application form. Tourist cards are valid for
a period of up to one month, but can be extended in Cuba for further periods
of one month up to a limit of 6 months. This can be arranged for a fee of
US$25. You should obtain stamps to this amount at a branch of the Banco de
Crédito y Comercio (Bandec), and take them, to the Dirección de Inmigración
which has offices in most major towns. Bring your passport and your airline
ticket.
A **visa** costing US$25 is required for business trips and for anyone intending to
stay with friends or with a family.

Customs

In order to be admitted to Cuba, visitors must have booked **2 nights in a
hotel**. Customs officials normally just ask for the name of the hotel and will
take your word for it. Travellers without proof of a reservation having been
made may be made to book into a hotel there and then, though this is
unlikely.
Import regulations – Personal effects, including photographic equipment, up to
the airline limit of 20kg can be brought into Cuba without charge. Any gifts
must not exceed a value of US$100 and medicines and medical supplies are
subject to an upper limit of 10kg. The duty-free limit for alcohol is 3 litres, and
for tobacco 200 cigarettes or 50 cigars.
No firearms, explosives, narcotics, or pornographic material may be brought into
Cuba, nor may unprocessed foodstuffs like fresh fruit. Publications which may
be construed as hostile to Cuba and its regime may be confiscated.
Export regulations – The amount of alcohol and tobacco which can be taken
out of the country is limited to 2 bottles of spirits and 50 cigars. To keep a check
on contraband cigars, customs officers may ask for the receipt *(comprobante)* from
the outlet where they were purchased.
While in Cuba you may be offered objects made from endangered species like
coral or turtles. The Convention on International Trade in Endangered Species
forbids the export of such products and fines are levied on anyone attempting
to do so.

Vaccinations

Proof of vaccinations is not required for entry into Cuba. However, vaccinations
are recommended against tetanus, typhoid, polio and hepatitis A. Anyone
intending to stay more than 3 months in the country will have to undergo an
AIDS test.

Driver's licence

An international driver's licence is not required in Cuba; an ordinary driving licence is quite sufficient when hiring a car.

● Local currency

Cash

Three kinds of money are in circulation in Cuba, all confusingly identified by the dollar symbol ($). The national currency (*moneda nacional*) is the **peso**, used by visitors from abroad only to make local phone calls or buy things like snacks, bus tickets, or a copy of *Granma*, the Party daily. It is quite feasible to spend a holiday in Cuba and not use pesos at all.

Most tourist dealings are done in hard currency (*divisas*) in the form of US **dollars** or, to a much lesser extent, in **convertible pesos**, rated 1:1 with the dollar (ordinary pesos are worth 20 to the dollar). Convertible pesos came into circulation in 1994 in response to a shortage of dollar notes; despite their name, they are not convertible and have no value outside Cuba. They can be changed into dollars before leaving the country, at hotel desks or the bureau de change at the airport.

Dollar notes come in denominations of 100, 50, 20, 10, 5 and 1. Low denominations are much more useful as change is scarce in many places, and will often be given in convertible pesos rather than dollars. Attempting to pay for something with a $100 note will often result in a request to see your passport.

Coins come in denominations of 5, 10, 25 and 50 **centavos** (cents) (100 centavos = 1 peso). Convertible centavo coins are marked "INTUR" (Institute of Tourism) while ordinary centavos have "Republica de Cuba" written on them. All tourist services such as hotel accommodation, restaurants, car hire and flight tickets, must be paid for in hard currency. Cubans have been allowed to hold dollars since 1993 and are using them more and more to buy goods and services not available from State outlets. Every visitor soon learns to distinguish a "peso" establishment from a "dollar" one. In theory, peso shops cannot sell goods to foreigners, but some will find a way of getting round this.

Currency exchange

It makes sense to take as many dollars in cash as you feel comfortable with, though it is usually fairly straightforward to change money at your hotel or at a branch of the Banco Nacional de Cuba or the Banco Financiero Internacional. Pesos can be obtained at the same rate as the black market from the Cadeca Bank. There are plenty of local people anxious to change money, but it is as well to check on the going rate before entering into negotiations (in 1999 the rate was 20 pesos to one dollar). Bear in mind that pesos are quite difficult to spend, and cannot be changed back into hard currency when you leave the country. US$10 worth is likely to be more than sufficient for most stays.

Travellers' cheques

Any travellers' cheques should be in US dollars. They should be issued by Thomas Cook or Visa, since **American Express** travellers' cheques or those issued by any other US bank are not accepted in Cuba. Cheques can be changed at major hotels or at a branch of the Banco Financiero Internacional. The commission varies between 2% and 4% and is likely to be higher at hotels than at the bank, possibly higher still at the weekend. Once off the main tourist trail, it may be difficult to change travellers' cheques, another reason for taking rather more cash with you than usual.

Credit cards

Visa international, **Eurocard** and **Mastercard** credit cards can be used in Cuba, provided they have not been issued by an American bank. American Express cards are not accepted. Credit cards can be used to withdraw cash in some major hotels and at branches of the Banco Financiero Internacional and the Banco Nacional de Cuba. In theory at least, many places which are used to dealing with tourists from abroad will accept payment by credit card, but transactions can be frustrating; machines frequently fail to function, the call to the authorising centre can be cut off, or the supply of slips may simply have dried up. However, there is usually no problem in using a credit card for paying for car hire or for accommodation and meals in a major hotel.

• Spending money

Individual travellers staying in well-starred hotels, eating in State restaurants and hiring a car will not find a holiday in Cuba particularly cheap. But costs can be reduced dramatically if you have bed and breakfast in private homes and eat in *paladares*, private restaurants. Getting around by public transport (patience essential), allowing between US$15 and US$20 for a double room with breakfast and US$10 for a main meal, the total daily cost per person could come to around **US$40** per person. Paying someone to drive you around in a private car will cost approximately US$40 a day (divided by the number of passengers).

Allow **US$80** per person per day, not counting car hire, if you plan to stay in reasonable hotels and eat in unpretentious restaurants or in *paladares*. Car hire from State firms is charged at international rates (around US$60 a day for a vehicle in Category 1 with insurance and unlimited mileage). A litre of fuel costs 90 cents. You can easily double this daily sum, to say **US$200**, by staying in luxury hotels and dining in the best restaurants in Havana and Varadero.

These figures are approximate and based on sharing a double room and do not include entertainment and other purchases. Hotel and car rental costs can be reduced substantially by booking a holiday through a travel agent.

• Booking in advance

For a holiday in the high season (December/January and July/August) it is advisable to book hotel rooms well in advance. This can be done by phone or fax, but it is easier to use a specialist travel agent, who will also help plan a holiday to your individual requirements.

The same applies to seats on trains, ferries and internal flights, though outside the high season a number of places are usually reserved for foreign travellers paying in dollars. Travel operators can sometimes offer excellent deals on internal flights. Arranging car rental in advance is advantageous too, as rates are less when booked at the same time as a flight. Leaving hire of a car until you are in Cuba can lead to problems, as the number of vehicles available is very limited.

• Insurance

Travel agents and tour operators invariably try to get you to buy their favoured brand of travel insurance, but it is usually better value to arrange this yourself. Year-round travel insurance is available from a number of companies and is more economical for people who travel abroad several times a year. Make sure you are covered for cancellations and for medical expenses including repatriation if necessary. If problems arise once you are in Cuba, **Asitur** may be able to help with medical and legal problems as well as putting you in touch with your insurance company (*See page 147*).

• Gifts

The dearth of all kinds of consumer goods means that virtually anything brought with you is capable of being turned into a gift. Soap, toothbrushes, toothpaste, matches, cigarette lighters, medicines, clothes, perfume, pens, all make welcome presents. You do not necessarily have to encourage the children who hang around tourist locations hoping for handouts (though it can be difficult to resist their blandishments); it is better to give things to people whose acquaintance you have made (bed and breakfast hosts for example). And a good bottle of rum is always welcome if you are invited anywhere.

GETTING THERE

• By air

Direct scheduled flights from London Gatwick to Havana are operated by British Airways and by Cuba's national airline, Cubana de Aviación (Cubana for short). Cubana also has one flight a week to Havana from Manchester. An alternative is to fly Air France via Amsterdam or Iberia via Madrid.

There are various charter flights from London Gatwick and Manchester to Varadero, some of which stop at Holguín.

Flight times are around 10hr for the outward flight and 9hr for the return flight.

Cubana de Aviación – 49 Conduit Street, London W1R 9FB, ☎ (020) 734 1165. For its flights from the UK Cubana uses French-registered DC-10 aircraft. Standard fares are around £400/US$640, more in high season. Tropical and Club Class offer a greater degree of comfort and are correspondingly more expensive. There are four flights a week between London Gatwick and Havana. Cubana does not have the best reputation in the business for punctuality and general level of service, but its old epithet as the Caribbean Aeroflot is not really justified, at least as far as its intercontinental flights are concerned.

British Airways – ☎ 0345 222111, has one flight a week (on Saturday) between London Gatwick and Havana. The cost is about £100/US$160 more than Cubana. Charter flights are operated by **Airtours**, ☎ (01254) 358554, **Monarch**, ☎ (01582) 398333, and **Interchange**, ☎ (020) 8681 3812.

J.-F. Galmiche

Airport

Most intercontinental flights to and from Cuba are handled by the extensively modernised **José Martí Airport** some 25km southwest of central Havana. The airport has a reasonable range of services including car rental desks. The best way of getting into the city is by official taxi costing around US$20. Private cabs are somewhat cheaper. Shuttle buses serve various city centre hotels.

Confirmation

Confirm your return flight 72hr in advance with the appropriate airline.

Airport tax

Airport tax of US$20 is payable on leaving Cuba.

● By boat

Pleasure craft may land at a number of marinas around Cuba, including Havana, Playa del Este, Varadero, Cienfuegos, Guardalavaca, Santiago de Cuba and Cayo Largo. Before entering Cuban territorial waters (which begin 12 miles out), make radio contact with the port in question.

● Package deals

A growing number of tour operators offer inclusive trips to Cuba, ranging from coach tours around the whole island to individually tailored itineraries. A two-week holiday staying in Havana and a number of provincial centres will cost between £1 200/US$1 920 and £1 500/US$2 400 per person with car hire, a coach tour slightly less. Bargains can be had; an off-season week in a four-star Havana hotel has been offered for under £400/US$640, including flight.

Tour operators

Ashley Holidays – 35 Wood Lane, Wickersley, Rotherham, S. Yorks, S66 0JT, ☎ 01709 543626.

Cosmos – Tourama House, 17 Homesdale Road, Bromley, Kent, BR2 9LX, ☎ (020) 8464 3444.

Distant Dreams – Garrard House, 2-6 Homesdale Road, Bromley, Kent, BR1 9LZ, ☎ (020) 8313 0599.

Havanatour UK Ltd – 3 Wyllyots Place, Potters Bar, Herts EN6 2JD, ☎ (01707) 665570.

Hayes & Jarvis – 152 King Street, London W6 0QU, T (020) 8748 0088.

The Holiday Place – 240 West End Lane, London NW6 1LG, ☎ (020) 7431 0670.

Interchange – Interchange House, 27 Stafford Road, Croydon, Surrey CR0 4NG, ☎ (020) 8681 3612.

JMC Holidays – 29-31 Elmfield Road, Bromley, Kent BR1 1LT, ☎ (020) 8290 1111.

Progressive Tours – 12 Porchester Place, London W2 2BS, ☎ (020) 7262 1676.

Regent Holidays UK Ltd – 15 John Street, Bristol BS1 2HR, ☎ 0117 921 1711.

South American Experience – 47 Causton Street, London SW1 4AT, ☎ (020) 7976 5511.

The Travel Collection – Deepdene House, Dorking Surrey RH5 4AZ.

Tropical Places – Freshfield House, Lewes Road, Forest Row, East Sussex RH18 5ES, ☎ (01342) 825123.

Diving holidays

Aquatours Ltd – Shelletts House, Angel Road, Thames Ditton, Surrey KT7 0AU, ☎ (020) 8398 0505.

Scuba en Cuba – 7 Maybank Gardens, Pinner, Middlesex HA5 2JW, T 01895 624100.

The basics

THE BASICS

• Address book

Tourist Information

One or other of the nationalised **travel agencies** will have a desk in any of the major hotels, where staff will help you plan sightseeing and excursions. The following are the office addresses of the most important agencies in Havana:

Havantour (or Tour & Travel) – Edificio Sierra Maestra, Avenida Premiera between Calle O and Calle 2, Miramar, ☎ (7) 24-2161/0166.

Cubatur – corner of Calle 23 and Calle L. ☎ (7) 33-4111, and at Calle F between Avenida Novena (9th Avenue) and Calle Calzada, ☎ (7) 33-4155.

Horizontes – a hotel chain, offers hotel and fly-drive packages throughout Cuba for between US\$700 and US\$4050 per week, Calle 23 no156 between Calle N and Calle O, ☎ (7) 66-2161/33-4042, Fax (7) 33-3722, crh@horizontes.hor.cma.net, www.horizontes.cu

Gaviota – another hotel chain, also acts as a travel agency: La Marina, Avenida del Puerto, 3rd floor (Old Havana), ☎ (7) 66-6777, Fax (7) 33-2780, reserva@nwgaviot.gav.cma.net

Rumbos – specialise in day trips with dinner in one of its numerous restaurants scattered throughout the country: Calle 23 between Calle O and P, ☎ (7) 70-3075/24-9628, or Calle O between Avenida Primera a and Avenida Tercera a, Miramar, ☎ (7) 24-9626, Fax (7) 24-7167, director@rumvia.rumb.cma.net

Cubamar – manage campsites at a number of attractive locations and offer "green tourism" packages of several days: corner Calle 15 and Paseo, ☎ (7) 30-5536, Fax (7) 33-3111.

Roots Travel – Calle 4 no512 between Calle 21 and Calle 23, ☎ (7) 3-7770 or 30-6843 or at Hotel Colina room 201, ☎ (7) 55-4005. Reservation of hotels or private accommodation throughout Cuba plus bus and train tickets.

Maps and plans are difficult to find except in Havana and Varadero and any you need should be bought from the El Navigante bookshop in Havana *(See page 103)*. Road maps given out at hotels are not particularly accurate. A superior publication is the "Mapa geográfico" on sale at the airport, bookshops and major hotels, while the "Guía de Carreteras" (Road atlas) may be obtainable from your car rental firm.

Embassies and Consulates

United Kingdom – Calle 34 no708 between Calle 7 and Calle 17, Miramar, ☎ (7) 331771/2 or 331286 or 331299 or 331049 or 331880.

Canada – Calle 30 no518 on corner with Avenida 7, Miramar, ☎ (7) 332516 or 33251 or 33252 or 332382 or 332752.

United States – United States Interests Section, Calzada between Calle L and Calle M, Vedado, ☎ (7) 333543-47, or 333551-59.

• Opening and closing times

Banks

8.30am-3pm, closed weekends. Expect to queue. Money can be changed at other times at a hotel bureau de change.

Post Offices

8am-6pm except Sunday. Major hotels sell stamps and accept mail at all times.

Shops
10am-6pm except Sunday. Hotel boutiques and souvenir shops generally open daily to 7pm.

Restaurants
Lunch from 11.30am. Last service for dinner generally around 8.30pm except in main tourist centres where some restaurants remain open later. In smaller provincial towns restaurants may close as early as 7.30pm, but paladares keep more flexible hours.

Offices
9am-5pm generally with an hour's break for lunch. Most offices close at the weekend.

Museums and archeological sites
9am-5pm, closed Sunday afternoon from 1pm and all day Monday. Closing day may vary from place to place. Most churches only open for services.

● Museums, monuments and archeological sites
Admission charges
Admission charges range from US$1 to US$3. Some museums may make a charge for photography. Allow US$1 as a tip for a guided tour. There is no charge for admission to churches unless they have a museum but donations are welcome.

● Mail
You may well be approached by local people with a request to post a letter for them. International mail from Cuba takes around 3 weeks to reach its destination, and Cubans who correspond with people abroad rely on tourists to take their letters home with them and mail them there. Stamps can be bought for pesos in post offices and for dollars in hotels (a postcard costs 50 centavos, a letter 75). Urgent mail can be dealt with by DHL in Havana and Varadero (*See page 147 and page 194*).

Telephone and fax
Cuba's telecom infrastructure is sadly dated and telephoning can be problematic. Getting a telephone installed can take years, and many homes are without one. Local people get round this by sharing a line between several dwellings or getting someone to take all calls (*recados*) and pass on messages.

International calls
With a little patience, it can often be less difficult to make an international call than a local one. To make a call at the **telecom centre** in larger towns, give the number to the employee at the counter. They will do the dialling and direct you to a cabin when the call comes through. At a **hotel**, calls are generally made via reception, though larger hotels have direct dialling from the bedside phone. International calls from Cuba are very expensive. One way of economising is to buy a **phone card** which can only be used at a designated card phone. These are now appearing in increasing numbers, especially in areas frequented by tourists. Cards are available to a value of US$10, US$25 and US$40.

Local calls
A local call from a battered public telephone box costs 5 centavos. Long distance calls are better made from a telecom centre, a hotel or from a card phone.

Codes
International codes vary according to which phone is being used.

From Cuba to the UK from a hotel room
88 + 44 + UK local code (minus 0) + subscriber's number

From Cuba to the UK from a card phone
119 + 44 + UK local code (minus 0) + subscriber's number
Local calls in Cuba
Subscriber's number
Long-distance calls in Cuba
0 + local code + subscriber's number
Local codes in Cuba
Below are the codes for provincial capitals and main tourist centres. These codes
are given in brackets in the Making the most of... sections of the guide.

Baracoa	21	Matanzas	61
Bayamo	23	Pinar del Río	82
Camagüey	322	Sancti Spíritus	41
Ciego de Ávila	33	Santa Clara	422
Cienfuegos	432	Santa Lucia	32
Guantánamo	21	Santiago de Cuba	226
Guardalavaca	24	Trinidad	419
Holguín	24	Varadero	5
Havana	7	Viñales	8
Las Tunas	31		

Charges
Hotels put a stiff surcharge on all calls made from your room. Use of a phone
card can help keep costs down, but remember that international calls are very
expensive, around US$6 per minute to phone the UK. Reverse charge calls are
not possible.
The larger hotels usually have telex and fax facilities. Sending a fax costs around
US$15 plus US$1 per page payable by the recipient.
Directory Enquiries
Dial 113. Major hotels have a copy of the *Directorio Turístico de Cuba*, an annually
revised publication with all numbers likely to be of interest to visitors.

● Local time
See page 76

● Public Holidays
I January: Liberation Day
I May: Labour Day
26 July: (plus 25 and 27 July): National Rebellion Day
10 October: Anniversary of the outbreak of the First War of Independence (1868)
A number of other anniversaries are marked by celebrations though they are not
public holidays. Any visitor to Cuba soon realises how important history is to
Cubans, who have a whole array of patriots and revolutionaries to honour.
Celebrations usually take the form of a procession, perhaps with the unveiling
of a statue in the presence of TV cameras. The following are some of the most
important dates in Cuban history:
28 January: birthday of José Martí
13 March: anniversary of the 1957 attack on the Presidential Palace
19 April: anniversary of the defeat of the Bay of Pigs invasion
8 October: death of Che Guevara
28 October: death of Camilo Cienfuegos
7 December: death of Antonio Maceo

• Carnival

Cuba's carnivals are sensational. The most famous is at **Santiago de Cuba** (*See page 288*), where, on 26 July, the city's streets are filled with costumed revellers dancing to the throb of drums and the shrill sound of *cornetines chinos* (Chinese cornets). The **Parrandas Remedianas** (*See page 225*) is an almost equally spectacular event, not to be missed if you are in Villa Clara province at Christmas. Cuba's "Special Period" has not been kind to the cause of Carnival; parades have been watered down or cancelled altogether. The **Havana** carnival vanished from the festive calendar for several years, but has recently reappeared in all its splendour. It takes place twice a year on the Malecón, in January / February and July / August. If you are tempted to join in the fun, check locally where, when and in what form Carnival is taking place.

GETTING AROUND

There is plenty of evidence in Cuba that the country is heir to what was the best developed transport system in the Caribbean, with 8-lane motorways, parkways and double-track railway lines. But much of this infrastructure is now in a sorry state, and the onset of the "Special Period" has turned fuel into a scarce commodity. People have turned improvisation into a fine art in their efforts to maintain personal mobility. Detroit's high-finned gas-guzzlers of the late 1950s were only meant to last a couple of years before being traded in for something even more spectacular; here, famously, their life has been miraculously extended, far, far beyond the concepts of planned obsolescence. Resprayed, re-engined, sometimes totally rebuilt, they queen it over a highway scene full of lesser vehicles. There is a small number of equally venerable European automobiles, Volkswagens, Austins, and Fiats, and a whole generation of more recent but rapidly decaying Ladas, Skodas and Moskvitches. Modern motoring is represented by an occasional Toyota or Daewoo (most likely a hire car driven by a visitor from abroad). Further down the hierarchy come an array of scooters and motorbikes, many of the latter with the sidecar long done away with elsewhere. Bikes there are a-plenty, a million of them donated by a friendly China, some of them ingeniously fitted with what looks like a home-made motor. Goods are shifted in trolleys and handcarts, or trucked in smoky Russian lorries. Public transport is provided, inadequately, in Havana by the "camel", a hump-backed trailer pulled by the front half of an articulated lorry, and in the country by open trucks whose only concession to comfort may be a handrail to cling to. Small towns have seen the revival of the horse-bus.

The visitor from abroad may well be confused by all this exotic variety, but in reality the options for anyone wanting to see a lot of Cuba in a short time are fairly limited. A hire car is expensive, but its convenience compared with public transport is almost priceless. It is also worthwhile considering an internal flight, which can save a lot of driving time when travelling from one end to the other of what is a very long country.

• By car
Rental
To hire a car you must be more than 21 years old (23 for a Mercedes) and have an ordinary driving licence. The hire car may only be driven by the people whose names appear on the hire contract. The car is identified by a "Turismo" number plate, and police will stop it if it is obviously being driven by a Cuban.

There are several rental companies with offices around the country and charges vary little from one to the other. **Havanautos** and **Transtur** (formerly Transautos) have representatives in more places than **Micar, Cubacar, Via,** or **Panautos**, but their standard of service has tended to deteriorate. Check that the vehicle offered is a recent model and make sure that all charges have been agreed before setting off. The whole of the cost of hiring a car must be paid at the time the contract is signed. This includes the rental, insurance, a tankful of fuel and a deposit, and can be paid by credit card, travellers' cheques or cash. There are two kinds of insurance. The cheaper (around US$10 per day) covers theft of the vehicle but not of parts, and the more expensive version (around US$18 per day and called cover B) only excludes theft of a wheel. Hotel car parks usually have a security guard, but anyone intending to stay in private accommodation is strongly advised to take out the more comprehensive version, as a car parked overnight in the street may attract the attention of dealers in spare parts. Wheels are a favourite target, and if your hire vehicle is a 4-wheel drive you should make sure the spare mounted on the outside is well secured. To reduce the risk of theft, some wheel nuts may require the use of a special spanner. Check that this is provided when hiring the car.

The daily rate for a basic vehicle is around US$60 with unlimited mileage and comprehensive insurance, with some reduction for weekly or fortnightly hire. (though not with Havanautos). For a fee, it is usually possible to leave a car at an outlet of the hire firm other than the one from which you have rented it; the drop-off charge for leaving a car picked up in Havana at Santiago will come to just over US$100. If the car you have hired needs a service (usually every 20 000km) during the rental period, you will need to take it to one of the firm's outlets or to a garage approved by them. Allow more time for this procedure than you would at home.

The number of cars for hire is limited, particularly in provincial areas, and it is advisable to arrange hire well in advance, especially in the high season. This can be done by travel agents, or directly with **Havanautos**, ☎ (53 7) 24-0646/7, www.havanautos.cubaweb.cu, **Transtur**, ☎ (53 7) 24-5532, webmaster@transtur.com.cu, and **Micar**, ☎ (53 7) 24-3457/55-3535, micar@columbus.cu and **Transautos**, ☎ (53 7) 33-5532.

Road network
Cuban roads suffer from a lack of maintenance, with a few exceptions like the Via Blanca between Havana and Varadero. The motorway (*autopista*) network is not extensive (total length around 700km); some sections are under construction while

stretches of the existing network are already showing signs of age. Particularly in eastern Cuba, the motorway can come to an end abruptly without any warning. The broad carriageway (up to four lanes in each direction) may be blessedly free of other motor vehicles, but drivers need to keep a watch out for pedestrians and for cyclists pedalling in the wrong direction, as well as for potholes.

Motorways have only partly replaced the pre-war two-lane *Carretera Central*, which runs from one end of Cuba to the other. It is a more interesting drive than the autopista, but much slower. The rest of the network consists of secondary highways and unsurfaced roads. There are plenty of surprises along the way. As well as ubiquitous and carefree cyclists, there will be agricultural vehicles of one kind or another, horsemen, free-ranging animals, and, in coastal areas, swarms of crabs waiting to lacerate your tyres. Hire of a 4-wheel drive vehicle should be considered by anyone thinking of venturing off the beaten track into remoter areas. Driving at night is not advisable. Road lighting is poor or non-existent and there are unlit vehicles and bicycles. Road marking is equally sub-standard and signing is erratic, even on motorways. You will almost certainly have to ask your way more than once.

Highway code

Rules of the road are much the same as in continental Europe or North America. Drive on the right (though the state of the road will not always make this possible). Speed limits are 100kph on motorways, 90kph on ordinary highways and 50kph in built-up areas. Tourists used to be treated leniently by the Cuban police, but those carefree days are over, and if you are caught for speeding or another offence you will be required to pay an on-the-spot fine *(multa)* in US dollars. Whatever the speed limit, you should exercise caution at all times, and always expect the unexpected. Town driving requires special care because of the numbers of bicycles, horse-drawn vehicles and pedestrians. Lose any inhibitions you may have about using the horn when overtaking or to warn cyclists and pedestrians (especially schoolchildren) of your approach. Always obey the "Halt" sign *(Pare)*, and stop at the frequent unguarded level crossings.

Fuel

Rental cars run on *gasolina especial*, sold at 24-hour petrol stations belonging to Servicupet, Cimex and Oro Negro. *Especial* costs US$0.90 a litre, and can be paid for by credit card (if the machine works) or in dollars. It is a good idea to fill up whenever possible, as outside towns service stations are few and far between. There is a black market in petrol, and you may well be offered fuel at around US$0.50 a litre. Quality cannot of course be guaranteed, and splicing with water is not unknown. Another reason for keeping the tank topped up whenever possible.

Parking in town

Risk of theft or damage can be minimised by leaving your car in an attended hotel car park. Elsewhere, people will offer to look after the car in your absence. They may well do so, but payment in advance is unwise. There are secure car parks in some of the larger towns, usual fee US$1.

In emergencies

If you are involved in an accident, contact the police immediately, ☎ 116, and inform your hire firm. If the police report *(acta de denuncia)* holds you responsible for the accident, you may have to pay a deposit for the damage caused.

Getting around

• By taxi

Official or dollar taxis are identified by the illuminated sign on the roof. They congregate at the airport and around hotels, are usually fitted with air-conditioning, and are reasonably comfortable. There is a basic hire charge of US$1, then a mileage, or rather a kilometrage charge calculated by taximeter. For longer trips or to hire a vehicle for a whole day, it makes more sense to use the services of a private taxi or to rent a car yourself.

In 1996, the government legalised so-called **peso taxis**. These are privately owned vehicles – frequently a Lada – identified by the "taxi" sign on the windscreen. Only Cubans are supposed to use them, but some drivers will accept foreign visitors as passengers, in which case the charge will be payable in dollars. There is no taximeter, so the charge should be agreed in advance. The larger vehicles known as **collective taxis** (*colectivos*) operate on much the same principle, but pick up individuals and small groups travelling in the same direction. Finally, there are plenty of owners of **private cars** willing to chauffeur foreign visitors around. This could be in a battered Lada, or possibly in one of Detroit's finest from the 1950s. The cost will be less than in a taxi, but it is illegal as well as perhaps less reliable. If stopped by the police, the driver will be liable to a steep fine. Nevertheless, owners of such vehicles are always on the lookout for customers, rather than the other way round. Hire could be for a few hours or as much as several days. There is of course no meter, and the charge (in dollars) should be agreed in advance, as well as establishing who is responsible for buying petrol.

• By train

Daily trains link Havana to most of the larger provincial cities, but services are slow and cancellations and long delays are a normal part of the Cuban railway scene. Nevertheless, travel by train is a good way to get the feel of the country and its people.

One particularly useful train for tourists is the overnight express between Havana and Santiago de Cuba. The journey lasts around 16hr and is cheaper than flying. As a rule, it costs around US$4 per 100km to travel by train. Tickets can be bought from the **Ladis agency** in the main stations (still referred to by its old name, Ferrotur). It is best to book in advance, though some seats are usually reserved for passengers paying in dollars, and it is quite often possible to get a place on the day of travel.

• By bus and coach

Most towns have a municipal bus service of sorts, and the network of coach services linking towns and cities is far more extensive than the rail network. (But all services have been hit badly by the "Special Period", and travel by bus (*guagua* pronounced wha-wha) should be avoided by anyone in a hurry.) Bus services in towns tend to start early in the morning and finish early – perhaps as early as 6pm or 7pm. Long waits are common and the overcrowding is enough to discourage most visitors from abroad. Anyone tempted to join the fray should check where the end of the queue is by asking "¿el ultimo?". Fares are in pesos. Long-distance services have recently been vastly improved, at least as far as tourists are concerned, by the creation of a network of routes run by **Viazul**. The coaches have comfortable seats and air-conditioning, and, unusually for Cuba, run on time. Most of the popular tourist destinations are served, including Pinar del Río, Viñales, Varadero and Matanzas, Trinidad and Santiago de Cuba via Santa Clara, Sancti Spíritus, Ciego de Ávila, Camagüey, Las Tunas, Holguín

Getting around

J. F. Galmiche

and Bayamo. Fares are reasonable (Havana-Santiago US$51, services three times a week). Seats should be booked a day in advance (though some may be available on the day of travel) at Viazul, Avenida 26 and Zoológico in Nuevo Vedado,☎ (7) 81-1413/5652/1108.

Travellers with considerable reserves of patience who are interested in investigating long-distance travel as experienced by Cubans should make for the Estación de Ómnibus, which is usually sited at some distance from the town centre. There may be two such coach stations, one for travel within the province, one for travel between different provinces. However, in general terms, the demand for places is so intense and services so few, that long-distance bus travel is not a very realistic option for visitors from abroad. Any attempt to do so should involve booking in advance and confirming reservations an hour or two before the advertised departure.

In Havana and Varadero, there is a special **Vaiven** bus service for tourists which calls at a number of hotels and visitor attractions.

• Renting a bike

Two-wheelers of all sorts, from push-bikes to motor-scooters, can be hired at most seaside resorts in Cuba. Elsewhere in the country, it is difficult to hire a bicycle, even in Havana. It may be possible to hire a bike from an individual, but it should be borne in mind that this is likely to deprive them of their only means of transport. Anyone wanting to get around the country in the saddle should bring their own bicycle with them, along with spare parts and a secure lock. Punctures (*poncheras*) are no problem, as Cuba has no shortage of bicycle repairmen.

• Hitch-hiking

The deficiencies of public transport means that for many Cubans, hitching a lift (*coger botella*) is the only way of getting around, and in many places it is done in an organised way. Uniformed officials, called *amarillos* (yellows, after the colour of their uniforms), marshal would-be hitchers according to their destination and flag down approaching vehicles. Tourist cars are generally ignored. Not many tourists attempt to hitch-hike their way around the country. It is perfectly feasible, though anyone doing so should be ready to contribute to costs, and might also bear in mind that they are probably depriving a local person of the chance of a lift. Picking up people yourself will earn you great gratitude, and is one way of making contact with Cubans.

Getting around

• Domestic flights

An internal flight is the most expensive, but by far the easiest way of covering long distances in Cuba. There are flights between Havana and some of the larger provincial cities, including several services a day to and from Santiago de Cuba. Other useful connections are flights linking Pinar del Río with Nueva Gerona on the Isle of Youth and Varadero with Cayo Largo, and there is a weekly flight between Santiago and Baracoa. Costs work out at around US$10 per 100km. Although some seats may be set aside on domestic flights for foreign travellers, it is still best to book in advance. Internal flights are cheaper if paid for before leaving your home country.

The three airlines operating domestic flights all have offices close to the Hotel Nacional in Havana.

Cubana de Aviación – corner of Calle Infanta and Calle Humboldt, Vedado, ☎ (7) 33-4949. Cubana operate the majority of scheduled internal flights.

Aerocaribbean – corner of Calle 23 and Calle P, Vedado, ☎ (7) 33-4543. This charter firm serves most of Cuba's main tourist centres.

Aerotaxi – corner of Calle 27 and Calle N, Vedado, ☎ (7) 32-8127. This firm's small planes fly to a limited number of the main tourist areas.

• Organised tours and excursions

Most of the larger hotels as well as travel agencies in some towns (*See page 146*) have information on a variety of organised tours, ranging from a round-the-town sightseeing trip to longer tours of several days. They may also offer boat trips or guided walks. Even people who are averse to going on such tours may find that a guided tour around Cuba is the best and easiest way of seeing a lot of the country in a short time. And simply looking at what is on offer can help you decide where to go on an individual basis.

BED AND BOARD

• Where to stay

Cuba's network of hotels includes one or more three-star establishments in each of the larger towns, making it feasible for visitors from abroad to plan a trip around the whole country. However, anyone wanting to make a longer stay in a particular area should consider staying in one of the resorts which have been specially developed for foreign tourists. These are invariably in an attractive setting, offer a wider choice of accommodation, and have plenty of visitor facilities.

• Types of accommodation

The rapid expansion of tourism means that the choice of places to stay has greatly increased. Before the Revolution, Cuba had some of the world's most glamorous hotels, designed to pander to every whim of a dollar-laden international elite. The following decades added monolithic, Soviet-style structures, intended to make package tourists from eastern Europe feel at home. Nowadays, the emphasis is on the rapid construction of beachside resorts and luxury hotels, once again in the hope of attracting dollars. In addition, a number fine old colonial-era buildings have been restored and reopened. And, a real plus, private people are now allowed to rent out rooms to visitors from abroad, creating an inexpensive option for independent travellers and an excellent way of getting to know the country and its people.

Hotels

All overnight stays made by foreigners must be paid for in dollars. This means that so-called **peso hotels** are normally off-limits for visitors from abroad. Any foreigner who does succeed in staying in a peso hotel is almost certain to have to settle their bill in dollars anyway, at the official rate of US$1 = 1 peso. This will work out at between US$15 and US$20, no bargain, given the low standard of most hotels of this type (cuts in the water supply, antiquated plumbing and lack of air conditioning). However, most towns have at least one three-star hotel, with rooms costing between US$25 and US$50. These establishments usually belong to the Horizonte or Islasul chains, and their design will often recall the popularity of reinforced concrete in the 1960s and 70s. Rooms, with (in theory functioning) air-conditioning, TV and shower, will have a basic level of comfort. The plumbing will probably be showing its age, and hot water should not be relied upon. However, some three-star hotels are not without character and charm, and their standard of comfort can be quite acceptable. Examples include Los Jazmines in the Viñales valley and El Castillo in Baracoa.

The cost of rooms in **four-star hotels** can be anything between US$50 and US$100, and establishments in this category range from run-of-the-mill resort hotels to the Hotel Moka, a minor masterpiece of architecture and landscape design high up in the Sierra del Rosario. Service is usually good, and some of the staff will speak English. Rooms will have working air-conditioning, a private bathroom – possibly with a bath as well as a shower – and satellite TV. Nevertheless, such hotels are not immune to the problems affecting the country as a whole, and you should not expect perfection.

A room in a **five-star hotel** will cost upwards of US$100. In towns, this means rooms and service of a standard comparable to anywhere in the world, plus business facilities like photocopying, conference rooms, and secretarial services. Rates will be much lower if booked as part of a package holiday. In places like Varadero, the larger five-star hotels resemble self-contained holiday villages, with a whole range of recreational and sporting facilities, and plenty of organised entertainment. The all-in price usually includes buffet meals.

Camping

There is no point in bringing your own tent to Cuba. There are no camp sites as such and camping in the wild is prohibited. The Cuban term *campismo* refers not to tented sites but to places with an array of permanent cabins or chalets (as at Pinar del Río and Jibacoa). Such places are cheap, but comfort is rudimentary.

All inclusive

A number of all-inclusive resorts have been developed in the most popular beach holiday areas on the mainland as well as on the cayos, and since 1997 Varadero has had a Club Méditerranée. Bookings should be made through a travel agent.

Bed and breakfast

A private room is not only the least expensive sort of accommodation, but is also an excellent way of getting to know local people, especially if you speak some basic Spanish. Private accommodation can range from the spare room in a family home to an entire house, fully furnished. Whole families have been known to pack their bags at the last minute and decamp elsewhere, simply in order to make room for a guest from abroad. Individual house owners are now permitted to let rooms, but have to pay a special tax in dollars. When this tax was subjected to a big hike in 1997, many budding entrepreneurs went out of business, while other

J. F. Galmiche

proprietors of *casas particulares* continued to let rooms clandestinely despite the risk of a hefty fine.

Some bed and breakfast establishments have a sign in front of the house to attract custom, but wherever you go in places frequented by tourists, you are more than likely to be approached by people offering you private accommodation – some going as far as throwing themselves bodily in front of your vehicle. Their commission will be added to the cost of the room, so if you already have an address, do not allow yourself to be led to it. Outside tourist areas, enquire locally if anyone has a room to let (¿Donde podría alquilar una casa?). The cost of a double room for a night varies between US$10 and US$25. Do not accept the offer of a room until you have found out where it is and inspected it. In Trinidad, US$15-20 could just as easily get you a room in a lovely colonial-era mansion just off Plaza Major as lodgings in a suburban back yard. In Havana, a room will cost upwards of US$20.

• Eating out

Menus hardly differ from one place to another, and the shortage of supplies outside the main tourist areas means that your request for a particular item will often be met with the response, *"se acabó"* (It's off). Private restaurants, *paladares*, are generally the best bet if you want a straightforward meal at a reasonable price.

In hotels

Most hotels have a cafeteria or a restaurant, but the choice is likely to be limited and the food undistinguished. Larger hotels may have a more varied menu, with international dishes, or, especially in beachside resorts, food may be presented in buffet form, with main meals costing around US$15 and breakfast around US$7. A small number of luxury hotels have gourmet restaurants serving international cuisine, at a price.

In restaurants

Tourist areas have an increasing number of restaurants offering international dishes, creole food, and possibly some regional specialities. Standards are very variable. The bill is likely to come to around US$10-15 per person, higher in more pretentious places.

Every town has peso restaurants intended for the use of local people. There will be very little choice of food, and once the bill has been converted at par into dollars the meal may not be particularly cheap.

In paladares

The "Special Period" has witnessed a boom in the provision of *paladares* (literally, "palace" or "taste"). These private restaurants, which owe their name to a popular TV programme from Brazil, are often an excellent alternative to State restaurants, offering complete meals for around US$7. Seating is limited to a maximum of 10312 places, and many *paladares* have simply been installed in the family's dining room. Some are as elaborately decorated as any official restaurant, perhaps with a bar in the corner. In others, guests will eat at a table covered in oilcloth, next to the TV set. Just as in the case of private rooms, many *paladares* are completely legal (and taxable), while others operate on an unofficial basis, making it impossible to list them in any travel guide. You will have to enquire locally. If there is no menu, check the total cost of the meal before ordering.

On the hoof

There is not much choice of fast food on the streets of Cuban towns. However, soft drinks (*refrescos*) are usually available from stalls and kiosks, along with excellent milk shakes (*batidos*), and confectionery. More substantial offerings may be limited to *pan con lechón*, a slice of fatty pork shoved between two chunks of bread. Try markets for a selection of fresh fruit and vegetables. The defrosted pizzas offered by individuals at their doorstep are unlikely to be particularly appetising. However, they can fill a gap when you are feeling peckish, as can the biscuits and other snacks available in some service stations.

SPORTS AND PASTIMES

Many visitors to Cuba rely on the leisure activities provided by their hotels. Nevertheless, in many places it is quite feasible to find all sorts of interesting things to do by exercising your own initiative. And serendipity can lead to interesting adventures, perhaps a fishing trip with a local boatman during the day, or a 100% Cuban party at night.

• Cross country

Walking

Cuba's sierras are excellent hiking country. Mountain walking is rapidly becoming popular with visitors from abroad, usually in the company of a guide provided by a hotel. In the west, there are trails leading through the Sierra del Rosario and the Viñales valley, in central Cuba there is fine walking around Lake Hanabanilla in the Sierra del Escambray, and in the east there are a number of paths in the country around Baracoa. Check locally whether it is possible to make the long hike to the highest point in Cuba, the summit of Pico Turquino in the Sierra Maestra National Park. At the time of writing, it was off-limits to the public.

Tennis

Many of the beachside holiday resorts have their own tennis courts.

Horse riding

Fantasies of galloping along the beach can be turned into reality, since most of the seaside resorts with any pretensions have a riding centre. Further inland, there is good riding country in the Sierra del Rosario and the Viñales valley. Enquire at the local hotels.

Golf

Despite the game's apparent popularity with the Cuban leadership, the country is far from being a golfer's paradise. Choice is limited to the 9-hole diplomats' club on the way to Havana airport, ☎ (7) 33-8919, or the 9-hole course by the Dupont Mansion at Varadero, due to be extended to 18 holes.

• The Sea
Swimming
With its immensely long coastline and crystal-clear sea, Cuba can hardly fail to please anyone who loves the water. The beaches on the north coast of the island or on a *cayo* are generally speaking far superior to the southern beaches (with the exception of the beautiful white sands to the south of Trinidad, and the southern shore of the Isle of Youth). Jellyfish can sometimes be a nuisance – a face-mask can help here.

In the mountains, you can splash around in streams and waterfalls.

Boat trips
Where it is possible, the larger beachside hotels organise day trips out to a cayo, usually with lunch included.

Scuba diving
Cuba is surrounded by countless coral reefs, including one of the longest in the world. All the beach resorts have diving centres catering both for practised divers and beginners, but the two finest sites are those at María la Gorda, in the far west, and on the "pirate coast" in the southwest of the Isle of Youth. Diving holidays are offered by a number of specialist travel agencies *(See page 82)*. Diving conditions are at their best in the dry season, when the water is at its clearest.

Watersports
Beach resort hotels usually have a whole range of equipment to enable their guests to windsurf, jet-ski, water-ski, or go sailing. Hire of some of this equipment will be included in the price of the package, though there is usually an extra charge for the use of motorised equipment.

Fishing
Cuba offers both sea and freshwater fishing. The best time for deep-sea fishing (for marlin or swordfish) is spring and summer, when a number of competitions are held. The most prestigious of these is in May at the Marina Hemingway in Havana *(See page 141)*. Scattered around the country are several large artificial lakes stocked with trout, at their biggest in winter.

• Night Life
With a few exceptions, like Havana, Santiago and Varadero, night life in Cuba takes place almost entirely in hotels.

Concerts
Going to a salsa performance at least once is a must – what happens on stage and among the audience is an experience not to be missed! Havana has several venues where Cuban groups perform, some of them, like Los Van Van, El Médico de la Salsa and Charanga Habanera, with an international reputation. Every town in Cuba has a **Casa de la Trova**, where there are usually several sessions a week of traditional music. The Casa de la Trova in Santiago is almost a national institution.

J. F. Galmiche

Cuba is a country in which it is quite difficult to avoid hearing music wherever you go – there are musicians playing in bars, restaurants, airports, even in the streets.

Live shows
Some hotels put on cabaret shows, of very variable quality. The spectacular show at Havana's Tropicana is justly famous, and accordingly expensive.

Cinema
Every large provincial town has at least one cinema. The films are mostly shown in the original version, with subtitles in Spanish. The choice is limited even in Havana, and there is little money to spend on importing the latest blockbuster. Many of the US films shown are doing the rounds for the nth time.

Theatres
Some theatre buildings are attractions in their own right. You should try and see a performance in Havana's Gran Teatro, or in one of the trio of superb provincial theatres – the Milanés in Pinar del Río, the Terry in Cienfuegos and the Sauto in Matanzas. Enquire locally about performances.

Bars and nightclubs
Most night owls, Cuban or foreign, head for the bars and discotheques in the larger hotels, where the music alternates between salsa and techno. A greater degree of intimacy and authenticity is likely to be found by having a drink and a dance in the *Casa de la Trova*, or going to a show at the *Casa de la Cultura*.

SHOPPING

All the goods described below are for sale to tourists from abroad and must be paid for in dollars.

• What's on offer

Arts and crafts
The tourist influx has encouraged the production of souvenirs which have little to do with traditional Cuban crafts. The same sort of articles like wooden statuettes, carved coconuts, necklaces, hats made from palm straw, and little figures representing the various *Santería* deities turn up everywhere.

Cigars
To return from a Cuban holiday without bringing back examples of the country's most famous product would almost count as sacrilege. The choice is huge, ranging from slender cigarillos to cigars of Churchillian corpulence. The price varies according to size, thickness, and brand. Connoisseurs will also consider colour, aroma and the "give" of the leaf. Fine quality cigars like **Montecristo**, **Partagás**, or **Romeo y Julieta** bought here cost around half the price charged in continental Europe, and far less than the UK price. Reckon on paying about US$300 for a box of 25 Cohibas. Cigars should be purchased at the last possible moment before returning home, then kept in a humidifier. Avoid buying cigars on the street at impossibly low prices. The quality is likely to be abysmal, and lack of proof of purchase could cause problems at customs.

Rum

Rum, like cigars, is an excellent buy. Bottles of **Havana Club** are on sale everywhere. There is three-year old white rum for making cocktails with, a golden five-year old rum, and a dark, matured rum (seven years or more), which can be drunk on its own or on the rocks. Reckon on paying between US$5 and US$10. There are a number of other national brands, and some distilleries sell their products directly.

Records and CDs

Souvenir shops usually have CDs and cassettes for sale, though the choice may be limited to current favourites. CDs cost around US$15.

Musical instruments

Craft markets and souvenir shops often have a range of drums and other percussion instruments for sale, including *claves*, *maracas*, *congas* and *tumbadores*. The shop at the Casa de la Música in Trinidad has a larger than usual choice of instruments.

Clothes

As well as the inevitable Che Guevara T-shirt, you might consider buying a *guayabera*, the pleated cotton shirt traditionally worn by Cuban men. Lace garments (and other items) are good buys, with a wide selection on sale in Trinidad as well as in Havana.

Books

All large towns have at least one bookshop, but the choice is sadly limited. There are usually a few books in English as well as in Spanish. For those who read Spanish, the same selection of key works turns up in every shop: the novels of Alejo Carpentier, essays by Fernando Ortiz, memoirs by Che Guevara, books on Cuban music or *Santería*, the thoughts of Fidel Castro. In addition to these official outlets, individuals sell secondhand books from improvised stalls outside their front door. And in Havana, you can browse for bargains at the daily **book market** in the sumptuous setting of the city's Plaza de Armas.

Fine art

Most towns have a gallery in which there are works for sale by contemporary Cuban painters and sculptors. If you buy anything, make sure you get a receipt to show to customs.

• Where to shop

What to buy where

The best shops and the widest range of things to buy are in Havana, particularly in Old Havana. Trinidad too has a good selection of shops.

Local markets

There are regular open air markets in the larger towns, selling books, cassettes, craft work and souvenirs of all kinds.

Factory outlets

Cigars and alcohol can often be bought directly from the manufacturer. Cigar factories offer visitors their whole range of products, and the rum and liqueur distilleries (like the *guayabita* distillery at Pinar del Río) usually have a shop of some kind.

Other shops

Goods beyond the reach of ordinary Cubans with only pesos to spend are sold in dollar shops. Boutiques at the major hotels sell CDs, alcohol, cigars and souvenirs, as well as more mundane items like soap. Artex shops specialise in cultural products.

Tobacco sheds

J. F. Galmiche

• Customs regulations and proof of purchase

Before leaving Cuba, make sure you have receipts for any works of art purchased in the country, and, if necessary, an export permit. Travellers entering or returning to EU countries are allowed to import 50 cigars and 1 litre of spirits free of duty.

• Mailing things home

The most straightforward way of getting your purchases back home is to take them yourself, or get someone else to do so. Mailing things home is definitely a last resort; if you have to, it is best to do it through the courier service **DHL**, which is expensive, but relatively reliable.

HEALTH AND SAFETY

• Precautions

Cuba is free of tropical diseases, and any medical problems experienced by visitors to the country are likely to be linked to either heat or diet. Take time to get used to the heat by avoiding over-exertion, and protect yourself from the sun with a generous application of blocking lotion and by wearing a sun hat of some kind. Dehydration can be avoided by drinking plenty of water, carrying a supply with you on long walks, and by making sure your diet contains enough salt. Tummy troubles often occur simply because of the change in diet, and the high fat content of some Cuban food may prove indigestible.

Even though no particular precautions need to be taken, it is as well to make sure anything you eat is fresh. This applies especially to seafood and shellfish. Eating barracuda is risky because of the poisonous algae which are part of its diet. But barracuda is never served in restaurants. While there are practically no dangerous animals in Cuba, mosquitoes can be a real problem. Local mosquitoes are hardy creatures, able to penetrate air conditioning systems and lie low until you go to sleep. Bring plenty of repellent with you and apply it lavishly, especially if you are staying near stagnant water of any kind. Some beaches are plagued at sundown by swarms of midge-like *gegenes*. The severe itching caused by a bite from one of these unpleasant little insects can be treated with an antihistamine.

Like the rest of the world, Cuba has been affected by AIDS (SIDA in Spanish), though the number of those infected remains low. The government is tough with sufferers, isolating them in special sanatoria (one per province), and claiming that this both increases their lifespan and protects the public. It is a policy that has caused much controversy, and in any case has not created an AIDS-free environment outside. So the usual precautions are necessary for anyone considering having unprotected sex with a stranger.

● Medical kit
Your medical kit should include bandages for minor injuries, disinfectant, aspirin, antiseptic cream, antihistamine, something for stomach upsets, any medicines you have been prescribed, plus suntan lotion and mosquito repellent, and a supply of tampons if required. Syringes could come in useful if you are hospitalised in a remoter area. The shortage of pharmaceuticals means that your kit will be much appreciated if you drop it at a medical centre or clinic before leaving Cuba.

● Health
Health care has long been considered one of the success stories of the Cuban Revolution, but this has been undermined by the acute lack of medical supplies and other material. Traditional cures have made a comeback, including herbal remedies of all kinds. The network of clinics for foreigners extending across the whole of the country has been largely exempt from these difficulties, and treatment in them is of a high standard. Cuba has established a good reputation for certain treatments, and thousands of foreigners come here every year for medical care.

First aid
To call an ambulance, contact the nearest clinic. First aid is available at all the larger hotels (*See the "Making the most of" sections of the guide*).

Hospitals
Hospital treatment is free for Cubans, but foreigners are treated in a network of international clinics run by the Servimed organisation. All fees must be paid in dollars, with a consultation with an English-speaking doctor normally costing between US$20 and US$30. There are *Servimed* clinics at Havana, Playas del Este, Varadero, Cienfuegos, Trinidad, Santa Lucía, Guardalavaca and Santiago de Cuba. Your embassy should be contacted if your case is severe enough to warrant repatriation.

Chemists / Pharmacies
All the major towns have at least one pharmacy, but it is unlikely to be well stocked. Bring with you all the medicines and pharmaceuticals you think you might need.

Doctors
Cuba has one of the highest ratios of doctors per head of population in the world, many of whom received their training in the countries of the Communist bloc. Most doctors working in international clinics speak English.

● Emergencies
Police, ☎ 116
Fire brigade, ☎ 115

A TO Z

• Addresses

Addresses in Cuba consist of the name of the street, followed by the building number, then possibly by the names of the two streets which run at right angles and which define the city block (*cuadra*) in which the building is located. So an address which reads: Convento de Santa Clara, Calle Cuba no610 e/Sol y Luz, means that the Santa Clara Convent is located at no610 in Calle Cuba, between Calle Sol and Calle Luz. If the building is on a corner (*esquina*), then only the two streets which meet there are mentioned. Thus: Hotel Deauville, esq. Galiano y Malecón, means that the hotel is on the corner of Calle Galiano and the Malecón. Lots of street names have been changed since 1959, but many local people continue to use the old name (given in brackets in the town plans).

• Bargaining

Haggling is not a Cuban tradition. However, the growth of tourism has brought with it a readiness to bargain over the price of at least some goods and services. This does not apply to any sort of official transaction, but there is nothing to stop you attempting to make a deal with individuals, whether it concerns the rent of a room or the cost of a ride in a private taxi. Bear in mind that, outside the main tourist areas, Cubans are not used to bargaining, and may refuse to lower even what is obviously an exorbitant price.

• Conversion table

Cuba uses the metric system, but a number of venerable units of measure are still current, such as the *caballería* (13.43ha) for tobacco plots. And the *arroba* (11.5kg) for sugar.

• Drinking water

Tapwater can be drunk in tourist areas, but in more remote places the quality may be variable and the supply is subject to interruption. Mineral water is widely available.

• Electricity

Power cuts (*apagones*) are a big headache for ordinary Cubans, but tourists are rarely affected, since the larger hotels all have their own generators.
Current is normally 110 volts, 60 Hz, and plugs are US-style. Recently-built hotels may have current at 220 volts.

• Laundry

All the major hotels have a laundry service. There is usually a price list in the bedroom. In other establishments, the chambermaid may help you out.

• Newspapers

The national daily paper is **Granma**, the official organ of the Central Committee of the Cuban Communist Party, and there is a weekly edition in various languages including English. Some foreign newspapers and magazines can be bought in the larger hotels, usually several days after publication.

• Radio and television

Among the national radio stations, **Radio Taino** has some English-language programmes for tourists. In some areas it is possible to pick up broadcasts from Florida.

TV is very much part of everyday life in Cuba. There are two channels, **Cubavisión** and **Tele-Rebelde**, broadcasting only from late afternoon to around 11pm. Everyone stays in for the soaps (*telenovelas*) and the Saturday night American blockbuster. The television sets in the rooms of major hotels are usually tuned in to a number of satellite channels.

● Smoking

Despite government attempts to get Cubans to cut down, there are lots of unre-constructed smokers around, and very few smoke-free zones. Compared with cigars, Cuban cigarettes are rough. The most popular brand is, funnily enough, *Popular*. Some American brands are sold in dollar shops, hotel bars and service stations.

● Taking photographs

Cuba is a most photogenic country, with its brightly uniformed schoolchildren, characterful faces, cherished old cars, subtly coloured facades, silver sands and clear waters. Most Cubans are more than happy to have their picture taken and will pose if you ask them.

Hotel shops and Photoservice branches have a limited range of colour films (but no black and white).

● Thefts

Cuba is a relatively crime-free country, certainly compared with many of the other Latin American countries. However, the continuing economic crisis has brought with it an outbreak of pick-pocketing, particularly in Old Havana and along the Malecón, and you should take special care with camera and handbag. Many hotels have a room safe where valuables can be left for a small charge.

● Tipping / gratuities

With the growth of tourism and the legalisation of the dollar, tipping has become widespread, and gratuities make up an important part of many people's earn-ings. The car park attendant, the museum guide, the car washer, the waiter and the chambermaid should all be tipped. The usual rate is US$1, more for excep-tionally good service, but it is bad form to over-tip.

● Units of measurement

Distances in this guide are given in kilometres. As a rule of thumb, one kilo-metre is five-eighths of a mile: 5 miles is therefore about 8 kilometres, 10 miles is about 16 kilometres and 20 miles is about 32 kilometres.

Consult the table below for other useful metric equivalents:

Degrees Celsius	35°	30°	25°	20°	15°	10°	5°	0°	-5°	-10°
Degrees Fahrenheit	95°	86°	77°	68°	59°	50°	41°	32°	23°	15°

1 centimetre (cm) = 0.4 inch
1 metre (m) = 3.3 feet
1 metre (m) = 1.09 yards
1 litre = 1.06 quart
1 litre = 0.22 gallon
1 kilogram (kg) = 2.2 pounds

● Weather forecasts

National TV has a weather forecast as part of the 8pm evening news programme. Cubans find weather a topic of endless fascination, especially during the hurri-cane season.

A to Z

LOOK AND LEARN

• General
GELDORF Lynn, *Cubans*, Bloomsbury Press, 1992.
GONZÁLEZ-WIPPLER Migene, *The Santería Experience*, Prentice-Hall, 1982.
GUILLERMO Jorge, *Cuba: Five Hundred Years of Images*, Abaris Books, 1992.
INFANTE Guillermo Cabrera, *Mea Cuba*, Faber & Faber, 1994.
OSPINA Hernando Calvo, *Salsa – Havana Heat, Bronx Beat*, Latin American Bureau, 1995.
PATULLO P, *Last Resorts: The Cost of Tourism in the Caribbean*, Cassell, 1996.

• History before the Revolution
BETTELL L, *Cuba: A Short History*, Cambridge University Press, 1993.
RIPOL Carolos, *José Martí: A Biography in Photographs and Documents*, Senda Nueva de Ediciones, 1992.
SZULZ Tad, *Fidel: A Critical Portrait*, Hodder & Stoughton, 1986.
THOMAS Hugh, *Cuba, or the Pursuit of Freedom*, Da Capo, 1998.

• The Revolution and after
ANDERSON John Lee, *Che Guevara: A Revolutionary Life*, Bantam, 1997.
BALFOUR Sebastian, *Castro*, Longman, 1995.
GEYER Georgie Anne, *Guerilla Prince: the Untold Story of Fidel Castro*, Little, Brown, 1991.
PÉREZ Louis A, *Cuba – Between Reform and Revolution*, Oxford University Press, 1988.
RIUS, *Cuba for Beginners*, Pathfinder Press, 1970.
THOMAS Hugh, *The Cuban Revolution*, Weidenfeld & Nicolson, 1986.

• Topical commentary
BARCLAY Juliet, *Havana, Portrait of a City*, Cassell, 1993.
HATCHWELL Emily & CALDER Simon, *Cuba in Focus: A Guide to the People, Politics and Culture*, Latin American Bureau, 1995.
LORENZ Marita and SCHWARZ Ted, *From Castro to Kennedy: Love and Espionage in the CIA*, Warner Books, 1994.
MILLER Tom, *Trading with the Enemy: A Yankee Travels through Castro's Cuba*, Athaeneum, 1992.
OPPENHEIMER Andres, *Castro's Final Hour: The Secret Story Behind the Coming Downfall of Communist Cuba*, Simon and Schuster, 1992.
SMITH Stephen, *The Land of Miracles*, Abacus, 1998.
TIMERMAN Jacobo, *Cuba – A Journey*, Picador, 1994.
WILLIAMS Stephen, *Cuba : the Land, the History, the People, the Culture*, Michael Friedman, 1994.

• Literature
BARNET Miguel, *The Autobiography of a Runaway Slave*, 1968.
CARPENTIER Alejo, *Explosion in the Cathdral*
GREENE Graham, *Our Man in Havana*, Penguin, 1962.
GUILLÉN Nicolás, *Patria o Muerte! The Great Zoo and Other Poems*
HEMINGWAY Ernest, *To Have and Have Not*, MacMillan, 1962, *The Old Man and the Sea*, 1952, *Islands in the Stream*, 1970.
INFANTE Guillermo Cabrera, *Three Trapped Tigers*, Faber 1989.
IYER Pico, *Cuba and the Night*, Quartet Books, 1995.

● Miscellaneous

The Cigar Companion, Apple Press, 1993.
DAVIDOFF Zino, *The Connoisseur's Book of the Cigar*, McGraw-Hill, 1967.

● Picture books

KUFELD Adam, *Cuba*, WW Norton, 1994.
SUGARMAN Martin A, *A Storm over Cuba*, Sugarman Productions, 1995.

● Films

REED Carol, *Our Man in Havana*, 1959.
STURGES John, *The Old Man and the Sea*, 1958.
GUTIÉRREZ ÁLEA Tomás and TABÍO Juan Carlos, *Strawberry and Chocolate*, 1993, and *Guantanamera*, 1995.
WENDERS Wim, *Buena Vista Social Club*, 1998. Traces the making of the award-winning album recorded in 1996 by stalwarts of the Havana musical scene of the 40s and 50s. Havana itself is as much the star as the musicians.

● Recordings

See the section on music page 58

Below are some of the best recordings of contemporary salsa. This world-conquering phenomenon has tended to overshadow the delights of more traditional Cuban music, a few examples of which are also listed.

Pachito Alonso y sus kini kinis, Ay! Que bueno está (World Music). A worthy successor to his father Pacho Alonso – inventor of *pilón* rhythm – Pachito and his band burst with vitality.

Afro-cuban All Stars, A toda Cuba le gusta (World Circuit). Fabulous fusion of styles on a single disc.

Buena Vista Social Club (World). The music that inspired the film of the same name.

La Charanga Habanera, Hey, you, loca (Magic Music). The Havana Street Players are famed for aggressive, polyrhythmic salsa.

Compay Segundo, Antología (East West). One of the best representatives of traditional *son* on the European scene.

Cuba "Evening": Crazy nights of the fifties (Auvidis). Series of recordings evoking the hot-house atmosphere of Havana in the days (or rather nights) before the Revolution.

De Cuba su Música, several compilations (EGREM). Down memory lane with historic recordings by stars of the past like Rita Montaner and Orquestra Sublime.

Cuba: the Trova, (World). Trovas as they were played in the old days, with just a singer, guitar, and laud (twelve-string guitar).

Isaac Delgado, Otra idea (RMM). Delgado may have quit NG la Banda, but has kept his compelling voice.

Introducing... *Rubén González* (World Circuit). Piano virtuoso González of the All Stars recorded his first solo album at the age of 77.

Los Guanches, Venga Guano (EGREM). Carefully crafted traditional sounds.

Manolin "El Médico de la salsa", Para mi gente (Caribe Productions). Cubans have lost count of the hits made by their "salsa doctor".

Benny Moré, Baila mi son (Caney). A wonderful compilation of numbers by the flashy "Barbaro del ritmo" (Wild Man of Rhythm).

NG La banda, Best of (Milan Latino). The pioneers of New Generation sounds.

Guillermo Portabales, El Carretero (World Circuit). Great selections from one of the greats of *guarija*.

Look and learn

Los Van Van, *Lo último en vivo* (Magic Music). Banded together now for three decades and hardly a wrinkle between them, the Van Van are still making fabulous music under the direction of Juan Formeil.

● **Maps**

Carta stradale Cuba 1:1 250 000, Litografia Artistica Cartografica. Published in Italy, this road map has plans of Havana, Cienfuegos, Camaguey, Santiago de Cuba, the Eastern Beaches and Varadero.

Mapa geográfico 1:1 250 000, ediciones GEO. From hotels and airport shops. A good quality road map, with plans of Havana, the Eastern Beaches, Varadero, Cayo Coco, Cayo Largo, Cayo Guillermo and Santiago de Cuba.

Mapa turistico "Ciudad de La Habana", ediciones GEO. A useful map covering the whole of the capital and the surrounding area.

La Habana Vieja, 1:2 500, Instituto cubano de geodesia y cartografía. Historical guide to Old Havana with street index. Practical information dates from 1991.

USEFUL WORDS AND EXPRESSIONS

All Spanish words used in the text, together with their equivalents in English, are given on the reverse of the rear cover of the book.

Anyone who visits Cuba with no knowledge of Spanish will find a pocket English-SpanishSpanish-English dictionary a great help in reading menus, understanding signs, and generally communicating with local people.

Cuban Spanish is full of "Cubanisms", that is, words or expressions which do not exist or have another meaning from the Spanish spoken in Spain (Castilian Spanish). Cubanisms appear in *italics* in the following list.

With some exceptions, Spanish is spoken as it is written, though the letter "h" is not pronounced. The "j" is like a harsh English "h", as is "g" when followed by an "e" or "i"; "ll" is pronounced like "y" in "yes"; "n" is like "n" in onion. Spanish "v" is almost identical to "b". The "th" sound in Castilian Spanish does not exist anywhere in Latin America.

The stress in Spanish is normally on the last syllable but one, though words ending in a consonant have the emphasis on the final syllable. In other cases, the stress is indicated by an acute accent.

Numbers

one	uno	sixteen	dieciséis
two	dos	seventeen	diecisiete
three	tres	eighteen	dieciocho
four	cuatro	nineteen	diecinueve
five	cinco	twenty	veinte
six	seis	twenty-one	veintiuno
seven	siete	thirty	treinta
eight	ocho	forty	cuarenta
nine	nueve	fifty	cincuenta
ten	diez	sixty	sesenta
eleven	once	seventy	setenta
twelve	doce	eighty	ochenta
thirteen	trece	ninety	noventa
fourteen	catorce	hundred	cien
fifteen	quince	thousand	mil

Days of the week

Monday	lunes	Friday	viernes
Tuesday	martes	Saturday	sábado
Wednesday	miércoles	Sunday	domingo
Thursday	jueves		

Months and seasons

January	enero	September	septiembre
February	febrero	October	octubre
March	marzo	November	noviembre
April	abril	December	diciembre
May	mayo	Spring	primavera
June	junio	Summer	verano
July	julio	Autumn	otono
August	agosto	Winter	invierno

Common expressions

Yes, no	Sí, no	Thank you	Gracias
Good morning	Buenos días	Thank you very much	Muchas gracias
Good afternoon, evening	Buenas tardes	You are welcome	De nada
Good night	Buenas noches	Excuse me	Perdón, disculpe
Hello	Hola	I don't understand	No entiendo
Goodbye	Adiós (or ciao)	I don't speak Spanish	No hablo espanol
See you later	Hasta luego	Mr, sir	Señor
Pleased to meet you	Encantado (a)	Mrs, madam	Señora
How are you?	¿Qué tal?	Miss	Señorita
Please	Por favor		

Time

When?	¿Cuándo?	Yesterday	Ayer
What's the time?	¿Qué hora es?	Tomorrow morning	Mañana por la mañana
Now	Ahora		
At once	Enseguida	Tomorrow afternoon	Mañana por la tarde
Date	Fecha		
Year	Año	Tomorrow evening	Mañana por la noche
Century	Siglo		
Today	Hoy		

Directions and visiting

Where is?	¿Donde está?	Turn	Doblar, girar
Address	Dirreción	Near	Cerca
On the right	A la derecha	Far	Lejos
On the left	A la izquierda	Corner	Esquina
Straight on	Recto	Map, plan	Mapa

Public transport

Ticket	Pasaje	To hitch-hike	Coger botella
Plane	Avión	Fine	Multa
Train	Tren	Car park	Parqueo
Return	Ida y vuelta	Forbidden	Prohibido
Bicycle repair man (punctures)	Ponchera		

Hotel

Reception	Carpeta	Single room	Habitación sencilla
Receptionist	Carpetero (a)		
Hotel guest	Huésped	Double room	Habitación doble

Bathroom	Cuarto de baño	Key	Llave
Bed	Cama	Toilet	Servicios, baño
Sheet	Sábana	Air-conditioning	Aire
Bed-cover	Manta		acondicionado

Restaurant

To eat	Comer	Lunch	Almuerzo
To drink	Beber	Dinner	Cena
I would like	Quisiera	Bill	Cuenta
Breakfast	Desayuno	Menu	Menú, carta

Dishes

Avocado pear	Aguacate	Butter	Mantequilla
Rice	Arroz	Apple	Manzana
Sugar	Azúcar	Seafood	Mariscos
Sandwich	Bocadillo	Bread	Pan
Sweet potato	Boniato	Potato	Papa
Prawn	Camarón	Fish	Pescado
Roast meat	Carne asada	Mince	Picadillo
Pork	Cerdo	Pepper	Pimienta
Fried pork	Chicharrón	Banana	Plátano
Rice and beans	Congrí	Fried chicken	Pollo frito
Lamb	Cordero	Dessert	Postre
Beans	Frijoles	Pork	Puerco
Ice cream	Helado	Cheese	Queso
Egg	Huevo	Beef	Res
Ham	Jamón	Salt	Sal
Lobster	Langosta	Veal	Ternera
Sucking pig	Lechón	Cassava	Yuca
Lettuce	Lechuga	Carrot	Zanahoria

Drinks

Tea	Té	Soft drink	Refresco
Black coffee	Café solo	Ice	Hielo
White coffee	Café con leche	Pineapple juice	Hugo de pina
Cocoa,		Grapefruit	Toronja
hot chocolate	Chocolate	Papaya	Fruta bomba
Mineral water (still)	Agua mineral (sin gas)	Milk shake	Batido
		Beer	Cerveza
Mineral water (sparkling)	Agua mineral (con gas)	Rum	Ron
		Wine	Vino
Tap water	Agua de la pila		

Shopping

How much?	¿Cuánto es?	Credit card	Tarjeta de crédito
Dear	Caro	Shop	Tienda
Cheap	Barato	Farmers' market	Agromercado
Hard currency,		Queue	Cola
Dollar	Divisas, dólar	Bill, receipt	Comprobante, recibo
Cuban			
currency	Moneda nacional	Cigar	Puro, tabaco
Cash	Efectivo	Cigarettes	Cigarillos

Post office

Envelope	Sobre	To telephone	Llamar por teléfono
Stamp	Sello		
Letterbox	Buzón	International call	Llamada internacional
Post office	Oficina de correos		

Visiting

Entrance	Entrada	Ticket desk, window	Taquilla
Exit	Salida		
Open	Abierto	Guide	Guía
Closed	Cerrado	Floor	Piso
Works	Obras		

Some common Cuban expressions

Great, cool	*Chévere*	Money	*Guaniquiqui*
To hitch-hike	*Coger botella*	How goes it, pal?	*?Qué bola, asere?*
Comrade	*Compañero (a)*	Mate	*Socio*
Freak, marginal person	*Friki*	Foreigner	*Yuma*

Useful words and expressions

107

Exploring Cuba

Colourful Trinidad

HAVANA ★★★
(CIUDAD DE LA HABANA)

The political, economic and cultural capital of Cuba
Capital of Havana province
Area 725sqkm – Pop 2.2 million
Harbour 180 km from Florida

Not to be missed
A stroll through the streets of Old Havana.
Eating an ice-cream at the Coppelia.
Browsing through the bookstalls in the Plaza de Armas.
Salsa!

And remember...
Reckon on a stay of at least two days.
Monday is closing day for most museums.
When driving watch out for cyclists, especially at night.

Havana holds its visitors spellbound for many reasons, but it is the city's magically preserved mixture of architectural styles which make it seem so timeless. Splendid facades evoke a glamorous but faded past, especially along the waterfront, where sun, sea-spray and tropical downpours have dimmed but not erased a gorgeous palette of pastel colours. Behind the waterfront is the colonial core of the city, a labyrinth of streets, alleyways and cracked pavements, with heady aromas emanating from the dilapidated but still grand buildings. Further west, there are wide avenues lined with fine villas and the occasional high building, together with luxuriant tropical vegetation which in places seems about to smother the architecture with its exuberant growth.

Kept going by endless ingenuity, American automobiles from the 1950s fight for pride of place on the city's streets with beat-up Ladas, but the kings of the road are now the countless bicycles, some of them sagging beneath the weight of a whole family.

Havana cityscape

Cuba's "Special Period" with all its shortages has affected Havana just as much as the countryside. Life has slowed down and the city has a look of the past about it, a situation not without its appeal to the visitor from Europe or North America who will be struck by the absence of skyscrapers, garish advertising signs, or shopping malls at every turn. But for local people unable to get petrol or spare parts for the car, or having to cram into an overloaded *guagua* (bus) after an interminable wait, the "Special Period" is synonymous with frustration and the daily struggle for existence, *la lucha*.

Adaptation has taken a variety of fascinating forms, all of which enliven the townscape in one way or another. An old Dodge in the middle of the carriageway might look as if it has been dumped, but in fact it is being resprayed, another layer of paint being added to the many already encrusting its battered bodywork. A building fronting on to the street is having its living room converted into a *paladar* where the family will shortly be serving home-made meals to all-comers. All sorts of services are on offer at the roadside, from the repair-man negotiating a price for patching the inner tube of a passing cyclist to the expert able to give a new lease of life to a disposable cigarette lighter. And as daylight fades on the Malecón, creatures of the night emerge, each having poured herself into the tightest of fluorescent shorts in the hope of tempting some tourist into parting with precious dollars.

As the years of privation have continued, the city's face has been altered in other ways. The gardens of both private houses and official buildings have been transformed into vegetable patches, while the rooftops populated by pigs and poultry in daytime are converted at nightfall into impromptu dance floors.

Open air life has continued to flourish despite frequent cuts in the gas and electricity supply, with light and warmth provided by makeshift flares and braziers. In the face of all their daily difficulties, the people of Havana have lost none of their human warmth or sheer love of life, and the city soon pulls every visitor into its sensual embrace. Smiles are common, sulky faces rare. Any excuse is good enough to start a celebration. Music seems to seep from every stone. Every evening, roused by salsa, Havana shakes off its tropical langour and dances to the intoxicating rhythms of its Afro-Cuban heritage.

An attractive prize

Every 16 November the people of Havana celebrate their city's birthday in front of the little Classical building in the Plaza de las Armas known as the Templete. It was on that date in 1519 that the Spanish conquistadors attended the solemn mass marking the foundation of **San Cristóbal de la Habana**. The site of the town had already been moved twice, but this was its final location. Its name may have come from the native leader Habaguanex, though it is thought by some to be derived from the English "*haven*", and the city's fortunes have certainly been closely tied to the development of its harbour.

The courtyard of the Palace of the Captains-General

J. F. Galmiche

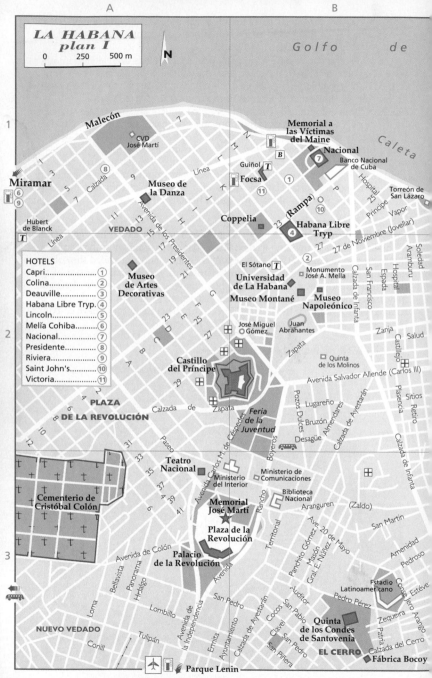

LA HABANA plan I

0 250 500 m

N

Golfo   de

Caleta

Malecón

CVD
José Martí

Miramar

Calzada

Línea

Memorial a
las Víctimas
del Maine

Nacional

Banco Nacional
de Cuba

Guiñol

Focsa

Museo de
la Danza

Avenida de los Presidentes

VEDADO

Hubert
de Blanck

Línea

Coppelia

(Rampa)

Habana Libre
Tryp

Torreón de
San Lázaro

Vapor

27 de Noviembre (Jovellar)

Hospital

Príncipe

25

251

HOTELS

Capri.................. ①
Colina................. ②
Deauville............. ③
Habana Libre Tryp. ④
Lincoln............... ⑤
Melía Cohiba......... ⑥
Nacional.............. ⑦
Presidente........... ⑧
Riviera............... ⑨
Saint John's......... ⑩
Victoria.............. ⑪

El Sótano

Museo
de Artes
Decorativas

Universidad
de La Habana

Museo Montané

Monumento
José A. Mella

Museo
Napoleónico

Calzada de Infanta

San Francisco

Soledad

Aramburu

Espada

Hospital

José Miguel
Gómez

Juan
Abrahantes

Zanja

Salud

Castillo
del Príncipe

Zapata

Quinta
de los Molinos

Avenida Salvador Allende (Carlos III)

Castillejo

Retiro

PLAZA
DE LA REVOLUCIÓN

Calzada   de   Zapata

Feria
de la
Juventud

Pozos Dulces

Lugareño

Bruzón

Desagüe

Boyeros

Almendares

Calzada de Ayestarán

Plasencia

Sitios

Calzada de Infanta

Cementerio de
Cristóbal Colón

Paseo

Teatro
Nacional

Ministerio
del Interior

Ministerio de
Comunicaciones

Biblioteca
Nacional

Aranguren

(Zaldo)

Memorial
José Martí

Plaza de la
Revolución

Palacio
de la Revolución

Avenida de Colón

Bellavista

Panorama

Hidalgo

San Pedro

Avenida

Rancho

Territorial

Ave. 20 de Mayo

Panchito Gómez

Masón

Gral. E. Núñez

San Martín

Amenidad

Pedroso

NUEVO VEDADO

Loma

Lombillo

Tulipán

Conill

Avenida de
la Independencia

Calzada de Ayestarán

Ermita

Ayuntamiento

Auditor

Cocos

San Pablo

Clavel

San Pedro

San Piñera

Estadio
Latinoamericano

Pedro Pérez

Quinta
de los Condes
de Santovenia

EL CERRO

Consejero Estévez

Zequeira

Patria

Consejero Arango

Calzada del Cerro

Fábrica Bocoy

Parque Lenin

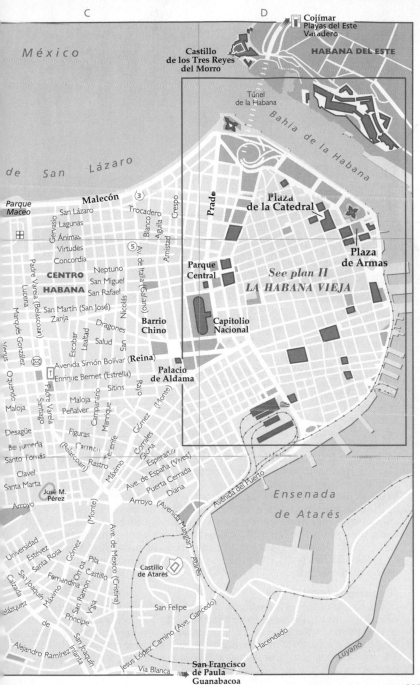

C

D

Cojímar
Playas del Este
Varadero

HABANA DEL ESTE

Castillo
de los Tres Reyes
del Morro

México

Túnel
de la Habana

Bahía de la Habana

de San Lázaro

Parque
Maceo

Malecón ③

San Lázaro
Lagunas
Ánimas
Virtudes
Concordia
Neptuno
San Miguel
San Rafael

Trocadero

Blanco
Aguila
Amistad

Crespo

Prado

Plaza
de la Catedral

Plaza
de Armas

⑤ Av. de Italia (Galiano)

Gervasio

Padre Varela (Belascoaín)

CENTRO
HABANA

Lucena
Marqués González
Venus
Oquendo
Maloja

San Martín (San José)
Zanja

San Nicolás

Escobar
Lealtad

Dragones
Salud

San

Barrio
Chino

Parque
Central

See plan II
LA HABANA VIEJA

Capitolio
Nacional

Avenida Simón Bolívar (Reina)

Enrique Bernet (Estrella)

Palacio
de Aldama

Padre Varela
Santiago

Maloja
Peñalver
Figuras

Campanario
Manrique

Sitios

Rayo

Gómez (Monte)

Desagüe
Benjumeda
Santo Tomás
Clavel
Santa Marta
Arroyo

Vicente
Carmen

Corrales
Gloria
Esperanza
Puerta Cerrada
Diaria
Arroyo (Avenida Magalí)

(Belascoaín)
Rastro

Máximo

Ave. de España (Vives)

Avenida del Puerto

José M.
Pérez

Ensenada
de Atarés

Universidad
Estévez
Santa Rosa
Calzada
San Joaquín
Velázquez

Gómez

Ave. de México (Cristina)

Orroa
Pila
Castillo

Famandina
Máximo
San Ramón
Vigía
Príncipe

Atarés

Castillo
de Atarés

San Felipe

Hacendado

Luyanó

Alejandro Ramírez

Infanta
San Joaquín

de

Jesús López Camino (Ave. Gancedo)

Vía Blanca

San Francisco
de Paula
Guanabacoa

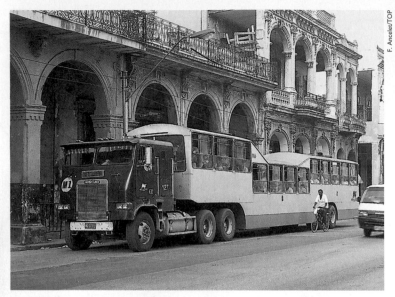
A camello

Havana's strategic position between Europe and the Americas led to early commercial success. Merchants built their homes on the waterfront the better to supervise the loading and unloading of ships laden with sugar, tobacco, slaves, gold and precious stones. But these cargo vessels brought in their wake a horde of pirates, buccaneers and corsairs who as often as not were in the pay of Spain's European rivals. To discourage their depredations, the Castillo de la Real Fuerza was built between 1538 and 1544. The first of Havana's fortresses, it was unable to withstand an attack by the French pirate Jacques de Sores, who seized the city in 1555. But new and stronger defences were constructed, and the city's commerce was soon flourishing even more than before. In the middle of the 16C the Spanish governors moved here from Santiago de Cuba and Havana became the island's capital.

In the 16C and 17C the city was subjected to repeated attacks by the English, its 10 000 inhabitants finally falling into British hands on 13 August 1762 after a two-month siege. But less than a year later Spanish rule was reinstated under the terms of the Treaty of Fontainebleau which compensated the British with Florida. British rule left few physical traces; its main effect was to open up Cuba and its capital city to the world and encourage it to trade more widely than ever before.

A modern capital city

In the course of the 19C most new building was in the form of palaces and other large private dwellings, though public works included a sewerage system and provision of street lighting. The city spread beyond the fortifications which, except for the defences at the entrance to the harbour, were demolished in 1863. The city's historic core, now known as *Habana Vieja*, was neglected in favour of the newer districts to the west such as Centro Habana.

After independence in 1902 it was the turn of the areas known as the Vedado and Miramar, where development took place on the familiar North American pattern, with a grid of streets designated by letters and numbers. As the city grew and US influence increased, it was here that many Americans settled, patronising the luxury hotels and casinos and building themselves magnificent villas on the far side of the Río Almendares. But with the triumph of the Revolution the old Caribbean capital of gambling and prostitution was stripped of its casinos and brothels and many of the larger private dwellings were confiscated.

The old districts in the centre of Havana have undergone very little in the way of architectural change since the Revolution. Most post-Revolutionary building has been on the outskirts of the city, for example in Nuevo Vedado or even further out at Alamar and Habana del Este. More recently, a number of modern hotel buildings have appeared in the Vedado and Miramar areas in an attempt to accommodate the ever increasing number of tourists.

The districts of Havana (Plan 1)

Ciudad de la Habana (City of Havana) is a province divided into fifteen administrative areas known as *municipios*.

The **Habana Vieja** *municipio* takes in almost all the city's colonial building heritage. Facing Havana Bay, it stretches east from Paseo de Martí (Prado) to the harbour and extends to the southwest beyond the central railway station as far as the Regla area. This historic core is partly enclosed by a ring road laid out along the line of the old fortifications.

To the west of Habana Vieja and the *municipio* of **Centro Habana** is the **Plaza de la Revolución** district. It includes an area to the north of the Columbus Cemetery known as the Vedado, the busy modern centre of the city and quite distinct from the populous Nuevo Vedado residential area to the south of the cemetery. The **Vedado** has numerous hotels and restaurants and other tourist facilities such as travel agencies and airline offices.

Beyond the mouth of the Río Almendares is the *municipio* of Playa which includes the **Miramar** area, a prestigious residential district with luxury hotels and restaurants as well as most of the city's foreign embassies.

Opposite Old Havana on the far side of the harbour is the *municipio* of **Habana del Este**, which extends from the fortresses guarding the harbour entrance to the Eastern Beaches. This area forms part of Havana but is described in another chapter (see page 178).

Old Havana north★★★
From Calle Obispo to the Cathedral
Allow half a day

A stroll through the narrow streets of Old Havana is a journey backward in time through 400 years of architecture, a rich and harmonious mixture which earned this part of the capital UNESCO World Heritage status in 1982. But despite its wealth of palaces, churches and squares the historic core of the city is far from being just a museum of buildings; it's a lived-in place, where overloaded bicycles compete for road space with broken-down cars and wandering pedestrians, and where shouted conversations from one balcony to another can just about be heard above the latest hits blaring out from ancient wireless sets with the volume turned up as far as it will go. A glance through the open windows reveals interiors whose dilapidated state contrasts with the newly renovated colonial edifices around the Cathedral and the Plaza de Armas.

The streets of Old Havana are often obstructed by building sites and it's best to get around on foot or by pedecab. Street lighting is poor so keep an eye on your possessions at night.

If your time in Havana is limited to a few hours go straight to Plaza de la Catedral and Plaza de Armas (see plan III page 119).

Leave the Parque Central by Calle San Rafael between the Manzana de Gómez and the Centro Asturiano. Turn right into Avenida de Bélgica (Monserrate) and immediately left by the El Floridita restaurant.

Calle Obispo★★ (Plan II A3, B2 and Plan III A2, B2)

Named after a bishop (*obispo*) from the neighbouring diocese who enjoyed strolling here, Calle Obispo remains an authentic local shopping street despite its location in a tourist area. But the empty shelves of many of its establishments are in sad contrast to the flashy galleries selling expensive works of art to foreign visitors; the street exemplifies Cuba's current contradictions just as much as its fascinating mixture of buildings from all eras testifies to the country's often dramatic history.

At the beginning of the pedestrianised area stands a splendid Art Deco structure housing what used to be the city's biggest bookshop, the Moderna Poesia, reopened in 1983 after having been used for years as a warehouse. The staff's determined efforts to make the place attractive despite shortages of stationery and books included Saturday book signings and other special events. Unfortunately the **Moderna Poesia** has had to shut its doors once again for an indefinite period, but books can be bought from a couple of dealers opposite (*see Making the most of Havana*).

Hemingway in Havana
Between 1930 and 1940 Ernest Hemingway lived at Calle Obispo No.153, the Hotel Ambos Mundos, not far from the Plaza de Armas. The simply furnished room (No.511) where he wrote For Whom the Bell Tolls is open to the public. Whenever his old war wounds began to bother him, Hemingway would leave his lodgings in search of solace in the local bars. His nocturnal wanderings would invariably take him to the Floridita at the corner of Calle Obispo and Avenida de Bélgica. After downing a few daiquiris or Papa's Specials (daiquiri with a double shot of rum) he would proceed down the Calle Obispo to the Plaza de la Catedral and from there to the nearby Bodeguita del Medio where he would settle down with one of the café's famous mojitos. From here it would be just a step to the harbour and the prospect of one of those fishing trips which would provide him with material for The Old Man and the Sea.

On the corner of Calle Aguiar is the **Droguería Johnson★**, one of the street's two fine old pharmacies; it is currently undergoing refurbishment. The superb early 19C Joaquín Gómez palace on the same side of the street is now an elegant hotel. One block further on, at No.155, is Calle Obispo's second pharmacy, the **Farmacia y Droguería Taquechel★★**, with venerable chandeliers, rows of porcelain jars and other tools of the pharmacist's trade like a water purifier and a human skeleton. Close by, No.159 is a fine **structure in Art Nouveau style**.

No 117-119 is Havana's oldest house. It's a little blue and white structure under a pretty roof of old tiles, built around 1648 though parts of it may date from the previous century.

The adjoining building houses the **Museo de Plata** (Silver Museum) (*9.30am-6.30pm. Admission charge. For details of collective ticket see below under Museo de la Ciudad*) with fine examples of the silversmith's work including weapons, jewellery and timepieces.

LA HABANA VIEJA
plan II

0   100   200   300 m

N

Castillo de los Tres Reyes del Morro

Castillo de San Salvador de la Punta

Monumento a los Estudiantes de Medicina

Malecón

San Lázaro

Capdevila

Ave. de los Estudiantes (Carcel)

Parque de los Mártires

Máximo Gómez

Paseo de Martí (Prado)

Cárcel

Ave. Carlos M. Céspedes

Túnel de la Habana

Bahía de la Habana

Canal de Entrada

Fortaleza de San Carlos de la Cabaña

Refugio

Industria

Consulado

Colón

Trocadero

Ánimas

Virtudes

Zulueta

Morro

N. Plaza 13 de Marzo

Museo de la Revolución

Memorial Granma

Sevilla ⑨

Museo Nacional de Bellas Artes

Ave. de las Misiones

Ave. de Bélgica (Monserrate)

Casa de Pérez de la Riva

Palacio Pedroso

Cuarteles

Chacón

Santo Angel Custodio

Tejadillo

Compostela

Empedrado

Progreso

Plazuela de San Juan de Dios

Edificio Bacardí

O'Reilly

Calle

Ave. Carlos M. Céspedes (Ave. del Puerto)

T

Parque Céspedes

Tacón

See plan III Historic Centre

Plaza de la Catedral

Obispo

Plaza de Armas ⑧

③

Casa de la Obrapía

①

Calle

Neptuno

Manzana de Gómez

⑤ ⑥

Parque Central ④

Floridita

Centro Asturiano

Gran Teatro

Industria

Agramonte

Ave. Bélgica (Monserrate)

Bernaza

Cristo

Villegas

Aguacate

Obrapía

Aguiar

Cuba

Lamparilla

Amargura

Santo Cristo del Buen Viaje

Brasil (Teniente Rey)

Muralla

Sol

San Ignacio

Mercaderes

②

Museo Carlos J. Finlay

Casa de las Hermanas Cárdenas

Casa del Conde de Jaruco

②

Plaza Vieja

Habana

Oficios

Baratillo

⑩

✉

Plaza de San Francisco

Fuente de los Leones

Convento de San Francisco de Asís

B

San Pedro

Regla

Capitolio Nacional

Fábrica Partagás

Parque de la Fraternidad

Máximo Gómez (Monte)

Corrales

Economía

Agramonte

Cárdenas

Egido

Fuente de la India (Reina)

Luz

Convento de Santa Clara ⑦

Santa Clara

Cuba

San Ignacio

Luz

Inquisidor

Oficios

San Pedro

Convento de Belén

Espíritu Santo

Arco de Belén

Convento de la Merced

Acosta

Jesús María

Merced

Damas

Compostela

San Isidro

Picota

Leonor Pérez (Paula)

Desamparados

Curazao

Palacio Balboa

Casa Natal de José Martí

Muralla

Fundición

San Francisco de Paula

Bahía de la Habana

HOTELS

Ambos Mundos .... ①
Condes de Villanueva.. ②
Florida .... ③
Inglaterra .... ④
Parque Central .... ⑤
Plaza .... ⑥
Residencia Santa Clara ⑦
Santa Isabel .... ⑧
Sevilla .... ⑨
Valencia .... ⑩

Embedded in the outside wall is a Grecian mask, its mouth wide open. It is a **letter box**★ *(buzón)*, Cuba's oldest, though one other example can be found on the Plaza de la Catedral.

Plaza de Armas★★ (Plan III B2)

Laid out in 1582, Havana's oldest square was used as a parade ground by the troops of the Spanish garrison, then served as the centre of the city's political and cultural life until the end of the colonial era. In 1776 it was extended to its present size and in 1929 it underwent a thoroughgoing restoration. In the centre, honouring the "father of the country", stands a **statue of Carlos Manuel de Céspedes**, completed in 1935 by the sculptor Sergio Lopez Mesa.

The Plaza de Armas begins to liven up when the book-dealers arrive and start setting up their makeshift stalls all around the square. Book-lovers will find plenty to interest them here; as well as classic novels by Cuban authors like Alejo Carpentier, there are illustrated books from the Batista era and cigarette-card accounts of Revolutionary history in lurid colour. Any bargains purchased can then be studied in one of several open-air cafes. The square is probably the best place in Old Havana to simply sit and take in the busy scene, to the constant sound of musicians cranking out the traditional Cuban repertoire. Shaded by magnificent palm trees, the **formal garden**★ in the centre of the square is a fine spot from which to appreciate the magnificent buildings which give the Plaza de Armas its distinctive character.

Palacio de los Capitanes Generales★★★ – This masterpiece of Spanish colonial Baroque architecture fills the whole of the western side of the square and was built on the site of Havana's first parish church which dated from around 1550. The palace was begun in 1776 on the orders of the Governor, the Marquis de la Torre, who employed as his architects Antonio Fernadez de Trevejos y Zaldivas and Pedro Medina. The work was completed around 1792, but the building only took on its present form in 1834 when major alterations were carried out by Governor Miguel Tacón. It served as the seat of government, both in colonial times and during the first three Republics. In 1920 it became Havana's City Hall, then, after the Revolution, was converted to house the **Museo de la Ciudad**★★ **(City Museum)** *(10.30am-5.30pm; 9am-12.30pm Sunday; closed Monday. Admission charge. A ticket is available here which for US$9 gives admission to several of Old Havana's museums)*. The palace's rooms give on to the lovely **courtyard**★★ whose luxuriant vegetation is the setting for occasional concerts. In the centre of the courtyard is a **statue of Columbus**, completed in 1862 by the Italian sculptor Cucchiari.

The museum has a fine array of works of art, documents, furniture and other items relating to important episodes in the history of Cuba and its capital. Set in the wall on the ground floor of the courtyard is the oldest relic of colonial times, a **tablet** commemorating the fate of Dona Maria de Cepero y Nieto, the Governor's daughter, who died as a result of an unfortunate encounter with an arquebus. To the right of the entrance at the foot of the stairs is the original bronze sculpture of the **Giraldilla** (the one crowning the fortress tower of the Real Fuerza is a copy).

On the first floor are the museum's collections of furniture, porcelain and pictures, expertly arranged to evoke the life of the country's colonial-era aristocracy. One interior is hung with flags and banners, including early versions of today's distinctive national flag. Here too is an epic painting entitled *The Death of Maceo* by the Cuban artist Armando Menocal, which depicts the last moments of this

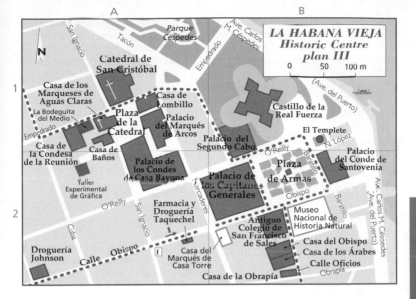

LA HABANA VIEJA
Historic Centre
plan III
0   50   100 m

hero of the Cuban struggle for independence as his comrades carry his body from the field of battle.

Among the bars and restaurants at the corner of Calle Obispo and Calle Oficios is the old **Bishop's Palace** (*Antiguo Colegio de San Francisco de Sales*) dating from the 17C. It is now a *casa del agua*, where those in the know can refresh themselves with a drink of water of exceptional purity.

On the corner of Calle Baratillo stands the **Palacio del Conde de Santovenia**★. This lovely 18C aristocratic mansion with its delicate wrought iron balconies was first converted into a hotel in 1867 and after thorough restoration at the end of the 20C was reopened as one of the city's most prestigious places to stay (*see Making the most of Havana*). Beyond is the **Museo Nacional de Historia Natural** (*9.30am-6.30pm; closed Monday. Admission charge*). A great favourite with children, the museum's displays explain the origin of the Earth and how life began. There is a fine array of stuffed animals, while life in the seas around Cuba is dealt with on the upper floor. The open-air café-restaurant has a fine view over the square.

At the northeastern corner of the square stands the **Templete**★, the city's first neo-Classical building (*9.30am-6.30pm. Admission charge*). The little temple was built in 1827 to commemorate the first mass held in Havana, in 1519. Inside are three **pictures** (possibly removed for

Governing passions

Dona Isabel de Bobadilla was the wife of Hernando de Soto, the Spanish Governor who ordered the city to be fortified in 1538. When her husband left on official business for Florida, Dona Isabel took over his duties, thereby becoming the first woman to rule over Cuba. Every day she climbed the tall tower of the fortress in the hope of catching sight of the ship bearing her loved one home. The couple exchanged many passionate letters, some of which only reached Dona Isabel long after the death of her partner who perished on the banks of the far-away Mississippi in 1542.

restoration) painted to celebrate this event by an artist of French origin, Jean-Baptiste Vermay; they are entitled *The First Mass*, *The First Meeting of the Council*, and *The Inauguration of the Temple*. The original *ceiba* tree around which people used to gather to commemorate the founding of the city has long since gone, its site marked by a column erected in 1754 by Governor F. Cajigal de la Vega. But close by is another stately *ceiba*, reputed to be the successor to nine others planted here; it is the focus of the annual celebrations on 16 November, when thousands of *Habaneros* wait patiently for their turn to walk round it three times and make a wish.

The Castillo de la Real Fuerza** on the far side of Calle O'Reilly on the northeast side of the square was constructed in 1558 as the city's first fortress. On the ground floor is the **Museo de la Cerámica** *(8am-7pm. Admission charge)*. The museum's dimly-lilt vaults house pottery and ceramics in a variety of styles, from realistic to conceptual. Among the works on show are pieces by 20C artists like Wilfredo Lam and Amelia Peláez. Prize-winning examples of the work of contemporary ceramicists are often on display following the biennial exhibition which is held here.

The fortress has a terrace restaurant with a fine **view**** over Old Havana and the fortifications on the far side of the entrance to the harbour. The weathercock in the form of a woman is the **Giraldilla**, created in 1632 by the sculptor Jerónimo Martínez Pínzon, the original of which is now in the City Museum.

To the left of the fortress is the structure built originally in 1772 by the Marquis de la Torre as a post office *(casa de correos)*. Later it housed the Royal Financial Administration before being turned over to the military and then, as the **Palacio del Segundo Cabo**** (Palace of the Second-in-Command), becoming the official residence of the Deputy Captain-General of the island. At the beginning of the 20C it became the seat of the Senate, then, in 1929 the home of the Supreme Popular Tribunal, Cuba's High Court. It is now the National Institute of Books with a pair of relatively well-stocked bookshops on the ground floor. The library and the superb **courtyard*** are also open to the public.

If there is time to spare, go down Calle Oficios and visit the Church of St Francis of Assisi before continuing to the Plaza de la Catedral.

Calle Oficios* (Plan III B2)

This street has been restored in very much the same way as Calle Obispo and is lined with refurbished buildings containing art galleries and museums. Fifty metres from the Plaza de Armas is the **Casa del Obispo***. The residence of the city's bishops from the 17C to the first half of the 19C, the building was then converted into a pawnshop. It now houses the **Museo Numismático** *(10am-5pm; 10am-4pm Saturday; 10am-1pm Sunday. Admisssion charge)* with a fascinating collection of coins and banknotes evoking the island's history.

Just beyond the Museo Numismático the Al Medina restaurant *(See Making the most of Havana)* is housed in the former **Colegio San Ambrosio**★ of 1689. The **patio**★ with its vine is particularly attractive. Adjoining it is the **Casa de los Arabes** (9.30am-7pm. Admission charge). The House of the Arabs has fine examples of traditional Islamic art given to Cuba by various Middle Eastern countries. On the opposite side of the street at No.13 is the **Sala del Transporte Automotor** (9am-7pm. Admission charge), housing an unlabelled assortment of historic vehicles ranging from prewar roadsters to the gas-guzzlers of the late 1950s, one of which belonged to Che Guevara.

Go one block along Calle Obrapía to the corner with Calle Mercaderes.

A lovely example of late 18C/early 19C palace architecture, the **Casa de la Obrapía** (10.30am-5.30pm; 9.30am-12.30pm Sunday. Admission charge) served as an orphanage in the 17C, hence its name ("pious works"). The building is on the grandest of scales, with an especially fine Baroque doorway. Furniture and fittings date from the 19C.

On the far side of the street are several little museums housing gifts received by Fidel Castro from various countries. They include the Casa de Mexico, the Casa de Africa, and, on Calle Mercaderes, the Casa de Asia.

Church of St Francis of Assisi

Go back to Calle Oficios, turn right towards Plaza de San Francisco.

J. F. Galmiche

Plaza de San Francisco★ (Plan II C3)

The beauty of this square is not enhanced by its great size and the proximity of the quayside with its customs buildings. But it is a good place to stop and take one's bearings and perhaps have a drink in one of a couple of elegant cafes. The lovely **Fuente de los Leones** (Lion Fountain) is the work of the Italian sculptor Gaggini and was completed in 1836. It was moved from here in 1844, then from one site to another and only finally returned to its original location here in the plaza in 1963. The Plaza de San Francisco was laid out towards the end of the 16C in front of the church and convent of the same name. The commercial buildings which now line it, such as the former **Lonja del Commercio** (Commodities Exchange) to the north or the **Customs House** to the east were erected at the beginning of the 20C.

The Church and Convent of St Francis of Assisi★★ *(9am-7pm and for evening concerts. Admission charge)* have had a colourful history. The idea of building a Franciscan convent was first mooted in 1570, but construction only began ten years later. Following its completion in 1591, the establishment became one of the most important in the whole of Latin America, its religious and cultural influence extending over much of the continent. By the beginning of the 18C it was in a neglected state, and between 1719 and 1733 was completely rebuilt. Its end as a religious institution came with the 1842 laws expropriating the clergy, when the buildings were converted into a warehouse. Then, four years later, it was battered by a hurricane which destroyed the chancel.

Since 1990 restoration work has given the church a new lease of life and a series of archeological investigations have been carried out. Concerts are held in the lofty nave, while the archeological finds are displayed on the ground floor of the restored north wing of the cloisters. They include **ceramics** and **pottery** dating from the 16C. There is also a fine **collection of religious objects★**, while on the upper floor of the recently renovated second cloister there is a collection of contemporary paintings. The cloisters themselves are due to be converted into a conservatory of music.

The studio and residence of the Venezuelan painter Carmen Montilla is a good place to terminate this part of the walk.

Return to the Plaza de Armas, then turn into Calle Tacón to the left of the Palacio del Segundo Cabo.

Calle Tacón No.12 is a pretty little house from the beginning of the 18C. It houses the **Gabinete de Arqueología** *(10.30am-5pm; 9am-1pm Sunday. Admission charge)* with an exhibition of pre-Colombian objects from Cuba, Mexico and Peru arranged by the resident archeologists.

Turn left by the Don Giovanni restaurant. Calle Empedrado leads directly to the Plaza de la Catedral.

Plaza de la Catedral★★★ (Plan III A1)

To see the square at its best get here early in the morning before the crowds of tourists arrive. A good time to take photographs is just after a downpour when the wet surface of the square produces brilliant reflections.

The square only gained its present name at the end of the 18C when the church, originally built by the Jesuits, became the city's cathedral. The area's earlier history had been distinctly watery. First called Plaza de la Ciénaga (Marsh Square) because of regular waterlogging in the rainy season, in 1587 it became the location of a large cistern built to supply ships with fresh water. Five years

Plaza de la Catedral

later a *chorro* (a small canal, literally a jet of water) was constructed and linked to the royal aqueduct to supply not only shipping but also the local population. In the 18C the colonial aristocracy lined the square with their mansions, fine buildings nearly all of which have been converted into museums. Nowadays the plaza is an essential stop on the tourist trail, not least because of the presence here of one of the city's most glamorous café-restaurants whose tables spill out into the square.

When skies are grey, the **Cathedral of San Cristóbal**★★★ (*10.30am to 3pm; Sunday mass 10.30am*) is a massive, solemn presence in the square, but as soon as the sun comes out it is transformed, and all is Baroque light and joy. The central **stained-glass window**★ is especially striking. Harmonising perfectly with the surrounding mansions, the cathedral's sensuously undulating facade is flanked by two asymmetrical towers, their bells long since silent.

The cathedral was supposedly designed by the Jesuits, but the architects' identity remains unknown to this day. Building began in 1748 but was interrupted in 1767 when the Spanish king ordered the expulsion of the Jesuits. The great building was completed ten years later and was made a cathedral in 1788. Its official dedication is to the Virgin of the Immaculate Conception, but it is universally known as the Cathedral of San Cristóbal in honour of Christopher Columbus. The cathedral was in fact the resting place of the great explorer's remains for more than a hundred years, but they were removed to Seville when Cuba gained its independence.

The austere interior was remodelled in Classical style in the early 19C and has little of the exuberance of the facade. The central nave is flanked by aisles with side chapels opening off them. In the centre of the choir is the **altar**★ with fine metalwork and statues by the Italian sculptor Bianchini, whose fellow-countryman Giuseppe Perovani was responsible for the **mural paintings*** above. The cathedral has a copy of the famous statue of the **Virgin de la Caridad del Cobre** the original of which is in Santiago *(see page 294)*.

On the left-hand side of the square is the elegant façade of the **Casa de los Marqueses de Aguas Claras**** which was built between 1751 and 1775. It now houses the well-known **El Patio** restaurant *(see Making the most of Havana)*. Even on the hottest of days the **courtyard*** is kept deliciously cool by a fountain and there is a fine **view*** over the square from the balcony on the upper floor.

On the same side of the square, the **Casa de Banos** (public baths) was erected in the 19C on the site of the cistern built here in 1587. The ground floor has been converted into an art gallery. Set in the wall at the corner with Callejón del Chorro is a delightful little **fountain** which, together with a plaque marks the line of the old aqueduct.

The **Palacio de los Condes de Casa Bayona**** opposite the cathedral is the oldest edifice in the square. It is also called the Casa de Luis Chacón, after its first owner Luis Chacón, who began building it in 1720. His palace later housed Havana's College of Registrars, and then the offices of one of the Republic's daily newspapers before becoming the headquarters of a nationalised rum corporation.

The building is now the **Museo de Arte Colonial**** *(9.30am-7pm. Admission charge)*. The museum's extensive collection of furniture covers the whole of the colonial period and includes fine items from churches as well as from other buildings. There are also architectural features such as wrought iron grilles, balustrades, and splendid door-knockers. Of special interest are the *medipuntos*, the features made of coloured glass or wood and placed above windows in order to lessen the fierce glare of the Caribbean sun. A number of the museum's own windows are filled with fine **stained glass**.

Built in 1741, the **Palacio del Marqés de Arcos*** occupies the southeast corner of the square but its main entrance is on Calle Mercaderes. The seat of the Royal Treasury until 1796, it served as the main post office until the middle of the 19C when it became the city's art school and literary academy. On completion of a restoration programme it will house a luxury hotel. Columns and wrought iron balconies adorn the lovely Baroque façade and set into one of the walls is a **letterbox** identical to the one in Calle Obispo. The palace has a perfectly matching neighbour, the **Casa de Lombillo***. It was built in the first half of the 18C for the Pedroso y Florencia family whose descendants were raised to the aristocracy in 1871. Three stories high, with fine ironwork, stencilled wall-paintings and wooden fittings painted in a striking shade of blue, this fine residence has been restored and will once more be open to the public.

Only a few steps from the cathedral on Calle Empedrado between Calle Cuba and Calle San Ignacio is the famous **Bodeguita del Medio** *(see illustration page 73 and Making the most of Havana)*, which never seems to be lacking for customers. Its ground floor bar is where the *mojito* is supposed to have been invented and was once the haunt not only of Hemingway but of other writers and intellectuals. A good way to spend the time while waiting for a table is to look into No.215, the **Casa de la Condesa de la Reunión****. This fine example of a colonial mansion dating from around 1820 has an attractive **courtyard*** and a striking **staircase***. No longer a private house, it is now the home of the **Centro de Promoción Cultural Alejo Carpentier** *(8.30am-3.30pm; closed Saturday and Sunday; no charge)*, devoted to the work of this famous Cuban author (1904-80), in particular to his book, *El Siglo de las Luces* (1962) (The Age of Enlightenment), set in the Caribbean at the time of the French Revolution.

Go four blocks along Calle Cuba to the corner with Calle Tacón

A good way to end this walk is at the **Palacio Pedroso**★ (Plan II B2) named after the Mayor of Havana who built it in 1780. Also known as the **Palacio de la Artesanía**, this gracious mansion is now devoted to satisfying the needs of tourists, with a selection of cigars, rum, T-shirts, books and records and CDs in the shops opening off its courtyard.

Old Havana south★

Allow two hours including visits

This part of Old Havana attracts far fewer visitors despite its wealth of fascinating but mostly decrepit buildings and the chance it offers to experience something of the sheer vitality of everyday city life.

Plaza Vieja★ (Plan II C3)

With the Plaza de Armas reserved for use by the military, the Plaza Vieja was intended for the public at large. Then called Plaza Nueva, it was laid out in the second half of the 16C, subsequently becoming a slave market and then an ordinary covered market which was demolished at the beginning of the 20C. In 1952 the square was seen as a suitable location for the construction of an underground car park. This monstrous eyesore eventually became derelict and has thankfully been removed. The square has now regained much of its former glory, with attractive new paving and a splendid central fountain. While a number of the buildings around the Plaza Vieja remain in an advanced state of decrepitude, others have been sensitively restored, and it seems more than likely that the square will once more become a focal point of urban life, for local people as much as for tourists.

The little structure at the corner of Calle Brasil and Calle San Ignacio bears the name of the two sisters who had it built at the end of the 18C. In 1824 the **Casa de las Hermanas Cárdenas** became the seat of the city's orchestral society. It has now been converted into the **Centro de Desarollo de las Artes Visuales** (Centre for the Development of the Visual Arts) which stages regular exhibitions of the work of contemporary artists.

On the eastern side of the square, more or less opposite, is the **Casa de Esteban José Portier**. Dating from 1752, this fine building with its delightful patio is now the home of the Fototeca de Cuba, which stages exhibitions of photographers' work. The wooden fittings inside are decorated in Moorish style. The southeastern corner of the square is graced by a striking example of Art Nouveau architecture, the former Hotel Viena, dating from 1906 and now subdivided into numerous family apartments.

At the corner of Calle San Ignacio and Calle Muralla is the most remarkable building in the square. The **Casa del Conde de Jaruco**★ dates from 1737 though it was much altered not long afterwards. Like many of its neighbours it suffered severely through neglect in the post-Revolutionary period, but unlike most of them it has been restored, allowing the charm of its façade and its **courtyard**★ to be appreciated once more. It is a good spot to stop for a drink. The building is now used by the cultural foundation called the Fondo de Bienes Culturales which puts on art and craft exhibitions.

Walk north from the square along Calle Ignacio, turn left into Calle Amargura and continue along it for one block.

The imposing building at the corner of Calle Amargura and Calle Brasil was originally the Augustinian Convent founded at the beginning of the 17C. In 1863 it became the Academy of Science. Today, after much rebuilding, the **Museo Histórico de Ciencias Carlos J. Finlay** (Plan II B3) *(8am-5pm; 9am-3pm Saturday; closed Sunday. Admission charge)* is housed behind its ornate façade. The museum traces the evolution of the sciences in Latin America and pays tribute to Carlos J. Finlay, the Cuban scientist who proved that yellow fever was transmitted by mosquitoes. There is also an intriguing replica of a 19C pharmacy.

Continue south along Calle Cuba.

Church and Convent of Santa Clara** (Plan II B2, C2) *(9am-4.30pm; closed Saturday and Sunday. Admission charge)*, the first convent in Cuba, was begun in 1638 and completed six years later. In the early years of the 20C the nuns lost their privacy when new buildings were put up nearby and they were obliged to move out. The convent was sold in 1919, becoming the headquarters of a construction firm and then the home of the National Centre for Conservation, Restoration and Museology. With very little in the way of resources, the Centre's team of devoted specialists have gained a reputation for their meticulous restoration of works of art. Apart from the church itself, the convent has been completely restored. Visitors should ask for a guide to show them around the hall where furniture and religious objects are displayed.

The convent's **cloisters**** are full of the lushest vegetation imaginable, with palm-trees, native *ceibas* and *yagrumas* and a glorious array of other plants and flowers, over which rises a pretty tiled roof. In the middle of this luxuriant garden stands the city's very first fountain, the **Fuente de la Samaritana**, dating from the 17C.

All around the garden the nuns' cells have been transformed into workshops where textiles, pictures, furniture and statues are painstakingly restored. Some of the cells still have the original **wood carving*** dating from the period of the convent's construction. The convent's church with its large rectangular nave and imposing ceiling is completely devoid of ornament.

The adjoining set of cloisters has been converted into a residence intended mainly for young people studying restoration techniques *(see Making the most of Havana)*.

Also in Calle Cuba, at the junction with Calle Acosta, is the **Iglesia del Espiritu Santo** (Plan II C4), Havana's oldest remaining church. Built in 1632 by a group of freed slaves it was the second place of worship to be built in the city following the construction of the church on the site of the Palace of the Captains General. The church's sober façade, together with its left aisle, were added in the late half of the 19C.

Two blocks further along on the right, at the corner with Calle Merced, is the **Church of Nuestra Senora de la Merced*** (Plan II C4). Begun in 1755 but only completed in the 19C, this is perhaps the most popular of all Havana's churches, not least because of the association of its statue of the Virgen de Merced (Virgin of Mercy) with the santería deity Obatalá. It is also the city's most ornate church, covered in trompe l'oeil **frescoes*** and richly fitted out with altarpieces and statuary. The grotto-like chapel at the eastern end of the north aisle is devoted to Our Lady of Lourdes.

Continue along Calle Cuba to the next junction, then turn left into Calle Leonor Pérez (Paula).

On the little square facing out on to the harbour stands the **Church of San Francisco de Paula**★, (Plan II C4) built between 1730 and 1745. The church was originally attached to a women's hospital, but this was destroyed in 1946 along with the choir. The rest of the building, including its lovely **cupola**★, was spared and is currently under restoration.

At Calle Leonor Pérez No.314 is the modest **Casa Natal de José Martí**★ (Plan II B4) *(9am-5pm; 9am-1pm Sunday; closed Monday. Admission charge)*, the birthplace of José Martí, the "Apostle of Cuban Independence". The great man was born in this little house on 28 January 1853 and spent the first four years of his life here. The museum dedicated to him was founded as early as 1925; on display are personal effects associated with the struggle for the island's independence, among them a photograph showing a smiling Martí with his son on his knee. There is also the only known portrait of him, painted by the Swedish artist Hermann Norrman in 1891.

On the left at the beginning of Calle Egido by the railway lines are remains of the old **fortifications** *(muralla)* which were demolished in 1863.

Go north along Calle Egido leaving the railway station on your left and turn right into Calle Acosta just beyond the Puerto de Sagua restaurant.

Calle Acosta is bridged by a Baroque archway. This is the **Arco de Belén (Bethlehem Arch)**, built in 1772 to link the Bethlehem Convent with the buildings on the opposite side of the street.

Just beyond the archway turn left into Calle Compostela. The little square in front of the convent has market stalls with fresh fruit and vegetables.

Church and Convent of Nuestra Senora de Bélen★ (Plan II B4), dating from 1718, was the first example of Baroque architecture in Havana and occupies the whole of a city block. It was acquired by the Jesuits in 1856, then became one of the seats of the Cuban Academy of Sciences.

The church and cloisters are currently undergoing major restoration intended to return them to their former glory.

From the Capitol to the Prado★

Allow half a day if visiting all the museums

This walk around the area to the west of Old Havana takes in many of the city's museums. Because some of the streets it leads through are heavily trafficked it's more of a purposeful walk than a stroll, though towards evening the Prado is calmer and you may be tempted to linger under its canopy of trees.

The Capitolio Nacional★★ (Plan II A3) *(9am-5pm; closed Sundays. Admission charge)*, more than 200m long is crowned by a splendid 90m dome and is one of Havana's great landmarks.

A massive reminder of the days of American domination, the great edifice is a copy of the Capitol in Washington DC and was built in 1929 during the regime of the US-backed dictator Machado. Until the 1959 Revolution it was the seat of the Cuban Parliament and now houses the country's Academy of Sciences. The viewing gallery giving a superb panorama over the city is currently closed for renovation.

The main entry hall is directly beneath the dome. It contains a huge **gilded bronze statue**, 14m high, of a female figure representing the Republic. Set in the floor is a **diamond** marking kilometre zero, the point from which all distances in Cuba are calculated.

The immensely long **Salón de los Pasos Perdidos★** (Hall of Lost Footsteps), so-called because of its strange acoustical effects, leads to offices and conference rooms as well as to the chamber where Cuba's parliamentarians once met.

The **Salón Martí** has particularly fine wall and ceiling paintings, while the **Library of Science and Technology★** has superb fittings made from rare woods. A tour of the Capitol can be finished off with a drink or a meal in the open-air at either end of the great building, overlooking the Prado or the Parque de la Fraternidad.

The **Parque de la Fraternidad** (Plan II A3) is the scene of much activity because of its strategic location between Old Havana, Central Havana and the Cerro. Like Parque Central to the north it's nearly always full of people waiting for their *guagua* (bus) or simply meeting beneath the shade of its palm trees. In the middle of the square stands the *ceiba* tree planted to mark the sixth Pan-American Conference of 1928; it was set in soil brought here from all the participating countries.

In the southeast corner of the park at the meeting point of three broad avenues stands the **Fuente de la India**, a famous symbol of Havana. Also called Noble Habana, it was sculpted in 1837 by the Italian artist Giuseppe Gaggini and represents a young Indian girl brandishing a shield embossed with the city's coat of arms.

To the west of the park at the junction of Avenida Simón Bolivar and Calle Amistad is the **Palacio de Aldama★★** (Plan I C2), a fine mansion of 1840 consisting of twin neo-Classical pavilions. Built for Don Domingo de Aldama y Arréchaga, it was sacked during the Ten Years War and confiscated by the Spanish government which suspected the family of secretly sympathising with the independence movement. The palace now houses the Institute of the History of the Working-Class Movement and the Socialist Revolution and is not officially open to the public. However, it is usually possible to get permission from the caretaker to see the two **courtyards★**, the first of which has a little lion-head fountain while the second has walls faced with *azulejos*.

Behind the Capitol at No.520 in Calle Industria is the **Fábrica de Tabacos Partagás★** (Plan II A3). This is one of the country's oldest cigar factories, though the date of 1845 on the front of the factory refers to the foundation of the company rather than the building itself which only began operation in the early years of the 20C. There are guided tours and the factory is one of the best places in which to appreciate the various stages in the manufacture of a cigar *(tours start at 10am and 2pm. Admission charge)*. The shop has an exceptionally wide range of cigars for sale at reasonable prices *(see Making the most of Havana)*.

Parque Central★ (Plan II A3)

Not many foreigners frequent Havana's palm-shaded Central Park, essentially a meeting place for local people, whose shouted conversations compete with the roar of traffic to make it the very opposite of a peaceful retreat. A particularly noisy spot is the Esquina caliente (hot corner) where the baseball results are endlessly argued over.

As much as anywhere in the city, the park is a place where the passing tourist is likely to be approached by young men hoping to be offered a beer or a dollar tip.

Ch. Cheadle/SCOPE

The Gran Teatro

The west side of the park is dominated by two of Havana's outstanding buildings from the early years of the 20C. Between Calle San José and Calle Rafael stands the **Gran Teatro de La Habana**★, also known as the **García Lorca** after the name of its main auditorium. The Grand Theatre's origins date from 1837, when the Teatro Tacón was built; in the early 1900s this theatre was incorporated into the ornate structure built to accommodate the Centro Gallego, one of several clubs catering for people from the various regions of Spain, in this case the Galicians. The lavish neo-Baroque façade has an overload of decorative features; the array of statuary in bright white marble includes angels posted at each corner tower, seemingly poised to take flight.

Guided tours of the building (*10am-7pm; closed Monday. Admission charge*) take in the various auditoria and during the week there is the chance to watch dance rehearsals, a fascinating experience. Access to the interiors on the upper floors is by a splendid marble **staircase** built overlooking a fine mosaic on the ground floor. In the evening there are operas, plays, and classical music concerts as well as performances by the National Ballet of Cuba, directed by **Alicia Alonso**, a key figure in the country's post-Revolution cultural life.

On the far side of Calle San Rafael stands the neo-Classical building of the **Hotel Inglaterra** (*see Making the most of Havana*), the equal of the Gran Teatro in ornate exuberance and a designated national monument. A long-term focus of the city's social life, it's busy night and day, not least because of the **El Louvre** café beneath its arcades. The *Acera del Louvre* (Louvre pavement) has become one of the places where the young of Havana gather in the expectation of picking up a few dollars. In the 19C the hotel was a rendezvous much favoured by opponents of the colonial regime. It was here on 27 November 1871 that a Spanish officer named Nicolás Estévanez publicly smashed his sword and resigned his commission in protest at the execution of a group of medical students involved in the independence movement. The students are commemorated by a memorial at the end of the Prado close to the entrance to the harbour.

In the middle of Central Park stands the **José Martí statue** (*see photo page 24*). With its elaborate iconography celebrating Cuba's "Apostle of Independence", the monument was completed in 1904 by the Cuban sculptor Villalta de Saavedra.

On the east side of the park between Avenida Zulueta and Calle San Rafael and difficult to overlook is the massive **Manzana de Gómez**, a once-splendid early 20C shopping arcade taking up an entire city block (*manzana* in Spanish). Now occupied by a few empty-shelved shops, its days of glory have long since passed away.

On the other side of Calle San Rafael, the Supreme Court of Justice is housed in a four-towered structure which was once the **Centro Asturiano**, the social centre for people originating from Spain's Asturias region. Begun in 1924 and completed four years later, the building was designed by the Spanish architect Manuel del Busto.

Continue the walk either by going down Paseo de Martí (the Prado) or by going directly to Avenida de Bélgica via Calle Neptuno to the right of the Hotel Plaza.

The Prado★ (Plan II A1-2)
This broad thoroughfare divides Centro Habana from Habana Vieja and links Central Park to the waterfront. At one time the place where the city's aristocracy came to see and be seen, it's now frequented by old folk enjoying a siesta in the shade of its palm trees and by children playing frenzied games of *pelota* (baseball). The buildings lining it are in a variety of styles, some heavily weighed with

rococo decoration, all without exception showing the signs of age and neglect. The avenue down the centre of the Prado is lined with splendid wrought-iron street-lights and is one of the city's most attractive and popular promenades.

Turn right towards Avenida de Bélgica which runs parallel to the Prado.

Standing out from the other buildings at the corner of Avenida de Bélgica and Calle Progreso is the **Edificio Bacardí***, a stylish Art Deco skyscraper. It was built at the end of the 1920s for Emilio Bacardí, the wealthy owner of sugar plantations and of the distillery bearing his family name. The tower is decorated with the bat emblem that appears on all bottles of Barcardi rum.

Further along Avenida de las Misiones is the **Museo Nacional de Bellas Artes** (Fine Arts Museum) *(under reconstruction)*, housed in a grim-looking concrete structure dating from the 1950s. As well as Egyptian antiquities and Graeco-Roman ceramics, the museum's holdings include fine examples of European painting as well as a large collection of Cuban art featuring such painters as Wilfredo Lam.

Just to the west of the museum entrance on Calle Trocadero is the **Hotel Sevilla**, behind whose unremarkable façade is a fascinating interior decorated in Hispano-Moorish style. The restaurant on the top floor has a **fine view**** over the whole of central Havana *(see Making the most of Havana)*.

The square opposite the Fine Arts Museum is occupied by the glass pavilion containing the **Granma** *(see page 27)*, the 20m yacht from which Fidel Castro and 81 fellow-revolutionaries disembarked in eastern Cuba in 1956 in their ill-fated attempt to start an uprising. Other relics of the revolutionary struggle on show around the pavilion include aircraft, home-made tanks, a Soviet ground-to-air missile and the bullet-riddled lorry used in the attack on the Presidential Palace on 12 March 1957.

Access to the Granma is only via the main entrance of the **Mueso de la Revolución**** (Museum of the Revolution) *(10am-5pm; closed Monday. Admission charge)* housed in the former **Palacio Presidencial*** (Presidential Palace). No expense was spared to build a palatial residence for the presidents of the Republic. Construction began in 1913, with responsibility for interior decoration given to Tiffany's of New York and the building was ready for occupation in 1920. In 1957 the building witnessed the failure of a rebel attack intended to assassinate dictator Batista.

All four storeys of the palace are now devoted to an extremely thorough chronological presentation of the history of Cuba, from the colonial period to the Revolution and its achievements. At least two hours are necessary even for a superficial look at the extensive displays of photographs, documents and many other items, including a fascinating diorama of Che Guevara and Camilo Cienfuegos emerging from the forest of the Sierra Maestra. Anyone staying the course will hardly need to visit any other of the country's numerous museums dealing with the revolutionary struggle.

At the point where Avenida de las Misiones meets Calle Cárcel a somewhat incongruous architectural note is struck by an elegant Italian façade in close proximity to the swirling traffic of the Parque de los Mártires. This is the **Casa de Pérez de la Riva***, which was built in 1905 and houses the **Museo Nacional de la Música** (National Music Museum) *(9am-4pm; closed Sunday. Admission charge)*. Inside is a highly variegated collection of musical instruments from Cuba and other parts of the world, including Indian sitars and Haitian drums, balalaikas, pianos and musical boxes. There are also pictures of musicians and musical scores. Lucky visitors may find themselves watching a salsa rehearsal in the little ground-floor rehaersal room. The museum has a small shop with a god selection of CDs, cassettes and a few musical instruments.

Opposite the museum towards the waterfront stands the imposing **statue of General Máximo Gómez**, one of the heroes of the wars of independence. To the left is the **medical students' memorial** erected in honour of the young men executed by the Spaniards in 1871 *(see page 130)*. The monument stands in front of the **Castillo de San Salvador de la Punta** (Plan II A1), the fortress constructed at the end of the 16C as part of the defences associated with the building of the Castillo de los Tres Reyes del Morro on the far side of the harbour mouth.

The Fortresses★

*The fortresses on the far side of the harbour mouth can be reached
by bus or taxi through the La Habana Tunnel.
Cycles are carried through the tunnel without charge on a special bus.*

Guarding the harbour mouth on the high ground of the eastern shore stand two fortresses, now the basis of the Parque historico-militar Morro-Cabana. The park's attractions include not only the fortresses and their museums, but bars and restaurants *(See Making the most of Havana)* and fine views over the bay to the city beyond.

In the past the harbour could be blocked by a chain stretched across its mouth from the San Salvador de la Punta fortress in the west to the **Castillo de los Tres Santos Reyes del Morro★** (Plan 1 D1) *(8.30am-8pm. Admission charge)* in the east.

J. F. Galmiche

View from the La Cabana fortress

The earlier of the strongholds on the eastern shore, it was built between 1589 and 1630. The **lighthouse** at the seaward end of the fortifications was added in the 19C. The ramparts give a superb **panorama*** over Havana.

On the battery below is the **Doce Apostoles** (Twelve Apostles) restaurant, which owes its name to the dozen cannon mounted here. Despite their presence, the British succeeded in occupying Havana in 1762. When the Spanish recovered the city a year later, King Carlos III ordered the defences to be strengthened by the construction of a modern stronghold to the south of the Morro fortress.

Completed in 1774, the **Fortaleza de San Carlos de la Cabaña*** (Plan 1 D1) (8.30am-10pm. Admission charge) was one of the largest fortresses ever to be built in Latin America. In the early 20C it was converted into a military prison, then immediately after the Revolution it served for a while as Che Guevara's headquarters.

Che's career is evoked in one of the Cabana's museums, the **Museo de la Comandancia de Che Guevara**, which has a number of his personal effects as well as contemporary photographs and documents. The fortress's other museum, the **Museo de las Armas**, has an extensive collection of weaponry and traces Cuba's military history from early colonial days onwards. There's also a fascinating model showing the successive stages in the growth of Havana.

The Cabana remains open in the evening for a military parade with soldiers dressed in uniforms of the colonial period. The action starts at 8.30pm and concludes with the traditional **Canonazo de las Nueve** (Nine o'clock gun) which in days gone by signalled the closing of the city gates.

More guns are mounted on the battery below the Cabana, where there is also the Divina Pastora restaurant. From its terrace there is an outstanding view of the city all the way from the waterfront of Old Havana to modern Vedado.

Central Havana (Plan 1 C1-2)
Allow 1hr. At night avoid unlit and deserted streets.

While foreign visitors throng Old Havana and the La Rampa area (known as "green zones" because of the dollars they spend there), very few venture into the *municipio* of Centro Habana despite its strategic location between the two districts.

Usually referred to simply as "Centro", Central Havana is the densely populated inner city area stretching westwards from the Paseo de Martí (Prado) to the Vedado, and bounded to the south by Avenida Arroyo (Manglar) and to the north by the famous waterfront of the Malecón.

Though there are few tourist attractions as such it's still a fascinating experience to wander at will among Centro's crumbling buildings and enjoy the local colour and the vivid street life.

Central Havana was the first neighbourhood to be built outside the line of the old city walls. Consisting mostly of rundown apartment blocks, the district has hardly benefited from the renovation

Swapping apartments
The windows of Central Havana are full of signs saying "se permuta 1 x 2" (exchange large flat for two small ones), a sure sign of overcrowding. The State has outlawed any kind of housing market, but allows people to swap one dwelling for another.

For Cubans anxious to move house, the lively Bolsa de las Permutas (Dwelling Exchange) held regularly on the Prado has become one way out of their problems.

activity which has done so much to restore the appearance of parts of Old Havana. Sea spray and tropical rainfall have left their mark on buildings already suffering from an almost complete lack of maintenance. Over-population and the desperate shortage of housing has contributed to urban decay, particularly through the subdivision of already cramped quarters; home-made mezzanines (*barbacoas*) are commonly inserted between the existing floors, putting further pressure on outside walls already weakened and liable to collapse into the street. A pedestrianised stretch of **Calle San Rafael** leads westwards into Centro from the Gran Teatro in the Parque Central. Despite the lack of goods in the stores, there's plenty of activity, from hairdressers on the pavement exercising their skills to old men playing dominoes.

Continue along Calle San Rafael to Calle San Nicolas, the second street on the left after Avenida de Italia.

The Barrio Chino (Chinatown) (Plan 1 C2) occupies several city blocks between Calle Zanja and Avenida Simón Bolívar (Reina).

In the second half of the 19C more than 120 000 Chinese were brought to Cuba mostly to replace the black slaves whose tendency to revolt made them less than reliable labour. Some of the Chinese eventually moved to this part of Havana where they formed a cohesive community of some 15 000 in the years before the Revolution. Few of them are left now, but there are stalls offering Chinese food at the *agromercado*, the little farmers' market at the junction of Calle Zanja and Calle Rayo.

Continue along Calle Rayo or one of the streets running parallel to it as far as Avenida **Reina** (Simón Bolívar). Colonnades run the whole length of this avenue, part of the reason why Havana has sometimes been called the City of Columns. The continuation of the avenue is called Avenida Salvador Allende (Carlos III) which leads directly to the Vedado.

The best way to explore Centro Habana is simply to wander at will. Losing one's way is unlikely, at least in rough weather; since half the streets lead to the Malecón, north will be indicated every now and again by a great burst of spray filling the space at the end of a street.

The Malecón★, Havana's waterfront

Havana's broad and curving seafront boulevard runs for 8km between the Castillo de San Salvador de la Punta and the Miramar district. Drivers use it as a quick way of getting around the city and to avoid venturing into the streets of Centro Habana, but above all it's a promenade and meeting place for the city's population and their visitors. It's perhaps at its best on a calm evening when the last rays of the sun caress the washed out pastel colours of its buildings and give them something of their former glory, but it's also impressive in stormy weather when the waves break over the rocks and sea wall.

People come to the Malecón at all times of day and night, fishermen to fish, children to play tag with the waves, young men to flatter a passing beauty with a *piropo*.

The art of "piropear"

Staring, hissing, or paying a verbal compliment, a piropo, are pleasures no self-respecting Cuban male could possibly deprive himself of when encountering a lady worthy of his admiration. No response whatsoever is required on her part (unless her admirer has expressed himself with exceptional wit).

"Si el amor toca a tu puerta, permitele entrar, estoy seguro que él te hará una maravillosa y bella compania" (when love knocks at your door let him in, I am sure he will be a wonderful companion).

The Cerro (Plan 1 B3)
5km southwest of Parque Central

This area of the city to the south of Centro Habana is crossed by Calzada del Cerro, the continuation of Avenida Máximo Gómez (Monte). Partly industrial, the Cerro is characterised by hospitals and great mansions built towards the end of the 19C and start of the 20C. Just as decayed as the rest of the city, it also has something of the attractive atmosphere of a provincial town.

On the way into the district, No.1417 Calzada del Cerro is the **Fábrica Bocoy** (*6.30am-2pm; closed Sundays*), a rum distillery whose product can be tasted.
Opposite the distillery, between a vegetable garden and a little park where fountains play a track leads to the **Quinta de los Condes de Santovenia**. Built in 1832, this was the summer residence of Count Santovenia, converted 50 years later into an old people's home run by nuns.
In the morning one of the nuns may be on hand to show visitors around the main building with its twin aisles, as well as the little chapel dedicated to the Virgen de la Caridad del Cobre, Cuba's patron saint.

The Vedado★ (Plan 1 A1-2, B1-2)
Allow half a day

Part of the Plaza de la Revolución *municipio*, the Vedado is laid out on a grid which extends from Centro Habana in the east to the banks of the Río Almendares in the west. The fine villas built by the rich moving out from Old Havana in the early 20C have been joined by a number of skyscrapers but the area's well-tree'd streets still have something of the charm of an American town of the 1950s. As elsewhere in the city, the passage of time and the lack of maintenance means that many buildings are on the point of collapsing, while at the same time a considerable amount of new construction is taking place.

A respectable suburb?
Until the end of the 19C, building was strictly prohibited in the Vedado (literally: "forbidden"), in order to maintain a clear field of fire in case of attack. When, at the beginning of the 20C, the city's upper classes began to quit the constricted streets and pungent odours of the old city, they built themselves splendid residences in this freshly developed area. Their palatial villas were followed by hotels and casinos, and parts of the Vedado became synonymous with gambling and prostitution, a trend which reached its peak in the Batista years. Despite all the post-Revolutionary changes the Vedado is still the city's main entertainment area.

The centre of the capital
Like it or not, and however short their stay, all visitors to Havana become familiar with the Vedado. Here are the majority of the capital's hotels and services, restaurants and *paladares*, most of them along the Rampa, the city's principal artery. The cigar sellers, car owners and assorted *jineteras* seem more numerous here than elsewhere in Havana, announcing their services to the foreign passer-by with a "psst!" in the ear, the traditional Cuban way of attracting attention. Their favourite hang-outs are at the entrances to the international hotels but they can pop up anywhere. The best way of dealing with them is with a polite refusal.

M. Gotin/SCOPE

The Malecón

The Vedado covers a large area and a car is the best way of getting around. Use the taxi stands in front of the major hotels or negotiate a rate with one of the private vehicles parked along the Rampa.

Finding your way around the Vedado is relatively easy thanks to the system of street numbering, indicated by signs at most intersections. Roads running northeast-southwest have odd numbers starting from the Malecón, while the roads at right angles are designated by letters from the east of the Paseo to the waterfront and by even numbers from there to the River Almendares.

A number of high buildings make useful landmarks, including the Hotel Habana Libre on the Rampa and the Hotel Meliá Cohiba at the lower end of the Paseo.

La Rampa★ (calle 23) (Plan 1 B1)

Calle 23 runs for more than 2km through the Vedado from the Malecón to the Columbus Cemetery and is lined with travel bureaux, airline offices and banks. The section linking the Hotel Nacional to the Habana Libre is known as the Rampa.

Full of bustle in the daytime, the Rampa has an equally frenetic nightlife once the hotel bars and discos have opened their doors.

The seaward end of the Rampa is dominated by the great Art Deco edifice of the **Hotel Nacional*** (Plan 1 B1) on its promontory. Completed at the beginning of the 1930s as Cuba's most prestigious hotel it still has something of the atmosphere of the era when it was patronised by film-stars and mobsters. The hotel garden is a good place to enjoy a drink while taking in the view across the bay.

A short distance to the west at the junction of the Malecón with Calle 19 are the twin columns of the **Monument to the Victims of the Maine** (Plan 1 B1). The memorial is a reminder of the explosion which destroyed the *USS Maine* on 15 February 1898, the incident which triggered the Spanish-American War *(see page 25)*. The warship's remains are preserved close to the memorial which is inscribed with the names of those who died in the disaster. Inaugurated in 1925, the monument was intended to celebrate the friendship between Cuba and the US. Damaged a year later in a hurricane, it suffered further indignity after the Revolution when, in protest against US policy towards Cuba, the bronze eagle surmounting it was removed along with the busts of American presidents.

The **Edificio Focsa** (Plan I B1), a 1950s apartment block, is the tallest building in Havana. From its top storey bar and restaurant (*see Making the most of Havana*) there is an unbeatable **view**** over the whole of the city.

The great landmark of the Rampa is the **Hotel Habana Libre** (Plan I B1), the former Hilton (*see Making the most of Havana*). Completed in 1957 and a powerful symbol of the American presence on the island, it was an inevitable candidate for early nationalisation after the Revolution. Its many facilities make it a useful stopping-off point for foreign visitors exploring the Vedado.

Opposite the Habana Libre, in the centre of an attractive square stands a rather plain circular structure, the famous ice-cream parlour known as the **Coppelia****. This city institution was immortalised in the film *Fresa y Chocolate* by the director Tomás Guitiérrez Alea. Despite the film's title, vanilla is often the only flavour available, but the quality is such that locals are prepared to stand in line for hours for one of the Coppelia's delicious offerings. Visitors from abroad have the luxury of a separate, and much shorter queue.

Go back past the Habana Libre on Calle L as far as Calle 27

The University of Havana (Plan I B2) was moved from Old Havana to its present slightly elevated site in 1902. The memorial at the foot of the monumental stairway leading to the university buildings honours the student leader and founder of the Cuban Communist Party José Mella, assassinated in 1929 on the orders of dictator Machado. Beyond the neo-Classical façade of the main university building is a lush little garden, a favourite spot for students to sit and revise.

The University is home to the **Museo Antropológico Montané** (*9am-midday; 2.30-4.30; closed Sundays. Admission charge*) with an extensive collection of pre-Columbian artefacts giving an overview of human life on the island before the Spanish Conquest.

Beyond the University at Calle San Miguel No.1159 is the **Museo Napoleónico*** (Plan I B2) (*11am-5.30pm; closed Sundays. Admission charge*). The museum's fascinating collection of Napoleonic memorabilia is housed in the Italian-style villa built by Julio Lobo, a millionaire obsessed by Bonaparte and his career. As well as Sèvres porcelain and Empire furniture, there's a painting by Jean-Georges Vibert of Napoleon planning his coronation and a library full of books about the Emperor and the age in which he lived.

To the south of the University on the far side of Calle G (Avenida de los Presidentes) a number of medical establishments stand at the foot of a hill. At the rear of the Hospital Ortopédico is the **Castillo del Principe** (Plan I A2), a fortress constructed in 1779 to command the surrounding area and deter an attack on the city from the west.

Once used as a prison, it is now in the hands of the military and not accessible to the public but there is a fine view over the city from the top of the hill.

Plaza de la Revolución* (Plan I A3, B3)

This vast 4.5ha expanse became famous all over the world because of the great national rallies and demonstrations held here, when up to a million people would listen to Castro delivering one of his epic speeches. People still come here in their thousands on the annual holidays of 1 January, May Day and 26 July, though popular fervour has abated somewhat since the early years of the Revolution. At other times the plaza is strictly policed and lingering is discouraged because of the presence of numerous government buildings. The only photography allowed is of the José Martí memorial and the giant portrait of Che Guevara.

The plaza was begun in the 1950s under the Batista regime, but only completed after the Revolution. The centre is dominated by the **José Martí Memorial**, a 142m-high obelisk in the shape of a five-pointed star. Once off-limits to the public, it is now a museum *(9am 5pm; closed Sunday. Admission charge)*. A gigantic **statue** of Martí in white marble stands at the base of the obelisk, while the museum devoted to the life and work of the "Apostle of Independence" makes use of sophisticated techniques, rare elsewhere in Cuba, like videos and holograms. From the top of the memorial *(additional charge)* there is a view of the concrete buildings around the square as well as of the city as a whole, though because the viewing area is enclosed by glass this is not the place to take an award-winning photograph.

To the north the façade of the Ministry of the Interior is graced with a huge **portrait of Che Guevara** in black metal.

To the right of Minint (as the Ministry of the Interior is usually known), the Ministry of Communications houses the **Museo postal cubano** *(9am-5pm, closed at weekends. Admission charge)*, which concentrates on extensive collections of stamps from all over the world rather than on the performance of the national postal service.

To the east, the National Library stands opposite the **Teatro Nacional**, while to the south of the square is the vast **Palacio de la Revolución**, the seat of the Central Committee of the Cuban Communist Party and the offices of the President.

Go down Calle 23 to the west of the Plaza de la Revolución and turn left into Calle 12

Cementerio de Cristóbal Colón★
(Christopher Columbus Cemetery) (Plan I A3)

(7am-6pm. Admission charge.) Pastel yellow walls enclose this vast cemetery straddling the boundary between the Vedado and Nuevo Vedado. It is entered through an immense **gateway** in Romanesque style designed by the architect Calixto de Loira in 1870. Inside the cemetery there are tombs in every imaginable size and style, from simple slabs to monuments of the utmost expressiveness. Most of the people who have shaped Cuba's cultural and political life over the years are buried here.

The paths and burial plots are laid out on a grid pattern with the chapel at the centre, making it easy to find one's way around. In neo-Byzantine style, the chapel has a 19C **fresco** painted by Miguel Melero.

The tombs are far too numerous to be described, but some of them have more than local interest. In a dominant position on the central avenue stands the huge sculptural group called the **Monumento a los Bomberos**, commemorating the tragic death of 28 firemen on 17 May 1890. The main figure of the Angel of Death holding a torch in her hand is accompanied by further heavy symbolism in the shape of a nun with a pelican at her foot.

Another tomb which attracts much attention is that of Dona Amelia de Gloria Castellano Pérez, better known as *La Milagrosa* (The Miracle Woman). Dona Amelia died in childbirth in 1901. Mother and child were entombed together; later, when the tomb was opened, the child was found in its mother's arms whereas it had originally been placed at her feet. The apparent miracle brings a steady stream of people hoping for help in their troubles.

The composer Hubert de Blanc has a big double-three domino piece atop his tomb, commemorating his death through a heart attack when a game was in progress. Other tombs include those of Alejo Carpentier and of Cirilo Villaverde, the famous 19C novelist. Villaverde lies not far from Cecilia Valdés, the mulatto woman who was the inspiration of his most celebrated tale.

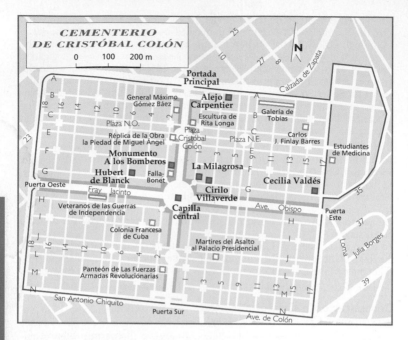

CEMENTERIO DE CRISTÓBAL COLÓN

0   100   200 m

N

Portada Principal

Calzada de Zapata

General Máximo Gómez Báez

Alejo Carpentier ■

Galería de Tobías

Plaza N.O.

Escultura de Rita Longa

Réplica de la Obra la Piedad de Miguel Ángel

Plaza Cristóbal Colón

Carlos J. Finlay Barres

Plaza N.E.

Estudiantes de Medicina

Monumento A los Bomberos

Hubert ■ de Blanck

Falla-Bonet

La Milagrosa

Cecilia Valdés

Puerta Oeste

Fray Jacinto

Cirilo Villaverde

Ave. Obispo

Puerta Este

Veteranos de las Guerras de Independencia

Capilla central

Colonia Francesa de Cuba

Mártires del Asalto al Palacio Presidencial

Panteón de Las Fuerzas Armadas Revoluciónarias

San Antonio Chiquito

Puerta Sur

Ave. de Colón

Loma Julia Borges

Back in the direction of central Vedado, on Calle 17 between Calle D and Calle E is the **Museo de Artes Decorativas**⋆ (Plan I A2) *(11am-6pm; closed Sundays and Mondays. Admission charge)*. This splendid mansion was completely remodelled in the early 20C by the fashionable Jansen firm from Paris, and is luxuriously furnished and fitted. There is Sevres and Meissen porcelain, fine 18C French furniture, and an Art Deco bathroom in pink marble.

Go down Avenida de los Presidentes towards the Malecón.

Havana boasts a new **Museo de la Danza** *(10am-1pm and 4pm-7pm; closed Sundays and Mondays. Admission charge)*, located on the corner of Avenida de los Presidentes and Avendia Linea. Established to celebrate the 50th anniversary of Cuba's National Ballet, it pays tribute to the company's guiding spirit, **Alicia Alonso**. The history of dance is evoked in photographs, costumes, paintings and much more.

Miramar⋆ (Plan I towards A1)
Miramar extends over a wide area and is best explored by car

With its sumptuous villas set in lush gardens along tree-lined avenues, Miramar is part of the exclusive district stretching west from the Río Almendares. As well as fine residences, Miramar is known for its embassies, hotels, restaurants and shops *(see Making the most of Havana)*, its cosmopolitan and sophisticated population, and its general atmosphere of discreet luxury.

Miramar has even-numbered avenues running from north to south, odd numbers from east to west.

The seafront road, Avenida I, can hardly be said to rival the Malecón. But since transport problems have made the Eastern Beaches difficult to get to, many families make good use in summer of the scruffy little beach called **playita del 16** tucked away between Calle 12 and Calle 16.

Quinta Avenida★ (Fifth Avenue)

A tunnel under the Río Almendares connects the Malecón in the Vedado with Miramar's Fifth Avenue.

Lined with embassy buildings, Miramar's Fifth Avenue has something of the prestige and allure of its New York namesake and is certainly one of Havana's most elegant thoroughfares. Its carriageways are separated by a central promenade with stone benches shaded by palms and laurels. In the Parque Emiliano Zapata between Calle 24 and Calle 26 a little bandstand is half hidden among the giant *jagüey* trees.

At the junction of Fifth Avenue with Calle 14 is one of Havana's most unusual museums. The **Museo del Ministerio del Interior** *(9am-5pm; closed Sundays, Mondays and in August. Admssion charge)* is devoted to the undercover activities of the United States in its confrontation with Cuba. There are displays on the various abortive attempts to assassinate Castro and a roomful of diabolically ingenious CIA gadgetry.

An excellent way of getting an overview of Havana's growth and development is to visit the **Maqueta de la Ciudad**, on Calle 28 between Avenida Premiera (1st Avenue) and Avenida Tercera (3rd Avenue) *(9.30am to 5.30pm; closed Sunday and Monday. Admission charge)*. This huge model measuring 22x10m shows the various stages in the city's evolution as well as current town planning and architectural projects.

The tall concrete structure visible from far away between Calle 62 and Calle 66 is the Russian Embassy, a useful Miramar landmark.

One block short of the Russian Embassy at the junction of Fifth Avenue and Calle 60 is the **National Aquarium** *(10am to 11pm Mondays and Fridays; 10am to 6pm other days; weekdays closing 11pm in summer; closed Mondays in winter. Admission charge)* featuring a great variety of tropical fishes and a dolphin display.

Miramar's luxury shops and its well-stocked *diplomercados* are famous. Ever since the legalisation of the dollar the diplomatic shops are no longer just for tourists and diplomats but for anyone with dollars, though it has to be said that most of the articles on sale are priced well beyond the means of virtually all local people. Those Cubans with access to dollars are very much in evidence at **La Maison** at the corner of Avenida 7 and Calle 16. Housed in a fine old villa, this elegant private establishment sells jewellery, perfume, and the latest in local chic. It also puts on evening fashion parades, where the alluring models sometimes upstage the outfits they are wearing.

Continue for about 20min along Avenida 5 towards the port of Mariel, passing the Palacio de las Convenciones. Immediately after the Río Jaimanitas a sign indicates the entrance to the Marina Hemingway.

Located in the Jaimanitas district, the **Marina Hemingway** is a vast marine leisure complex, which, together with its restaurants, bars, hotels and discos covers an area of five square kilometres *(see Making the Most of Havana)*. In May the marina is the venue for the deep-sea fishing competition founded by Hemingway which attracts participants from all over the world.

Miramar

The attractive southeastern part of Miramar is called Kohly. Calle 49-C runs parallel to the Río Almendares through woodland, the **Bosque de La Habana**. A walk here seems a thousand miles away from city bustle and traffic noise, with footsteps silenced by the thick layer of foliage and sunlight filtered through great swathes of creepers.

There are a number of military installations in this area and parking is not allowed. One way of enjoying the cool green landscape here is to hire a motorbike.

The surroundings of Havana

All the places described in this section belong to one or other of the *municipios* which make up the province of Ciudad de la Habana. As the province covers an area of 725sqkm, and several of the municipalities are some distance from the city centre, they are treated separately.

Regla
Reached by ferry every 15min from the quayside at the end of Calle Santa Clara (Plan II C3). The crossing takes 5min and costs 10 centavos.

On the far side of the harbour, the *municipio* and industrial town of Regla is also a stronghold of *Santería*. Streets lined with single-storey colonial houses have something of the atmosphere of a small fishing village and make for a pleasant stroll well away from the tourist crowds.

Just opposite the ferry terminal, a little white-painted house with yellow doors attracts a constant stream of visitors. Inside there is an **altar** dedicated to the *Virgen Negra* (Black Virgin), the patron saint of Havana. Clad in a blue robe, this Virgin is also a sea-goddess, known as Yemayá in the Yoruba religion (*see page 55*), who watches over ships and sailors.

On the left side of the square from the ferry is the **Church of the Santisima Virgen de Regla**, one of the main centres of Santería and the starting point of a lively Procession held on her saint's day, **8 September**, when the church's altar is ablaze with candles lit in her honour.

Go down Calle Martí opposite the ferry landing and continue through the town square.

At No.58 Calle Martí, the small **Museo Municipal de Regla** (*9am-6pm; 9am-1pm Sundays; closed Mondays. Admission charge*) has displays on the history of the municipality, the cult of Yemayá and a special exhibition on the town's first *babalao* (*see page 56*).

Guanabacoa★ (Plan 1 towards C3)
Reached via Calzada de Infanta. At the roundabout just beyond the Diez de Octubre Clinic go left along Via Blanca for about 5km.

Now engulfed in the Havana suburbs, Guanabacoa is in fact one of the oldest towns on the island, founded in the 17C. Once a thriving centre of the slave trade, it still has a large Black population and is one of the chief centres of *santería*. The town is proud of the spirited guerrilla-type resistance it put up to the invading British in 1762. Numerous fine churches are evidence of Guanabacoa's past prosperity, while its museum boasts the country's most extensive collection of Afro-Cuban religious exhibits.

To the south of Guanabacoa, crowning a little hill, is the **Potosí Hermitage**, built in 1644 and one of the island's oldest churches.

The fine old colonial mansion at Calle Martí No.108 houses the **Museo histórico de Guanabacoa*** *(9am-4pm; closed Sundays)*. The museum's displays are an excellent introduction to the country's Afro-Cuban religions and the attendants are happy to give further information. Here are the principal figures of *Santería*, all identifiable by their bright colouring and their different attributes *(see page 54)*, as well as a reconstructed altar and the Batá drums used in ceremonies. The rooms tracing the history of Guanabacoa since colonial times may be closed for repairs.

San Francisco de Paula (Plan I towards C3)

15km southeast of Havana. Go towards Guanabacoa but leave the Via Blanca 800m beyond the Río Luyanó and turn right on to the Carretera Central towards Parque Virgen del Camino, following signs to Güines.

In 1939 Ernest Hemingway rented the late 19C country house known as Finca la Vigía, and a year later bought it outright. The little hilltop estate in the village of San Francisco de Paul remained his home until he returned to the United States in 1960. Hemingway left the house and all its contents to the Cuban people; it is now the **Museo Hemingway*** *(9am-4pm; 9am-midday Sundays; closed Mondays)*, with furniture, fittings and personal effects exactly as he left them. In the interests of conservation and to prevent pilfering, the inside of the house is not accessible, and visitors have to content themselves with peering through the open windows. The great man's typewriter stands among an array of weapons and hunting trophies and shelving collapsing beneath the weight of books, though he also used a study in the tower behind the house. In the palm-shaded grounds is his little yacht, *the Pilar*, as well as the graves of four of his dogs.

Cojímar (Plan I towards D1)

10km east of Havana, allow 15min by car. Leave Havana by the La Habana Tunnel towards the fortresses. At the roundabout 2km beyond the Villa America sporting facilities turn left off the Via Monumental and go down Calle Martí as far as the port of Cojímar.

Founded in the 17C, this charming fishing village is guarded by a colonial Spanish **fortress** at the mouth of the Río Cojímar. Built in 1643 and called La Chorrera, the fortress failed to repel the British naval attack in 1762 despite the bravery of its garrison.

But Cojímar's present fame really only dates from the arrival here of Ernest Hemingway, who immortalised the place in the novel *The Old Man and the Sea*. It was here that he kept his fishing boat *Pilar*, now transferred to the grounds of the Museo Hemingway at San Francisco de Paula *(see above)*. On the waterfront, **La Terraza** restaurant has mementoes of the man everyone referred to affectionately as "Papa Hemingway", among them photographs of the many fishing trips the novelist undertook with his skipper and faithful companion, Gregorio Fuentes.

Hemingway is also commemorated by a seaward-gazing **bust** placed close to the fortress by local fishermen in 1962.

In the summer of 1994 Cojímar was roused from its habitual slumber when its harbour was filled with thousands of *balseros* preparing to make the perilous crossing to Florida *(see page 31)*.

The Old Man and the Sea

His features ravaged by a century's exposure to sea and sun, the fisherman Gregorio Fuentes skippered Hemingway's Pilar for nearly 30 years, accompanying the writer on all his many deep-sea fishing trips and inspiring the writer to create the unforgettable figure celebrated in The Old Man and the Sea, the novel which won Hemingway the Nobel Prize in 1954. At the end of the 20C Fuentes was still a familiar figure in Cojímar, taking his meals at La Terraza and receiving visitors (for a small fee) in his home.

On the far side of the river mouth loom the grim apartment blocks of the **Alamar** district, built in the 1970s by "micro-brigades" in a brave attempt to demonstrate one kind of solution to the country's desperate housing problem. Made of prefabricated panels on the Soviet model, the flats were constructed by the would-be occupiers themselves under the direction of a State-employed architect.

Parque Lenin (Plan 1 towards A3)

20km south, allow 30min. Follow Avenida Rancho Boyeros towards the airport and turn left just beyond the bridge over the Río Almendares.

This big out-of-town leisure area was laid out in the 1970s. The park used to be extremely popular with city dwellers, but its distance from the centre means that it has suffered from the deterioration in public transport and it is rarely crowded any more.

The park covers an area of 670ha, centred on an artificial lake. There is an amphitheatre, an art gallery, a rodeo ring, a theatre, several cafeterias and a famous restaurant, **Las Ruinas** *(see Making the most of Havana)*. These attractions are open 9am-5pm between Wednesday and Sunday, but the park itself is accessible on the other days of the week too, when it is even less crowded than usual.

Some 3km to the south of the restaurant is the **Jardin Botánico Nacional** *(8am-5pm; closed Mondays and Tuesdays. Admission charge)*. The country's principal botanical garden has an array of plants from Cuba and the rest of the world. There's also a **Japanese garden**. It's possible to drive round the gardens or enjoy them aboard a tractor-drawn train.

On the far side of the main road stand the pavilions of **ExpoCuba**, devoted to celebrating the *logros* (achievements) of the Revolution in all spheres, cultural and scientific as well as economic. The park is also the venue for the annual Havana International Fair.

Making the most of Havana

COMING AND GOING

By air – Havana's international airport is the *Aeropuerto Internacional José Martí*, 17km south of the city centre on Avenida Rancho Boyeros, ☎ (7) 45-3133. It handles direct flights to and from London Gatwick (Cubana and British Airways) and Manchester (Cubana), as well as indirect flights to Britain via Madrid (Iberia) and Paris (Air France). All leave from Terminal 3. A tax of US$20 is payable on departure. Domestic flights use Terminal 1. There are daily flights to and from Santiago de Cuba, Varadero, Holguín, Camagüey and Nueva Gerona, and several flights a week to other major provincial towns. Internal flights are relatively inexpensive. The airport is linked to the city centre by hotel shuttle bus or by taxi (c US$15 to the Vedado).

By train – The imposing *Estación Central de Ferrocarriles* (Plan 1 D2), ☎ (7) 61-4259, on Avenida Egido at the southwestern corner of Old Havana, is the capital's rail terminus. There are several trains a day to the main provincial cities, but speeds are low and the trains are often full. Tourists from abroad have the privilege of using a special booking office, on the left of the entrance to the station. There is no queueing, but fares are payable in dollars. There are three types of train: the daytime "regular", and the air-conditioned "especial" or "azul" overnight services. The single fare to Santiago varies between US$30 and US$40 according to the type of train, and the trip takes about 14hr. Cancellations and delays are common. Places should be booked a day in advance at the latest.

By bus – *Viazul*, corner of Avenida 26 and Avenida Zoológico, Nuevo Vedado, ☎ (7) 81-1413/5652/1108, runs a newly-introduced coach service specifically for visitors from abroad. Its air-conditioned vehicles are comfortable and the service is reliable. Coaches run to all the major cities as well as to Viñales, Varadero and Trinidad. The service between Havana and Santiago de Cuba (three times weekly, 15hrs, single fare US$51) calls at Santa Clara, Sancti Spíritus, Ciego de Ávila, Camagüey, Las Tunas, Holguín and Bayamo. Along with the internal air services it is probably the best way of getting around Cuba.

The normal *Terminal de ómnibus Interprovinciales* (Plan 1 B2) is on Avenida Rancho Boyeros to the north of the Plaza de la Revolución. It is a place where the reigning chaos has put off more than one enterprising traveller, even though visitors from abroad have their own information bureau (on the loft of the entrance) and booking office (2ⁿᵈ door on the right). Services are operated by Astro, and payment is in dollars. Bear in mind that delays and cancellations are common. Bookings can be made on the day of travel or the previous day. The trip to Santiago costs US$35 and takes 14hr.

By taxi – There are several types of city taxi in Havana (see Getting Around Havana, below). Both official and private taxis can be hired for long-distance journeys. Private taxis are cheaper but their standard of maintenance may leave something to be desired. Check when agreeing on a rate whether petrol is included or not.

GETTING AROUND HAVANA

The historic city centre is best explored on foot, or possibly in one of the two-seater pedecabs which have recently appeared. For the other parts of the city like Vedado and Miramar, where the attractions are more scattered, a car is the best option, though you could hire a bike and join the throngs of Habaneros negotiating the potholes on their sturdy Chinese machines.

By bus – A sightseeing bus called the Vaiven is run by *Rumbos*, ☎ (7) 66-9758. It leaves from the Floridita restaurant at the corner of Calle Obispo and Calle Bernaza, and calls at all the major hotels in the Vedado and Miramar, the cemetery, the Plaza de la Revolución, the Museum of the Revolution, and the Morro-Cabana Fortress (the last bus allows you to see the Nine O'clock Gun ceremony). The bus runs between 9am and 9.40pm and an all-day ticket costs US$4.

Ordinary city buses are infrequent and use of the service involves long queues and even longer waits. Definitely not for anyone in a hurry. A ride aboard a crowded "camello" (one of the hump-backed vehicles pulled by a converted truck) in the company of several hundred habaneros is an experience not easily forgotten. Fares in pesos.

By taxi – Most of the places frequented by tourists have stands for taxis operated by the official companies *Taxi Transtur*, ☎ (7) 36-6666, *Taxi-OK*, ☎ (7) 24-9518/19, and *Fenix*, ☎ (7) 63-9720/9580. Fares are in dollars and rates per kilometre are non-negotiable. There is an initial charge of US$1. The yellow vehicles operated by *Pantaxi*, ☎ (7) 55-5555, are cheaper but not always easy to find.

Cheaper still are the cars with the "taxi" identification on the windscreen. Rates are negotiable.

Last but not least are the "taxis particulares", private vehicles plying for hire illegally. They include American models from the 1950s as well as Ladas. Payment should be made discreetly as the drivers are liable to a heavy fine if caught.

Car hire – There are now several official car hire agencies, and the number of cars available has increased significantly. Nevertheless, bookings should be made in advance, either through a travel agent or directly with the rental company. Firms include: *Havanautos*, corner of Avenida Premiera (First Avenue) and Avenida 0, 3rd floor, Miramar, ☎ (7) 24-0646/8176; *Transtur*, Calle L between Calle 25 and Calle 27, ☎ (7) 24-5532, Fax (7) 24-4057, comerc@rentcar.transtur.com.cu; *Micar*, Calle 0 No 306, Miramar, ☎ (7) 24-3457/2444. Offices at the airport and in most of the major hotels. More details on page 86.

Bicycle hire – Bikes are now only available from private owners. If you hire one, make sure it is securely locked whenever you leave it anywhere, preferably in a guarded bicycle park.

FINDING YOUR WAY
See "Addresses" p 99

ADDRESS BOOK

Tourist information – Details of cultural events of all kinds can be obtained at the *Buró de Información Cultural*, in the craft gallery to the left of the Gran Teatro, ☎ (7) 63-6690, 9.30am-6.30pm. Tourist information, for both Havana and Cuba as a whole, from the offices of *Infotur*, open 8.30am-8.30pm. Like the various travel agencies, they can make hotel reservations, arrange car hire and organise excursions, all without charge. Also available are telephone cards, town plans and souvenirs. There are offices in Old Havana, Calle Obispo between Calle Habana and Calle Compostela and at the corner with Calle San Ignacio and the corner with Bernaza, ☎ (7) 33-3333. There is an office in Miramar at the corner of Avenida Quinta (Fifth Avenue) and Calle 112, ☎ (7) 3-7770, and another at the airport.

Roots Travel, Calle 4 No. 512 between Calle 21 and Calle 23, ☎ (7) 3-7770 or 30-6843.

Banks / currency exchange – All the major hotels have "cajas de cambio", exchange facilities. There are no cash machines, but cash can be obtained with travellers' cheques or by using a credit card at the *Banco Nacional de Cuba*, at the corner of the Malecón and the Rampa, and at the *Banco Financiero Internacional* (8.30am-3pm except at weekends), at the corner of Avenida Linea and Avenida O (near the Hotel Nacional), at the corner of Calle Oficios and Calle Brasil in Old Havana, and at the Centro Comercial Carlos III on Calle 18 between Avenida Premiera (First Avenue) and Avenida Tercera (Third Avenue) in Miramar.

Dollars can be changed into pesos at the same rate as the black market (20 pesos = US$1 in 1999) and with no risk at Cadeca, on the corner of Calle Aguiar and Lamparilla (Plaza de San Francisco), open 8.30am-6pm, 8.30am-12.30pm Sunday.

Post office / Telephone – Most major hotels can deal with mail, telephone calls and have fax facilities. Charges are more expensive than elsewhere, and must be paid in dollars (See also page 84). There is a post office on Plaza

San Francisco. The growing numbers of **Etecsa** public telephone boxes accept telephone cards which can be purchased at tourist localities. Available in denominations of 10, 20 or US$45, these are the least expensive way of making international calls (around US$4 a minute to Europe).

Medical service – Havana has numerous hospitals, though these are mainly intended for the use of local people. Foreigners should turn for medical help to the **Clinica Central "Cira García"**, Calle 20 No 4101 at the junction with Avenida 41 in Playa, between Miramar and Kohly, ☎ (7) 33-2811/14, Fax (7) 33-1633. High charges, payable in dollars. English spoken.

Some hotels have clinics and pharmacies.

The **Diplofarmacia** on the corner of Avenida Quinta (Fifth Avenue) and Avenida 42 in Miramar is a relatively well-stocked pharmacy, though it too is subject to shortages.

Embassies – United Kingdom, Calle 34 No. 708 between Calle 7 and Calle 17, Miramar, ☎ (7) 331771/2, 331286, 331299, 331049 or 331880; **Canada**, Calle 30 No. 518 on corner with Avenida 7, Miramar, ☎ (7) 24-2611, 24-2729, 24-2527; **United States, United States Interests Section**, between Calle L and Calle M, Vedado, ☎ (7) 333543/47, or 333551/59.

Airline companies – The main airline offices are located around the Rampa (Calle 23) (Plan I B1) in the Vedado. Check return flight times 72hr in advance.

Cubana de Aviación, corner of Calle 23 and Calle Infanta, Vedado, ☎ (7) 33-4949/50 or 33-4446. The office dealing with internal flights (same telephone nos) is a block away on the corner of Calle Infanta and Calle Humboldt.

**Servicupet petrol stations –
Vedado**; corner of Calle L and Calle 17; corner of the Paseo and Malecón (Hotel Riviera). Miramar: corner of Calle 31 and Calle 18; corner of Avenida 7 and Avenida Segunda (Second Avenue); corner of Avenida Quinta (Fifth Avenue) and Calle 112; corner of Avenida 5a and

Calle 120; several petrol stations along Avenida Rancho Boyeros on the way to the airport.

Other – Asitur (Tourist Assistance), Prado No. 254, Old Havana (Plan II A2), ☎ (7) 33-8920/8527/8339, www.asitur.cubaweb.cu, open 24hr all week. This organisation can be contacted in cases of lost property, missing documents, medical emergencies or need for repatriation, and may be able to offer legal or financial help.

WHERE TO STAY

Most of the hotels in Old Havana are in renovated colonial-era buildings of considerable charm. By contrast, the Vedado and Miramar hotels are mostly large-scale modern structures.

Havana has a large number of rooms in private dwellings. Those in the Vedado are generally the most attractive. The charge for a double room in a private house or apartment varies between US$15-30 according to the level of comfort, the facilities provided, and the length of stay. Breakfast is extra.

• **Old Havana** (Plan II)

Between US$20-30

🏠 **Residencia Académica Convento de Santa Clara**, Calle Cuba No. 610 between Calle Sol and Calle Luz, ☎ (7) 61-3335 or 66-9327, Fax (7) 33-5696 – 8rm. (30 beds). ♨ ⚞ ✗ ℘ Charming university pension in the Santa Clara convent, one of the most peaceful spots in Old Havana. Spacious rooms for between one and five people plus a suite with a balcony overlooking the cloisters. Attentive service. Breakfast (minimal) included.

Noemi Moreno Fuentes, Calle Cuba No. 611 between Calle Luz and Calle Santa Clara, 1st floor, ☎ (7) 62-4117 – 25rm. ♨ 🗐 ✗ A useful alternative to the Santa Clara opposite, Noemi's rooms are plain but well-kept and very reasonably priced for this type of accommodation in Old Havana. Her upper-floor neighbour, Miriam, has similar rooms. Good breakfasts and possibility of bike hire.

Around US$50

Hostal Valencia, Calle Oficios No. 53 between Calle Lamparilla and Obrapía, ☎ (7) 57-1037, Fax (7) 33-5628 – 12rm. A short step away from the Plaza de Armas, a lovely colonial-era building with spacious and tastefully decorated rooms overlooking a shady courtyard. The "Paella" restaurant is reckoned to serve the best dish of this kind in town. Book well in advance.

Under US$100

Hotel Inglaterra, Prado No. 416 between Calle San Rafael and Calle San Miguel, ☎ (7) 60-8594/97, Fax (7) 60-8254 – 83rm. Car hire, bureau de change, medical services. This imposing neo-Classical building is a designated national monument, for its historical as well as its architectural importance. Restaurant with Seville ceramics, palm trees, and stained glass. Attractive bar on the first floor terrace. Some of the plain rooms overlook the internal courtyard, others (with or without a balcony) give on to the clamorous city centre activity on Parque Central.

Hotel Plaza, corner of Calle Zulueta and Calle Neptuno, ☎ (7) 60-8583/90, Fax (7) 33-8569 – 188rm. Car hire, bureau de change, medical services. On the edge of Parque Central, this distinguished century-old palace was completely refurbished in 1991. The foyer with its fountains is particularly elegant, but the rooms overlooking the courtyard or the park lack period charm.

Around US$100

Hotel Florida, corner of Calle Obispo and Calle Cuba, ☎ (7) 62-4217, Fax (7) 62-4117 – 25rm. Good location in the heart of the old city, between the working-class west and the tourist east, this private palace dating from 1835 has been superbly restored. The refined bedrooms overlook a lovely neo-Classical courtyard. High standards of service and comfort, which also characterise the restaurant, one of the city's best.

Hostal Conde de Villanueva, corner of Calle Mercaderes and Calle Lamparilla, ☎ (7) 62-9293, Fax (7) 62-9682, hconde@ip.etecsa.cu – 9rm. Between Plaza de Armas and Plaza Vieja, this 18C palace has a cigar theme, including warm brown panelling and a "casa de Habano". Quiet and intimate atmosphere. Each of the rooms bears the name of a famous brand of cigar.

Hotel Ambos Mundos, corner of Calle Obispo and Calle Mercaderes, ☎ (7) 60-9530, Fax (7) 60-9532 – 51rm. Close to the Plaza de Armas, this is the legendary establishment where Ernest Hemingway used to stay when in town, along with any number of other celebrities whose portraits grace the walls of the hotel's bar. Pleasant rooms furnished in 1930s style.

More than US$100

Hotel Santa Isabel, Calle Baratillo No. 9 between Calle Obispo and Calle Narciso López, ☎ (7) 33-8201, Fax (7) 33-8391 – 27rm. Right on the Plaza de Armas, one of the loveliest squares in Havana, and thus only a few steps from most of the city's colonial-era sights, this is a luxurious establishment in the sumptuous setting of an 18C palace. The limited number of rooms means it is essential to reserve well in advance.

Hotel Sevilla, Trocadero No. 55 between Calle Zulueta and the Prado, ☎ (7) 60-8560, Fax (7) 60-8582, secre@sesvilla.gca.cma.net – 192rm. Car hire, bureau de change, medical services. Superb neo-Moorish interiors with ceramic decoration, plus a delightful courtyard. Service and rooms do not measure up to the rates charged, but this could improve with the change in ownership anticipated in 2000. Panoramic view over the city from the top-floor restaurant.

Parque Central, Calle Neptuno between the Prado and Calle Zulueta, ☎ (7) 66-6627/29, Fax (7) 66-30, sales@gtpc.cha.cyt.cu – 278rm. Bureau de change and tourist information office, car hire. Facing the tree-lined square of the same name, this brand-new hotel is part of the Golden Tulip chain. It offers a wide range of services and has rooms of the highest standard to suit its largely business clientele. The top floor bar and swimming pool have panoramic views over the city.

• Centro Habana
This densely built-up inner city area just to the west of Old Havana is very conveniently located, but has a slightly dubious after-dark reputation. Despite the presence of policemen everywhere, it is advisable to keep a tight hold on personal possessions when walking around in the evenings.

Between US$30-50
Hotel Lincoln (Plan 1), Calle Virtudes No. 164 on the corner with Avenida de Italia (Galiano), ☎ (7) 33-8209 – 135rm. ⌘ 📠 𝒫 📺 ✕ Showing its age, this hotel is a favourite with honeymooning local couples. The rooms are nothing very special, but this is a convenient location half-way between Old Havana and the Vedado. Pleasant bar and restaurant on the terrace of the top storey.

Around US$50
Hotel Deauville (Plan 1), Avenida de Italia (Galiano) No. 1, on the corner with the Malecón, ☎ (7) 33-8812, Fax (7) 33-8148 – 148rm. ⌘ 📠 𝒫 📺 ✕ ⏃ Car hire, bureau de change. 14-storey high rise by the Malecón between Old Havana and the Vedado. Decent rooms with balconies and fine views. Ask for a room on the upper floors away from the traffic noise of the Malecón.

• Vedado
Between US$20-35
Silvia Vidal, Paseo No. 602 between Calle 25 and Calle 27, ☎ (7) 34-165 – 3rm. ⌘ 📠 𝒫 Close to Plaza de la Revolución, a superb mansion dating from 1925 with prettily furnished and well-kept rooms, some of which are family-sized and have a separate entrance. Garage.

Marta Vitorte, Avenida de los Presidentes No. 301 at the corner with Calle 13, # 14, ☎ (7) 32-6475 – 3rm. ⌘ 📠 On the 14th floor of a block of flats in the heart of the Vedado, this fine apartment has an unequalled view over city and ocean. Rooms are comfortable and the proprietress, a lover of modern art, speaks several languages.

Marta Valentin, Calle Calzada No. 904 between Calle 6 and Calle 8, ☎ (7) 30-2898 ⌘ 📠 In the leafy western part of the Vedado, not far from the Malecón, this fine house has a number of decent rooms. Friendly reception. Garage.

Between US$40-70
Hotel Colina, corner of Calle L and Calle 27, ☎ (7) 33-4071, Fax (7) 33-4104 – 79rm. ⌘ 📠 𝒫 📺 ✕ The least expensive hotel in its category. Good location opposite Havana University. Outside appearance and foyer off-putting, but unpretentious and clean rooms.

Hotel Saint John's, Calle O No. 216 between Calle 23 and Calle 25, ☎ (7) 33-3740, Fax (7) 33-3561 – 94rm. ⌘ 📠 𝒫 📺 ✕ ⏃ Bureau de change, medical services. Excellent value for the location in the heart of the Vedado, close to the Rampa. Make sure of getting a room as far away as possible from the 14th floor night-club.

Between US$60-100
Hotel Capri, Calle 21 between Calle N and Calle O, ☎ (7) 33-3747, Fax (7) 33-3750 – 215rm. ⌘ 📠 𝒫 📺 ✕ ⏃ Car hire, bureau de change, medical services. This establishment was at its peak in the 1950s, since when a certain decline has set in, but it still enjoys a prime location, and has a roof-top swimming pool and night-club.

Hotel Victoria, corner of Calle 19 and Calle M, ☎ (7) 33-3510, Fax (7) 33-3109 – 31rm. ⌘ 📠 𝒫 📺 ✕ ⏃ 🆑 Car hire, bureau de change. The most expensive establishment in its category, but the one with the most personal service. The attentive staff and the small size of the hotel contribute to a cosseted atmosphere. Favoured by business clientele. The best rooms are those in a corner position with two sets of windows. Rates constant throughout the year.

More than US$100
Hotel Riviera, corner of the Paseo and the Malecón, ☎ (7) 33-4051, Fax (7) 33-3739 – 330rm. ⌘ 📠 ✕ 📺 ✕ ⏃ 🆑 Car hire, bureau de change, medical services. 1950s grand hotel, famous for its Palacio de la Salsa cabaret. Just behind the Hotel Meliá Cohiba and some way from the centre. The topmost

two floors are reserved for business people and the remaining rooms are currently being refurbished.

Hotel Habana Libre Tryp, Calle L between Calle 23 and Calle 25, ☎ (7) 33-4011, Fax (7) 33-3141, hotel@rllibre.tryp.cma.net – 524rm. ⌂ 🖳 🔊 TV ✕ ⌖ CC Car hire, bureau de change, medical services. The 25-storey building of the old Havana Hilton is the great landmark of the Rampa. Luxurious, recently refurbished rooms. Complete range of tourist services.

Hotel Nacional, corner of Calle 21 and Calle O, ☎ (7) 33-3564/7, Fax (7) 33-5054, ejecut@gcnacio.gca.cma.net – 426rm. ⌂ 🖳 🔊 TV ✕ ⌖ CC Car hire, bureau de change, medical services. High above the Malecón, one of Havana's finest hotels, a source of national pride when it was opened in 1930 and entirely renovated in 1992. The impressive hall and salons give on to attractive gardens. By comparison, the bedrooms are slightly characterless. The best are the ones with a sea view.

Hotel Meliá Cohiba, Paseo between Calle 1 and Calle 3, ☎ (7) 33-3636, Fax (7) 33-455 – 462rm. ⌂ 🖳 🔊 TV ✕ ⌖ CC Car hire, bureau de change, medical services. Built in 1995, this tall glass tower alongside the Hotel Riviera epitomises the Cuban tourist industry of the 1990s. It is one of the most expensive places to stay in Havana, and generally comes up to 5-star standards, though the standard rooms and suites are rather charmless. Numerous boutiques, bars and restaurants.

The Hotel Presidente is closed for renovation at present.

● **Cojimar** See directions on Plan 1
Around US$50

Hotel Panamericano, corner of Calle A and Avenida Central, ☎ (7) 95-1242/1010, Fax (7) 95-1021 – 81rm. ⌂ 🖳 🔊 TV ✕ ⌖ 🕸 CC Car hire. Built in 1991 to house athletes taking part in the Panamerican Games, this modern complex is 1km from the harbour at Cojimar, on the way from Havana to the Eastern Beaches. The villa accommodation is very suitable for families. There are shops in the town of Cojimar, between the hotel and the sea.

WHERE TO EAT

Finding somewhere to eat is not a problem in Havana. With a few exceptions, all the hotels have a restaurant, and there are plenty of good "paladares", especially in the Vedado. Paladares tend to come and go, and you should not be surprised if some of those listed below have closed. But others will have opened in their place.

● **Old Havana** (Plan II)
Under US$10

Hanoi, corner of Calle Brasil and Calle Bernaza (Plan II A3), ☎ (7) 57-1029, midday to 11pm. Small courtyard house, three blocks from the Capitol. Despite the name and the decor, this is no longer a stronghold of South East Asian cuisine; the food is creole, the price very reasonable. Patronised mostly by local people.

La Moneda, Calle San Ignacio No. 77 between Plaza de la Catedral and Calle O'Reilly (Plan III A2). Strategically located on a popular tourist thoroughfare, this paladar has a decor of coins and notes from all over the world. Good quality standard offerings of meat or fish plus rice and banana fritters and a salad of green beans, avocado or cucumber.

Teresa, Calle Mercaderes No. 111 between Calle Obrapía and Calle Obispo (Plan III B2). The outside may not be much to look at, but inside all is good cheer, with a collection of miniature porcelain figurines, an aquarium, and a TV to watch as a succulent lobster is prepared for you by the genial proprietress.

La Torre de Marfil, Calle Mercaderes No. 111 between Calle Obrapía and Calle Obispo (Pla III B2), ☎ (7) 57-1038, midday-10pm. Authentic Chinese atmosphere and copious chop suey.

Between US$10-20

🙂 **La Bodeguita del Medio**, Calle Empedrado No. 207 between Calle Cuba and Calle San Ignacio (Plan III A1), ☎ (7) 57-1374/5, midday-12.30am. Just a short step from the Plaza de la Catedral, the Bodeguita del Medio has been an Old Havana landmark for half a century. Its walls are covered in the photos and the signatures of the famous and not so famous. Good creole food and a range of cocktails including its own renowned "mojito". Open-air section upstairs with local musicians. Best to reserve.

Al Medina, Calle Oficios No. 12 between Calle Obispo and Calle Obrapía (Plan III B2), ☎ (7) 50-1041, midday-11pm. A short distance from the Plaza de Armas, the interior of this lovely 17C palace has a Middle Eastern charm. Mutton, falafel, and houmos served on large copper plates. The rather high prices are justified by the setting.

El Patio, corner of Calle San Ignacio and Calle Empedrado (Plan III A1), ☎ (7) 57-1034/5, midday-11pm. Comprises an arcade café overlooking the Cathedral square, plus dining tables set out around the delightful courtyard of the palace which once belonged to the Marquess of Aguas Claras. The musical accompaniment to the excellent creole cuisine can sometimes be overwhelming.

Café del Oriente, corner of Calle Oficio and Calle Amargura (Plan II C3), ☎ (7) 66-6686, midday to midnight. International cuisine on the Plaza de San Francisco. Refined retro decor.

More than US$20
Roof Garden, Trocadero No. 55 between Calle Zulueta and the Prado (Plan II A2), ☎ (7) 60-8560. Midday-midnight. Closed Wednesday. The high-ceilinged, century-old ballroom at the very top of the Hotel Sevilla has magnificent views over the city and food and service to match.

El Floridita (Plan II A3), corner of Calle Obispo and Avenida Bélgica, ☎ (7) 57 1300. 11.30am-midnight. Luxury establishment which counted Ernest Hemingway as one of its most faithful clients. Fish and seafood specialities. High standard of service and even higher prices. Famous for its cocktails.

• Eastern Havana
(Plan I D1 or Plan II B1, C1)
Between US$10-20
Los Doce Apostoles, Castillo de los Tres Reyes del Morro, ☎ (7) 63-8295. 12.30pm-11pm. This little restaurant serving creole food is in one of the buildings of the Morro Fortress facing Old Havana across the harbour mouth. Good food at a more reasonable price than in the other fortress restaurant.

More than US$20
La Divina Pastora, Castillo de San Carlos de la Cabana, ☎ (7) 60-8341. Midday-11pm. Overlooking the city on the far side of the entrance to the harbour, this rather expensive establishment in the Cabana fortress has one of the finest settings in Havana. As well as serving excellent seafood specialities, it is among the best places in town to savour an aperitif while enjoying the view.

• Centro Habana
A pair of restaurants facing each other in Havana's Chinatown serve Chinese dishes for less than US$3:
Muralla and **Tientan**, Calle Cuchillo between Calle Rayo and Calle San Nicolas, Another possibility is **Pacifico**, Calle San Nicolas (closed Monday).

Under US$10
La Guarida, Calle Concordia No 418 altos between Calle Gervasio and Calle Escobar (Plan I C2), ☎ (7) 62-4940. This paladar featured in the successful film *Fresa y Chocolate*.

• Vedado (Plan I)
Under US$10
🐌**Paladar El Helecho**, Calle 6 between Calle 11 and Avenida Linea (Plan II A2). Midday to 11pm. Sparklingly clean dining room full of ferns. Meticulously prepared creole meat and fish dishes plus delicious desserts. Excellent value for money. Family atmosphere and efficient service.

Between US$10-20
Dona Nieves, Calle 19 No. 812 between Calle 2 and Calle 4 (Plan II A2), ☎ (7) 30-6282. Midday-midnight except Monday. Refined food served in a delightful Vedado villa with Tiffany interiors. Lobster bouillabaisse a speciality. Much in favour with the Havana art crowd. Best to reserve.

Amor, Calle 23 No. 759 between Calle B and Calle C, second floor (Plan I A2). Midday-midnight. Wonderful colonial-era decor and fine food, especially fish in béchamel sauce. The establishment's very success has led to a falling-off in the standard of service.

Nerei, corner of Calle 19 and Calle L (Plan 1 B1). Midday-midnight; 6pm-midnight Saturday and Sunday. Close to a number of major hotels, this paladar is more like a full-blown restaurant, with a lovely terrace next door to a fine old mansion. Squid and octopus specialities.

La Casona de 17, Calle 17 No. 60 between Calle M and Calle N (Plan II B1)

☎ (7) 33-4529. Midday-midnight. This chic little restaurant opposite the Focsa Building serves traditional Cuban cuisine at above-average prices, but the pizza and fried chicken in the open-air café section are less expensive.

🍴*Paladar El Bistrot*, corner of Calle K and the Malecón (Plan I A1), ☎ (7) 32-2708. An open-air paladar overlooking the Malecón serving French-style food, with a frequently changing menu. Starters and desserts from the buffet.

Between US$10-20

La Casa Colonial, Calle 11 No. 509 altos between Calle D and E (Plan I A1), ☎ (7) 32-5411. A paladar with something of the style of a much larger restaurant. Courteous welcome from the proprietor and tasty family food from the kitchen.

Restaurante 1830, Malecón No. 1252 at the corner with Calle 20, ☎ (7) 55-3090/2. Midday to midnight. Sited on a little promontory the River Almendares meets the ocean, this villa restaurant is famous for its Japanese-style gardens. It is a good spot to stroll, listen to music, and dance the evening away. International cuisine and fish specialities.

More than US$20

La Torre, Edificio Focsa, corner of Calle 17 and Calle M (Plan II B1), ☎ (7) 32-5650. Midday to midnight. This restaurant occupies the top floor of the Focsa Building, the tallest in Havana. From the big windows there is an unequalled view over the city, but the cuisine and service are less impressive.

• **Miramar** (indicated on Plan I A1)
Most of the city's smartest restaurants are in this area.

Under US$10

Doctor Café, Calle 28 No. 111 between Avenida Premiera (1st Avenue) and Avenida Tercera (3rd Avenue), ☎ (7) 23-4718. Holiday atmosphere guaranteed in this secluded garden close to the Malecón. Try the delicious rabbit, prepared with garlic or beer.

El Laurel, Avenida Quinta (5th Avenue) No. 26002 between Calle 260 and Calle 262, Santa Fé, ☎ (7) 29-7767. Just beyond the Marina Hemingway, an attractive shoreline setting and a varied menu including good fish dishes.

Between US$10-20

🍴*El Alijibe*, 7ma Avenida (7th Avenue) between Calle 4 and Calle 26, ☎ (7) 24-1584. Midday-midnight. Lively evening atmosphere in an informal setting. Chicken is the speciality here, notably "pollo criollo" with unlimited rice, salad, potatoes and fried bananas. Copious food, served quickly. Some of the best value for money in Havana.

More than US$20

El Tocororo, corner of Calle 18 and Tercera Avenida, ☎ (7) 24-2209. Midday-11pm. Chic establishment much in favour among foreign diplomats. Richly decorated interiors with lush indoor landscaping populated by "tocororos" (Cuba's national bird). The vegetation is real, but the little winged creatures are not. The menu measures up to the surroundings. Seafood specialities including excellent lobster.

La Cecilia, Quinta Avenida (5th Avenue) between Calle 110 and Calle 112, ☎ (7) 24-1562. Midday-midnight. Several restaurants and a night-club hidden among luxuriant greenery. All the rooms open on to the grounds and a pullover may be necessary in winter. Wide range of creole and international cuisine, exotic meat dishes and excellent fish. The quality of the food and the setting justify the high prices.

La Ferminia, Quinta Avenida (5th Avenue) No. 18207 between Calle 182 and Calle 184, ☎ (7) 36-6555. Midday-midnight. The rooms of this elegant mansion have been turned into private dining rooms. Panelling in rare woods, a wealth of indoor plants, embroidered tablecloths all contribute to the luxurious atmosphere. Tasty grills of meat and fish can be enjoyed in the garden. Popular with business clientele.

• **Cojimar** (indicated on Plan I D1)

Between US$10-20

La Teraza, Calle Real No. 161, ☎ (7) 33-8702. 11am-11pm. Chic establishment with a friendly reception. The broad veranda has a fine view over the bay. Ernest Hemingway was a regular here, as is evident from the number of photos of the great man which adorn the walls. Seafood specialities and paella. Very expensive, but the prices are on a level with the high standard of food and service.

• Parque Lenin

(indicated on Plan I A3)

More than US$20

Las Ruinas, Calle 100 and Cortina de la Presa, ☏ (7) 57-8286. Midday-midnight. Closed Monday. In the middle of Lenin Park, this is a modern building set among the ruins of an old sugar mill. The planting and the colonial-era furnishings give the place a kind of stylishness, as does the stained glass by the Cuban artist René Portocarrero. Fish specialities of variable quality. Some visitors may be quite happy simply to have a drink on the terrace overlooking the park.

HAVING A DRINK

The weekly publication "Cartelera" gives listings of events and places of entertainment in Spanish and English. It is available in all the major hotels.

Bars – "My mojito at the Bodeguita, my daiquiri at the Floridita", was how Hemingway is supposed to have described his daily drinking routine, and you could do worse than follow in his footsteps.

La Bodeguita del Medio (Plan III A1), Calle Empedrado No. 207 between Calle Cuba and Calle San Ignacio, ☏ (7) 57-1374. Midday-12.30am. Crowded bar but relaxed atmosphere. Be prepared to force your way through the throngs of drinkers to get your mojito. Expensive.

El Floridita (Plan III A3), corner of Calle Obispo and Avenida de Bélgica, ☏ (7) 57-1300. 11.30am-midnight. The daiquiris are served in the Floridita's plush interior by red-jacketed waiters. This is where the famous cocktail was invented in 1914. "Papa's Special" came a little later, when Hemingway asked for, and got, an extra measure of rum in his daiquiri. Expensive.

Jazz Café, corner of Premiera Avenida and Paseo. 7.30pm-2am. On the first floor opposite the Melia Cohiba, a busy bar with Latin jazz and inexpensive cocktails.

Casa de la Amistad, Paseo between Calle 17 and Calle 19 (Plan I A2). 11am-11pm. Prestigious building with a garden. Evening concerts, fashion shows, or possibly just good conversation. Drinks, fried chicken and pizza at reasonable prices.

UNEAC, corner of Calle 17 and Calle H. This is the home of the Cuban Association of Writers and Artists. Exhibitions, concerts, conversation.

A number of the larger hotels have attractive bars where the drinks are not overpriced.

Concerts – Music oozes from every stone in Havana, and it is impossible to give anything approaching a full list of places to go to hear it. Some of the places where the best music is likely to be found are given below, and you should also scan the latest edition of Cartelera.

Café Cantante, corner of Paseo and Calle 39 (Plan I A3). 10pm-5am. Admission US$10. The biggest salsa groups play in this hall beneath the Teatro Nacional in Plaza de la Revolución. Discotheque when there is no live music.

Casa de la Música, corner of Avenida 35 and Calle 20. Music from 11pm to 4am. Admission US$15 maximum. Internationally famous "saleros" play here.

La Cecilia, Quinta Avenida (5th Avenue) between Calle 110 and Calle 112, ☏ (7) 24-1562. Music in an attractive garden setting, Thursday-Sunday from 9.30 onwards. Details posted at the entrance to the restaurant.

Habana Café, Hotel Melia Cohiba, Paseo between Calle 1 and Calle 3, ☏ (7) 33-3636. Midnight-2am. 1950s decor incorporating an aeroplane hanging from the roof, and high calibre music including appearances by groups like Compay Segundo. Minimum charge for drinks or food US$10. Book in advance.

El Gato Tuerto, Calle O between Calle 17 and Calle 19 (Plan I B1), ☏ (7) 55-2696. 11pm-4am. Admission US$5 including a drink. Intimate space, sombre and appealing, like some of the music played here, for example excellent bolero. This is where many famous artistes from the 1960s first made their mark. A favourite with couples.

Casa de la Cultura, corner of Calle Aguiar and Calle Teniente Rey (Brasil) (Plan II B3). Admission US$2. Good traditional groups to dance to, in the company of Habaneros. Depending on the evening, rumba, son and salsa from 7pm onwards.

Shows – *El Palacio de la Salsa* is currently closed for renovation.

La Tropicana, corner of Calle 72 and Avenida 43, Mariano, ☎ (7) 27-0110 or 27-1717. 9pm-3am, closed Monday. Admission between US$50 and US$70 depending on where you sit and whether you have dinner (US$60 if booked through a hotel or travel agency, including transfer and quarter bottle of rum). Opened in 1939, the world-famous Tropicana has been a showcase for international stars like Nat King Cole and Maurice Chevalier. Nowadays, it puts on the most spectacular show in Cuba twice nightly, featuring more than 200 elaborately costumed (but skimpily dressed) dancers in an open-air setting of tropical greenery. Expensive, but often fully booked, so reserve well in advance.

A number of major hotels have their own night-club with cabaret. The *Salon Rojo* in the Hotel Capri, open 10.30pm-4am, has a particularly entertaining show at 11.30pm. Admission US$10 including drink.

El Turquino, on the top floor of the Habana Libre has a show every night at 1030pm. Admission on US$15.

El Pico Blanco, on the top floor of the St John's Hotel, has bolero in a pleasant setting. Much favoured by habitués of the genre. From 10pm. Admission US$5.

El Sabado de la Rumba, Calle 4 No. 103 between Calzada and Calle 5, Vedado, ☎ (7) 31-3467. Performances by the Conjunto Folklórico Nacional every other Saturday afternoon, with African drumming and dancing. Admission US$5.

Discotheques – Many of the places listed above have discotheques following the evening show. Discos were once notorious for the crowds of "jineteras" ready to pounce on any stray foreign male, but a recent crack-down has largely eliminated this phenomenon. Among the most rated discos is the one in the Hotel El Comodoro, or try *Havana Club*, every evening from 10pm-5am, admission US$10.

OTHER THINGS TO DO

Excursions – The travel agencies listed above and their hotel branches will help in choosing and organising one day or longer trips out of the city, to destinations like Trinidad or Cayo Largo.

Theatres – The *Gran teatro de la Habana* (Plan II A3) on Parque Central is the home of the Ballet Nacional de Cuba directed by Alicia Alonso, and also has performances by the National Opera. An opera or ballet is an excellent reason for making a visit to this magnificent building. Programmes are advertised in front of the theatre. ☎ (7) 61-3075/9.

The *Teatro nacional* (Plan I A3) on Plaza de la Revolución is a frequent venue for performances by theatre companies from abroad. There are also concerts by Cuba's National Symphony Orchestra. ☎ (7) 79-6011.

Cinemas – Havana has more than 200 cinemas, but most films are run-of-the-mill except during cinema festivals. These are usually held in the *Ciné La Rampa*, at the corner of Calle 23 and Calle O, by the Hotel Nacional (Plan I B1). In December, the International Latin American Film Festival is held at the *Ciné Charles Chaplin*, Calle 23 between Calle 10 and Calle 12, close to the main entrance to the Colón Cemetery (Plan I A2).

Outdoor pursuits – The *Marina Hemingway*, corner Calle 248 and Quinta Avenida (Fifth Avenue), Santa Fé, has facilities for all kinds of watersports, including scuba-diving, deep-sea fishing and water-skiing. For information and bookings, ☎ (7) 24 1150/55, Fax (7) 29-7201.

Baseball fans can take in a game at the *Estadio Latinoamericano* (Plan 1 B3), corner of Calle Patría and Pedro Pérez in the Cerro area. Games begin on Thursday and Saturday at 8pm, and on Sunday at 1.30pm. The baseball season lasts from November to June.

SHOPPING

Rum, coffee and cigars – *Casa del Rón* (Plan III B2), Calle Baratillo No. 53 at the corner with Calle Obispo, Old Havana, close to Plaza de Armas. The House of Rum offers the opportunity of tasting different types of rum, and has cigars for sale as well. Next door is the *Casa del Café*, where the different kinds of coffee grown in Cuba can be bought. There are tastings in the bar on the first floor.

Fábrica Partagas (Plan II A3), Calle Industria No. 524. Just behind the Capitol, 9am-5pm, closed Sunday. Wide selection of cigars for sale on the ground floor of this venerable tobacco factory. There are tours of the factory itself at 10am and 2pm.

Sala del Habano, Calle Mercaderes between Calle Obispo and Calle Obrapía (Plan III B2), 10am-5pm, 9am-1pm Sunday. Closed Monday. Just one among the many cigar shops and other outlets (eg hotels), but this example dates from the 18C and is a museum too, telling the whole story of tobacco and smoking, from native rite to mass production.

Arts and crafts – There are souvenir stands every day except Sunday in Parque Céspedes (Plan III A1) to the rear of the Cathedral, and more in the Vedado, at the junction of the Rampa and Calle M (Plan I B1). The merchandise includes straw hats, Che Guevara T-shirts, lacework a cross-section of the Cuban souvenir industry.

Palacio de la Artesanía, in the Palacio Pedroso (Plan II B2), Calle Cuba No. 64, between Calle Pena Pobre and Calle Tacón. 9.30am-7pm. Two blocks away from Plaza de la Catedral, a fine old 18C mansion with a wide selection of books, cassettes and CDs, musical instruments, rum and cigars. Souvenir shopping made convenient.

El Quitrín, corner Calle Obispo and Calle San Ignacio (Plan III A2). Lace makers in an Old Havana residence. A popular here is a well-made and relatively inexpensive "guayabera", the traditional Cuban shirt.

Art galleries – A good number of artists' studios are open to the public, especially in Old Havana. The **Taller experimental de gráfica** (Plan III A2), Callejón del Chorro. 10am to 4pm, closed Sunday. A large studio with examples of contemporary engraving, some for sale.

Galería La Acacia, Calle San José No. 114 between Calle Industria and Calle Consulado, to the north of the Capitol (Plan II A3). 10am-4pm, closed Sunday. Works by some of Cuba's finest artists, at correspondingly high prices.

Centro Wilfredo Lam, corner Calle San Ignacio and Calle Empedrado (Plan III A1). No works by Lam himself, but interesting exhibitions of the work of contemporary artists.

Casa de Guayasamín, Calle Obrapía between Calle Mercaderes and Calle Oficios (Plan III B2). The Ecuadorian artist best known for his portrait of Castro has his Cuban studio here. There are sculptures, paintings, ceramics and jewellery. The Casa de México opposite has Mexican arts and crafts for sale.

Bookshops – There are improvised little bookstalls all over the town, often set up in the owner's doorway. But there is not much choice, the same books turn up over and over again.

There is an **open-air book market** every day except Sunday on the Plaza de Armas (Plan III B2), with the occasional treasure to be unearthed among the works of Fidel Castro, Che Guevara, Fernando Ortiz or Nicolás Guillén. The asking prices are high, but bargaining is possible.

La Internacional (Plan II A3), Calle Obispo No. 526 between Calle Bernaza and Calle Cristo. 10am-5.30pm except Sunday. Close to the Parque Central, this bookshop has foreign-language books and magazines.

El Navegante (Plan III A2), Calle Mercaderes No. 115 between Calle Obispo and Calle Obrapía. 8.30am-midday, and 2pm-5pm, closed Sunday. This shop has a good selection of maps, charts and town plans, and is the best place to stock up on such items, as they are rarely available elsewhere in the country.

Shopping centre – Centro Comercial Plaza Carlos III (Plan I B2), Avenida Salvador Allende (Carlos III) between Calle Retiro and Calle Arbol Seco. The opening of this large-scale shopping centre in Centro Habana was a major event. There are four floors with an array of shops selling footwear, clothes, books, domestic appliances, hi-fi's etc. Daily 10am to 8pm, Sunday 10am-3pm.

Market – Fruit, vegetables and lots of local colour at the Vedado "agromercado", Calle B between Calle 17 and Calle 19.

"Guajiro" and ox-team at work

WESTERN CUBA

This is one of Cuba's most fascinating regions, its land-scapes, townscapes and people an inexhaustible source of picturesque images and impressions. Who could forget the sight of the mist clearing over the *mogotes* in the valley of Viñales like the smoke curling from a cigar from the Vuelta Abajo, the country's finest tobacco-growing area? And who could fail to respond to the smile cracking open the weather-beaten features of a farmer as he turns his team of oxen at the end of a furrow ploughed in the rich red earth? With its little *bohíos* scattered over the countryside, its charming little towns and its deserted beaches, western Cuba tempts discerning travellers to take time to discover its many delights.

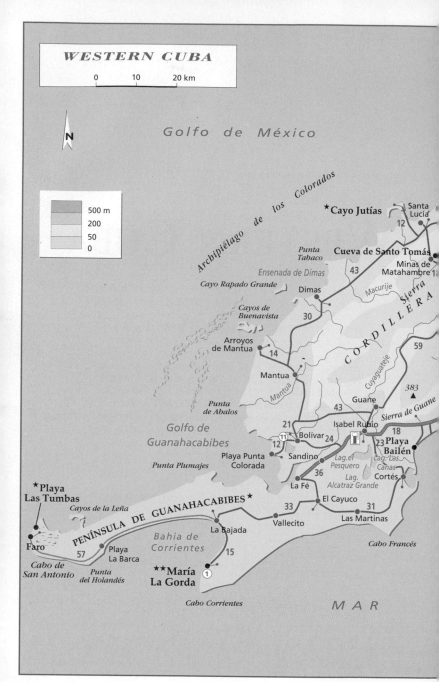

WESTERN CUBA

0   10   20 km

N

Golfo de México

Archipiélago de los Colorados

★ **Cayo Jutías**

Santa Lucía

12

500 m
200
50
0

Punta Tabaco

Cueva de Santo Tomás

43

Minas de Matahambre 1

Ensenada de Dimas

Cayo Rapado Grande

Dimas

Macurije

C
O
R
D
I
L
L
E
R
A

Sierra

Cayos de Buenavista

30

59

Arroyos de Mantua

14

Cuyaguateje

Mantua

Mantua

Guane

383 ▲

Punta de Abalos

43

Sierra de Guane

Golfo de Guanahacabibes

21

Isabel Rubio

18

12

Bolívar

24

23 **Playa Bailén**

11

Playa Punta Colorada

Sandino

Lag. el Pesquero

Lag. Las Cañas

Punta Plumajes

36

Lag. Alcatraz Grande

Cortés

★ **Playa Las Tumbas**

Cayos de la Leña

La Fé

★

PENÍNSULA DE GUANAHACABIBES

33

El Cayuco

31

Las Martinas

Faro

57

Playa La Barca

La Bajada

Vallecito

Cabo Francés

Cabo de San Antonio

Punta del Holandés

Bahía de Corrientes

15

★★ **María La Gorda**

1

Cabo Corrientes

M A R

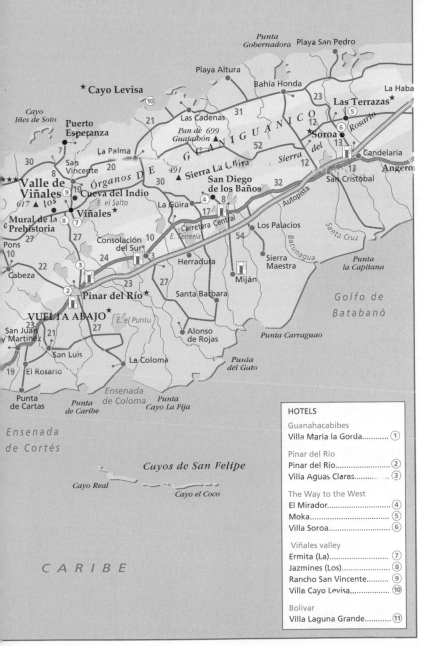

HOTELS

Guanahacabibes
Villa María la Gorda............ ①

Pinar del Río
Pinar del Río........................ ②
Villa Aguas Claras.............. ③

The Way to the West
El Mirador............................ ④
Moka..................................... ⑤
Villa Soroa........................... ⑥

Viñales valley
Ermita (La)........................... ⑦
Jazmines (Los)..................... ⑧
Rancho San Vincente.......... ⑨
Villa Cayo Levisa,,.............. ⑩

Bolivar
Villa Laguna Grande............ ⑪

THE WAY TO THE WEST★
FROM HAVANA TO PINAR DEL RÍO

Havana and Pinar del Rìo Provinces
Around 250 km – Allow a whole day if visiting all the attractions described
See map page 158

Not to be missed
Walking in the Sierra del Rosario.
Cooling off beneath the Soroa waterfall.

And remember...
If time is short drive directly to Pinar del Río: allow 2hr by motorway (180km).
Nights in the sierra are cool – take some warm clothes.

The Guaniguanico range of mountains and the Vinales Valley can be reached from the north by the coast road *(see page 174)* or from the south by the *Carretera Central* (Central Highway) and the *autopista* (motorway) which run more or less parallel to each other between Havana and Pinar del Río.

A trip down the *Carretera Central* reveals the extent to which the Cuban countryside has slipped back into a pre-industrial age, a time-warp with hardships as well as abundant attractions. Carts and carriages are more in evidence than cars, and ploughs are pulled by horses rather than tractors. A characteristic sight is the *guajiro*, the classic Cuban country-dweller astride his steed; straw-hatted, cigar clamped between his teeth, machete hanging from his belt. Whole families wait patiently by the roadside in the hope of getting a lift from the occasional passing motorist or clamber up into the back of a lorry to join the dozens already there.

Drying the harvest on the motorway

B. Brillion/MICHELIN

Despite its three lanes in each direction, this is far from being a conventional motorway. In many ways it's a joy to drive along; jams are unknown and there is very little distraction from other motor traffic, just the occasional car, bus or lorry. The *autopista* is laid out on a beautifully sweeping alignment, which brings it tantalisingly close to the sierra to the north. On the other hand, drivers have to watch out for pedestrians sauntering across the road, cyclists pedalling nonchalantly in the wrong direction, and vehicles drawn by horses or teams of oxen. Some of the interchanges have the usual slip roads and overbridges, but other junctions with the motorway simply consist of a dirt road running off at right angles. Signs are few, though progress westward is shown by green kilometre markers in the central reservation. Though seemingly remote from towns and villages, the *autopista* is something of a social centre. People shelter in the shade of a bridge which may also serve as a bus stop or hitch-hiking point, while other folk proffer strings of garlic or contraband cigars to the passing traffic.

While the Central Highway and the motorway both lead directly to Pinar del Río it's far more interesting to turn off onto the side roads which climb up into the sierra. What the mountains lack in height they more than make up for with fresh air and welcome relief from the heat of the plain. And, with an inviting network of footpaths, they are fine walking country.

Leave Havana by Avenida Rancho Boyeros in the direction of the airport. About 10km from the city centre the motorway to Pinar del Río is signposted on the right. Leave the motorway after 46km in the direction of Artemisa. 7km further on a pair of stone pillars on the left marks the entrance to the Angerona coffee plantation.

■ Angerona coffee plantation

■ **Angerona coffee plantation** – A red dirt road leads through fields of sugar-cane to an old coffee plantation dating from the 19C and called the "garden of Cuba". It's a place of great tranquillity and rustic charm. Ghosts of masters and slaves still seem to inhabit the ruins of what was once a thriving enterprise; a Classical statue evokes former splendours among the broken-down walls of the great house, and here too are the remains of the *barracón*, the quarters lived in by the slaves. Abandoned equipment rusts away in the embrace of luxuriant vegetation. More than 400 slaves once worked here.

It's quite feasible to walk around this haunted place on one's own, but the attendant at the entrance can provide all sorts of fascinating detail about the plantation and its past.

Go back the way you came and continue along the motorway. Near the km51 marker leave the motorway and follow signs to the Las Terrazas Motel. Non-residents must pay a toll at a checkpoint on the road through the sierra.

■ **Las Terrazas★** – This rural community had its origin in the early 1970s as part of a regional reafforestation programme. About 1 000 people, many of them artists and craft workers, live in the terraced dwellings zigzagging along the slopes above the lake of San Juan. Living conditions in the village contrast strongly with the luxurious facilities and the lavish landscaping of one of the country's finest hotels, the Moka (*see Making the most of the Way to the West*), beautifully sited high above the valley.

Las Terrazas makes an excellent starting point for exploring the **Sierra del Rosario**, a designated UNESCO Biosphere Reserve. Information on walks is available at the hotel which can also provide guides. Signposted footpaths lead to waterfalls, places to swim and old coffee plantations which have fallen into disuse. Accessible on foot 2km to the northeast of Las Terrazas is the old **Buenavista Coffee Plantation**, its restored buildings now housing a restaurant.

On leaving the Hotel Moka turn left on to the main road for 12km. At the check-point turn left again and continue for 8km to Soroa. The Hotel Villa Soroa is on the right just before the bridge.

■ **Soroa** – This little settlement is also called the "Rainbow of Cuba" because of its famous falls whose spray sparkles with all the colours of the spectrum. Founded by a coffee grower of Basque origin who had to flee from Haiti, Soroa is a good centre for exploring the Sierra del Rosario. At the start of the road leading to the Castillo de las Nubes (Castle in the Clouds) restaurant, a gateway marks the entrance to the **Orquideario** *(9am-3.30pm. Admission charge)*. Spreading over the hilly terrain, this splendid orchid park contains more than 700 varieties of orchid, 250 of them endemic to Cuba. The best time to visit is in the flowering season which lasts from November to March, though the grounds are attractive at all times of the year.

Soroa's **Salto**, its 20m high cascade, is reached by a path which starts from the restaurant beyond the bridge. A walk of about 20min is rewarded by the sight of water falling into a basin which serves as a delightful, and deservedly popular swimming pool. Those in search of a more solitary splash in the water should go a little further upstream.

Continue along the mountain road towards Candelaria and on reaching the motorway turn right. At Km 116 turn towards San Diego de los Banos and continue for 14km.

■ **Sierra de Güira** – Cool forests of pine and cedar characterise the short drive through this sierra.

San Diego de los Banos on the banks of the San Diego river is a tiny spa surrounded by mountains. Some people come here for a cure, others just to get away from it all.

Leave San Diego in the direction of La Güira, crossing the river one block beyond the park. Continue for 5km as far as the entrance to the La Cortina hacienda.

La Güira Park extends over the old La Cortina property which was destroyed by fire.

It is a romantic place, with ruins, a lake and a cascade, and a Japanese house currently being restored. There is a restaurant, and very basic accommodation for an overnight stay.

Beyond the tourist complex the road climbs through coniferous forest into the Sierra de Güira. Some 10km further on there is a sign pointing to **Cueva de los Portales**. This is a cave with an underground river, of considerable historic interest since it was here that **Che Guevara** had his headquarters during the Cuban Missile Crisis of October 1962.

From Cueva de los Portales there is a choice of routes, leading either directly to the Viñales Valley or continuing towards Pinar del Río.

Viñales Valley (40km). Do not turn left at the Cueva de los Portales junction; the road to the west of San Andrés is only suitable for four-wheel drive vehicles. Take the road towards La Palma and after 10km turn left towards Pinar del Río. After 20km turn left again by the "Entronque de la Palma" restaurant. Vinales village is 10km further on.

Pinar del Río (82km). After leaving Parque de la Güira turn left on the road towards Herradura. After 25km rejoin the motorway. Pinar del Río is 37km further on.

COMING AND GOING
This route can only be followed using your own transport (hire car, taxi or similar).

ADDRESS BOOK
Servicupet service stations – Autopista, between the exits for Soroa and Candelaria; San Diego, Carretera San Diego Km 9; Consolación del Sur, Avenida 51 Final.

WHERE TO STAY
AND EATING OUT
Under US$10
There are three camp-sites in the area, mostly used by Cuban holidaymakers, with permanent accommodation in the form of chalets with a fairly basic level of comfort and facilities. ☜ ✗
El Taburete, part of the tourist complex at Las Terrazas; **La Caridad**, on the way into Soroa; **La Cueva de los Portales**, close to the cave used by Che Guevara.

• Las Terrazas
From US$70 to US$120
☜ **Hotel Moka**, autopista Km 51, Candelaría, ☎ (7) 33-5516 or (85) 2921/2996, Fax (7) 33-3814/5516, hmoka@telda.gate.cma.net – 26 rm. ☜ ▤ ☞ ✗ ☜ ☜ ☞ cc Built in 1994, the hotel is perfectly integrated into the mountainous surroundings of the Sierra del Rosario. A massive tree rises from the floor of the hall to an opening in the tiled roof. Tropical vegetation seems about to engulf every part of the building, including the luxurious bathrooms with their bay windows opening on to the forest. The spacious and tastefully decorated rooms offer every comfort. Those on the ground floor have a spectacular view down into the valley while the first floor rooms look directly into the trees. Prices are reasonable for a hotel of such a high standard.

• Soroa
Around US$20
Casa Pepe, Carretera Soroa Km 3.5. On the left of the road to Soroa, 4km from the motorway exit. ☜ ▤ Clean and friendly bed and breakfast establishment.
From US$30 to US$50
Villa Soroa, Carretera de Soroa km8, Candelaría, ☎ (85) 2122 or 2041 - 49 rm. ☜ ▤ ☞ TV ✗ ☜ Bureau de

change, medical facilities. Most of Soroa's tourist facilities are to be found in this hotel complex. Accommodation is in chalets set around a swimming pool which gets very popular at the height of the summer season (closed for repairs). The rooms are strictly functional but offer a reasonable degree of comfort. Quieter family accommodation is available in separate buildings scattered around the foot of the hill close to the orchid park.

• San Diego de los Banos
Under US$50
Hotel El Mirador, Calle 23 Final, ☎ /Fax (85) 33-5410 or 78-338. ☜ ▤ ☞ TV ✗ ☜ cc Next to the spa building, 30 tastefully refurbished rooms with a delightfully sylvan view. Various medical treatments available.

WHERE TO EAT
• Soroa
El Castillo de los Nubes, Soroa, ☎ (85) 2041. Open 9am-5pm. The road climbing up from the Orquideario leads to this "Castle in the Clouds" at the top of the hill with its wonderful view over the Sierra del Rosario. This is a good place for a refreshing drink or something from the grill.

OTHER THINGS TO DO
• Las Terrazas
Information about walking in the Sierra Rosario is available from the Hotel Moka. The hotel also hires out horses and mountain bikes.

• Soroa
There is splendid walking in the mountains around the Villa Soroa with an English-speaking guide. Longer treks with overnight stays with local farmers can also be arranged. Baths and massage available at the entrance to the Salto.

SHOPPING
Crafts – At Las Terrazas there are craftspeople making wonderful creations from various fibres as well as potters, sculptors, painters and silk-screen printers (8am-5pm; closed Saturday and Sunday).

THE VIÑALES VALLEY★★★

Pinar del Río province
205km from Havana – 25km from Pinar del Río
See map page 158

Not to be missed
Watching the sun go down over the "mogotes".
Viñales village.
A meal in the restaurant at the Mural de la Prehistoría.

And remember...
Spend at least one night in one of the valley hotels.

Hidden among the mountains, the Viñales Valley is one of Cuba's most striking landscapes, its strange rock formations known as *mogotes* forming the backdrop to a relaxed way of life. A glorious variety of shades of green is set off by the rich soil whose reddish tint echoes the blooms of the royal poincianas growing throughout the area. Further splashes of colour are added by the farmers' *bohíos*, brightly painted little houses with roofs thatched with palm leaves.

The valley can be reached from the north via La Palma or from Pinar del Río via the road known as the **carretera de los Borrachos**, 25km of hairpin bends through the sierra. Why this mountain road should be called the Drunkards' Highway is a matter of dispute. One explanation is that the labourers who built it were paid in rum rather than pesos. Local drivers tend to take it at full tilt, but visitors are advised to proceed with caution.

The church in Viñales

J. F. Galmiche

Geological oddities

The Sierra de los Órganos (literally the Organ Range) consists of several ridges running more or less parallel to one another as well as the isolated hills known as **mogotes**. In between runs a series of fertile valleys. The *mogotes* are made up of Jurassic limestone. A fascinating example of karst scenery, they once were part of a limestone plateau which has been worn away by the action of underground rivers. Softer strata were eroded, forming caverns whose roofs eventually collapsed, leaving the strange sugar-loaf shapes of the mogotes standing in isolation.

Karst country
"This area owes its existence to water penetrating the porous limestone and dissolving it from within. It is as if the very substance of the country was being washed away, leaving it to crumble in upon itself".
(M Derruau).

Tour of the valley

Allow at least one day to explore the valley on foot

Paths and tracks make the Viñales Valley perfect for exploration on foot or on horseback. The best starting point for many walks and rides is Vinales village itself.

Vinales village ★ — This charming little place with its population of around 3 000 has something of the character of a town from the Wild West, though nowhere could be more tranquil. Shaded by pine trees, the main street, the Calle Cisneros, is lined with single storey houses beneath whose columned porches the locals take their ease in rocking chairs. Every now and then the scene is enlivened by a mounted *guajiro* guiding his steed towards the drinks stand set up on the pavement. The only disturbance to the peace and quiet is likely to come from the raised voices of a group of village elders setting the world to rights.

Few visitors are able to resist the spell of this sleepy settlement where the days slip by in perfect tranquillity. A good place to relax is on one of the benches of the main square, the **Parque José Martí**, with its church and its statue of this national hero. On the north side of the square stands the old building housing the **Casa de la Cultura** where concerts are held from time to time. Leisurely evenings can be spent in Viñales sipping a *mojito* and listening to local musicians, perhaps on the terrace of the Casa de Don Tomás, the town's oldest building. On the left-hand side of the road north out of the village is a charming little botanical garden.

Leave Viñales on the main road towards Pinar del Río and at the southern end of the village follow signs for 4km to the Mural de la Prehistoria.

Mural de la Prehistoría — The "Prehistoric Mural" is an extraordinary sight, an incongruous work of art 120m high and 180m long painted on the cliff-like face of one of the valley's *mogotes*. Completed in 1961 by Leovigildo González Murillo, a follower of the Mexican muralist Diego Rivera, it's an ambitious evocation of the evolutionary process leading from the humble amoeba to "Socialist Man". The never-ending task of touching up the gaudy colours of its ammonites, dinosaurs and other creatures is entrusted to a team of painters with no apparent fear of heights.

The *mural* is a compulsory stop for tour groups, who are ushered into the vast restaurant at its foot where they are fed on succulent local pork and serenaded by musicians. To appreciate the tranquil scenery of the valley it's best to come here early or late in the day and pass a leisurely hour or two beneath the restaurant's huge canopy, perhaps with your back to the mural.

Concealed among the trees to the right of the mural is a path which leads to the summit via a series of ramps and ladders. The superb view is worth the climb.

Go back through Viñales and at the northern end of the village turn left towards La Palma.

Caves – The **Cueva de San Miguel**, 3km north of Viñales, has been turned into a "prehistoric" bar and discotheque where you can drink and dance among stalactites and stalagmites.

One km further on, the **Cueva del Indio** (*9am-6pm. Admission charge*) has become a tourist attraction. The Indian's Cave is so-called because it served as a refuge for the Guanahatabey people during the Spanish Conquest in the 16C. Part of the visit is on foot, part in a motorboat on an underground river. Although the cave seems popular, the tour doesn't last long and there is little in the way of explanation or interpretation.

A third cave is the **Cueva de Santo Tomás**, beyond the Mural of Prehistory on the road towards Minas de Matahambre and Cayo Jutías. This is one of the most extensive caves in Latin America, 25km long and with an underground river. Full kit is provided for budding speleologists.

Making the most of the Viñales Valley

COMING AND GOING

If you do not have your own transport, cars can be hired in Pinar del Río.

By bus – There is a *Viazul* service every other day from Havana to Viñales (Calle Salvador Cisneros 63A) via Pinar del Río and vice versa. Fare US$12 and the trip takes 3hrs15mins.

GETTING AROUND

Car hire – All three hotels in the valley have a car hire desk: *Havanautos* at La Ermita ☎ (8) 93-6071, *Transautos* at Los Jazmines ☎ (8) 93-6205 and at the Rancho San Vincente ☎ (8) 9-3200. Hire should be arranged well in advance as the number of cars available is limited, particularly in season.

Taxi – Taxis can be ordered at all the hotels.

ADDRESS BOOK

Servicupet service stations – There are service stations on the road into Viñales from the north and at San Cayetano (12km north towards Puerto Esperanza), but they do not always have supplies, so to be on the safe side drivers should fill up at Pinar del Río.

WHERE TO STAY

Between US$30-60

Las Jazmines, Carretera de Viñales Km 25, ☎ (8) 93-6205, Fax (8) 93-6215, – 78 rm. ⌕ 🍴 📺 ✕ 💧 cc 4km from Viñales village on the road to Pinar del Río, the hotel consists of a number of buildings set into the hillside overlooking the valley. The broad terrace with its swimming pool offers one of the finest views of the area's celebrated "mogotes". The spacious and comfortable rooms all have balconies.

La Ermita, Carretera de La Ermita Km 2, ☎ (8) 93-6071, Fax 93-6091 – 62 rm. ⌕ 🍴 📺 ✕ 💧 cc The Ermita is within walking distance of Viñales village, 2km away. The accommodation is arranged around a busy swimming pool. The setting and the views over the valley are comparable with Las Jazmines. The rooms at the far end of the most recently built wing have the best views.

Rancho San Vincente, Valle de San Vincente, ☎ (8) 9 3200/01 – 43 rm. ⌕ 🍴 📺 ✕ 💧 cc 7km north of Viñales village beyond the Cueva del Indio. The chalets dotted around the grounds are perfectly decent but the hotel doesn't quite match up to the charm of the places described above, though it also boasts a number of sulphur springs. The main building is under reconstruction.

Because of its proximity to the Viñales Valley and because there are no tourist facilities of any kind along the coast road (*see page 174*), the only hotel on Cayo Levisa is included at this point.

Between US$50-100
Villa Cayo Levisa, Cayo Levisa, ☎ (82) 3207/08 or (7) 66-6075 – 20 rm. 🗄️📖✂️📺✕🏊♨️♿️cc The 20 chalets of this unspoilt little island's only hotel are strung out along a delightful sandy beach fringed by palm trees. This setting alone justifies the relatively high prices charged. Because accommodation it limited it should be reserved well in advance. Reservations can be made through a number of tour operators in Havana.

Under US$10
Campismo Dos Hermanas, at the foot of the "mogote" to the right of the Mural of Prehistory, ☎ (82) 9-3223. 🗄️✕ 🏊 54 concrete chalets in the centre of the camp-site. Guided walks and horse-riding. Often fully booked during the Cuban summer holidays.

Under US$20
Viñales village is very popular with visitors and there is no shortage of private accommodation. Rooms are mostly quite simple but decent, the welcome is warm and the meals are often excellent. **Olga Martinez**, Calle Mariana Grajales No.1, between the two main streets. 🗄️ 🍴 Nondescript house but amazing hospitality and delicious food.
Fernando Diaz Arenciba, Calle Salvador Cisnero No.142 (next to Casa de Don Tomás). An attractive house on the main street with a charming host.
Motel colonial azul, Calle Salvador Cisnero No.64. Large and beautiful blue house with dormitory-type rooms suitable for groups.

WHERE TO EAT

Between US$5-10
Casa de Don Tomás, Calle Salvador Cisneros No.141, Viñales, ☎ (8) 93-6300. Open 10am-10pm. On the edge of the village on the road to Pinar del Río, this restaurant is housed in an attractive wooden building, one of the oldest in Viñales. The terrace on the upper floor has a view of the main street

through the trees shading its garden. Recommended: "Las Delicias de Don Tomás", a tasty paella made from fish, rock lobster, pork, chicken and chorizo.
Paladar "La Fiesta", Calle Salvador Cisnero final No 3, Viñales. At the northern end of the village, a modest paladar, unimpressive from the outside but with a warm welcome and generous helpings, especially of succulent local pork.
Mural de la Prehistoria, Viñales Valley, ☎ (8) 93-6260. Open 12pm-4pm. This enormous establishment specialises in catering for the tour groups making their compulsory stop at the Prehistoric Mural. Despite this, the food is acceptable and the portions generous. Pride of place on the menu goes to "puerco asado estilo Viñales", pork soaked in a special marinade and grilled. Service is more attentive once the coach parties have departed.
Le Palenque, 3km north of the village, at the end of the Cueva de San Miguel, ☎ (82) 93-6280. 8am-5pm. Visitors braving the twists and turns of this cave eventually come to this open-air restaurant, hidden away in a spot which was once a refuge for escaped slaves. The speciality is chicken flavoured with citronella.

HAVING A DRINK

Bars – There are no bars as such in the valley but all the hotels and restaurants listed are good places to relax and order your favourite drink.

Discos – The **Cueva de San Miguel** is a discotheque and bar set up inside a cave, 3.5km north of Viñales village ☎ (8) 9-3203. Open daily 9pm-2am.

OTHER THINGS TO DO

Excursions – The valley has a network of paths and tracks suitable for walkers. Further information available at Las Jazmines and La Ermita. The guided walk from La Ermita introduces visitors to local farmers and gives them the opportunity to sample local crops, from coconuts to oranges and guavas.

Outdoor pursuits – Horse riding can be arranged by the hotels or by enquiring in the village.
The area's caves can be explored in the company of a guide. The hotels will make arrangements.

PINAR DEL RÍO★

Capital of Pinar del Río Province
Vuelta Abajo Region
180km from Havana – Pop 120 000

Not to be missed
Sampling Guayabita liqueur.
Inspecting a cigar factory.
And remember...
Staying overnight is quieter and cooler in the Viñales Valley.
The best time to visit the Vuelta Abajo area is during the tobacco harvest.

Tobacco is king in this area, since it is here that the leaves are grown which are turned into Cuba's world-famous cigars.

For visitors coming directly from the bustle of Havana, Pinar del Río has an instant charm, especially in the early evening when friends and neighbours gather around the porches of its low-slung, pastel-coloured dwellings after a long day spent in the *vegas* (tobacco fields) or in the local factories.

On the other hand, after the peace and quiet of the Viñales Valley, the rapidly expanding provincial capital may seem a hyperactive sort of place, with its hordes of young people dashing around on bicycles and propositioning visitors with offers of every imaginable kind, from cheap cigars to bed and breakfast at a seriously improbable price. But if it all gets too much you can always retreat to Viñales or move on towards the Vuelta Abajo tobacco-growing area.

Exploring the town
Allow 2hr

Calle José Martí

The main street of Pinar del Río runs east-west through the city from the end of the *autopista* from Havana. Always bustling with activity, it is here or in the adjoining streets that most of the town's shops and tourist attractions are to be found.

Set among the arcaded buildings lining the street are two structures with some claim to architectural distinction.

The **Palacio Guasch★** stands on the corner of Calle José Martí and Calle Commandante Pinares close to the end of the *autopista*. In a strange mixture of Gothic and Moorish styles, the palace was built in 1917 for the wealthy Doctor Francisco Guasch. It now houses the **Museo de Ciencias Naturales Sandalio de Noda** *(9am-4.30pm; 9am-11.30am Sundays; closed Mondays. Admission charge)*. Like most of Cuba's natural history musuems, this establishment has displays on local plant and animal life but its unique feature is a collection of dinosaur sculptures in the courtyard.

Three blocks further on the same side of the road at the corner with Calle Colón is the **Teatro José Jacinto Milanés**, a city institution and one of the most important theatres in the whole country. Built entirely of wood in 1883, and inspired by the Teatro Sauto at Matanzas, it can seat an audience of 540 people.

Beyond the theatre at José Martí No.58 on the corner of Calle Isabel Rubio and Calle Colón is the **Museo Provincial de Historia** (*9am-4pm, 9am-1pm Sundays; closed Mondays*) the regional history museum, dealing with native life before the Conquest, the history of Pinar del Río from the time of its foundation in 1774, and the Wars of Independence.

Products of Pinar del Río

The city is famous for two main products, tobacco and guayabita liqueur, and guided tours are available around the places where they are made.

Guayabita is made from a locally-growing fruit of the same name, smaller but otherwise not dissimilar to guava. The fruit is fermented with rum and spices and distilled into a liqueur available in both sweet and dry versions. Unique to Pinar del Río, it is made in the **Casa Garay** (*8.30am-4.30pm; closed weekends. No charge*) located on Calle Isabel Rubio between Calle Frank País and Calle Ceferino Fernández. Visits to the factory are rounded off by a tasting.

Since 1961 the **Fábrica de Tabacos Francisco Donatién*** (*7.30am-4.30pm, 7.30am-11.30am Saturdays; closed Sundays. Admission charge*) has been housed in the old prison building at Calle Antonio Maceo No.157 close to the Plaza de la Independencia, and is the town's most important tobacco factory. The most fascinating part of the tour is the sight of the *torcedores* side by side at their wooden workbenches effortlessly rolling one identical cigar after another (*see page 39*). A shop sells the various cigars produced by the factory.

The Vuelta Abajo*

42km there and back – Allow 2hrs

Of Cuba's four main tobacco-growing regions it is the Pinar del Río area whose soil and climate make it exceptionally suitable for growing the leaves used to make the country's very best cigars (*see page 38*). The tobacco plantations which have helped make the reputation of the Havana cigar occupy a triangular area to the southwest of the provincial capital.

The "vegas" – *Leave Pinar del Río by Calle José Marti, turning left on Calle Isabel Rubio beyond the Museo Provincial de Historia. Turn left after 13km on to a road leading to the village of San Luis (8km) and after a further 8km to San Juan y Martínez.*

The Vuelta Abajo tobacco-growing area is triangular in shape, its corners marked by the villages of **San Luis** and **San Juan y Martínez** and by Pinar del Río. The tobacco plantations change constantly with the changing seasons. In summer the fields are left bare while the red soil recovers its fertility, then in winter, after reseeding, many of them disappear beneath vast canopies of protective white muslin which protects the crop from excessive sunlight. Finally the large fleshy leaves are ready for the harvest, the best time of the year to visit the area, not only for the spectacle of the *vegueros* working in the fields but also for the chance to find out at first hand something about the painstaking preparation of the material which goes into a fine cigar.

■ **Visiting a tobacco plantation** – *Shortly before entering San Juan y Martínez turn right into the entrance of the Despalillo Vivero Plantation (Open 7am-midday/1pm-4.30pm; closed Sundays and every other Saturday and during the first half of August and January. Admission charge).*

How the tobacco leaves are brought from the fields, hung up to dry, and then sorted ready for dispatch to the factory (in Cuba or abroad) is all explained in this fascinating tour of a working plantation.

Making the most of Pinar del Río

COMING AND GOING

Western Cuba is poorly served by public transport and use of a car is highly advisable.

By air – The **Aerotaxi** company flies once a week between Pinar del Río and Nueva Gerona, the capital of the Island of Youth. Pinar del Río's **aeropuerto Alvaro Barba** ☎ (82) 6-3248 is 3km to the north of the city centre via the Carretera Central.

By train – One train a day (sometimes every other day) to Havana (6hr) leaves from the **Estación de Ferrocarriles** ☎ 2272, Calle Ferrocarril between Calle Rafael Ferro and Calle Comandante Pinares three blocks south of the Palacio Guasch.

By bus – Run by **Viazul**, the only reliable bus service to Havana calls at Pinar del Río (Calle Colón) every other day on its way from Viñales (3hr journey, fare US$11). In theory, but only in theory, there are 3 services a day to Havana from the nearby **Terminal de Ómnibus**.

By taxi – Some colectivos are ready to pick up foreign passengers despite the risk of a fine. They can usually be found at the bus station.

GETTING AROUND

The city centre can be explored on foot but a vehicle is essential for getting out into the surrounding countryside.

By taxi – The official taxi company **Turistaxi** has a stand in front of the Hotel Pinar del Río and provides a 24-hour service. ☎ (82) 78-078.

Car hire – There is a **Transautos** office ☎ (82) 5071/76 in the Hotel Pinar del Río and a **Havanautos** office, ☎ (82) 78-015, in the nearby car park.

ADDRESS BOOK

Tourist Information – The hotels catering for foreign visitors will provide information on the town and the surrounding area.

Banks / Currency exchange – The Hotel Pinar del Río will change foreign money. **Banco Financiero Internacional** on Calle Rosario No.2 between Calle Martí and Calle Gómez.

Post office / Telephone – Use the facilities at the Hotel Pinar del Río

Health – The Hotel Pinar del Río has a medical unit. 24-hour **pharmacy** on the corner of Calle Martí and Calle Isabel Rubio.

Servicupet service stations – **Siboney**, Carretera Central 88, Reparto 10 de octubre, 3km from the city centre in the Havana direction; **Oro Negro**, not far from the town on the Carretera Central Km 87; **América**, Calle Rafael Morales No.238 on the road south out of town.

WHERE TO STAY

Private accommodation can be an attractive alternative to the somewhat rudimentary comforts of Pinar del Río's central hotels.

Between US$15-20
Tebelio Robaina, Calle Colón No.106 between Calle Mariana Grajales and Calle Delicias, ☎ (82) 2280. ⌂ 🖂 Hotel standard room, with privacy and in a good location. Superior breakfast.

Leila Cheche, Calle Celestino Pacheco No.115 between Ignacio Agramonte and Calle Roldán, ☎ (82) 2613 (next door), 🛏 🍽 On the eastern side of the town not far from the centre, this is an attractive house with welcoming hosts. The rooms are quiet and well kept.

Under US$30

Villa Aguas Claras, Carretera de Viñales km7.5, ☎ (82) 98-427 – 100 rooms. 🛏 🍽 🅿 ✗ ⚓ In a parkland setting on the edge of town in the direction of the Viñales Valley, this is the best place to stay in Pinar del Río. Its 50 chalets are simply furnished but well maintained, the surroundings are attractive, the staff friendly, and charges reasonable.

Between US$25-50

Hotel Pinar del Río, Calle José Martí (no number), ☎ (82) 5070/74, Fax 4449 – 136 rm. 🛏 🍽 🅿 TV ✗ ⚓ CC Car hire, bureau de change, medical services. The Pinar del Río is an unmissable reinforced concrete structure on the way into town from the autopista. Basic rooms but good range of visitor facilities

EATING OUT

Pinar del Río only has a few restaurants but there are a number of paladares as well as several pizza stands under the arcades along Calle José Martí.

Under US$10

Nuestra Casa, Calle Colón altos (south side) between Calle Virtudes and Calle Vandama. Generous main course served on a terrace.

Around US$10

Rodrigo, Calle Colón No.167 between Calle Mariana Grajales and Calle Labra. Tasty regular menu served in a prettily panelled room.

Casa 1890, on the corner of Calle Rafael Ferro and Calle Sol, not far from the station. An attractive place to eat a reliable "pollo con queso y jamón" (chicken with cheese and ham) to a musical accompaniment.

Between US$10-20

Rumayor, Carretera de Viñales km1, ☎ (82) 63-007. Midday-10pm. 2km from the city centre on the road leading to the Viñales Valley, this restaurant occupies a thatched building with a garden

sloping down to a river. Inside, there is a welcoming atmosphere and decor featuring African masks. The Rumayor's reputation owes a lot to the house speciality of "pollo ahumado", chicken smoked over a fire using wood chips from the guava tree.

OTHER THINGS TO DO

Bars – The garden of the **Rumayor** is a quiet and pleasant place.

Concerts – The **Casa de la Música** close to the Hotel Italia on the corner of Calle Medina and Calle Antonio Rubio stages occasional concerts of traditional music.

Discotheques – Disco dancing at the **Rumayor** following the evening show. Alternatively at the **Hotel Pinar del Río** from 9pm-3am except Monday (US$2).

Cabaret – The delightful grounds of the **Rumayor** are the setting every evening (except Mondays) at 11pm (US$5) for music and cabaret in the open air.

Excursions – All the hotels in Pinar del Río offer organised trips into the surrounding area, especially to the Viñales Valley.

Close to the village of San Juan y Martínez, the **Centro experimental de cultura de tabaco** carries out research into new varieties of tobacco. Permission to visit can be obtained from Cubatabaco, Calle O'Reilly No.104 between Calle Tacón and Calle Mercaderes, Habana Vieja, ☎ (82) 62-5463, Fax (82) 33-8214.

Outdoor pursuits – The Villa Aguas Claras can arrange horseback riding. The **Centro de artes visuales**, Calle Luz Sardival between Calle Martí and Calle Maceo puts on exhibitions of contemporary art.

SHOPPING GUIDE

Market – Calle Rafael Ferro, near the station. 8am-6pm, 8am-2pm Sunday.

Rum – Casa del Ron, Calle Maceo No.161.

Art and crafts – Close to the station at the corner of Calle Rafael Ferro and Calle Frank Pais is the **Palacio de la Artesanía**, with a good range of local craft products (9am-5pm).

GUANAHACABIBES PENINSULA★

Pinar del Río province
125km from Pinar del Río
See map p 158

Not to be missed
Scuba-diving off María la Gorda.
The peninsula's wonderfully deserted beaches.

And remember...
Allow 4hr for the drive from Pinar del Río.
Fill up with petrol at Isabel Rubio.
Don't drive at night.
A 4-wheel drive vehicle is best for exploring the National Park.

See map p 158

At the westernmost end of Cuba, the two-pronged Guanahacabibes peninsula protrudes into the Yucatán Channel between the Gulf of Mexico to the north and the Caribbean to the south. It is a remote area, with deserted beaches and a National Park which is a designated UNESCO **Biosphere Reserve**. The only resort of any kind is at María la Gorda, with a beach that tempts many visitors to stay a day or three longer than they may have intended to.

From Pinar del Río drive first to San Juan y Martínez then continue towards Isabel Rubio.

Once past the Vuelta Abajo area the tourist trail is left behind for a part of Cuba still unused to foreign visitors. It's much more difficult to get around here than in other parts of the country, with a network of poorly maintained roads which are generously studded with potholes (the road to Maria la Gorda is an exception). Driving is made even more hazardous by a whole array of obstacles, including sheep and horses grazing nonchalantly by the roadside and cows dozing in the centre of the carriageway, quite unfazed by the sound of your horn. Closer to the coast, the road surface is littered with crabs, forcing drivers and cyclists into slalom-like avoiding action.

20km short of Isabel Rubio a huge sign points left to Playa Bailén

■ **Playa Bailén** – 8km from the main road, this beach has been developed for use by Cubans, and visitors from abroad are not allowed to stay in the chalets along the shoreline. This alone gives it a special atmosphere, though the beach has neither the lovely fine sand nor the ultra-clear waters of the north coast. What foreign tourists there are tend to come for the day from Pinar del Río and leave early in the evening before the little midges known as *gegenes* start to bite (their sting can cause unpleasant itching).

Return to the Carretera Central and continue for 15km to Isabel Rubio, turning left 200m beyond the Servicupet service station in order to stay on the main road (the turn to the right leads to the Villa Laguna Grande). Carry on for 26km to La Fé then continue towards Manuel Lazo. After El Cayuco (11km) take the road towards La Bajada, 32km further on. At the checkpoint, turn left and follow the shoreline route for 14km.

■ **María la Gorda**★★ – The interminable drive is finally rewarded by what at first seems like a mirage, a long and splendid beach lined with coconut palms. This is María la Gorda (Big Mary), a diving resort on the Bahía de Corrientes (Bay of Currents). The place owes its name to a large lady who either came from

Western Cuba

Venezuela or was the daughter of a Spanish sea-captain. Whatever her origin, she is supposed to have learnt useful skills on board ship which she then put into practice here, procuring female companions for passing pirates.

With its unspoilt shore running for miles along the turquoise sea, Maria la Gorda is an idyllic place, one of the remotest spots in the whole of Cuba and ideal for anyone wanting to get away from the crowds. Diving is the main attraction, but it's just as suitable for families looking for a quiet holiday.

■ **Guanahacabibes National Park** – *Entry permit from the Hotel María la Gorda.* The National Park stretching out along the peninsula is home to numerous species of animal including deer and wild pigs. Most of it is wild and remote, particularly the marshy northern shore with its mangrove swamps, but in the south there is a track running parallel to the shore.

From María la Gorda return to the checkpoint at La Bajada and continue for 70km towards the tip of the peninsula.

All along the way are the caves which were the last refuge of the native people during the Spanish Conquest.

Cuba's westernmost point is marked by the **San Antonio lighthouse**, but the road continues another 4.5km to **Playa las Tumbas***, a stunning and almost completely deserted beach overlooking the Yucatán Channel.

Making the most of Guanahacabibes

COMING AND GOING

This remote and undeveloped area is only accessible by car. In the rainy season hire of a four-wheel drive vehicle is advisable.

ADDRESS BOOK

Servicupet service station – The only filling station in the area is the one at Isabel Rubio halfway between Pinar del Río and María la Gorda.

WHERE TO STAY AND WHERE TO EAT

Under US$30

Villa María la Gorda, Centro Internacional de Buceo, Península de Guanahacabibes, ☎ (874) 3121 – 15 rm. ☏ ⊟ [TV] ⚲ This tourist complex consists of a series of chalets overlooking the magnificent beach. The rooms are acceptable. The little resort caters for families as well as for scuba-divers. There are no restaurants anywhere in the vicinity and

buffet-style full board is compulsory; breakfast around US$5, main meals US$15.

Accommodation should be reserved in advance through Marsub, Calle B 310 between Calle 13 and Calle 15, Vedado, Ciudad de la Habana, ☎ (7) 33-3055/60, Fax 33 3481.

Villa Laguna Grande, take the right turn after leaving Isabel Rubio towards Sandino, then turn left at Bolívar – 12 chalets. ☏ ⊟ [TV] 🐎 Sited on the banks of a large trout-stocked lake. Bird-watching, bike-riding, horses for hire. Enquire at Islazul, Martí No.127, Pinar del Río, ☎ (82) 2303.

OTHER THINGS TO DO

Excursions – The biosphere reserve at the far end of the peninsula has fascinating plant and animal life.

Sports and recreation – María la Gorda is above all an international diving centre. Equipment can be rented.

THE COAST ROAD★
FROM LA FÉ TO HAVANA
Pinar del Río and Havana provinces
380km partly on poorly maintained roads
See map p 158

Remember...
Check tyres and fill up with petrol before leaving Isabel Rubio.
Set out early in the morning and reckon on a long day's drive.
The only visitor facilities are at Viñales or on Cayo Levisa (see p 166).

The road along the coast to the north of the Guaniguanico range passes through a succession of tiny settlements hidden among sugar plantations, rice fields and pastureland. Every now and again it turns inland to run along the foot of the mountains where the landscape is dotted with the palm-leaf roofs of lonely *bohíos*. Elsewhere it drops down into little fishing villages where local boatmen may well offer to take you out to a completely deserted island. Just visible a few miles off the coast is the line of *cayos* which make up the **Archipelago de los Colorados.** A whole day is necessary in order to really savour this succession of landscapes between sea and mountain, but visitors who are pressed for time can easily cut the journey short and rejoin the main road and motorway by crossing the cordillera *(see p 160)*.

From La Fé drive 16km along the Carretera Central and then turn left towards Bolivar (see previous page for the Villa Laguna Grande). Before reaching Bolivar turn right for 4km on an unsurfaced road towards El Batey, turning left towards Mantua when this road comes to an end. Shortly after leaving Mantua the road divides; take the road on the left in the direction of Las Guásimas and keep straight ahead.

70km beyond Mantua and 3km short of the village of Santa Lucía a road under construction leads to a cayo. Note that the road sign can only be seen when coming from Santa Lucía.

■ **Cayo Jutías★** – Now that it is linked to the mainland, this island is likely to become a major tourist attraction, but in the meantime its mangrove swamps and idyllic sandy beach (where you can have lunch) are a haven of perfect peace.

■ **Puerto Esperanza** – 40km from Santa Lucía, this little coastal town with its harbour is easily accessible from Viñales, only 25km inland.

The coast road east of Puerto Esperanza is in very poor condition. Avoid it by detouring inland towards Viñales, then after 15km turn left at San Vincente towards La Palma.

In La Palma go towards Palma Rubia and turn left after 23km towards Cayo Paraíso. The landing stage for the ferry to Cayo Levisa is 3km beyond a banana plantation.

■ **Cayo Levisa★** – The island is served by a daily ferry *(departs 11am, returns 5pm, return fare US$15, US$25 with lunch)*. Surrounded by coral reefs offering excellent scuba diving, it also has tempting sandy beaches and a solitary hotel *(see p 167)*.

Back on the mainland, the badly maintained road leads eastwards through sugar plantations and cattle ranches, giving occasional glimpses of the attractive and deeply indented coastline. Some 95km from Palma Rubia the road passes close to the port of **Mariel**, the scene in 1980 of a massive exodus of refugees *(see p 30)*.

5km after the turn to Mariel you join the autopista. Havana is 55km away.

B. Brillion/MICHELIN

On the beach at Varadero

THE NORTH COAST

The *Via Blanca* eastward out of Havana takes its name from the white sand of the beaches stretching out along this Cuban Riviera. But there is much more to this part of the country than swimming and lazing in the sun. As well as jet-skis, millionaires' villas and ultra-modern hotels, there are horse-drawn carriages rattling past the faded houses of old colonial cities, and as well as raucous discotheques, the sound of traditional music and the songs of Cuban "troubadours".

Dazzling white sand, brilliant blue sea...rivalled only by the gorgeous palette of colours in the fertile Yumurí River valley.

THE EASTERN BEACHES★

Havana Province
Between 18km and 40km from Havana
30min by car to Santa Maria del Mar

Not to be missed
Riding along the beach on horseback.

And remember...
The best places to stay are Santa Maria del Mar and Guanabo.
Don't leave personal possessions unattended on the beach.

The series of lovely beaches to the east of Havana are called the *circuito azul* (literally Blue Circuit) and are very popular with the citizens of the capital. At least they were, until the "Special Period" made getting there much more difficult. But the beaches are lively enough, especially at weekends, when people manage to get to them in one way or another, some by bus, some by bike, others by hitching a lift. For visitors from abroad, the Eastern Beaches are a good place to spend a few days relaxing in the sun or simply to escape the city for a while. They can also be visited on the way further east to Varadero.

Leave Havana by the harbour tunnel and follow the Via Monumental to the roundabout (on the left, Calle Martí leads to Cojimar, see page 143). 2km further on turn left on to the Via Blanca. After 6km the road crosses the Rio Bacuranao where the first of the beaches is located.

The delightful little cove at the mouth of the Rio Bacuranao is only 18km from the city. Its beach, **Playa Bacuranao**, is graced by a solitary hotel.

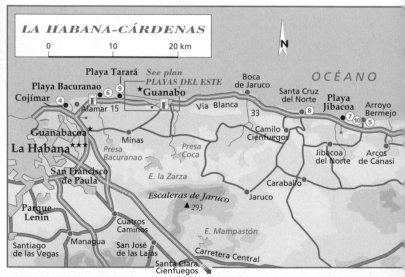

The North Coast

On the left, 3km further along the Via Blanca by the little beach of **Playa Tarará**, are the buildings and recreational facilities of the **Ciudad de los pioneros José Martí** (Pioneer Village). This is where children who have done especially well at school are sent for their holidays. In a reminder of the fraternal links which existed between Cuba and the former Soviet Union, the village continues to welcome children affected by radiation from the Chernobyl disaster.

Beyond Tarará there are four beaches spread along a 10km stretch of coastline, all with a range of tourist facilities.

The sand dunes at **Playa el Mégano** continue westward as far as **Santa Maria del Mar★**, a magnet for foreign tourists (mostly Italian). Santa Maria has a good number of hotels, most of them close to the broad beach with its coconut palms. On the far side of the mouth of the Itabo river is **Playa Boca Ciega** followed by **Guanabo★**, a resort catering more for holiday-making Cubans than for visitors from abroad. The town museum (*9am-4pm, 9am-midday Sunday. Admission charge*) at the corner of Calle 504 and Avenida 5 is limited in size and mostly devoted to natural history, but it organises interesting walks around the local nature reserves with good birdwatching opportunities.

From the Eastern Beaches to Matanzas

The first of a number of oil installations appears about 3km east of Guanabo and the Via Blanca is lined with them as far as Santa Cruz del Norte. On the road out of Santa Cruz is the distillery which produces the **Havana Club** brand of rum (*some hotels organise a visit*). A short distance to the south of the town is the Central Camilo Cienfuegos, a huge sugar-mill built by the Hershey Chocolate Co. of Pennsylvania, US which was of course nationalised soon after the Revolution. Hershey's also built Cuba's only electric railway, the line running along the coast between Havana and Matanzas.

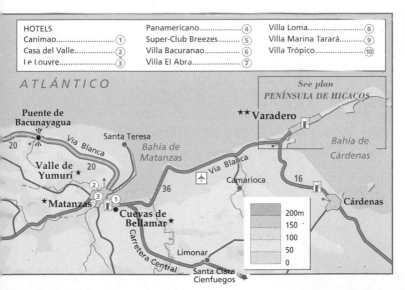

HOTELS		
Canimao............................①	Panamericano..................④	Villa Loma...........................⑧
Casa del Valle..................②	Super-Club Breezes..........⑤	Villa Marina Tarará...........⑨
Le Louvre..........................③	Villa Bacuranao................⑥	Villa Trópico......................⑩
	Villa El Abra.....................⑦	

The main road continues for 6km to where a turning to the right leads to **Playa Jibacoa**, a beach famous for its coral reef.

The Bacunayagua Bridge 20km beyond Jibacoa straddles the boundary between Havana Province and Matanzas Province.

The Bacunayagua Bridge, 110m above the fertile **Yumuri Valley⋆**, is the highest in Cuba. Many people stop to admire the **view⋆**, which takes in both the valley (to the right) and the ocean (to the left), and is especially alluring at twilight. 20km or so beyond the bridge the harbour town of Matanzas comes into view.

Making the most of the Eastern Beaches

COMING AND GOING
The only reliable way of getting from Havana to the Eastern Beaches is by car.

Bus – Havana is linked to Guanabo by service no.400 departing from the corner of Calle Egido and Calle Gloria.

Taxi – Private taxis charge about US$25 for a whole day trip from Havana.

Boat – The **Marina Tarará** (Puertosol Company) has 25 berths with water, fuel and electricity link-ups.

GETTING AROUND
The best way of getting around is on foot or by hiring a bike.

Taxi – Official taxis outside most of the hotels in Santa Maria del Mar.

Car hire – *Havanautos* and *Transautos* have desks in the larger hotels.

Bicycle and moped hire – Information from the Hotel Tropicoco.

ADDRESS BOOK

Tourist information – Most of the larger hotels have an information desk.

Banks / Currency exchange – *Banco de Crédito y Commercio*, 5ta Avenida between Calle 470 and Calle 472, or at a hotel.

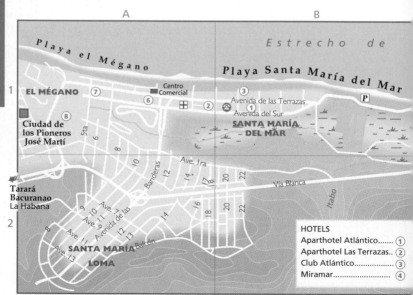

Post Office / Telephone – *Centro de telecommunicaciones* (B1), Avenida de las Terrazas/Calles 10 and 11, Santa María del Mar. Open 8am-6.30pm.

Health – *Clínica Internacional* (A1), Avenida de las Terrazas No. 36, Santa María del Mar. ☎ (96) 2689.

Servicupet service station – *Bacuranao*, Via Blanca kilometre mark 15.5, on the road into Bacuranao.

WHERE TO STAY

The majority of the area's hotels are in Santa María del Mar, but private accommodation is usually easier to find in Guanabo.

• Playa Bacuranao
(See the map on page 178)
Between US$30-50
***Villa Bacuranao*,** Via Blanca Km 15.5, Celimar, ☎ 65-6332 – 51rm. 🍴 🖳 ✏ 📺 ✕ 🛋 🏊 The accommodation consists of a number of chalets close to an attractive small beach in a quiet location.

• Playa Tarará
Between US$50-100
***Villa Marina Tarará*,** Via Blanca Km 19, Tarará, ☎ (7) 97-1462, Fax (7) 94-

1333. 🍴 🖳 📺 ✕ 🛋 🏊 ♨ 🍸 💳 Private development of 60 two or three-roomed houses with cooking facilities. Close to the beach and very quiet.

• Playa Santa María del Mar (A1, B1)
Around US$50
***Aparthotel Atlántico*,** Avenida de las Terrazas/Calle 11 and Calle 12, Santa María del Mar, ☎ (7) 97-1494, Fax (7) 97-1203 – 65 apartments. 🍴 🖳 ✏ 📺 ✕ 🛋 🏊 🍸 💳 Bureau de change. One to three-room apartments 100 metres from the beach some with cooking facilities. 1970s furnishings, but spacious and with balconies, some with sea views.

***Villa Mégano*,** Via Blanca Km 17, Santa María del Mar, ☎ (7) 97-1610, Fax (7) 97-1624 – 61rm. 🍴 🖳 ✏ ✕ 🛋 🍸 💳 500 metres from the El Mégano beach, opposite the José Martí Pioneer Village. Well-shaded surroundings and pleasant atmosphere. Rooms have been renovated.

***Hotel Tropicoco Beach Club*,** junction of Avenida de las Terrazas and Avenida del Sur, ☎ (7) 97-1371, Fax (7) 97-1389 – 188rm. 🍴 🖳 ✏ 📺

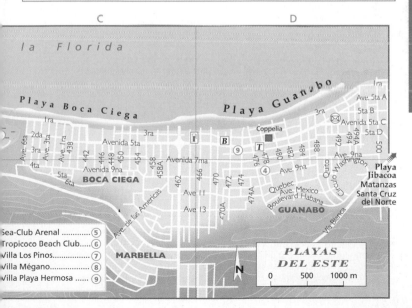

PLAYAS
DEL ESTE
0   500   1000 m

✗ ⚒ ⚘ ⚒ CC Car hire, bureau de change, clinic. Close to the beach, this large 1970s structure boasts a foyer like an airport terminal. The rooms are basic. Some have seaward-facing balconies. Non-residents can use the hotel's numerous facilities.

Between US$50 and US$100

Aparthotel Las Terrazas, Avenida de las Terrazas/Calle 10 and Calle Rotonda, Santa Maria del Mar, ☎ (7) 97-1344, Fax (7) 97-1316 – 89 apartments. ✻ ▤ ✎ ✗ ⚒ ⚘ CC Bureau de change. Similar facilities to Aparthotel Atlántico.

Club Atlántico, junction of Avenida de las Terrazas and Calle 11, Santa Maria del Mar, ☎ (7) 97-1085/7, Fax (7) 96-1532 – 92rm. ✻ ▤ ✎ TV ✗ ⚒ ⚘ CC Car hire, bureau de change. Not to be confused with the aparthotel with the same name. Good value, but often reserved for the exclusive use of Italian tour groups.

Around US$100

Sea-Club Arenal, Laguna de la Boca Ciega, Santa María del Mar, ☎ (7) 97-1272 Fax (7) 97-1287 – 169rm. ✻ ✎ TV ✗ ⚒ ⚘ ⚒ CC A fully-renovated hotel complex in the jewel-like setting of the lagoon and linked to the beach by a wooden bridge. Attractive rooms and pleasant service.

Over US$100

Villa Los Pinos, between Avenida de las Terrazas and Calles 4 and 5, Santa Maria del Mar, ☎ (7) 97-1361, Fax (7) 97-1524 – 70rm. ✻ ▤ ✎ TV ✗ CC Two and three-bedroom villas, some with a small swimming pool, spread over a wide area divided by roads. Rates vary with distance from the beach and level of service provided. Relatively expensive but reasonable value.

- **Playa Guanabo** (D1-2)

There is plenty of private accommodation in Playa Guanabo, but the price is the same as at the hotels listed below.

Under US$30

Villa Playa Hermosa, between 5th Avenue and Calles 472 and 474, Guanabo, ☎ (7) 96-2774 – 25rm. ✻ ▤ TV ✗ ⚒ One to three-room chalets in a garden setting a short distance from the beach. The accommodation is very basic but extremely cheap.

Hotel Miramar, junction of Avenida 7B and Calle 478, Guanabo, ☎ (7) 96-2507 – 24rm. ✻ ▤ TV ✗ ⚒ A small hotel on rising ground at some distance from the beach.

- **Playa Jibacoa** (See map page 178)

Under US$20

Villa El Abra, Playa Jibacoa, Santa Cruz del Norte, ☎ (692) 83-344 – 87 chalets. ✻ ▤ ✗ ⚒ ⚘ ⚒ ⚞ This camp-site has a very attractive setting and its straightforward but completely renovated facilities offer good value for money.

Under US$30

Villa Loma, Playa Jibacoa, Zona 6, Santa Cruz del Norte, ☎ (692) 83-316 – 39rm. ✻ ▤ ✎ TV ✗ ⚒ Bureau de change. 14 stone-built chalets in a garden setting overlooking the beach.

Over US$100

Super-Club Breezes, Playa Arrojo Bermejo, Vía Blanca Km 60, Santa Cruz del Norte, ☎ (692) 85-122, Fax (692) 85-150 – 143rm. ✻ ▤ ✎ TV ✗ ⚒ ⚘ ⚄ ⚞ CC Luxury tourist complex hidden away between hills and beach to the west of Jibacoa. Wide range of facilities.

Vila Trópico, Playa Jibacoa, Via Blanca Km 60, ☎ (7) 3305657, Fax (7) 33-7960 – 154rm. Identical conditions and facilities as above.

WHERE TO EAT

The Eastern Beaches have a very limited choice of places to eat. Most people make do with a quick meal from a beach kiosk or hotel restaurant. There are some good "paladares" in Guanabo.

- **Playa Santa Maria del Mar**

Between US$10-20

Mi Cayito, Avenida Las Terrazas, Laguna, Santa María del Mar, ☎ (7) 97-1339. 10am-10pm. Close to the Hotel Arenal between the lagoon and the beach. Sailing club and busy open-air restaurant with seafood specialities.

- **Playa Boca Ciega**

Between US$10-20

Casa del Pescador, Avenida 5 between Calles 440 and 442. Midday-11pm. excellent fish dishes.

• Playa Guanabo

Under 10US$
Piccolo Paladar, Avenida 5 between Calle 502 and Calle 504. Produce from this charming market garden finds its way directly on to diners' plates. The vegetables and the pork are the best choices.

Paladar Don Peppo, Calle 482 No. 503 between Avenida 5 and Avenida 5D (D1), ☎ (96) 4229. A simply decorated ground-floor room opening on to the street. As well as fish specialities, there are tasty pizzas.

Mirabel, Avenida 5 between Calle 480 and Calle 504. Creole and Italian specialities served in the open air.

Maeda, Calle Quebec No. 115 between Calle 476 and Calle 478. Grilled fish and other seafood specialities served either inside or in the garden.

El Brocal, corner of Avenida 5 and Calle 500. Lovely old wooden house with a terrace overlooking the road. Meat and fish dishes.

HAVING A DRINK

Discotheques – A number of hotels have discotheques and most of them organise dance evenings.

Guanabo Club, Calle 468 between Avenida 13 and Avenida 15, Guanabo (D2), Open 10pm-4am. US$5 per couple. On the high ground above Guanabo, this is an open-air disco patronised by local people as well as tourists.

Via Blanca, corner of 5ta Avenida and Calle 486, Guanabo. Nightly 9pm-2am. The musical theme changes nightly.

OTHER THINGS TO DO

Excursions – The hotel tourist offices run excursions to Havana as well as to other destinations in Cuba.

Outdoor pursuits – Most of the hotels have some facilities for water-sports. Scuba diving, fishing trips and other boat trips are run from the **Marina Tarará** and the **Villa El Abra**.
Tennis courts at the **Aparthotel Atlántico**, the **Hotel Tropicoco**, and at the **Atlántico Club**.

SHOPPING

Market – Calle 496 between 5ta Avenida and 5ta B Avenida.

Ice cream – Las Almendras is the local equivalent of Havana's Coppelia.

Sunday at the seaside

L. Sraney/RAPHO

MATANZAS ★

Capital of Matanzas Province
Pop 120 000
98km from Havana and 42km from Varadero by the Via Blanca
See map page 179

Not to be missed
The Ernest Triolet Pharmacy.
A drink at the Café Atenas in Plaza de la Vigía.
The caves at Bellamar.

The impression many visitors get of Matanzas as they hurry through on their way between Havana and Varadero is that of a modern harbour town built on a wide bay. But Matanzas has more to offer than the sight of an occasional oil tanker putting into port; its historic centre has a number of fine old colonial houses with wrought-iron trimmings, evidence of past prosperity and a high level of culture which gave it the now somewhat redundant name of the "Cuban Athens". The city has also been called the "Cuban Venice", and the presence of water in the form of the Rivers Yumurí and San Juan does lend it a certain charm. The rivers divide Matanzas into three distinct quarters, Versalles to the north, the city centre in the middle, and Pueblo Nuevo to the south. Practically all the city's historic sites are concentrated in the area defined by Calle 79 to the north, the San Juan River to the south, by the bay to the east and Calle 290 to the west.

A prosperous place

Matanzas was founded in 1693 on the site of an old abattoir, hence its name whose literal meaning is "slaughter". The town's location on Cuba's biggest bay meant that it soon became the most important economic centre in the country. Coffee and tobacco were already being exported in the 18C but Matanzas became famous in the early 19C as the capital of both the sugar and slave trades. The wealthy town also attracted numerous artists and writers as well as scientists, and its intellectual and cultural life was second to none. It was the heartland of Afro-Cuban music, as well as being the cradle of the *danzón*. But the city's days of glory gradually faded, and a kind of revival only came after the Revolution when the deep waters of the bay sheltered many a Soviet freighter and oil tanker. Matanzas is still Cuba's fourth largest port, but following the collapse of the Soviet Union the level of activity is much reduced.

The town
Allow 2hr

The Via Blanca runs through the northeastern part of Matanzas. At the waterfront, it turns right and becomes Calle 61. Plaza de la Vigía is three blocks beyond the bridge over the River Yumurí.

Cars, carts and carriages fill the old streets of the city centre, and the main road traffic trying to force its way through is reduced to a crawl.

Plaza de la Vigía ★

Close to the waterfront at the point where the town was originally founded, the plaza is laid out at the meeting point of several streets. There is no garden in the middle, and local people prefer to take their ease in the adjoining Parque de la Libertad. But the **Café Atenas** *(See Making the Most of Matanzas)* with its bougainvilleas makes a good vantage point from which to survey the buildings around the plaza. In the middle of the plaza is a statue of the Unknown Soldier, erected to commemorate those who died in the War of Independence of 1895.

To the east of the plaza is the **Teatro Sauto** *(Open 9am-4.30pm; 9am-midday Saturdays; 2pm-5pm Sundays; closed Mondays. Admission charge)*. Built in 1862, this splendid neo-Classical edifice was the model for two other famous theatres in Cuba, the Jacinto Milanés in Pinar del Río and the Terry in Cienfuegos. Originally called the Esteban, the Teatro Sauto was designed by the Italian theatre architect Daniele dell'Aglio who was also responsible for the **frescoes** in the main auditorium. The theatre gained its present name early in the 20C in honour of Ambrosio de la Concepción Sauto y Node, a prominent local pharmacist and politician. Many famous figures have graced the stage here, among them the actress Sarah Bernhardt in 1887 and the ballerina Anna Pavlova in 1915. Performances generally take place at the weekend.

Just to the north of the theatre is a prominent bright blue building, the **Palacio del Junco**. Dating from 1840, this splendid neo-Colonial residence is now the home of the **Museo Histórico Provincial★** *(Open 10am-midday and 1pm-5pm; 8.30am-midday Sunday; closed Mondays. Admission charge)*, which traces the history of the area from pre-Columbian times to the Revolution with an array of objects including furniture and old documents. The town's 19C role as sugar capital and centre of the slave trade is tellingly evoked by the collection of tools and instruments of torture.

The road opposite the Palacio del Junco runs down to the San Juan River which is crossed by the **Calixto García Bridge**. On the right before the bridge is the **Parque de los Bomberos**. This is the barracks of the Matanzas fire brigade, centred on a fine neo-Classical building. Old fire engines and a collection of photographs recall the past exploits of the city's firemen.

Go two blocks along Calle 83 (formerly Calle Milanés) which starts between the Teatro Sauto and the Palacio del Junco.

On the corner of Calle 282 and Plaza de la Iglesia stands the oldest church in Matanzas, the **Cathedral of San Carlos Borromeo** *(Open 8am-midday and 2.30pm-5pm; 8am-1.30pm Sunday; closed Monday)*. The original church dating from 1693 was destroyed by fire. Its replacement was built in 1730 in a neo-Romanesque style and given cathedral status in 1915. The interior with its **frescoes** is in a sorry state.

Continue for two blocks along Calle 83 as far as the city's central square.

Parque de la Libertad★

In days gone by the Parque de la Libertad was the place where criminals were executed in public. Nowadays it is the city's favourite meeting-place, especially towards the end of the day. In the middle, beneath the royal palms, stands a bronze **statue** of José Martí, erected in 1909 to commemorate Cuba's "Apostle of Liberty". The square is lined with fine colonial-era public buildings. The **Palacio de Gobierno** is now occupied by the *Poder Popular*; it is flanked by the former **Spanish Casino**, now the **public library**, at the junction of Calles 79 and 290.

On Calle 83 to the south of the square, a pink-painted building with a wrought-iron balcony houses the **Museo Farmacéutico★★** *(Open 10am-5pm; 10am-2pm Sundays. Admission charge and charge for photography)*. This perfectly preserved pharmacy was established in 1882 by a Frenchman, Ernest Triolet, and medicines were dispensed here right up to 1964, when it became a museum. Made from rare woods, the shelves carry row upon row of earthenware jars and porcelain pots, while old phials and medical instruments share counter space with fine old scales of bronze. The dispensary table won a bronze medal at the Universal Exhibition of 1900. Visitors can look up herbal recipes or inspect the hundreds of old labels kept in the apothecary's cabinet. The array of objects in the room behind the shop includes a very early feeding cup. On the far side of the courtyard is the old **laboratory**, still with its alembic, a cauldron and all kinds of copper instruments.

Immediately to the right of the pharmacy is the entrance to a little yellow building. This is the **Hotel El Louvre**, a convenient place to stay for people who had business with the provincial governor, who used to reside in the next-door palace. The interior of the Louvre hardly seems to have changed since the end of the 19C and its mahogany furniture, stained glass windows and a grand staircase give it a delightfully old-fashioned charm. Until recently only Cubans were allowed to stay here, but the hotel now accepts foreign guests. The palm-shaded **patio** is an excellent place to stop for a drink on a hot day.

Around Matanzas

Church of Nuestra Señora de Monserrate
From Parque de la Libertad go along Calle 83 as far as the junction with Calle 306 (formerly Calle Mujica). Turn right and continue for 1.5km.

The church was built in the 19C by immigrants from Catalonia in northeastern Spain. Only the west front has survived, but the climb up from the town centre is worthwhile for the **view***, which takes in the Bay of Matanzas to the east and the Yumurí valley to the north.

Cuevas de Bellamar* (Bellamar Caves)
5km southeast of the town centre. From Plaza de la Vigía go across the Calixto García Bridge along Calle 272, turning right after 800m. 20m further on turn left where a sign points to the caves. Open 9am-5pm. Admission charge. Conducted tour in English. Meals available.

The caves were discovered in the middle of the 19C by a shepherd, a slave searching for the wooden staff he had lost. The caves have not yet been fully explored, but the first 3km or so are open to the public. The process of crystallisation is particularly well developed in some of the caves, and the extremely pure deposits known as "crystal lamps" have no equivalents anywhere else in the world. Other strange calcareous formations have been given fanciful names like the Cloak of Columbus, the Woman's Hand, the Dancer, or, more prosaically, the Grated Coconut.

COMING AND GOING

By air – Matanzas is 20km from the Juan Gualberto Gómez international airport serving Varadero.

By train – The **Estación de Ferrocarriles** is on Calle 181 to the south of the San Juan River. Several trains daily to Havana. One train daily to Manzanillo and an overnight train to Santiago. Four services a day to Havana on the Hershey railway.

By bus – The **Terminal de Ómnibus Nacionales** is at the junction of Calle 272 (the continuation of the Calixto García Bridge) and Calle 171 to the south of the San Juan River. There are daily services to Havana (2hr), Varadero, Santa Clara, Camagüey and Santiago de Cuba.

By taxi – An official taxi will charge around US$20 for the trip between Matanzas and the airport.

HOW TO GET AROUND

The best way of exploring the town is on foot or by hiring a car.

ADDRESS BOOK

Tourist information – The hotels in Matanzas can provide tourist information.

Banks / Currency exchange – **Banco Financiero Internacional**, on the corner of Calle 85 (Medio) and 298 (2 deMayo).

Post office / telephone – Postal services available in the international hotels. **Correos** at the corner of Calles 85 and 290. Open 7am-8pm. **Centro de Telecommunicaciones** in Parque de la Libertad.

Health – **Farmacia Central**, on the corner of Calles 85 and 298. Open 24hr.

Servicupet service station – On the Varadero road on the eastern outskirts.

WHERE TO STAY

The hotels in the centre of Matanzas are normally reserved for the use of Cubans except for the Louvre. All the other hotels catering for foreign visitors are located on the outskirts of the town (See map page 179)

Under US$30
Hotel Louvre, Parque de la Libertad (next to the Museo Farmacéutico),

☎ (52) 4074 – 15rm. ⌂ 🖥 📺 ✕ Four attractive rooms with antique furniture and a view over the square (the best is No.4, the Governor's Room). Inexpensive. Attentive staff.

Hotel Canimao, Carretera a Varadero Km 3.5, Matanzas, ☎ (52) 6-1014 – 120rm. ⌂ 🖥 🅿 📺 ✕ ⌕ 🆑 7km from the town centre on the Via Blanca towards Varadero. Modern hotel built around a swimming pool. Decent and renovated but charmless rooms. Reasonable rates.

Between US$30-50
Hotel Casa del Valle, Carretera de Chirino Km 2, Valle del Yumurí, ☎ /Fax (52) 53-300 – 42rm. ⌂ 🖥 🅿 📺 ✕ ⌕ 🍴 🐎 🆑 Medical facilities. 7km north of the town in the lovely Yumurí valley. Most of the accommodation is of recent date, but there is also a fine old residence from the early years of the 20C. As well as a sauna there is an "anti-stress centre" and visitors can explore the valley on foot or horseback.

WHERE TO EAT, WHERE TO GO OUT

Enquire locally about paladares.

Under US$10
Café Atenas, Plaza de la Vigía, ☎ (52) 5493. Open 24hr. The café has a spacious interior cooled by fans. Light meals are served here and the open air section facing the Teatro Sauto is the best place in town to sit for a while with a drink.

OTHER THINGS TO DO

Ruinas de Matasiete, at the corner of Calle San Diego and Calle Cuni, on the east side of the Río San Juan overlooking the bay, ☎ (52) 9-1987. Open air bar and restaurant in an old warehouse. Evening dances and discotheque.

Casa de la Trova, at the corner of Calle 83 and Calle 304 (also at Calle 272 and 121), and **Casa de la Cultura**, Calle 79 between Calle 288 and Calle 290. Weekend music and dance sessions.

Excursions – Horse riding in the Yumurí valley and boat trips up the river. Apply to the Hotel Casa del Valle.

Theatre – **Teatro Sauto**, on the Plaza de la Vigía. Performances mostly take place at the weekend.

VARADERO ★★

Matanzas Province
140km from Havana and 42km from Matanzas via the Via Blanca
Water temperature: 25°C in winter, 28°C in summer

Not to be missed
Enjoying yourself in the water and idling in the sun.
Cocktails in the Du Pont mansion.

And remember...
A moped is the best way of getting around.
Reserve accommodation well in advance in the high season.

The tourist enclave of Varadero (literally "place of shipwrecks") occupies the whole of the Hicacos peninsula, which owes its name to the coco-plums which used to grow here in abundance. Some 20km long and only 500m across and cut off from the Cuban mainland by the Paso Malo lagoon, this narrow strip of land juts out at an angle into the ocean, separating the Strait of Florida to the north from the Bay of Cárdenas to the south.

Cuba's premier beach resort

There is one superb sandy beach after another all the way along the north shore of the peninsula to its tip at Punta de Morlas. The white sands, together with the crystal-clear water, the year-round summer climate, and a good range of luxury hotels, makes Varadero an ideal destination for anyone whose idea of a perfect holiday involves no more than sun-worship and/or watersports.

The centre of Varadero is an attractive place, not unlike a small town in Florida; its sunny streets are lined with timber houses and stone villas, some of them built to show off the wealth and ostentatious taste of their one-time owners. By contrast, the far end of the peninsula is still quite wild, though its luxuriant cover of hibiscus and coco-palms has begun to give way to large-scale tourist developments. Almost entirely given over to satisfying the needs of foreign visitors and with something like a third of all the hotels in Cuba, Varadero is at the cutting edge of the Cuban government's policy of encouraging international tourism in order to refresh the ailing economy with an infusion of dollars. It is a "green zone", an enclave where the dollar reigns supreme but where contacts with local people can be kept to a minimum. The access of Cubans to beaches and other facilities is strictly limited, and anyone staying here will meet more Canadians and visitors from Europe than local people, though from time to time the place has attracted swarms of *jineteras* (prostitutes) from all over Cuba. In an attempt to keep the number of these girls to a minimum, they have been subjected to

PENÍNSULA
DE HICACOS
plan I

0   1   2 km

N

★★ Varadero
See plan II
VARADERO

Isla del Sur

Matanzas
Playas del Este
La Habana

Vía   Blanca

Cárdenas

round-ups and the networks controlling them have been broken up. The well-manned local police force sees to it that tourists are left unmolested and also clamps down hard on all sorts of illegal commercial activity, such as letting private rooms to foreign visitors.

Varadero devotes itself whole-heartedly to the pleasures of the seaside and consequently attracts large numbers of visitors. But it is definitely not the place for the seeker of solitude nor for anyone wanting to experience the "real" Cuba.

From millionaires to mass tourism

For many years the peninsula's main role was as a source of sea salt, extracted here from the end of the 16C to the middle of the 18C. The town of Varadero was founded at the end of the 19C, when rich families from Cárdenas began to build themselves holiday villas here. The first hotel opened its doors in 1915, but a real tourist boom only began at the beginning of the 1930s.

In the 1920s, **Irénée Du Pont de Nemours**, a member of the Dupont industrial dynasty, bought land here at an extremely low price. He divided it up into plots which he then sold off to rich Cubans as well as to his wealthy fellow-countrymen. One plot he kept for himself, building on it the sumptuous villa which became a restaurant and then a hotel. Other millionaires began to build luxury homes here, then, when Americans were deprived of European holidays by the outbreak of the Second World War, Varadero took off as a tourist destination. The good times continued right up to the end of the 1950s, with fun-lovers being shuttled to and from Miami by direct flights.

With the coming of the Revolution, the millionaires fled and the casinos were closed. Sun-seekers came here in some numbers from Eastern Europe and the Soviet Union, but exploitation of the peninsula only began again in earnest with the declaration of the "Special Period" and the country's crying need for dollars. Nowadays there are direct flights from Canada and Europe to Varadero's airport, and tourist development is in full swing, financed from abroad and encouraged by the Cuban government.

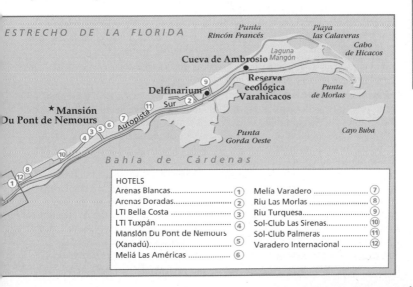

HOTELS

Arenas Blancas	①	Melía Varadero	⑦
Arenas Doradas	②	Riu Las Morlas	⑧
LTI Bella Costa	③	Riu Turquesa	⑨
LTI Tuxpán	④	Sol-Club Las Sirenas	⑩
Mansión Du Pont de Nemours (Xanadú)	⑤	Sol-Club Palmeras	⑪
Meliá Las Américas	⑥	Varadero Internacional	⑫

Varadero

Central Varadero

The town of Varadero extends from the Paso Malo lagoon as far as Calle 69. Finding one's way around is straightforward, thanks to the system of road numbering with *avenidas* running parallel to the beach and *calles* numbered 1 to 69 crossing them at right angles. Practically all the shops and tourist services are on the two main roads, **Avenida Primera** and **Avenida Playa**. In addition, there are a few – very few – visitor attractions.

One of the more interesting places to visit is on Avenida Primera (First Avenue) between Calle 56 and Calle 59. **The Retiro Josone★** (Plan II E2) (*Admission charge*) is an old property once owned by a wealthy Cuban. It consists of a pretty park with a number of restaurants (*See Making the most of Varadero*) centred on an artificial lake populated by (equally artificial) pink flamingos. Boats can be hired, and altogether this is a pleasant spot to spend a relaxing hour or two after a hard day on the beach.

Not far from the Retiro Josone, close to the beach on Calle 57, is a fine wooden residence painted blue, the home of the **Museo Municipal de Varadero** (Plan II E1) (*Open 9am to 6pm; closed Tuesday. Admission charge*). It has reproductions of cave paintings and fragments of pottery, mostly from the Cueva de Ambrosio, evoking the life of the Siboney tribespeople before the arrival of the Spaniards. There are also photographs of the town in the early years of the 20C, while the first floor is entirely given over to celebrating the achievements of Cuban athletes. Despite the fact that its displays are rather scrappy and not very different from those in other museums, the house offers the opportunity to see inside one of Varadero's prestigious residences. In addition it has a lovely terrace overlooking the beach and a garden full of *uvas caletas*.

The Hicacos peninsula
Allow 2hr by car

Beyond the town of Varadero, the peninsula remained virtually undeveloped until the beginning of the 1980s, since when luxury hotel complexes have sprung up along most of the way towards Punta de Morlas.

Leave Varadero town on Avenida de las Américas which begins at the junction with Calle 63 and continue for 4km to a house on a hilltop.

Dupont Mansion★ (Plan 1) (*Open 9am-1pm. Admission free*). Irénée du Pont's extravagant residence was completed in 1930 and given the name **Xanadu**. The famous lines "In Xanadu did Kubla Khan/A stately pleasure dome decree" from Coleridge's poem appear on one of the walls of the building, Photographs show the mansion as it was in its heyday, when fashionable regattas were held here. It now houses a fine hotel and restaurant.

High above the sea, the building was at the heart of a vast estate which included a private airport, a golf course, extensive gardens and a beach. Part of the grounds to the east have been acquired for hotel development, while to the west the mansion's original setting has been restored to some extent by the re-creation of a magnificent 18-hole golf course. As impressive in their own way as the natural setting, the opulent interiors of the mansion feature rare woods and marble. The terrace is a good place to stop for a drink and enjoy the ocean views.

Continue along the Autopista Sur for 5km to just beyond the Hotel Sol Palmeras.

The Delfinarium (Plan 1) puts on shows three times a day *(11am, 2.30pm and 4pm. Admission charge)* and visitors can take to the water with the dolphins in their lagoon *(Reservation necessary, US$35 per person)*.

Continue on the Autopista Sur.

This end of the peninsula is the only part which retains something of its original wild character. It is now a conservation area.

Beyond the Delphinarium and the Gran Hotel, a sign by the side of the *autopista* points left to the **Cueva de Ambrosio** *(Open 9am-4.30pm; closed Monday. Admission charge)*. Only discovered in 1961, the cave is supposed to have served as a hiding-place for escaped slaves, but more significant is the presence here of exceptionally fine examples of geometric wall-painting dating from the pre-Columbian period.

The **Reserva ecológica Varahicacos** (Plan 1) *(9am-4.30pm. Admission charge)*, the nature reserve established to conserve the flora and fauna around a lagoon, begins just beyond the next road junction. There are guided walks (some of the guides speak English) along interpretive paths, which also take in the three caves at the end of the peninsula, including the Cueva de Ambrosio. Among the things to see in the reserve are a 500-year old **giant cactus**, the old salt pans at **Las Salinas**, and **Playa Las Calaveras***, one of Varadero's few remaining deserted beaches.

The Hicacos peninsula

M. Gotin/SCOPE

Making the most of Varadero

COMING AND GOING

By air – Varadero is served by the *Aeropuerto Internacional Juan Gualberto Gómez*, 20km away off the Via Blanca towards Matanzas, ☎ (5) 61-3016/7015. There are weekly flights to Varadero from many cities in Europe, Canada, and South America, daily internal flights to Cayo Largo and Cayo Coco, and several flights a week to Santiago de Cuba and Holguín. Transport to and from the airport is by hotel bus, taxi (around US$25), or by the *Viazul* tourist coach which stops here on the way to Havana.

By train – Varadero is not on a railway line, but there are stations at Matanzas and Cárdenas.

By bus – The *Terminal de Ómnibus Interprovinciales* (Plan II D2) is at the junction of Calle 36 and the Autopista Sur. Tickets should be bought well in advance except for local journeys, e.g. to Matanzas and Cárdenas. There is a *Viazul* air-conditioned coach service to Havana via Matanzas 3 times daily (3hr, US$10), and a service every other day to Trinidad. For tickets, ☎ (5) 61-4886 or from the Terminal. The tourist desk at your hotel will give you advice on getting a day trip to Havana.

By taxi – Only official taxis have access to Varadero and the airport. There are police checkpoints, and private taxi owners risk a heavy fine if caught carrying tourists.

By boat – The *Marina Puertosol Dársena*, Via Blanca (turn left towards the lagoon on the approach to Varadero), ☎ /Fax (5) 66-8063/4/1, is the biggest marina in the area with 122 berths. Drinking water, fuel, electricity and good security. The other two local marinas specialise in boat trips: *Marina Chapelín*, Autopista Sur (on the right just before the Delfinarium), ☎ (5) 66-8440, Fax (5) 66-8441, and *Marian Gaviota*, Autopista Sur, final, ☎ /Fax (5) 66-7756 (*See "Other things to do", page 198*).

HOTELS		
Acuazul .... ①	Dos Mares .... ④	Pullman .... ⑧
Bellamar................................ ②	Iberostar Barlovento .... ⑤	Villa Caleta .... ⑨
Cuatro Palmas .... ③	Kawama .... ⑥	Villa Caribe .... ⑩
	Los Delfines .... ⑦	Villa Herradura .... ⑪

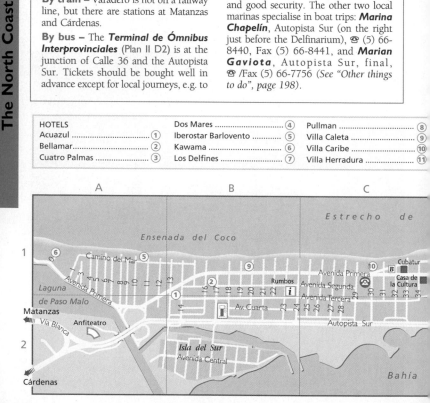

GETTING AROUND

It is easy to get around the centre of Varadero on foot, but for the rest of the peninsula your own transport is necessary.

By bus – There is a *Vaiven* service run by Rumbos on the same lines as in Havana, linking all the tourist spots between the Hotel Oasis and the Gran Hotel, 9am-11.15pm (every 1hr 15mins), flat fare US$1. A similar service, Tourbus, is operated by Transtur (every 30 to 45 mins).

By taxi – *Taxi Transtur*, ☎ (5) 61-4444 or 61-3377, and *Taxi-Ok*, ☎ (5) 66 9911, have vehicles with taximeters at most of the hotels. Reckon on about US$40 for whole-day hire.

Car hire – The State car hire firms all have offices in Varadero, as well as at the airport and in most of the hotels. *Havanautos*, corner of Avenida Primera and Calle 8 (Plan II A1) or 31 (Plan II C1), ☎ (5) 66-7029. *Transtur*, corner of Avenida Primera and Calle 21 (Plan II B1), ☎ (5) 66-7332/7715. *Micar*, corner of Avenida Primera and Calle 19 (Plan II C1), ☎ (5) 66-7326. *Via Rent-a-car*, Sol-Club Las Sirenas, ☎ (5) 66-7240.

Motor-bike and bicycle hire – Motor-bikes and scooters: *Transtur*, corner of Avenida Primera and Calle 21, *Rumbos*, corner of Avenida Primera and Calle 13, which also hires out bikes as do many of the hotels.

Horse and carriage – Hail a carriage on the street in the centre of Varadero. An hour's ride costs around US$3.

ADDRESS BOOK

Tourist information – Local information and excursion bookings at the *Rumbos travel agency* (Plan II B1) (8am-8pm) at the corner of Avenida Primera and Calle 23, ☎ (5) 66-6666. For trips around Varadero and to attractions in the surrounding area, *Cubatur*, (8am-5.30pm) at the corner of Avenida Primera and Calle 33 (Plan II D1), ☎ (5) 66-7217. Likewise *Havanatur* (Plan II D1), Avenida Playa between Calle 36 and Calle 37, ☎ (5) 61-3516, *Gaviota Tours*, at Villa Caleta, ☎ (5) 66-7864, and also at the tourist desks at most of the hotels.

Banks / Currency exchange – *Banco Finaciero Internacional* (8.30am-7pm), corner of Avenida Primera and Calle 32 (Plan II C1), ☎ (5) 66-7002 and *Plaza América*, autopista Km 11, ☎ (5) 66-8272. Travellers cheques cashed, cash with Visa card. Some hotels have a bureau de change.

Post office / Telephone – The *Correos* (Plan II D1), corner of Avenida Primera and Calle 36 is open 8am-6.30pm except Sunday. *Centro Teléfonico Etecsa*, corner of Avenida

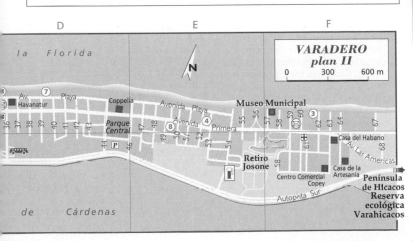

Primera and Calle 30. There are card-operated phones at the **Centro de Communicaciones Internacionales** (Plan II F2), corner of Calle 60 and Avenida Primera (US$10 and US$20 cards on sale at the counter). Open 8am-10pm. Express mail by **DHL**, also in the Centro de Communicaciones Internacionales.

Mail and telephone services also available in most of the hotels.

Health – The **Clínica Internacional** (Plan II F2), corner of Avenida Primera and Calle 60 opposite the Cuatro Palmas hotel, ☎ (5) 66-7711, specialises in medical treatment for visitors from abroad, and has a 24hr pharmacy. Fees payable in dollars. Some hotels have medical facilities.

Consulate – **Canadian Consulate**. Calle 7 opposite the Villa Tortuga, ☎ (5) 6-2078. Open 5pm-7pm, closed Thursday and at the weekend.

Airline offices – **Cubana** has an office for internal flights at the corner of Avenida Premiera and Calle 54 (Plan II E2), ☎ (5) 61-1823. **Aerocaribbean** shares the same address. **Aerotaxi**, corner of Avenida Premiera and Calle 24 (Plan II B1), ☎ (5) 61-2929, organises charter flights, minimum 11 people. These companies also have offices at the airport, ☎ (5) 61-3016, and tickets can also be purchased from hotel tourist desks.

Servicupet service stations – "17", at the junction of the autopista and Calle 17. **Dársena**, Via Blanca on the approach to Varadero near the Marina Dársena. **Complejo todo y uno**, at the junction of the autopista and Calle 54 (with supermarket and delicious coffee in the Casa del Café y Tabaco).

Others – **Asitur** (Tourism assistance), Calle 31 No. 101 (Plan II C1) (8.30am-5pm; 8.30am-midday Saturday; closed Sunday). This insurance company may be able to give financial and legal aid in emergencies such as loss of luggage or documents, hospitalisation or repatriation.

WHERE TO STAY

Varadero's less expensive hotels are located between the Paso Malo lagoon and Calle 53. The more modern luxury hotels built towards the eastern end of the peninsula are much dearer, though a package deal booked through a travel agency brings the price down considerably. Local people are not allowed to offer private accommodation in Varadero.

Between US$30-50

Dos Mares (Plan II), corner of Avenida Primera and Calle 5, ☎ (5) 61-2702, Fax (5) 66-7490 – 33rm. ⌇ 🖃 𝒫 TV ✗ Bureau de change. Pretty hotel in the middle of Varadero. Charming staff and the quality of the building compensate for the undistinguished rooms. Reasonably priced.

Villa Caribe (Plan II), corner of Avenida Primera and Calle 30, ☎ (5) 61-3310, Fax (5) 66-7488 – 124rm. ⌇ 🖃 𝒫 TV ✗ ⌇ 🍴 CC Bureau de change. Right in the middle of Varadero. Three-storey building divided into 2 and 3-room apartments with shared bathrooms. Very acceptable and reasonably priced accommodation in good location. Renovation project planned for 2000.

Bellamar, Calle 17 between Avenida Primera and Avenida Tercera (3rd - Avenue), ☎ (5) 66-7490 and ☎ /Fax (5) 66-7733 – 282rm. ⌇ 🖃 𝒫 TV ✗ 🍴 CC Bureau de change. Large structure with charmless rooms which should be improved by current refurbishment. Good value and friendly staff.

Around US$50

Pullman (Plan II), corner of Avenida Primera and Calle 49, ☎ (5) 66-7161, Fax (5) 66-7495 – 15rm. ⌇ 🖃 𝒫 TV ✗ CC 150m from the beach, this stone building has a certain old-fashioned charm. Basic rooms tastefully redecorated, terrace and garden, family atmosphere.

Villa Herradura (Plan II), Avenida de la Playa between Calle 35 and Calle 36, ☎ (5) 61-3703, Fax (5) 66-7496 – 79rm. ⌇ 🖃 𝒫 TV 🍴 CC Bureau de change. Horseshoe-shaped building with an attractive terrace overlooking the beach. 2 to 5-room apartments with a living room which may have to be shared in high season. The rooms are well kept, and those on the upper floor at the ends of the building have the best views.

Villa Caleta (Plan II), corner of Avenida Premiera and Calle 20, ☎ (5) 66-7080, Fax (5) 66-7194 – 46rm. ⌐ 🗐 🖉 TV ✕ 🔌 🏛 CC Car hire at the Gaviatour tourist desk. In a garden setting in the old part of Varadero, this hotel offers a choice between rooms in the main building or chalets with a shared living room for every 3 units. Completely refurbished rooms with cane furniture. Reasonable prices.

Acazul (Plan II), corner of Avenida Primera and Calle 13, ☎ (5) 66-7132, Fax (5) 66-7229 – 78rm ⌐ 🗐 🖉 TV 🔌 CC Bureau de change, medical facilities. Large and austere building dating from before the Revolution with spacious rooms with balcony. Rates are reasonable even though it is the most expensive of the trio of hotels forming a single complex. The others are the ***Varazul*** (being renovated) and the ***Villa Sotavento***.

Between US$60-100

🦞 ***Los Delfines*** (Plan II), corner of Avenida de la Playa and Calle 39, ☎ (5) 66-7720, Fax 66-7727 – 47rm. ⌐ 🗐 🖉 TV ✕ 🔌 CC Bureau de change. Quiet location despite being in central Varadero. One building is in rough stone, another, more recent, is closer to the beach. Comfortable and spacious rooms. An Italian tour operator has first choice of accommodation (Press Tours, piazza Grandi, 9. 20129 Milano, ☎ (02) 76 111 069) except in the off-season if rooms are available. The hotel is due to be enlarged and a swimming pool is planned. Half-board only.

Around US$100

🦞 ***Cuatro Palmas*** (Plan II), Avenida Premiera between Calle 61 and 62, ☎ (5) 66-7044, Fax (5) 66-7583 – 302rm. ⌐ 🗐 🖉 TV 🔌 🏛 CC Car hire, bureau de change, medical facilities. Main building in Spanish colonial style plus chalets. Sumptuous foyer with luxuriant vegetation and caged birds. Quiet and extremely attractive setting. Ask for rooms close to the beach as some are a fair distance away.

🦞 ***Mansión Du Pont de Nemours*** (Xanadú), Km 8.5, ☎ (5) 66-7788/8482, Fax (5) 66-0401 – 6rm. ⌐ 🗐 🖉 TV 🔌 CC Overlooking the sea on one side and a golf course on the other, this millionaire's mansion from the 1930s has exceptional decor and service. Rooms are spacious, with sea views, Art Deco furnishings and marble bathrooms. Varadero's most refined place to stay, still at a very reasonable price. But book well in advance.

Arenas Blancas, Calle 64 between Avenida Premiera and the autopista, ☎ (5) 61-4450, Fax (5) 61-4491 – 358rm and 81 chalets. ⌐ 🗐 🖉 TV ✕ 🔌 🏛 💧 🍴 CC Many additional facilities. On the beach at the northern end of Varadero, this brand-new establishment is run by one of the best Cuban hotel chains, Gran Caribe. Service is of a high standard, and despite the impersonal architecture the rooms are very pleasant.

Arenas Doradas, Autopista Km 17, ☎ (5) 66-8150, Fax (5) 66-8159 – 316rm. Same facilities as the above, slightly less luxurious and correspondingly cheaper. It is further along the peninsula, close to Los Tainos, the last beach, among luxuriant vegetation.

Between US$100-200

Kawama (Plan II), Calle 0 between Avenida Premiera and Camino del Mar, ☎ (5) 61-4416, Fax (5) 66-7334 – 204rm. ⌐ 🗐 🖉 TV ✕ 🔌 CC Located on the way into Varadero between the Paso Malo lagoon and a secluded private beach, the hotel's accommodation is in a number of separate buildings, some dating from before the Revolution, some more recent. The best is No. 420 which is close to the beach. The clientele is mostly from Germany. All-inclusive package only. Rates are likely to rise when the planned refurbishment is completed.

Varadero Internacional (Plan I), Carretera de las Américas (just beyond Calle 69), ☎ (5) 66-7038, Fax (5) 66-7246 – 163rm. ⌐ 🗐 🖉 TV ✕ 🔌 🏛 CC Car hire, bureau de change. This was Varadero's first luxury hotel, built at the beginning of the 1950s (under renovation). The hotel terrace overlooks a splendid beach. Comfortable rooms, and two magnificent but rarely available penthouse suites (Nos 601 and 602, undergoing renovation) for the same price.

Barlovento (Plan I), Avenida Primera between Calle 10 and Calle 12, ☎ (5) 66-7140, Fax (5) 66-7218 – 276rm. 🍴 📇 ✐ TV ✗ ⅄ ⅍ CC On the way into Varadero, this hotel complex with its imposing foyer is laid out around a swimming pool which is the focal point of the ambitious entertainment programme. The beach is 200m away. The hotel's chalets are a short distance away and are more secluded. The high standard of service reflects the all-in rates.

Starting in the early 1990s, the German chain LTI and the Spanish Meliá and Riu company have been building luxury hotels towards the far end of the peninsula, and Club Med has also opened one of its holiday villages. All offer the same kind of accommodation: a high standard of service, comfortable rooms, a range of services and recreational facilities and an entertainments programme. An all-inclusive package is much cheaper if booked through a travel agent (Plan I).

LTI Tuxpán, Carretera de las Américas Km 4, ☎ (5) 66-7560, Fax (5) 66-7561 – 233rm.

LTI Bella Costa, Carretera de las Américas, ☎ (5) 66-7210, Fax (5) 66-7205 – 382rm and chalets.

Meliá Las Américas, Autopista Sur Km 7. ☎ (5) 66-7600, Fax (5) 66-7625 – 322rm and chalets.

Meliá Varadero, Autopista Sur Km 7, ☎ (5) 66-701, Fax (5) 66-7012 – 490rm.

Riu Las Morlas, corner of Carretera Las Américas and Calle A, ☎ (5) 66-7215,Fax (5) 66-7215 – 143rm.

Riu Turqesa, Carretera Los Tainos, ☎ (5) 66-8471, Fax (5) 66-8495 – 468rm.

Sol Club Las Sirenas, between Calle C and Calle K, Reparto La Torre, ☎ (5) 66-8070, Fax 66-8075 – 434rm.

Sol Palmeras, Carretera Las Morlas Km 8, ☎ (5) 66-7009, Fax (5) 66-7008 – 600rm and chalets.

Club Med, Autopista Sur Km 11, ☎ (5) 66-8286, Fax (5) 66-8414 – 319rm.

WHERE TO EAT

There are no private restaurants in Varadero, all "paladares" having been forbidden in order to eliminate competition with State restaurants. But there is still a reasonable choice of places to eat.

Under US$5

Fast food round the clock at:

Calle 13, at the corner with Avenida Premiera. Fried chicken, pizzas and hamburgers.

FM17, at the corner of Avenida Premiera and Calle 17. Cocktails, snacks, and music in the evening.

El Bodegoncito, at the corner of Avenida Premiera and Calle 40. Fried chicken served in a pretty little wooden cabin.

Under US$10

El Criollo, corner of of Avenida Premiera and Calle 18 (Plan II B1), ☎ (5) 66-7793. Open 24hr. Close to the beach, a delightful house with a veranda. Tables set out beneath a straw canopy. Attractive setting and popular restaurant. Creole specialities based on pork and chicken. Good value for money.

🍴 **Lai-Lai**, corner of Avenida Premiera and Calle 18 (Plan II B1), ☎ (5) 61-3297, midday-10.45pm. A handsome stone building next door to the Criollo. Spacious dining rooms with oriental decor. Good Chinese food.

La Casa del Chef, Avenida Premiera between Calle 12 and Calle 13, ☎ (5) 61-3606. A good spot for people-watching on Varadero's "bulevar" where many of the town's restaurants are located. Very reasonably priced all-in menu available (bean soup, meat or fish dish, salad, dessert). Friendly staff.

Castel Nuovo, corner of Avenida Premiera and Calle 11 (Plan II A2), ☎ (5) 66-7786. Midday-11pm. On the way into Varadero, this quite smart Italian restaurant has a good choice of specialities including pizzas and pasta dishes.

Las Brazas, Calle 12 between Camino del Mar and Avenida Premiera. 12noon-10pm. Attractive open-air establishment close to the beach with a good range of Cuban dishes.

Between US$10-20

El Arrecife, corner of Camino del Mar and Calle 13. 12noon-11pm. Open-air restaurant with fresh seafood at a range of prices. Attentive service.

El Bodegón Criollo, corner of Avenida de la Playa and Calle 40 (Plan II D1), ☎ (5) 66-7784. 12noon-12pm. This is a replica of the Havana's famous Bodeguita del Medio. Cocktails served on the terrace, near the beach. Creole cuisine at a reasonable cost.

El Mesón del Quijote, Carretera las Américas (Plan 1), ☎ (5) 66-7796. Midday to 11pm. Guests arriving at this Spanish style tavern opposite the Hotel Riu Las Morlas are greeted by a sculpture of the Don on his mount. Specialities from Spain and lobster served in chandelier-lit surroundings.

Over US$30

🍽 **Las Palmas**, in the Hotel Cuatro Palmas (Plan II F1), ☎ (5) 66-7208. Romantic candle-lit dining on the beach. A la carte French specialities, but the best buy (some evenings only) is the "gastronomic menu", sophisticated eating at a reasonable price.

Retiro Josone Park (Plan II E2), Avenida Premiera between Calle 56 and Calle 59, makes a fine setting for a number of specialist restaurants of the excellent Cuban Palmares chain open 12.30pm-11pm.

La Casa de Antigüedades, ☎ (5) 66-7329, features 19C decor and interesting but expensive meat and fish dishes.

La Campana, ☎ (5) 66-7224, has a more rustic atmosphere which goes well with its creole specialities. **Dante**, ☎ (5) 66-7739 serves excellent pasta Italian-style, at a price, and **El Retiro**, ☎ (5) 66-7316, concentrates on meat dishes, lobster and seafood, best prices.

Las Américas, Carretera Las Américas (Plan I), ☎ (5) 66-7750. Midday-10.30pm. Refined French cuisine and one of the choicest wine lists in Cuba in the sumptuous setting of the Du Pont mansion. Outdoor terrace high above the ocean.

HAVING A DRINK

Bars – El Mirador, on the top floor of the Du Pont mansion (Plan 1). Elegant panelled setting, grand piano, spectacu-

lar ocean views (especially at sundown). Happy hour 5pm-7pm and jazz band and salsa from 9pm.

Concerts – Music is provided in most of the hotels by musicians of variable talent. International bands sometimes play in the open-air on Saturday evenings in Parque Central close to the Coppelia ice-cream parlour (Avenida Premiera between Calle 44 and Calle 46), or at the **Anfiteatro** (Plan 1 A2), close to the lagoon before the bridge on the way into Varadero. People come from as far away as Havana to dance to local groups such as Médico de la Salsa or Charanga Habanera. ☎ (5) 61-9938.

La Comparsita, corner of Calle 60 and Avenida Tercera. Intimate open-air cabaret with enjoyable Cuban music, popular with local people. Admission US$1. Daily except Monday 10pm-3am.

Night-clubs – The Cabaret Continental in the Hotel Varadero Internacional (Plan 1), ☎ (5) 66-7038, puts on what is probably the best show in Varadero, after which it becomes a conventional night club. Daily except Monday 10pm-2am. Admission US$25 or US$40 with dinner.

La Cueva del Pirata, Autopista Sur Km 11, ☎ (5) 61-3829. The Pirate's Cave – it is a cave – has a show followed by a discotheque. Daily except Sunday 9pm-3am. Admission US$10 or US$25 with dinner.

Casa de la Cultura, Avenida Premiera between Calle 34 and Calle 35 (Plan II C1). Sábado de la Rumba every Saturday evening (Afro-Cuban music and dancing) and Café Cantante every Thursday evening. Admission US$3.

Discotheques – Because Cubans are not allowed into Varadero except as service workers, the resort's discotheques are basically for foreign tourists.

La Bamba, the discotheque of the Hotel Tuxpan (Plan I), may well be Varadero's trendiest establishment. Video screens, high-tech decor and elaborate light show. Admission US$10. Daily 10pm-4am.

La Rumba, to the rear of the Hotel Bella Costa (Plan I). A rival to La Bamba. Admission US$10 (drinks included). 10pm-5am.

Havana Club, close to the Copey shopping centre (corner of Avenida Segunda and Calle 64) (Plan II F2).

Azúcar, corner Avenida Primera and Calle 25 (Plan II C1). Also known as La Cancha, this extremely laid-back establishment plays classic disco numbers as well as salsa. Daily 9pm-3am.

Nautilus, Marina Dársena, Via Blanca. Ship-shape decor on the upper floor of the sailing club. Music includes boléro, feelin' and jazz, and there is a show as well as dancing. Daily except Monday 11pm-5am. Admission US$3.

OTHER THINGS TO DO

Excursions – The tourist desks at hotels and travel agencies can give advice on excursions to a number of destinations, including Havana, Matanzas and other provincial towns and cities.
Varadero's three **marinas** offer boat trips aboard a catamaran or a glass-bottomed boat out to the coral reef or to the keys. Deep-sea fishing is also possible.

Cinema – Cine Varadero, Avenida de la Playa between Calle 42 and Calle 43 (Plan II D1), shows mostly Spanish-language films every evening at 6.30pm.

Sports – Many hotels have sports facilities and there are a number of sports centres as well.
The three **marinas** hire diving gear and equipment and also give instruction. The local diving specialist is **Club Barracuda** (Chapelin marina), corner Avenida Premiera and Calle 59 (Plan II F1), ☎ (5) 61-3841. Charges are about the same at all the diving centres (cUS$35 per dive).
Parachuting is possible at the **Centro Internacional de Paracaidismo**, opposite the Marina Dársena on the way into Varadero, ☎ (5) 66-7256.

The **Varadero Golf Club** is housed in the Du Pont mansion (Xanadú), ☎ (5) 66-7788 or 66-8482, Fax (5) 66-0401. 9 or 18 holes.

SHOPPING

Cigars – Casa del Habana (Plan II F2), corner Avenida Premiera and Calle 63. 9am-7pm. Wide choice of brands.

Crafts – Casa de la Artesania (Plan II F2), corner Avenida de las Américas and Calle 64. 9am-7pm. Shop with local crafts, jewellery and books.

Centro Commercial Copey (Plan II F2), Avenida Segunda between Calle 61 and Calle 63. 9am-7pm. Large shopping centre for tourists. Clothing, souvenirs, plus foodstuffs.

Art galleries – Taller y Galería de Cerámica Artistica (Plan II F1), corner Avenida Premiera and Calle 60. 9am-7pm except Sunday. A pottery with contemporary Cuban sculpture as well as ceramics.

Galería Varadero, corner Avenida Premiera and Calle 59 (close to the ceramics studio): good choice of painting and sculpture. Sol y Mar, close to the Casa de la Cultura, 10am-7pm. Plaza de Américas, shopping centre between the two Melía hotels.

Music – Artex, corner Avenida Tercera and Calle 60, next to the Comparsita. 9am to 9pm. Cassettes and CDs of Cuban music.

Bookshop – Hanoi (Plan II D1), Avenida Primera between Calle 46 and Calle 47. 9am-9pm. Good selection of books in Spanish plus a number of foreign-language publications. Also town plans, maps, records and cassettes.

R. Tixador/TOP

Clear water, silver sands: Varadero

CÁRDENAS

Matanzas Province
Pop 75 000
18km southeast of Varadero
See map p 179

And remember...
A visit to Cárdenas from Varadero takes a good two hours.

What a contrast between the frenetic activity of Varadero and this run-down old harbour town! Just a few kilometres away from the international hotels on the far side of the bay, sleepy Cárdenas seems untouched by the modern world, its arcaded buildings making a shabby backdrop to the bicycles and horse-drawn carriages which ply its streets. Although the town has little to offer in the way of conventional tourist attractions, a visit here is an essential corrective to the impression of Cuba given by a holiday confined to Varadero.

Public transport in Cárdenas

P. de Wilde/HOA QUI

City of the flag

In 1820 the founders of Cárdenas chose a marshy site for their town, but this didn't stop the place from growing, thanks to its location close to some of Cuba's most productive sugar and coffee plantations.

In the mid-19C the town was the scene of a bizarre event in the country's history. On 19 May 1850 an invasion force of 600 men landed here, having sailed across the Gulf of Mexico from New Orleans. They were led by a fervent opponent of the Spanish colonial regime, the Venezuelan **Narciso López**, who hoped to attach Cuba to the United States. But their brief occupation of Cárdenas was quickly brought to an end by local people, aided by Spanish troops. Nevertheless, this was the occasion when the Cuban flag flew for the first time, when the invaders raised it on the flagpole of the Hotel Dominica.

Town centre
Allow 1hr

Cárdenas is the finest example in Cuba of a town laid out on a grid pattern and it has an impeccably logical system of street-numbering. The central street is Avenida Céspedes; *avenidas* to the west (*oeste*) are designated by odd numbers,

those to the east (*este*) by even numbers, while the *calles*, the streets running at right angles to the avenues, are numbered from 1 to 29, beginning at the waterside. But there is a complication; local people tend to refer to the streets by their former names, none of which appear on signs or street plans. So it pays to be patient when finding one's way around.

Parque Colón is the town's central square, bounded by Calles 8 and 9 and crossed from north to south by Avenida de Céspedes. In the middle of the square is a bronze **statue of Christopher Columbus**, dating from 1862 and supposedly the oldest statue of the great navigator in the whole of Latin America. Columbus is shown pointing towards the American continent on the globe at his feet.

Beyond the statue is the **Cathedral of the Immaculada Concepción**, built in 1846 (*Irregular opening hours*).

Dilapidated they may be, but the neo-Classical buildings lining the square speak eloquently of past splendours. To the left of the Cathedral is the **Hotel Dominica** (*See Making the most of Cárdenas*), where the Cuban flag made its first public appearance. Designated as a national monument, the hotel carries a plaque recording the Narciso López invasion of 1850.

The Cuban flag
The national flag was designed by the writer Miguel Teurbe Tolón in 1849. Its three horizontal blue stripes stand for the old provinces of Occidente, Las Villas and Oriente and rest on a white ground symbolising peace. The three sides of the blood-red equilateral triangle on the left represent the Liberty, Equality and Fraternity of the revolutionary slogan, while the five-pointed white star in the centre is a symbol of freedom.

Go down Avenida de Céspedes leaving the Cathedral on your right. Three blocks down, turn left into Calle 12 (formerly Calle Calzada).

On Parque Echevarría at the corner of Calle Calzada and Avenida 4 is the **Museo Municipal Oscar Maria de Rojas** (*Open 10am-5pm; 8am-midday Sunday; closed Monday. Admission charge*) housed in the old town hall of 1862. The museum itself was founded in 1900 and is thus one of Cuba's oldest. It contains highly variegated collections of weaponry and coins as well as archeological items from the time of the indigenous Taino people. There are insects and butterflies, mineral specimens and painted shells, but pride of place goes to an imposing 19C **funeral carriage*** which continued in service until the 1950s.

On the opposite side of the street from the museum is the **Casa Natal de José Antonio Echevarría** (*Open 10am-5pm; 8am-midday Sunday; closed Monday. Admission free*). The birthplace of this student leader, assassinated on 13 March 1957 because of his opposition to the Batista regime, is now the **Museo de Historía** with displays on the Wars of Independence and the Revolution.

Go back up Calle 12, cross Avenida de Céspedes and continue for three blocks as far as the junction with Avenida 3.

The centre of **Plaza Malakoff** is occupied by a **covered market**. This splendid two-storey structure topped by a glittering metallic dome is of a pretension somewhat at odds with the architectural character of the rest of Cárdenas. But it has only been partly restored, and the few stalls it shelters only add to its general air of neglect.

Making the most of Cárdenas

COMING AND GOING

By bus – *Terminal de Ómnibus*, corner of Avenida de Céspedes and Calle 22. Several services daily to Matanzas and Havana.

GETTING AROUND

By carriage – The normal way of getting around the town is by horse-drawn carriage. Fares payable in pesos.

ADDRESS BOOK

Post office / Telephone – The **Correos** on Parque Colón is open 8am-6pm except Sunday. The **Centro telefónico**, Avenida de Céspedes between Calle 12 and Calle 13 , is open round the clock.

Servicupet service stations – On the way into town from Varadero, on Calle 13 at the junction with Calle 31.

WHERE TO STAY

Under US$30
Hotel Dominica, corner of Avenida de Céspedes and Calle 9, ☎ (5) 521502 – 25rm. ⌑ 🍴 🗏 ✗ On Parque Colón, this is the building where the Cuban flag was first raised in 1850. Its moment of glory long since past, it is now rather run down, and the accommodation is very basic. The clientele is basically Cuban, most foreign visitors preferring to stay in Varadero.

EATING OUT

The best way of getting a good meal at a reasonable price is to eat in a paladar. Make enquiries locally.
Las Palmas, on the corner of Avendia Céspedes and Calle 16. Midday-8.30pm. A lovely interior and good, inexpensive Cuban meals, followed by music and dancing.

HAVING A DRINK

Concerts – Traditional music can sometimes be heard at the **Casa de la Cultura**, Avenida de Céspedes between Calle 15 and Calle 16.

Making the most of Cárdenas

P. Cheuva/DIAF

Trinidad street scene

CENTRAL CUBA

A trip through Cuba's central provinces takes in landscapes ranging from marshlands rich in bird-life and
sweeping savannahs dotted with hump-backed oxen, to
invigorating uplands and lakes teeming with trout. On
both sides of the *Carretera Central*, this is the region
where today's Cuba meets the colonial past, represented by an array of old towns rich in history. There
is Cienfuegos, with its hints of a bygone France, revolutionary Santa Clara, pious Camagüey, and above all,
the colonial-era jewel of Trinidad, with its cobbled
streets and pastel-coloured houses.

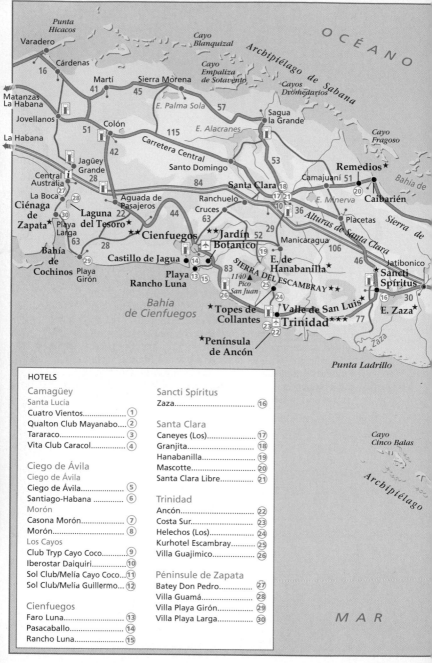

HOTELS

Camagüey
Santa Lucía
Cuatro Vientos................... ①
Qualton Club Mayanabo.... ②
Tararaco............................ ③
Vita Club Caracol............... ④

Ciego de Ávila
Ciego de Ávila
Ciego de Ávila.................... ⑤
Santiago-Habana .... ⑥
Morón
Casona Morón................... ⑦
Morón................................ ⑧
Los Cayos
Club Tryp Cayo Coco........... ⑨
Iberostar Daiquiri................ ⑩
Sol Club/Meliá Cayo Coco... ⑪
Sol Club/Meliá Guillermo... ⑫

Cienfuegos
Faro Luna........................... ⑬
Pasacaballo........................ ⑭
Rancho Luna...................... ⑮

Sancti Spíritus
Zaza................................... ⑯

Santa Clara
Caneyes (Los)..................... ⑰
Granjita.............................. ⑱
Hanabanilla........................ ⑲
Mascotte............................ ⑳
Santa Clara Libre............... ㉑

Trinidad
Ancón................................. ㉒
Costa Sur........................... ㉓
Helechos (Los).................... ㉔
Kurhotel Escambray........... ㉕
Villa Guajimico................... ㉖

Péninsule de Zapata
Batey Don Pedro............... ㉗
Villa Guamá....................... ㉘
Villa Playa Girón............... ㉙
Villa Playa Larga............... ㉚

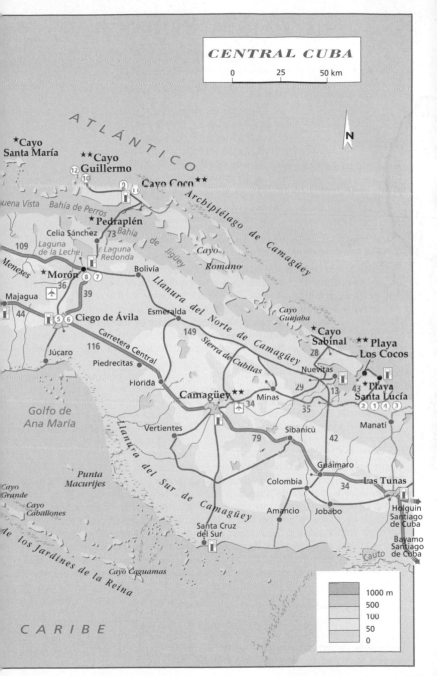

CENTRAL CUBA

0   25   50 km

N

ATLÁNTICO

★Cayo
Santa María

★★Cayo
Guillermo

⑫
⑩

② ①
Cayo Coco ★★

uena Vista   Bahía de Perros

★Pedraplén

Celia Sánchez   73 Bahía

109
Laguna
de la Leche

Laguna
Redonda

de
Jigüey

Cayo
Romano

Archipiélago de Camagüey

Meneses

★Morón
⑧⑦

36

Bolivía

Llanura del Norte de Camagüey

Majagua ✈

44   39

⑤⑥ Ciego de Ávila

116   Carretera Central

Esmeralda

149

Sierra de Cubitas

Cayo
Guajaba

★Cayo
Sabinal

★★Playa
Los Cocos

28

Júcaro

Piedrecitas

Florida

Camagüey ★★
✈ 34

Minas

Nuevitas

29   13

35

43 ★Playa
Santa Lucía
②①①③

Golfo de
Ana María

Llanura del Sur de Camagüey

Vertientes

79

Sibanicú

42

Manatí

Punta
Macurijes

Colombia

Guáimaro

34   Las Tunas

Cayo
Grande

Cayo
Caballones

Amancio   Jobabo

Santa Cruz
del Sur

Holguín
Santiago
de Cuba

Bayamo
Santiago
de Cuba

Cauto

de los Jardines de la Reina

Cayo Caguamas

CARIBE

1000 m
500
100
50
0

THE ZAPATA PENINSULA

South shore of Matanzas Province
3 300sqkm – Pop c 8 000
150km from Havana – Warm, wet climate
See map page 206

Not to be missed
A visit to the La Boca crocodile farm.
A boat trip on the Tesoro lagoon.
Birdwatching in Cuba's most important bird sanctuary.
Swimming among the tropical fish in the Cueva de los Peces.

And remember...
Take along a good mosquito repellent.
The dry season is the best time to visit, since much of the peninsula
is under water in winter.

From Havana, take the motorway towards Santa Clara. At the 140km mark, at Jagüey Grande, turn right towards Central Australia.

Bounded to the north by the Havana-Santa Clara motorway, the Zapata peninsula protrudes into the Caribbean Sea between the Gulf of Batabanó to the west and Cienfuegos Bay to the east. The Zapata Peninsula itself has the shape of a shoe, partly because of the long and narrow inlet which forms its eastern boundary, the **Bay of Pigs**. Part of the area is covered by the mangrove swamps which are characteristic of this tropical coastline. In winter, these flat lands are often flooded well into the dry season, causing the formation of peat, a useful source of carbon.

Before the Revolution, the warm and damp *ciénaga* (swamp) of Zapata was inhabited almost exclusively by an abundance of mosquitoes and crocodiles. Even now, after valiant attempts to rescue the region from its acute state of underdevelopment, the human population is still thinly spread and communications are poor. But the area covered by sugar plantations has been extended, major irrigation schemes have made it possible to grow citrus fruits, and the region is now one of Cuba's most productive agricultural areas.

Tourism has been developed too, around the national park as well as along the shore, and is attracting an ever-increasing number of visitors. The **Parque nacional de la ciénaga de Zapata** is home to a rich and diverse wildlife. The wetlands are a favoured habitat for waders and other endemic species, as well as migratory birds, while the Tesoro lagoon has a wealth of perch and trout, together with a small number of crocodiles lurking in the vegetation along its banks. Along the shore of the Bay of Pigs there are natural pools where it is possible to swim among multi-coloured tropical fish as well as in the sea itself. And the beaches of Playa Larga and Playa Gigón are awash with memories of one of the strangest episodes of the Cold War.

A watery wilderness
The original inhabitants of the peninsula were Tainos, members of a group who practised agriculture and who were wiped out by the Spaniards. The village of Guamá is named after one of their tribal chiefs who led a spirited resistance against the invaders at the beginning of the 16C.

For centuries the region was more or less abandoned, used only as a lair by the pirates who were the curse of the Caribbean. During the 19C, a few charcoal burners lived here, transporting their product along the channels which threaded their way through the endless swamps.

Soon after taking power, Fidel Castro took a close interest in this near-virgin land, hoping to rescue it from its backward state. In the course of several trips taking in some of the most remote and inaccessible parts of the peninsula, he acquired a detailed knowledge of the area which was later put to good use at the time of the Bay of Pigs invasion. A determined anti-illiteracy campaign waged during the 1960s was accompanied by the provision of a basic infrastructure of schools and clinics, followed later by the tourist developments at Playa Girón and Playa Larga.

A symbolic victory: the Bay of Pigs

Soon after the Revolution, relations between Cuba and the United States deteriorated rapidly, especially after the trade embargo imposed on 18 October 1960. The two sides began an escalating process of military confrontation, which culminated in the Bay of Pigs invasion of 1961. On 15 April, air raids on a number of airfields by American planes piloted by Cuban exiles resulted in seven dead and 50 wounded. On 16 April, in a defiant speech, Castro came out with a frank admission of where Revolutionary Cuba stood in the Cold War – firmly in the Socialist camp. On 17 April, a brigade of 1 400 Cuban exiles, trained by the CIA in Nicaragua and Guatemala and escorted by American warships, attempted a landing on Beach Blue (Playa Girón) and Beach Red (Playa Larga) in the Bay of Pigs. Two of the cargo boats taking part in the operation were sunk by Cuban aircraft, part of an air force numbering all of seven planes, and the remaining ships fled. Within two days, 20 000 of Castro's men had assembled in the peninsula ready to repel the *invaders*. Castro himself led them, setting up his headquarters at the big Central Australia sugar mill, 30km north of the theatre of operations. Deprived of the back-up they had been led to expect from the United States, the invaders were forced to acknowledge the failure of their mission. On 20 April, three days after the landing, hostilities ceased, and the 1 183 survivors of the operation were taken prisoner. They were subsequently ransomed, exchanged for the tractors and the medical supplies denied Cuba by the embargo.

The scene of operations is marked by an array of memorials in honour of the defenders, while giant hoardings proclaim this "first victory over American imperialism".

The Parque Nacional de la Ciénaga de Zapata★

Allow 2hr to visit all the sights around the Laguna del Tesoro

The National Park is entered 6km after leaving the motorway. The flat landscape continues as far as La Boca, the starting point for boat trips to Guamá, a tourist village based on a reconstruction of an indigenous settlement. The rest of the National Park is a nature reserve, which is only accessible via a track starting from Playa Larga.

Just 2km from the motorway exit, the otherwise unremarkable **Central Australia** sugar mill has gone down in history as the place where Fidel Castro set up his headquarters during the invasion of the Bay of Pigs. The episode is commemorated in the **Museo de la Comandancia** *(Open 8am-5pm; closed Monday. Admission charge)*. The museum traces the history of Cuba from pre-Columbian times to the Revolution. Outside the building are the remains of an aeroplane shot down by Castro's forces.

From Central Australia drive south for 18km. On the left is a tourist resort and the landing stage at La Boca for the ferry for the Laguna del Tesoro.

■ **Laguna del Tesoro**★ – Legend has it that the lagoon – Treasure Lake – owes its name to an event which took place at the time of the Conquest. In flight from the Spaniards, a group of Taino carrying sacks of gold decided to sink their treasure in the waters of the lagoon rather than give it up to their pursuers. And there it remains to this day. Whatever the truth of the story, the 9sqkm freshwater lagoon is a treasure in its own right, teeming with trout, carp and *manjuarís*, a fossil-fish with a crocodile-like head.

La Boca is a tourist resort with several restaurants, souvenir shops and a pottery studio.

Close to the entrance to the resort is the popular attraction called the **Criadero de Cocodrilos**★ *(Open 9am-5pm. Admission charge)*. This crocodile breeding station was established at the start of the 1960s in order to save the species from extinction. The crocodiles, many hundreds of them, are held in a series of large tanks according to age and size; most spend their time lazing in the sun, waiting for feeding time. The establishment is worth a visit, despite the pervading stench and the clouds of mosquitoes.

"Indian village" at Gaumá

La Boca is the starting point for the ferries for Laguna del Tesoro. The boat follows an 8km channel bordered by reed-beds and mangrove swamps, which opens out on to the vast expanse of the lagoon. The trip can also be made by speedboat, which can get into the remoter parts of the lake which are inaccessible by ferry.

Visible from far across the lagoon, the resort of **Guamá** consists of a series of islands linked by wooden bridges, with accommodation in the form of bungalows built on stilts. Just beyond the resort is the **replica of a Taino village**, made up of *bohíos* (huts) and a *caney*, the dwelling of the tribal chieftain. On the grassy banks of the lagoon is an array of life-size **sculptures** of native people in a variety of poses; the work of the Cuban artist Rita Longa, they are intended to depict the everyday life of the village.

■ **Birdwatching** – *Access to the Ciénaga wildlife refuge is only possible from Playa Larga, 12km south of La Boca. You must be accompanied by a guide from the beach hotel.*
The **Santo Tomás** reserve, 30km west of Playa Larga, is an excellent place in which to observe the local birdlife. The species present include a number specific to the locality, among them the *carpintero jabado*, a woodpecker, the *fermina*, the budgerigar (which can also be seen on the Island of Youth), and the Zapata sparrow. There is also a good chance of seeing a *zunzuncito* (hummingbird).

Another road from Playa Larga runs along the western shore of the bay for 10km to La Salina.

The salt-water lagoon known as **La Salina** is home to various species of wader and is also frequented by a number of migratory species, but is perhaps most famous for its abundant pink flamingoes.

The Bay of Pigs (Bahía de Cochinos)
33km drive from Playa Larga to Playa Girón

There are two seaside resorts of the Bay of Pigs, one at its apex (Playa Larga), the other at its mouth (Playa Girón). The coast road linking the resorts is lined with memorials commemorating those who fell in defence of the Revolution in the course of the 1961 invasion. As well as this historic interest, there is also the possibility of enjoying a dip in a most attractive natural swimming pool.

■ **Playa Larga** – This is one of the two beaches where landings took place in 1961. Although the resort only has minimal facilities, the coral reefs just offshore offer attractive diving.

Continue on the main road from Playa Larga, following the shore for 15km as far as the El Cenote restaurant, half-way between Playa Larga and Playa Girón.

Just off the road and almost invisible among the luxuriant tropical vegetation is the **Cueva de los Peces**★ (Cave of Fish). This underwater cave forms a wonderful natural swimming pool some 70 metres deep, teeming with brightly coloured tropical fish. Organised diving parties come here regularly, but it is also quite feasible simply to hire a mask and snorkel from the nearby restaurant.

■ **Playa Girón** – Bounded by a massive concrete sea wall, the "Blue Beach" is far from idyllic, but is nevertheless a good centre for scuba diving. Facing the hotel is the **Museo Girón** *(Open 9am-5pm. Admission charge)*. One of the museum's rooms is devoted to the social progress made in the Zapata peninsula since the Revolution, concentrating particularly on the literacy campaign. The second section deals in some depth with the build-up to the invasion of the Bay of Pigs, the fighting itself, and its aftermath. Outside the building there are various items of military hardware including armoured vehicles and a British-made Sea Fury, which at the time of the invasion was one of the mainstays of the tiny Cuban air force

Follow the coast road southeast of Girón for 8km to Caleta Buena.

The pretty cove of **Caleta Buena** offers visitors the opportunity to swim among shoals of tropical fish. Equipment can be hired.

To continue towards Cienfuegos, return to Playa Girón and turn inland on the road heading northeast towards Yaguaramas. Turn right on reaching the Carretera Central which takes you to Cienfuegos via Rodas.

Making the most of the Zapata Peninsula

COMING AND GOING

The only way of getting to the Zapata Peninsula is by road. Other than coming here on one of the day trips run by coach operators from Havana and Varadero, you will need your own transport.

GETTING AROUND

A car is really the only way of getting around the area. A four-wheel drive vehicle is recommended for the more remote parts of the national park, especially in wet weather.

Car hire – Both **Transautos** ☎ (59) 4147 and **Havanautos** ☎ (59) 4110 are represented at the Villa Playa Girón.

By boat – The tourist complex at Guamá on the Tesoro lagoon can only be reached by boat. Ferries leave from the landing stage at **La Boca**, 20km from the motorway, at 10am, midday and 3pm in high season, and at 10am off-season. The trip to Guamá lasts about half an hour. US$10. An alternative is to hire one of the small boats with an outboard motor which does the trip in half the time for the same price.

ADDRESS BOOK

Tourist information – The **Rumbos** travel agency, **Australia No 1**, **Jagüey Grande**, or on the motorway at Km 142, ☎ (59) 3224/2535, can provide tourist information of all kinds.

Servicupet service stations – **Jagüey**, 1km from the motorway on the way into Jagüey Grande, and, somewhat off the beaten track, at Jovellanos, Colón, and **Aguade de Pasajeros** (autopista Km 172)

WHERE TO STAY

The location of the hotels is shown on the map page 206.

• **Parque nacional de la ciénaga de Zapata**
Under US$30
Batey Don Pedro Finca Fiesta Campesina, autopista Km 142, ☎ (59) 2045/3224, Fax (52) 5-3125 – 10rm. 🍴 ⛱ 📺 ✗ A group of delightful timber chalets with thatched roofs, close to Central Australia. Comfortable accommodation and friendly family atmosphere. A good place to get the feel of life in the Cuban countryside in a parkland setting.
Between US$30-50
Villa Guamà, Laguna del Tesoro, Ciénaga de Zapata, ☎ (59) 5515, Fax (59) 5551 – 56rm. 🍴 🗐 ☎ 📺 ✗ ⛱ 🆑 Bureau de change, medical facilities. Tourist complex on the Laguna del Tesoro in the form of a "native village" spread out over a dozen islands. Accommodation is in huts on stilts, reached by timber footbridges or by boat. The rooms are comfortable but rather damp. Mosquitoes can be troublesome, and an effective repellent is a must.

- **Playa Larga**
Between US$30-50
Villa Playa Larga, Playa Larga, Ciénaga de Zapata, ☎ (59) 7294, Fax (59) 4141 – 57rm. ⚐ 🍽 📺 ♨ 🆑 Bureau de change. A group of chalets scattered around a grassy expanse close to the beach. The rooms have been refurbished and are well-kept, but the setting is rather gloomy.

- **Playa Girón**
Between US$30-50
Villa Playa Girón, Playa Girón, Ciénaga de Zapata, ☎ (59) 4118 or 4110 – ⚐ 🍽 ♨ 📺 ✕ 🏊 ♨ Car hire, bureau de change, medical facilities. A group of comfortable chalets, conveniently located for a couple of beaches. Wide range of outdoor pursuits available – enquire at main reception.

EATING OUT
The only places to eat are around the hotels and at the main tourist attractions.

- **Parque nacional de la ciénaga de Zapata**
Under US$10
Complejo turístico Pio Cuá, Carretera Girón, Ciénaga de Zapata, ☎ (59) 5-3152. Midday-midnight. 4km from the motorway on the Playa Girón road. Big wooden tables set out beneath an immense thatched canopy. The clientele consists mainly of tour groups. The mainstay of the establishment is chicken in all its varieties, the house speciality being chicken in cheese sauce. Standard food at a reasonable price.
La Boca de Guamá, by the landing stage at the La Gaumá tourist complex. Creole specialities served beneath a big thatched roof. The clientele consists largely of tour groups. Crocodile can appear on the menu.

- **Between Playa Larga and Playa Girón**
Under US$10
Cueva de los Pesces (El Cenote), Km 45 Carretera a Península de Zapata, ☎ (59) 5667. 9am-4pm. 15km from Playa Larga on the Girón road. A lovely natural bathing pool close to the Cueva de los Pesces. Grilled fish and shellfish.

- **Caleta Buena**
Under US$10
Rancho Benito, Playa Caleta Buena, 8km to the east of Girón, ☎ (59) 5589. 9am-4pm. Another good spot to enjoy fine seafood.

OTHER THINGS TO DO
Excursions – The ***Villa Guamá*** and the ***Villa Playa Larga*** both organise birdwatching trips to remote parts of the peninsula.
Details of boat trips out to the deserted islands in the southwestern part of the Bay of Pigs from the reception at the ***Villa Playa Girón***.

Outdoor pursuits – The ***Villa Guamá*** organises trout fishing in the Tesoro lagoon, and boats can be hired for trips around the lagoon.
The diving centre called ***Centro Internacional de Bueco de Villa Playa Girón*** has equipment for hire and can provide instruction at all levels. Diving in the Caribbean and in the underwater caves of the Bay of Pigs.

SHOPPING
Arts and crafts – The souvenir shop by the landing stage at **La Boca** has postcards plus items made from crocodile skin. Open 9am-9pm.
Ceramics can be bought at the ***Taller de Cerámica***, a pottery in the same tourist complex.

Making the most of the Zapata Peninsula

213

CIENFUEGOS★★
Capital of Cienfuegos Province
Pop 125 000 – Cuba's third most important port – 256km from Havana
See map page 206

Not to be missed
The view over the city's rooftops from the Palacio Ferrer.
A performance at the Teatro Terry.

And remember...
The easiest way of getting to the castle at Jagua is by boat, rather than by the long
and complicated coast road.
The city has more than its fair share of "jinetero" hustlers.

*From Havana take the motorway towards Santa Clara. Leave the motorway at the exit
for Aguada de Pasajeros and follow the main road for 80km. Cienfuegos is entered via
the Paseo del Prado.*

Midway between the Zapata peninsula and the Sierra del Escambray, the harbour
city of Cienfuegos spreads out over a peninsula projecting into one of the
country's largest bays. This is almost an inland sea, extending over an area of
90sqkm and with a narrow mouth through which vessels making for the port
have to thread their way carefully. Sometimes referred to as the "Pearl of the
South", despite its unlovely industrial outskirts and workaday harbour,
Cienfuegos is laid out on spacious lines with broad avenues, as well as arcades
which provide a welcome refuge from the heat of the day. Main streets like Prado
and Malecón are thronged at all hours of the day and night by bicycles, carriages and crowds of people, enjoying their city to the full.

Founded by the French
For many years, the area around the bay was regularly pillaged by pirates based
in Jamaica and the Island of Pines. To deter them, the fortress called Castillo de
Nuestra Senora de los Angeles was built at the entrance to the bay in 1745. But
the wonderful natural harbour still lacked a port and a town. This was only built
three-quarters of a century later by a group of New Orleans French, who had
emigrated to the bay area when Louisiana became part of the United States in
1803. In 1819 they founded the town of Fernandina de Jagua, named in honour
of the Spanish King Fernando VII. Ten years later the town was renamed
Cienfuegos after Don José Cienfuegos, the then Governor of Cuba, who had
encouraged them to settle here in order to redress what was seen as an
unfavourable racial balance. Following their arrival, a strict colour bar was put
into operation, which included measures like separate pavements for whites and
blacks on the town's principal thoroughfare, the Prado.

Industrialisation
After the Revolution, Cienfuegos became one of Cuba's major industrial centres,
largely thanks to aid from the Soviet Union. When the country's administrative
structure was reorganised in 1976, the city became a provincial capital. As well
as several large sugar refineries and a number of flour mills, Cienfuegos boasts
the country's biggest cement works and an important naval base. Cuba's only
nuclear power station is also located here, though due to the collapse of the
Soviet Union it has remained unfinished.

The town
Allow half a day

It is easy to find one's way around Cienfuegos thanks to its regular grid-iron street pattern. The *avenidas* running east-west have even numbers, while the north-south *calles* have odd numbers starting from the waterside. Calle 37 is called the Malecón as far as Avenida 46 where it becomes Paseo del Prado; it links the smart old district of Punta Gorda with the historical centre of the city, Pueblo Nuevo, where there are fine examples of neo-Classical architecture, particularly around Parque José Martí, the main square.

Parque José Martí★ (Plan B1 and inset)

The majestically proportioned square with its stately shade trees is lined with numerous fine buildings dating from the late 19C/early 20C. Most visitors begin their exploration of the town here, and unless the police have persuaded them to perpetrate their hassles elsewhere, the square has more than its fair share of *jineteros*. But most of the time it is cloaked in somnolent silence, interrupted only when the municipal band strikes up some stirring salsa from the *glorieta*, the bandstand.

There are several reminders of Cuba's historic past. Beyond the pair of marble lions guarding the eastern entrance to the square, a **roundel** showing the original outline of the town is set into the paving. The lines of trees all converge on the **statue of José Martí**, the national hero, while a **triumphal arch** commemorating Cuban independence closes off the western end of the square.

The **Cathedral de la Purisima Concepción** (*Open 7am-1pm; 7am-1pm and 2pm-4pm Saturday. Admission free*) dominates the eastern end of the square. Completed in 1869, the neo-Classical building has two towers of dissimilar design and an interior with **stained glass** depicting the Twelve Apostles, as well as a splendid **altar★** with Corinthian columns.

To the left of the Cathedral on the corner of Calle 27 is the **Teatro Tomás Terry★★** (*Open 9am-6pm; 9am-midday Sunday. Admission charge*), named in honour of a sugar magnate of Venezuelan origin whose statue graces the foyer. Built in 1889, it is one of the country's great trio of colonial-era theatres (the other two being the Jacinto Milanés at Pinar del Río and the Teatro Sauto at Matanzas). The theatre's neo-Classical façade had been renovated, but the auditorium still has its original wooden seating for an audience of 950. The sober elegance of the dress circle and the boxes contrasts with the ornate ceiling **fresco★**. Visitors can tread the boards once graced by the likes of Sarah Bernhardt and Enrico Caruso.

On the corner of Calle 54, beyond the triumphal arch, stands an Art Nouveau edifice with an ornate little tower. This is the **Palacio Ferrer★** (*Open 9am-9pm. Admission charge*), built at the very end of the 19C by another sugar millionaire, an immigrant from Catalonia. It is now the **Casa de la Cultura** and occasional concerts are held in its sadly neglected interior. The tower is worth climbing for the fine **view★★** over the city's red-tiled roofs towards the bay.

On the corner of Avenida 54 and Calle 27 is **El Palatino** (*See Making the most of Cienfuegos*), one of the city's most venerable buildings, a fine arcaded residence of 1842, the home in turn of a café-restaurant, a patisserie and finally a wine bar.

CIENFUEGOS

0   250   500 m

A

B

SAN LÁZARO

La Habana

Avenida 70

Cayo Loco

Museo Naval

Avenida 70
Avenida 68
Avenida 66
Avenida 64
Avenida 62
Avenida 60
Avenida 58
Avenida 56

Avenida 64

PUEBLO NUEVO

Punta Verde

Cementerio de Reina

SEE DETAIL
Parque José Martí
Avenida 54

Prado

Avenida 50

Avenida 52

REINA

Avenida 48

Avenida 50

Avenida 48

Punta Arenas

Coppelia

Av. 44

Av. 42

Avenida 46

Avenida 44
Avenida 42
Avenida 40
Avenida 38
Avenida 36
Avenida 34

Av. 5 de Septiembre

Jardín Botánico

Cementerio Tomás Acea

Rancho Luna

Ensenada Marcillán

PUNTA GORDA

Avenida 30
Avenida 28
Avenida 26

Punta Majagua

Punta Revienta Cordeles

37 (Malecón)

Av. 22

Avenida 20

Bahía

de

Cienfuegos

(Jagua)

Avenida 18

Avenida 16

Avenida 14

Av. 12

Laguna del Cura

Av. 10

Marina Jagua

Av. 8

Punta

Gorda

Av. 6

Punta del Medio

Av. 4

Av. 2

Av. 0

Palacio de Valle

Punta Gorda

23   27
Teatro Tomás Terry

29
Avenida 58

Catedral
31

Avenida 56

25
Palacio Ferrer

Parque José Martí

Avenida 54

Palacio de Gobierno

El Palatino

Museo Provincial

Avenida 52

0   100 m

HOTEL

Jagua .... ①

216

On the far side of Calle 27 is the **Museo Provincial** *(Open 9am-4.30pm; 9am-midday Sunday; closed Monday. Admission charge)*, housed in the former Casino Español. The displays evoke the city's rich musical, literary and theatrical history and the museum also puts on exhibitions of the work of contemporary artists.

Adjoining the museum is the former **Palacio del Gobierno**, a grandiose blue structure topped by a dome. It is now the seat of the *Poder Popular Provincial* (Provincial Assembly).

The section of Avenida 54 between the square and the Prado has been pedestrianised. Lined with shops, this *bulevar* has the typical atmosphere of a provincial Cuban town, a strange mixture of bustle and langour.

Around Parque José Martí

Go down Avenida 56 towards the waterfront and turn right into Calle 21.

The **Museo Naval** *(Open 9am-5pm; 9am-1pm Saturday and Sunday. Admission charge)* is at the intersection of Calle 21 and Avenida 60 in the northwest part of the old city centre. The displays tell the story of shipping and of the Cuban navy, with special attention given to the naval revolt of 5 September 1957 against the Batista regime.

Go west down Avenida 48 as far as the railway and continue for four blocks to the bus depot. Turn right along a dirt road.

The little **Cementerio La Reina** (A2) at the far end of the La Reina district is an appealing example of a colonial-era cemetery. It dates from 1836 and among the poorly-maintained graves of Spanish soldiers and the city's French-speaking founding families is the *Bella Durmiente* (Sleeping Beauty), a marble statue of a girl who is supposed to have died of a broken heart at the tender age of 24.

Go down the Prado (Calle 37) which becomes the Malecón once it reaches the waterfront.

Punta Gorda★ (B 3-4)

The peninsula to the south of the city centre, known as Punta Gorda, was once THE place to live in Cienfuegos. The Malecón is now rather run-down, but its opulent villas were much in favour among wealthy Americans until the demise of the Batista regime. Avenida 37 continues south towards the tip of the peninsula, an area of lovely wooden houses in New Orleans style. Most of the city's tourist facilities are located here.

Right at the end of the avenue, and impossible to overlook, is the **Hotel Jagua**, a concrete structure built as a casino in the 1950s.

Close by, and surrounded by fine trees, is an edifice which seems to have sprung fully formed from the pages of *A Thousand and One Nights*.

The **Palacio de Valle★** is built in an extraordinary mixture of styles, ranging from Romanesque and Gothic to Baroque, though

The Palacio del Valle and Cienfuegos Bay

Bossu-Picat/HOA QUI

its main inspiration is Moorish. It is named after the wealthy Cuban who had it built at the beginning of the 20C and nowadays houses a restaurant and a bar. Calle 35 leads to the tip of the peninsula. It is lined by elegant **wooden villas**★★ built by the Louisiana French who founded the city. These delicious dwellings in pistachio green, mustard yellow and raspberry pink are adorned with balconies with lace-like woodwork. Unfortunately many of the villas' roofs were badly damaged in the October 1996 hurricane.

Calle 35 ends at what is somewhat pretentiously known as the beach. It is nevertheless a good spot to have a drink and take in the great sweep of the bay. During the daytime swimmers hang around the bar or doze in deckchairs and in the evening there is an open-air discotheque.

Carretera de Rancho Luna

34km drive – allow half a day including visits to attractions
See map page 206

Leave Cienfuegos via Avenida del 5 de septiembre towards La Milpa

Two kilometres from the city centre a grandiose replica of the Parthenon marks the entrance to the **Tomás Acea cemetery**. Laid out in the early 20C, the cemetery is huge. Its most striking monument is the one commemorating those killed in the uprising of 5 September 1957.

After leaving the cemetery continue for 10km as far as a bridge, then after a further kilometre turn left by a service station. Go to the end of this road and turn left (the right turn leads to Trinidad). After 2km look out for a white gateway on the left.

About 20km from the city centre, the **Jardín Botánico**★★ *(Open 8am-4pm. Admission charge)* is Cuba's oldest botanical garden, laid out in the early years of the 20C by the American sugar baron Edwin Atkins. In 1919 it was taken over by Harvard University as a tropical research station. Atkins planted trees in abundance and the 96ha site is more of a forest than a garden. Among the 2 000 species of tropical and subtropical plants are no fewer than 307 different kinds of palms. The guided tour concentrates on identifying the main species.

Return to the service station, turn left and continue for 5km.

Playa Rancho Luna is the nearest beach resort to Cienfuegos. The tourist facilities here make it a possible base for exploring the area provided visitors have their own vehicle.

Continue on the same road for 4km until you see the Hotel Pasacaballo and, on the far side of the narrow mouth of the bay, the Castillo de Jagua.

The fortress of Nuestra Senora de los Angeles de Jagua

Access by boat (See Making the most of Cienfuegos). The Castillo de Jagua cannot be reached easily by car, and the ferry operators seem less and less inclined to let foreigners on board. One not particularly convenient solution is to try and hire a boat at the Marina or the Hotel Pasacaballo.

On the western shore of the bay, the fortress rises over the delightful village of **Perché** with its timber dwellings built on stilts by 19C French settlers. The fortress was constructed in 1745 to defend the area against pirates. It is of no great architectural interest and most visitors are quite happy to look at it from the Hotel Pasacaballo rather than attempt to make the crossing.

Making the most of Cienfuegos

COMING AND GOING

By air – The **Aeropuerto Internacional Jaime Gonzalez** is 5km north of the city on the road leading to Trinidad. ☎ (432) 451299. Several flights a week to Canada.
Internal flights by **Aerocarribean** and **Aerotaxi**.

By train – The **Terminal de Ferrocarriles** (B1) is at the junction of Calle 49 and Avenida 58. Every other day, one train between Cienfuegos and Havana (journey time between 7 and 10 hr). Other trains serve a number of provincial towns.

By bus – The **Terminal de Ómnibus** (B1) is on Calle 49 between Avenidas 56 and 58, close to the railway station. The **Viazul** tourist coach stops here on its daily run between Havana and Trinidad (US\$20). Several normal bus services daily to Havana, Trinidad and Santa Clara, and one service every other day to Camagüey and Santiago de Cuba. Tourists must pay in dollars. Tickets should be bought in advance.

By boat – The **Marina Puertosol Jagua** (B3) on Calle 35 between Avenidas 6 and 8 has facilities for pleasure boats. ☎ (432) 451241/75.

GETTING AROUND CIENFUEGOS

By taxi – The official company **Taxi Transtur** (B4) has a stand in front of the Hotel Jagua. There is also a 24hr service, ☎ (432) 451600 or 451172.

Car hire – The **Havanautos** agency (B3) is next to the service station on the corner of Calle 37 and Avenida 16 in Punta Gorda, ☎ (432) 451211, and also has a desk in the Hotel Rancho Luna, ☎ (432) 48143. **Transautos** has a desk in the Hotel Rancho Luna, ☎ (432) 48120, and in the Hotel Jagua, ☎ (432) 451003.

Carriages – A city tour by horse-drawn carriage is a pleasant way of getting to know Cienfuegos and is not expensive.

ADDRESS BOOK

Tourist Information – The hotels can help with tourist information, as can the **Rumbos** travel agency at the corner of

Calle 20 and Calle 39, ☎ (432) 451175/21 (may move to the east of Parque Martí).
Intur shop (B1) at the corner of Calle 33 and Avenida 56 can provide information about the city and its surroundings. Alternatively try the Hotel Jagua.

Banks / Currency exchange – **Bannco Financiero Internacional**, at the corner of Avenida 54 and 29.
The reception desk at the Hotel Jagua has facilities for changing foreign currency.

Post office / Telephone – Letters can be posted from the hotel or at the **Correos** (B1) at the corner of Calle 35 and Avenida 56. The 24hr **Centro Telefónico** is one block away on Avenida 54 between Calles 35 and 37 (B1), and also has **DHL** facilities.

Health – The 24hr **Clínica Internacional** (B3) is located opposite the Hotel Jagua on Calle 37, ☎ (432) 451622. Consultations, ambulance service and hospital treatment must be paid for in dollars. There is also a pharmacy.

Servicupet service station – **Punta Gorda** (B3), junction of Calle 37 and Avenida 16, 700m from the Hotel Jagua. **Rancha Luna** by the hotel of the same name 20km from Cienfuegos.

WHERE TO STAY

Hotels are not the city's strong point and those that do exist are on the outskirts. But there is a good choice of private accommodation in colonial-era buildings in the city centre, particularly along the Prado or around Parque Martí.
Between US\$15-20
La China, Calle 25 No. 5407 altos between Calle 54 and 56, ☎ (432) 6527 – 1 or 2rm. 🍴📺 On the west side of Parque Martí with an unequalled view over the town and the square. A well-preserved colonial-era building and a warm welcome.
Ulises Jaureguí, Calle 37 No. 4202 between Calle 42 and Calle 44, ☎ (432) 9891 – 1 or 2rm. 🍴📺 On the busy Prado, a house with columns and high ceilings. Clean, attractive and quiet.

• **Punta Gorda**
More than US$50
Hotel Jagua, Calle 37 no1 between Avenidas 0 and 2, ☎ (432) 451003, Fax (432) 451245 – 144 rm. ⌂⌧ 🖋 📺 ✗ ⌑ ⌷ Car hire, bureau de change. Put up in the late 1950s, this building dominates the tip of the Punta Gorda peninsula with its pretty wooden houses from the early years of the 20C. The hotel has an impersonal atmosphere and most of its clientele are members of tour groups. Rooms are spacious and reasonably comfortable with balconies giving views over the city and the bay. If you want to stay in Cienfuegos itself, this is the only choice, but it cannot be said that the hotel really deserves its four stars. Full refurbishment is planned.

• **Around Cienfuegos**
Hotels are shown on map page 206.
Around US$30
Hotel Pasacaballo, off the main road to Rancho Luna at the Km 22 mark, ☎ (43) 96-013/121 – 188rm. ⌂⌧ 🖋 📺 ✗ ⌑ ⌷ Bureau de change. 25km from the city centre on the eastern side of the entrance to the bay, this imposing concrete structure faces the Castillo de Jagua on the far shore. The hotel enjoys superb views over the bay, especially from its terrace, and has a variety of visitor facilities as well as clean and comfortable rooms. A car is essential, as there are very few local attractions.

Between US$30-50
Hotel Faro Luna, Playa Faro Luna, ☎ (432) 48-162/5, Fax (43) 451162, www.cubanacan.cu – 40rm. ⌂⌧ 🖋 📺 ✗ ⌑ ⌬ Tourist information, medical facilities, bureau de change, car hire. 20km from the city centre, the most up-to-date accommodation in the area. Clean and attractive. The comfortable rooms overlook the swimming pool and most have a sea view. Diving centre.

Hotel Rancho Luna, Playa Rancho Luna, ☎ (43) 48-120) 22rm. ⌂⌧ 🖋 📺 ✗ ⌑ ⌬ Car hire ⌷ Adjacent to the Pasacaballo above. Accommodation is in a pair of modern buildings close to an attractive beach. The rooms

are acceptable though utterly devoid of charm. The hotel can organise trips to the Sierra del Escambray.

EATING OUT
Cienfuegos has no gastronomic restaurants and is one of those places where it might be best to rely on local advice and hope to find a good paladar.

• **City centre**
Under US$10
El Palatino, Avenida 54 between Calles 25 and 27 (B1), ☎ (432) 451244, 10am-10pm. This is one of the oldest buildings in Cienfuegos, with high wooden ceilings painted blue, a bar running the whole length of the spacious room, and an outside section beneath the arcades on Parque José Martí. Unfortunately, only light meals and the occasional fish dish are served in what is one of the city's most attractive eating places (at least when it is not crowded-out with a tour group).
La Verja, Avenida 54 between Calles 33 and 35 (B1), ☎ (432) 6311, open midday-3pm and 6.30pm-9.30pm except Tuesday. On the pedestrianised section of Calle 54 only a short distance from Parque José Martí. Attractively rustic interior and a courtyard. Popular with local people. Creole specialities, mostly based on pork. Unpretentious cooking at a reasonable price.
1819, Calle 37 between Avenida 56 and Avenida 58. Midday-3pm and 6.30pm-10pm. Attractive old building serving Cuban food at Cuban prices mostly to Cubans.

• **Punta Gorda**
Between US$10-15
La Cueva del Camerón, opposite the Hotel Jagua, ☎ (432) 451128. Midday-11pm. Delicious prawns served in a variety of sauces in a fine old house with tiled floors. Evening discotheque.

• **Outside town**
Under US$10
Finca La Isabella, on the road to the beach 5km south of town. Unexceptional and inexpensive food served in a quiet countryside setting.

WHERE TO HAVE A DRINK

Bars – In the middle of town, *El Palatino* is a good place to take a break from sightseeing. The Hotel Jagua has a bar looking out over its well-planted garden and swimming pool.

Concerts – The *Café cantante*, Calle 37 between Avenida 52 and Avenida 54 hosts traditional music groups in an authentically Cuban atmosphere. 9pm-2am, with occasional afternoon sessions from 3pm-7pm.

Discotheques – *Benny Moré*, Avenida 54 between Calle 29 and Calle 31. Bearing the name of the "Wild Man of Music" who was a native of Cienfuegos Province, this night club has a spacious floor and a mixture of Cuban and international music to dance to. Liveliest at the weekend. 9pm-3am except Monday, and from 5pm Friday to Sunday. Admission US$3.

Caribbean, Calle 35 between Avenida 20 and Avenida 22. Built out over the water, this is a favourite with the young of Cienfuegos for weekend action.

The "beach" at the tip of Punta Gorda is sometimes turned into an informal dance floor. And all else failing, the hotels also have discotheques.

OTHER THINGS TO DO

Excursions – The Hotel Rancho Luna arranges trips into the Sierra del Escambray.

There are boat trips from the Hotel Pasacaballo to the Castillo de Jagua.

Sports – Scuba diving from the Hotel Faro Luna.

SHOPPING

The main shopping street in Cienfuegos is the pedestrianised section of Avenida 54 known as the "bulevar" (boulevard). The well-stocked dollar shops contrast with the meagre offerings of the peso establishments.

Art Gallery – The *Galeria de Arte*, Avenida 56 No .2505, in the entrance to the Teatro Tomás Terry on Parque José Martí (B1) has a limited range of arts and crafts and recordings. Open 9am-6.30pm.

Bookshop – *The Edad de Oro*, Avenida 54 No. 3309 between Calles 33 and 35 (B1), just opposite the La Verja restaurant. Books in English as well as Spanish.

SANTA CLARA
Capital of Santa Clara Province
Pop 220 000
280km from Havana and 80km from Sancti Spíritus
See map page 206

Not to be missed
The Che Guevara trail.
The carnival at Remedios.
The beaches of the Sabana archipelago.

And remember...
Parque Leoncio Vidal is a favourite hang-out of the city's "jinetero" hustlers.
The best accommodation is on the outskirts.

Whether coming from Havana or Sancti Spíritus, leave the motorway to the west of Santa Clara and drive down the Calle 9 de abril. The Parque Leoncio Vidal is three blocks to the north of the junction of Calle 9 de abril and Calle Colón.

Santa Clara tends to be bypassed by tourists because of its lack of historical attractions, but it is a vibrant provincial capital whose bustle is in complete contrast to the sleepy towns of the surrounding countryside. One of the country's largest universities is here, and the large student population contributes to the lively atmosphere, especially at weekends.

Che Guevara

GAMMA

The city was founded towards the end of the 17C by settlers from the coast fleeing constant raids by pirates. They chose an inland site, half-way between the Caribbean and the Atlantic, at the point where the foothills of the Sierra de Escambray give way to the plain, with its grazing lands and plantations of sugar cane and tobacco. In the 19C Santa Clara became a provincial capital. In more recent times it has developed into an industrial city with factories turning out a variety of products, including domestic appliances from the giant Inpud complex. However, the historic centre has preserved some of the charm of colonial times, particularly around the handsome central square, the Parque Leoncio Vidal.

A number of day trips can be made from Santa Clara, notably to the charming little city of Remedios.

Che's city
The name of Santa Clara is inextricably identified with the **Battle of Santa Clara**, the final episode in the guerrilla war which led to the Revolution. After 18 months of fighting in the Sierra Maestra, **Che Guevara** and Camilo Cienfuegos were put in charge of the campaign to liberate the western half of the country. On 28 December 1958, the column led by Che arrived at the gates

of Santa Clara and fierce fighting broke out between the guerrillas and the government forces defending the city. The following day Dictator Batista ordered an armoured train loaded with troops and munitions to steam eastwards to stiffen the defence. But the reinforcements never arrived. Ambushed by Che's men, the train tried to escape by reversing in the direction of Havana. But the track had been sabotaged and it left the rails. Bombarded with Molotov cocktails by the handful of guerrillas, the hundreds of government troops resisted for a few hours, then surrendered. Arming themselves with the captured weaponry, the rebels took possession of Santa Clara on 31 December. On learning of this defeat Batista fled the country, leaving the way open for the bearded guerrilla fighters (los barbudos) to enter Havana on 2 January 1959.

The City

Santa Clara's grid pattern of streets make it relatively easy to find one's way around, but a car is useful as some of the sights are quite a long way apart.

The Parque Leoncio Vidal

The favourite rendezvous of *Santaclarenos* at all hours of the day, Santa Clara's pedestrianised central square is always busy, not least because of the welcome shade cast by its *guásimas*. At the weekend it fills up with students who come here to dance the night away to the sound of the bands performing from the *glorieta*. Close to this bandstand is the monument to Leoncio Vidal Sánchez, a prominent local man killed in the course of the struggle for independence in 1896.

At the corner of Calle Máximo Gómez on the north side of the square stands the **Teatro de la Caridad**, which has a much-appreciated programme of events and performances. Dating from 1885, it was paid for by Marta Abreu, a much-loved local lady philanthropist. The interior has ornate **frescoes** painted by Camilo Zalayas.

To the right of the theatre at the corner of Calle Luis Estévez, a fine old 18C building has been converted into the **Museo de Artes decorativas★** (*Open 9am-midday; 1pm-6pm Monday, Wednesday and Thursday; 1pm-6pm and 7pm-10pm Friday and Saturday; 6pm-10pm Sunday; closed Tuesday. Admission charge*). The museum has an extensive and beautifully presented collection of Cuban furniture and other items from the 17C onwards. A guided tour is available.

On the east side of the square, the imposing early 20C Governor's Palace has been renovated and now houses the provincial library.

The **Santa Clara Libre Hotel** on the opposite side of the square is where the last shots of the 1958 battle were fired, though the bullet-holes made then have subsequently been filled in.

Revolutionary memorials

Most of Santa Clara's monuments commemorate the guerrilla war, the Revolution, and Che Guevara's role in both of them, and most of them are outside the city centre.

From the Parque Leoncio Vidal go one block north up Calle Luis Estévez and turn right into Calle Independencia. Continue for 800m to the far side of the Rio Cubanicay.

Both ways round the square

Santa Clara's Parque Leoncio Vidal used to be famous in Cuba as the only square to have two-way traffic. In the 19C, at the time of the paseo, the ladies and gentlemen of the city's upper crust would stroll around the square in opposite directions. Only if a lady responded positively to a suitor's advances as they passed each other could he change direction and accompany her. The custom survived the Revolution, but has since fallen into disuse.

The famous **Monumento al asalto y toma del tren blindado** occupies part of the area between the river and the railway, close to the point where Che and his men carried out their attack on the armoured train on 29 December 1958. Sculptures depict explosions and the derailment of the train, and the bulldozer used to tear up the track is mounted on a plinth. Four of the 24 items of rolling-stock which made up the armoured train are here, two of them converted into a **museum** *(9am-5pm; 9am-midday Sunday. Admission charge)* with weapons and other items and contemporary photographs.

Return to the Parque Leoncio Vidal and go down Calle Rafael Tristá next to the Santa Clara Libre Hotel. Continue along this road for 1.5km.

On the edge of town, the vast ceremonial space of the **Plaza de la Revolución** needs a mass rally to fill it, but it is usually empty, except for children hoping for handouts from foreign tourists.

All the memorials in the square are devoted to the memory of Che Guevara. The most recent of them, and probably the most revered monument of its kind in Cuba, is his **mausoleum**, unveiled in October 1997. Here, accompanied by six of his comrades, Che lies in peace in surroundings evoking the tropical forest where he spent his last moments as a guerrilla fighter. On 12 July 1997, just before the thirtieth anniversary of his death, and after many years of investigations into the fate of his remains, Che's body was found at Vallegrande in Bolivia and brought back to Havana. For several days the masses flocked to the capital's Plaza de la Revolución to pay homage to their guerrilla hero before he was removed to his last resting place here in Santa Clara, in 1998.

The mausoleum is now a rival attraction to the giant **bronze statue** erected 10 years earlier. It shows Che, gun in hand, standing atop a plinth on which is written the slogan *"Hasta la victoria siempre"* (To final victory). Nearby, inscribed on a marble monument, is the text of the moving farewell letter Che addressed to Fidel Castro before leaving Cuba for Bolivia.

The **Museo de la Revolución**★ *(Open 9am-5pm; 9am-midday Sunday; closed Monday; Admission charge)* completes the array of Guevara memorials. On display are a number of his personal possessions as well as photographs tracing the life of this icon of the revolutionary struggle up to his assassination in Bolivia in October 1967.

San Juan de los Remedios★

45km north of Santa Clara – 45min by car.
See map page 206

Leave Santa Clara by driving east along Calle Independencia, passing the armoured train memorial and continuing in the same direction.

Normally referred to simply as Remedios, this little colonial town established in 1514 by Vasco Porcallo de Figueroa, is the oldest settlement in the region. In 1689, it was abandoned by some of its inhabitants, who moved inland and founded Santa Clara. They were joined three years later by other *Remedianos* fleeing from a disastrous fire which had destroyed a large part of the town. The subsequent development of Remedios has been overshadowed by the presence of its much larger neighbour only a short distance away. With a population of only 17 000, it is a quiet place, hardly touched by tourism, its tranquillity only interrupted once a year by the unique December festival which goes under the name of the **Parrandas Remedianas**.

Parque José Martí*

The usual starting-point for a stroll around the town, this majestic main square is surprisingly spacious. It is one of the few town squares in Cuba to have two churches facing each other.

The Church of San Juan Buatista* *(Open 9am-11am and 3.30pm-5.30pm. Admission charge. Access via the sacristy at the rear of the building if main door closed)* on the eastern side of the square was built in 1545 and reconstructed in 1939 following an earthquake. The exterior is less remarkable than the interior, thanks to the work of the artist Rogelio Atá. It features magnificent mahogany ceilings and a superb cedarwood altar covered in gold leaf.

The Church of Buen Viaje dates from 1852 and, attractive though it is, can hardly compete with its neighbour on the far side of the square.

On the north side of the square, the fine mansion which once belonged to Alejandro García Caturla now houses the **Museo de la Música** *(8am-5pm; 8am-midday Sunday; closed Monday. Admission charge)*. Caturla was a lawyer and a musician of great originality and personal integrity, whose work helped to introduce African rhythms into Cuban music. On display are personal items, musical instruments and original scores. One room is given over to press cuttings dealing with Caturla's assassination in 1940 at the untimely age of 34.

No-one should leave Remedios without visiting the **Museo de las Parrandas Remedianas*** on Calle Máximo Gómez between Calles Alejandro Río and Andrés del Río, 100m from the Parque José Martí *(Open 8am-midday and 1pm-5pm; 8am-midday Sunday; closed Monday. Admission charge)*. The museum's two floors trace the history of the carnival with photographs, banners, musical instruments, costumes, and models of *trabajos de plaza*, while a model of the square illustrates the manoeuvres that take place in the course of this strangest of competitions. Since the Revolution, the festival has taken place on the Saturday before the 26 December, the date of the liberation of the town by Che Guevara's men.

A noisy duel

The origin of Remedios' unique carnival goes back to Christmas Eve in 1821, when the parish priest sent a crowd of youngsters out into the town with instructions to keep his congregation awake for Midnight Mass by making as much noise as possible. This was taken as a challenge, and the following year the parishioners poured into the streets and made an even greater racket. Ever since, the districts of San Salvador and Del Carmen have sent costumed teams to compete on to the Parque José Martí at this time of year, armed with banners, musical instruments and fireworks, and an elaborate multi-storied structure called a *trabajo de plaza*, prepared in great secrecy throughout the year. The revels continue until dawn, or the onset of exhaustion and deafness.

North coast*

Visitors to the harbour town of **Caibarién** are greeted by a sculpture of a giant crab. From here a newly built causeway links the mainland to a chain of virtually uninhabited offshore islands forming part of the Sabana archipelago. Large-scale tourist development of the islands is inevitable, particularly on **Cayo Santa Maria*** with its great stretches of pristine beach. For the time being, however, there is only one restaurant here.

Embalse de Hanabanilla★
52km – allow 1hr by car

This great artificial lake in the Sierra de Escambray is most easily reached from Santa Clara (the sierra itself is described as part of the surroundings of Trinidad on page 235). A mountain road links Hanabanilla with Topes de Collantes and from there to Trinidad.

From the centre of Santa Clara go south down Calle Cuba towards Manicaragua, 29km away. A road sign in the square in Manicaragua points right towards Hanabanilla, 23km further on.

The Hanabanilla reservoir has a capacity of 286 000 000 cubic metres of water, held back by the dam built across the River Hanabanilla in 1961. A hotel, one of the first to be built after the Revolution, overlooks the reservoir. It is a tranquil spot, ideal for boating, fishing for the plentiful trout, or exploring the surrounding area on foot or horseback.

Making the most of Santa Clara

COMING AND GOING

By train – The **Estación de Trenes**, ☎ (422) 2895, is in the Parque de los Mártires to the north of the city centre. Several trains a day to Havana, one train a day to Santiago de Cuba.

By bus – The **Terminal de Ómnibus Nacionales**, on the Carretera Central on the northwestern outskirts of the city. The **Viazul** tourist coach between Havana and Santiago de Cuba stops in Santa Clara on Tuesday and Friday and on Monday and Thursday in the opposite direction.

GETTING AROUND

It is best to see the sights by car.

By taxi – The official **Turistaxi** firm has a 24hr service. To call a cab, ☎ (422) 4512/15. Other firms include **Cubataxi**, ☎ (422) 26-903, and **Taxi-Ok**, ☎ 3999.

Car hire – There is a **Havanautos** desk in the Motel Los Caneyes and a **Transautos** desk at the Santa Clara Libre.

Carriage rides – This is a convenient way of getting around.

ADDRESS BOOK

Tourist information – Information from **Cubanacan**, Calle Maceo between Calle General Roloff and Carretera Central, ☎ (422) 2-6169, and **Rumbos**, Calle Independencia No. 167 between Calle Alemán and Calle Toscano, ☎ (422) 27-292, at the **Café Europa** on the corner of Calle Indipendencia and Calle Luis Estéves, or from the various hotels.

Banks /Currency exchange – **Banco Financiero Internacional**, on the corner of Calle Cuba and Calle Rafael Trista, and **Cadeca**, in the adjoining building (*8.30am-6pm; 8.30am-midday Sunday*).

Post office / Telephone – **Correos** on Calle Colón between Calles Rafael Tristá and Eduardo Machado, but it is quicker to send mail or make phone calls from a hotel.

Health – Medical treatment is available at the Santa Clara Libre.

Servicupet service station – **La Estrella** and **Oro Negro**, both at the junction of Calle General Roloff (formerly Caridad) and Carretera Central to the south of Parque Vidal. There is another service station on the motorway at the Km 259 marker.

WHERE TO STAY

See map page 206
Do not rely on the offers of accommodation made by touts on the street in Santa Clara.

- **Santa Clara**

Between US$15-20

Olga Rivera Gómez, Calle Evangelista Llanes No. 20, ☎ (422) 5828. 🍴📧 An attractive room in a pretty house on a quiet square 5 blocks north of the centre via Calle Maximo Gómez. Warm welcome from charming proprietress.

Milan, Calle Villuendas No. 305 between Calle Nazareno and Calle Pastora, ☎ (422) 4022 - 2 rooms. Centrally located, fine colonial-era house with attractive decor and a courtyard. Warm welcome.

Under US$30

Hotel Santa Clara Libre, Parque Vidal No. 6 between Calles Padre Chao and Rafael Tristá, ☎ (422) 27548/50 – 151rm. 🍴📧 𝒫 📺 ✕ cc Car hire, medical services. This high building dating from the 1950s has not worn well and its rooms are small and skimpily furnished, but it is the only city centre hotel.

Between US$30-50

Motel Los Caneyes, junction of Avenida de los Eucaliptos and Circunvalación de Santa Clara, ☎ /Fax (422) 28-140 – 90rm. 🍴📧 𝒫 📺 ✕ 🏊 cc 3km west of the city centre beyond Plaza de la Revolución. Laid out like an "Indian" village, with huts in a well-wooded setting. The accommodation is spacious and attractive but not well-lit.

Hotel Granjita, Carretera Malezas km 2.5, ☎ (422) 26-051, Fax (422) 22-762 – 75 rms 🍴 📧 ☎ 📺 ✕ 🏊 cc Bureau de change, medical facilities and fitness centre. A group of concrete chalets, comfortable and well-maintained. Ideal for peace and quiet.

- **Remedios**

Between US$30-40

🍴 Hotel Mascotte, Parque Martí, ☎ (422) 39-5144 – 14rm. 🍴📧 𝒫 ✕ 🏯 cc Well away from the tourist trail, the hotel has recently been refurbished, and is ideal for anyone wanting to visit Cayo Santa María. The rooms have been enlarged and made more comfortable, and the rise in prices is quite justified.

- **Embalse de Hanabanilla**

Under US$30

Hotel Hanabanilla, Salto Hanabanilla, Manicaragua, ☎ (42) 8-6932, Fax (491) 3506 – 125rm. 🍴📧 𝒫 📺 ✕ 🏊 cc Medical services. A large 1960s concrete structure overlooking the Hanabanilla reservoir. Splendid surroundings. Most rooms have a view of the lake.

EATING OUT

The best restaurant in Santa Clara is the one in the Motel Los Caneyes. Otherwise take your chance in a paladar.

You can have an inexpensive meal among quite pleasant surroundings standing at the counter of **El Castillo**, at the corner of Calle Villeundas and Calle San Miguel, and also at **La Casona**, at the junction of the Carretera Central and Calle Marta Abréu (near the river on the south side of town).

Ice cream – A Coppelia ice-cream parlour occupies the whole of the building opposite the post office.

HAVING A DRINK

Bar – **La Marquesina**, next to the theatre. Busy, informal city centre bar.

Concerts – The **Casa de la Cultura**, on Parque Vidal advertises concerts. Also on the square is the **Casa de la Trova** which has traditional music. **Club Mejunje**, Calle Marta Abréu between Calle Zayas and Calle Fabbián also has trova (on Thursday), as well as disco music (Friday).

Discotheque – You could try the nightclub in the Hotel Santa Clara, a favourite with locals.

OTHER THINGS TO DO

Excursions – With a car it is possible to drive out on to the islands via the causeway linking the port of Caibarién with Cayo Santa María.

Theatre – **Teatro de la Caridad**. Programme details ☎ (422) 5548.

SHOPPING

Crafts – **Tienda Artex**, on Parque Vidal between Calles Tristá and Marta Abreu. Open 9am-6.30pm. This boutique has a limited stock of souvenirs, cassettes, books and postcards.

Books – **Llibrería Vietnam**, on Calle Independencia between Calles Luis Estévez and Independencia.

TRINIDAD ★★★
Sancti Spíritus Province
Pop 50 000
82km from Cienfuegos and 345km from Havana
See map page 206

Not to be missed
The colonial-era buildings around Plaza Major.
A stroll through the cobbled streets of the old town.
A show at the "Conjunto folklórico".

And don't forget...
Get off to an early start before the crowds arrive.
Stout footwear is a must on Trinidad's cobbled streets.
The town and its surroundings are worth more than a day trip.
Check brakes and tyres before driving up into the Sierra del Escambray.

Of the two routes linking Cienfuegos and Trinidad the more attractive is the coast road which runs between the Sierra del Escambray and the Caribbean shore. Watch out in winter for masses of migrating crabs crossing the road – they are definitely not good for your tyres. You are strongly advised not to use the stretch of mountain road between Cienfuegos and Topes de Collantes. Parts of it are very steep, unsurfaced, and spectacularly potholed.

Trinidad rooftops and the tower of St Francis of Assisi

M. Goin/SCOPE

Central Cuba

Sheltered by the Sierra del Escambray, secretive Trinidad kept itself to itself for well over a century. With the coming of tourism, this exquisite small town has finally emerged from its isolation, though it still seems to belong to a world which has long since passed, and the rattle of a horse-drawn carriage is more common than the roar of a diesel lorry. The 19C part of the town is laid out on the familiar grid, but the old centre consists of a tangled web of lanes still paved with the cobbles brought here as ballast aboard Spanish ships. In subtle shades of ochre, blue and pastel green and with only one storey, the characteristic Trinidad houses have spacious interiors, half-hidden from view behind elegant grilles.

Trinidad was declared a national monument in 1965, then in 1988 was added to the **UNESCO** World Heritage list. Restoration work has brought back the town's colonial-era charm, and hotel building has been deliberately limited in order to preserve its unique character. But Trinidad has inevitably become a compulsory stop for coach parties, and while its inhabitants mostly retreat indoors during the day from the heat of the sun, the centre of town can become crowded with visitors from abroad. Plaza Mayor is the focal point of tourist activity, leaving other parts of the town to cast their special spell on visitors who are prepared to explore a little. A reinforced police presence has discouraged the *jineteros* who used to make tourists' lives a misery.

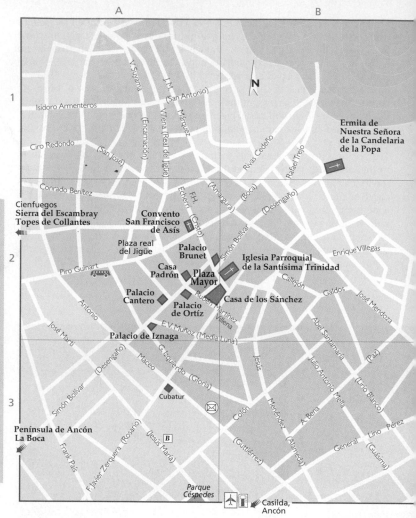

Ermita de
Nuestra Señora
de la Candelaria
de la Popa

Cienfuegos
Sierra del Escambray
Topes de Collantes

Convento
San Francisco
de Asís

Plaza real
del Jigüe

Palacio
Brunet

Casa
Padrón

Iglesia Parroquial
de la Santísima Trinidad

Plaza
Mayor

Palacio
Cantero

Casa de los Sánchez

Palacio
de Ortíz

Palacio de Iznaga

Cubatur

Península de Ancón
La Boca

Parque
Céspedes

Casilda,
Ancón

Past prosperity

The third of the seven colonial *villas* established by the Spaniards, Trinidad was founded by Diego Velázquez in 1514. The first settlers mostly occupied themselves in the hunt for gold. But the seams were soon exhausted, and as early as 1518 people left to take part in the conquest of Mexico under the leadership of Hernán Cortés. For two centuries Trinidad led a modest existence, its inhabitants making a living from sugar and tobacco and from cattle ranching. There was a thriving contraband trade, particularly with the British colony of Jamaica, and pirate raids were frequent. Sugar production increased in the second half of the 18C, and was given an extra boost when the rebellions led by Toussaint-Louverture destroyed the rival plantations in Haiti and pushed up the price of

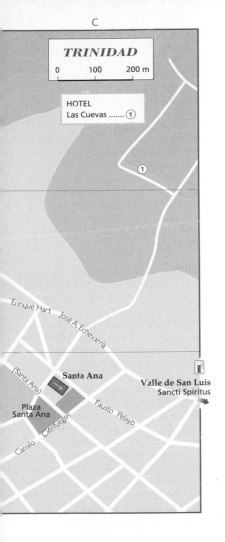

C

TRINIDAD

0   100   200 m

HOTEL
Las Cuevas .... ①

①

Enrique Hart

José A. Echevarría

(Santa Ana)

Santa Ana

Valle de San Luis
Sancti Spíritus

Plaza
Santa Ana

Fausto Pelayo

Camilo Cienfuegos

Cuban "white gold". Slaves were imported in large numbers to work on the newly extended plantations, and *Santería* has been widely practised in the area ever since.

At the beginning of the 19C there were as many as 43 sugar-mills in the nearby San Luis valley, and huge quantities of sugar were exported through the port of Casilda, 5km to the south of the town. Trinidad's boom-times lasted until the middle of the century, leaving their mark in the fine colonial-era buildings which are the pride of the town.

A Sleeping Beauty

As the 19C wore on, the development of the harbour at Cienfuegos and above all the rise of sugar-beet production in Europe brought Trinidad's glory days to an end. The docks at Casilda were virtually abandoned, but the final blow came with the abolition of slavery and the two wars of independence, in the course of which those symbols of Spanish rule, sugar mills and plantations, were destroyed by the rebels.

By the beginning of the 20C Trinidad was languishing in almost total obscurity, forgotten by the world.

Tour of the town
Allow half a day

Most of Trinidad's tourist attractions are located around the Plaza Mayor. But every visitor should spend at least some time wandering through the charming streets leading off the square. The majority of streets have two names, most residents preferring to use the older one, which is given in brackets on plans of the town.

Plaza Mayor★★★ (A2)

All the streets in the old part of Trinidad seem to lead to the town's main square. The centre of the square is bounded by a low wall, whose mellow ochre colour harmonises perfectly with the brightly-painted façades of the buildings all around. Steps guarded by a pair of elegant bronze greyhounds lead up to a quartet of floral parterres defined by low wrought-iron fences. But the scanty shade cast by the tall palms is not enough to attract many locals here in the heat of the day.

The Church of the Santissima Trinidad (*11.30am-12.30pm; 2.30pm-6pm Saturdays; 9am-8pm Sundays; daily Mass at 7pm*) spends most of the day slumbering behind its locked doors. Completed towards the end of the 19C, it boasts a superb altarpiece carved in precious woods and a Spanish figure of Christ of the True Cross dating from 1731. The church's austere façade which dominates the northeast side of the square is a useful point of reference when wandering around the town.

To the left of the church, at the corner of Calle Fernando Hernández and Calle Simón Bolivar, stands the splendid ochre building known as the **Palacio Brunet**✶✶. Built between 1740 and 1808 for the Spanish Count Nicolás de la Cruz y Brunet, it houses the **Museo Romántico**✶✶ (*Open 9am-5pm; closed Monday. Admission charge*). Arranged around the imposing courtyard, the palace's spacious interiors (currently being renovated) are filled with a fascinating collection of 19C furniture and decorative objects, evoking the very European life-style led by the Cuban upper crust in the 19C. In a splendid setting of marble and glittering mirrors, there are mahogany chests of drawers, bisque figurines, French opalines, and Sèvres porcelain (currently under reconstruction).

The **Casa Padrón**✶, at No. 457 Calle Simón Bolivar, dates from the 18C. In 1801 Alexander von Humboldt stayed here at the invitation of its owner; the great German explorer and naturalist was making a brief visit to Trinidad in the course of one of his expeditions.

The building now houses the **Museo de Arqueología Guamuhaya**✶ (*Open 9am-5pm; closed Saturday. Admission charge*). Guamuhaya is the indigenous name for the mountain range now known as the Sierra del Escambray to the north of Trinidad. The museum's somewhat chaotic collections consist mostly of objects from the pre-Columbian period, like skeletons, shells, jewellery and pottery, as well as an array of stuffed animals and a few items from colonial times. On the far side of the courtyard is a beautiful example of a tiled kitchen.

On the southwest side of the plaza, at Calle Rubén Martínez Villena No. 33, stands the 19C **Palacio de Ortíz**✶, traditionally thought of as the successor to the dwelling built by Cortez before he led his army of conquistadors off to conquer Mexico. The palace now houses an **art gallery** where works by contemporary artists are on sale. There is a fine view over the square from the first floor balcony.

On the right-hand side of the plaza, facing the church, is the **Casa de los Sánchez-Iznaga**✶, made up of two buildings, one dating from 1738, the other from 1785. The building is now the **Museo de Arquitectura colonial**✶✶ (*Open 9am-5pm; closed Friday. Admission charge*), which tells the story of the town's architectural development. There are plans and models showing the changes in building design and technique in the 18C and 19C, as well as exquisitely carved woodwork in the shape of doors, shutters, and grilles (which were also fashioned in wrought iron). In a small room off the courtyard is the ancestor of the jacuzzi, a steam shower dating from the early 20C. There is a guided tour, for the time being only in Spanish.

Around the Plaza Mayor (A2)

Unlike most of Cuba's colonial-era towns, which were laid out on the familiar grid pattern, Trinidad was unplanned, and its winding streets, paved with cobbles brought as shipboard ballast, form a complex and fascinating pattern.

The pretty pastel-coloured single storey houses alternate with the mansions of wealthy sugar planters, some of which have been restored thanks to their new status as tourist attractions.

One block to the southwest of the Plaza Mayor, at No. 423 Calle Simón Bolívar, is the **Palacio Cantero**★★, completed in 1828. Its sumptuous rooms are now used for the exhibits of the **Museo Municipal de Historia**★★ *(Open 9am-5pm; closed Saturday. Admission charge)*. The fine collection of decorative objects and of furniture, including fine Cuban pieces, gives an idea of the luxurious lifestyle of its sugar-millionaire owner. The building is topped by a tower which gives a superb **view** over the town and the Sierra.

On the other side of the street from the Palacio Cantoro, on the corner with Calle Gustavo Izquierdo, No. 416 Calle Simón Bolívar is the 19C **Palacio de Iznaga**★, once the luxurious residence of one of Trinidad's richest families. It is currently being restored for conversion into a hotel.

Return to the Plaza Mayor and go along Calle Fernando Hernández Echerri which leads northwest out of the square from the Museo Romántico.

About a hundred metres from the square stands one of Trinidad's most prominent landmarks, the tall tower of the **Convent of St Francis of Assisi**. The tower once belonged to a convent and church completed between 1726 and 1747, eventually used as a barracks by the Spanish army until the end of the colonial regime.

It was then used for a whole variety of purposes, including a chicken-farm, before becoming a school. Since 1984 it has housed the **Museo de la Lucha contra Bandidos**★ *(9am-5pm; closed Monday. Admission charge)*. Photographs, plans and models illustrate the struggle against the "bandits", the anti-Castro units who carried on guerrilla warfare in the Escambray mountains between 1960 and 1965. In the courtyard is part of an American U2 spy plane shot down during the 1962 Missile Crisis *(See p 29)*. From the top of the tower, the **view**★★ takes in the whole of the town, the Sierra, and the Caribbean.

From the convent go west along Calle Piro Guinart

The **Plaza Real del Jigüe** is one block down from the convent. A jigüe tree marks the spot where Trinidad's founding mass was celebrated by Father Bartlomé de las Casas in 1514.

Return to the Plaza Mayor and go up Calle Simón Bolívar between the Museo Romántico (Palacio Brunet) and the church. Continue for 700m to the top of the hill.

There is nothing left of the **Hermitage of Nuestra Senora de la Candelaria de la Popa** except the blocked up main facade, but the **view** over Trinidad makes the gentle climb well worthwhile.

Protector of the Indians
Bartolomé de las Casas (1474-1566) was a priest and landowner from Seville. In Cuba, he provoked a whole series of controversies, which continued to reverberate right up to the 20C. In 1512, he was granted an "encomienda", the right to use indigenous slaves as agricultural labourers, but soon turned against the injustice and tyranny to which they were subjected. Renouncing his own rights, this "Apostle of the Indies" appealed to the Spanish Crown against the natives' inhumane treatment by this system of forced labour, but only to the extent of envisaging their replacement by Africans. De las Casas was the inspiration behind the "Leyes Nuevas" of 1542, promulgated by Charles V, which opened the way to the dismantling of the encomienda system.

Street in Trinidad

Go back towards the town centre and turn left into Calle José Mendoza, the second road on the left. Continue for 800m.

Calle José Mendez is particularly attractive. It leads to the **Plaza Santa Ana**, a vast space which is in total contrast to the town's narrow, winding streets.

The **Church of Santa Ana** overlooking the square is awaiting restoration. The large yellow building occupying a corner of the square is the **former Royal Prison**, now transformed into a cultural complex mainly aimed at tourists, with a bar, restaurant, art gallery and craft shop.

Around Trinidad
See map p. 206

Part of the attraction of Trinidad is that it is close to several contrasting landscapes. To the north are the cool uplands of the Sierra del Escambray, with fresh air, waterfalls, and a luxuriant cloak of mosses, lichens, tree ferns and conifers. They are a paradise for walkers, with enticing glimpses of the Caribbean and the red roofs of Trinidad.

On the other hand, the mills and canefields of the San Luis Valley, protected like Trinidad itself by World Heritage designation, offer a trip back in time to the plantations as they used to be. Finally, on the coast to the south of the town are some of Cuba's finest beaches.

The coast★
15km drive (plus 12km with a detour to Casilda). Allow 20min. From Trinidad go west along Calle Simón Bolívar, and after crossing the railway turn right towards La Boca.

The nearest beach to Trinidad, **Playa La Boca**, is only 5km from town, at the mouth of the Río Guaurabo. La Boca is a fishing village, its not particularly attractive shoreline backed by little houses with verandas. Despite the lack of tourist facilities, it is a busy place, very popular with local people, but the better beaches are a little further on.

Continue south along the coast. After 5km, there is a turning to the left towards Casilda, which can also be reached directly from Trinidad via a road running alongside the railway.

Six kilometres to the south of Trinidad, the little **port of Casilda** shared in the town's former prosperity but is now a backwater, though there are fishing boats and some sugar is still exported. The detour here can be left out if time is short.

Return to the junction and continue along the coast road for 4km.

The sandy beaches of the **Ancón peninsula★** are easily the most attractive on Cuba's southern coast. Between them, **Playa María Aguilar★** and **Playa Ancón★** offer 4km of sun-bleached sand and each has a large hotel. Just out to sea is a coral reef, with excellent scuba diving. The peninsula is the best place to stay for anyone wanting to combine a beach holiday with a modicum of culture and the chance of getting to know something of the Cuban countryside and mountains.

San Luis valley★
13km, allow 20min. From Plaza Santa Ana go up Calle Camilo Cienfuegos and take the second turn on the right towards Sancti Spiritus.

Along with Trinidad itself, this fertile valley at the foot of the Sierra del Escambray was added to UNESCO's World Heritage List in 1988. Its other name is the Valle de los Ingenios (Sugar Mill Valley), and its landscape is very evocative of the 19C heyday of the sugar industry.

On its hilltop 5km from Trinidad, the lookout point called the **Mirador de la Loma★** has a clear view over the whole of the valley. There's also a convenient bar.

After 10km turn left towards a tall tower.

A track leads to **Manaca Iznaga**, a sugar plantation which in the 18C and 19C belonged to the wealthiest family in the area. The 44m high **tower** (*Admission charge*) which dominates the estate allowed the work of the slaves to be closely supervised. A bell was rung at the beginning and end of the working day and was also used to sound the alarm.

The *barracón* (the slaves' quarters) can be seen, as can the **Masters' mansion★**, now a bar and restaurant. Built in 1750, it is a huge structure, a witness to the lavish life-style of the Ignaza family.

Sierra del Escambray★★
20km, allow 45min. Go west along Calle Piro Guinart towards Cienfuegos and after 5km turn right by a cafeteria.

Sometimes known by its indigenous name of Guamuhaya, the Sierra del Escambray was the scene of two episodes in Cuba's Revolutionary history. The mountains served as a refuge, firstly for the guerrillas led by Che Guevara before their descent on Santa Clara in December 1958, then later for the last efforts of anti-Castro fighters between 1960 and 1965.

To the north of Trinidad, the uplands take in part of three provinces, Sancti Spíritus, Villa Clara, and Cienfuegos. Cienfuegos province is dominated by San Juan (1 140m), the highest summit in the range. The road from Trinidad to Santa Clara consists largely of hairpin bends, winding among slopes carpeted in lichens, mosses and tree ferns. As the plain is left behind, its fields of crops give way to coffee plantations and to conifers, a sure sign of the lower temperatures typical of the uplands.

20km north of Trinidad at an altitude of 700m is the settlement of **Topes de Collantes**★. Blessed with a cool climate (with an average temperature of 21°C), it is a health resort with a variety of visitor facilities. Among them is a huge structure from the 1950s, built as a sanatorium and now reverting to its original purpose after being used for a while as a teacher training college (*See Making the Most of Trinidad*). Spa treatments are being developed, based on the nearby thermal springs.

The mountains are threaded by walking trails. One path, 2.5km long, leads from Topes de Collantes to the **Salto de Caburní**★, where it is possible to splash around in the pools at the foot of a 62m high waterfall, a designated national monument.

The road from Topes de Collantes to Lake Hanabanilla is in very poor condition and the reservoir can be more easily reached from Santa Clara (see page 226).

Making the most of Trinidad

Central Cuba

COMING AND GOING
The Viazul tourist coach is the best way of getting to and from Trinidad for visitors without the use of a car.

By air – The tiny **Aeropuerto de Trinidad** (2km southwest of Trinidad towards Casilda, ☎ (419) 2547, has flights operated by **Inter** ☎ (419) 6212/4406 to Havana, Varadero, Cayo Largo and Cayo Coco, and by **Aerocaribbean** to Santiago.

By bus – The **Terminal de Ómnibus Interprovinciales**, is on Calle Piro Guinart between Calle Izquierdo and Calle Maceo. Trinidad is particularly well served by **Viazul** coaches. There are daily buses to Havana (3hr, US$25), Cienfuegos and Santa Clara, and every other day to Varadero and Sancti Spíritus.

Seats can be booked the day before or up to one hour before departure, either at the ticket office or ☎ (419) 4448. Arrangements can be made for coaches to pick up from the hotels.

GETTING AROUND TRINIDAD
Walking is the only way to enjoy the historic centre of Trinidad, but a vehicle is essential to explore the surrounding area. Most of the addresses given below are at Playa Ancón, 15km south of the town.

By taxi – **Turistaxi** ☎ (419) 2479 or 4011 and **Taxi-OK** both have a 24-hour service. There is a taxi stand in the car park of the Hotel Ancón.

Car hire – **Via rent-a-car** is at the junction of Calle José Martí and Calle Camilo Cienfuegos close to the Parque Céspedes, ☎ (419) 4101. **Transautos** has desks at the Motel Las Cuevas and the Hotel Ancón, and **Havanautos** is represented at the Ancón and the Costasur.

Bike hire – Bicycles can be hired for the day from the Hotel Ancón and the Hotel Costasur.

ADDRESS BOOK
Tourist information – **Cubatur** (A3) on the corner of Calle António Maceo and Calle Francisco Javier Zerquera, ☎ (419) 4414, runs trips around the town and its surroundings, and **Rumbos** is located beside the Mesón del Regidor on Calle Simon Bolívar.

Banks / Currency exchange – The **Banco Nacional de Cuba** (A3) on Calle José Martí between Calle Colón and Calle Francisco Javier Zerquera will change travellers' cheques and hard currency.

Post Office / Telephone – The **Correos** (A3) is on Calle António Maceo between Calle Colón and Calle Francisco Javier Zerquera, four blocks away from the Plaza Mayor. The **Centro telefónico** is on Paque Céspedes. But it is better to send correspondence and make international telephone calls from the larger hotels.

Health – The **Clínica Internacional** is at Calle Lino Pérez No. 130 at the junction with Calle Anastasio Cárdenas, ☎ (419) 3391. Consultations and 24-hour emergency service payable in dollars. Pharmacy attached.

Servicupet – **Trinidad** (C3) on the Sancti Spíritus road on the outskirts of town, and another branch (B3) 2km southwest on the way to Casilda

WHERE TO STAY

There is now so much private accommodation on offer in Trinidad that the choice is yours. But the following establishments are particularly recommended.

Between US$15-20
Fernandez de Lara, Calle F Hernánez Echerri No. 54, ☎ (419) 3634. ⚔ 🗴 Close to the Palacio Brunet and Plaza Mayor, this is a fine old dwelling-house with a spacious room opening on to its patio. The landlord knows his Trinidad back to front and is a good cook as well. Garage.

Lidice Zeuera Mauri, Calle Simon Bolívar No. 518, ☎ (419) 3485. ⚔ 🗴 Just up the hill from the square, this house is called a "little palace" by its owner, and well deserves it. Striking decor, billiards, a delightful bedroom, and a garage.

Estela, Calle Simon Bolívar No. 557 between Calle Márquez and Calle Mendoza, ☎ (419) 4329. ⚔ 🗒 A little further to the north of the town centre, Estela's is a well-known paladar as well as a beautifully decorated place to stay. The attractive rooms have a view over the town.

Carlos Soto Longo, Plaza Mayor No. 33 (south side), ☎ (419) 4169. In the heart of the town, this house has a fascinating art collection as well as pleasant accommodation overlooking a courtyard.

Casa Muñoz, corner of Calle Martí and Calle Olvido, ☎ (419) 3673. ⚔ 🗒 Superb colonial-era building with an

outdoor terrace; courtyard, peaceful rooms and garage. English-speaking and very knowledgeable proprietor.

Apart from the Motel Las Cuevas, all the hotels listed are in the area around Trinidad rather than in the town itself, in Topes de Collantes and Ancón. See map p. 206.

• Trinidad
Under US$30
Finca Ma Dolores, Carretera Circuito Sur, ☎ (419) 3581 – 20rm. ⚔ 🗒 𝒫 TV 🗴 ⚒ 3km from Trinidad on the road towards Topes de Collantes close to the Río Guarabo. A stay on this farm could include riding a horse through the surrounding countryside, watching the cows at milking time or betting on the outcome of a cock fight, as well as enjoying an evening fiesta of music and dance - after which the comforts of the modestly furnished chalets could seem doubly welcome.

Between US$30-50
Motel Las Cuevas, Finca Santa Ana, ☎ (419) 6133, Fax 6131 – 112rm. ⚔ 🗒 𝒫 TV ⚒ CC Car hire. One of the limited number of places to stay in town, and much used by tour groups, this motel is located on the hilltop to the north of Plaza Santa Ana with a fine view over the town and the sea. Some of the accommodation is in chalets of variable quality and it is best to ask for one of the more modern rooms overlooking the town.

• Ancón peninsula
Around US$50
Hotel Costasur, Playa Maria Aguilar, ☎ (419) 6174-6-8 – 131rm. ⚔ 🗒 𝒫 TV 🗴 ⚒ 🐾 Y CC Car hire, bureau de change. 14km from Trinidad and ideal for those with their own means of transport. Comfortable and clean rooms. Chalets are slightly more expensive than the main building, but are quieter and closer to the beach. Good range of recreational activities.

Over US$50
Hotel Ancón, Playa Ancón, ☎ (419) 6120/0, Fax (419) 6122 – 279rm. ⚔ 🗒 𝒫 TV 🗴 ⚒ 🐾 Y CC Car hire, bureau de change. This huge hotel dominates the lovely beach 3km south of the Hotel

Costasur and was extended in the late 1990s. The best rooms are those in the recent extension, some of which have balconies overlooking the beach. Much favoured by tour groups, and most guests are on a full board arrangement. Very wide choice of recreational and sporting activities.

• Sierra del Escambray

Between US$30-50

Hotel Los Helechos, Topes de Collantes, ☎ (42) 40-180/9 – 38rm. ⚑ 📧 🅿 📺 ✖ ⌁. In the heart of the sierra, this hotel makes an excellent base for exploring the mountains. It is small, quiet, and has a pleasant family atmosphere. Rooms are spacious and well-kept, and there is a gym, a sauna and a swimming pool fed from the thermal springs.

Kurhotel Escambray, Topes de Collantes, ☎ (42) 4-0180 – 210rm. ⚑ 📧 🅿 📺 ✖ ⌁ 🆑 The design of this sanatorium is reminiscent of the Hotel Nacional in Havana, though the antiseptic interior is more like a vast hospital. A whole range of medical services are on offer and the rooms are clean and comfortable, but for the ordinary visitor a better bet is the **Villa Caburní** on the way to the salto. Its collection of chalets have a fine view of the sierra and are quieter than the hotel.

Between US$50-100

Villa Guajimico, Km 42 on the Trinidad-Cienfuegos road, Guajimico, ☎ (432) 8125 or 6472 – 50rm. ⚑ 📧 🅿 📺 ✖ ⌁ 🏊 Y 🆑 Car hire. At the foot of the Sierra del Escambray halfway between Cienfuegos and Trinidad, this establishment is a recreational centre run by a French tour operator, with accommodation in the form of 50 chalets nestling by the bank of a river. Activities include scuba diving and learning how to sail a catamaran. Full board available.

EATING OUT

As elsewhere in Cuba, the best meals in terms of price and quality are those offered by the private paladares.

Under US$10

La Coruña, Calle Martí No. 430 between Calle Simon Bolívar and Calle Fidel Claro. A full menu in the attractive setting of a little patio. Friendly hosts, reasonable prices, and exceptionally good fresh fish.

Estela, Calle Simon Bolívar No. 557 (See "Where to Stay in Trinidad"). A spacious courtyard beneath an avocado tree, where you can enjoy a meal of several courses prepared and served with care.

Sol y Son, Calle Simon Bolívar No. 283 between Calle Martí and Calle Frank País. In the southwest part of the town, this paladar is prettily decorated and has a charming courtyard. But its standards may have deteriorated, as it has become something of a victim of its own success.

El Jigüe, at the junction of Calle Rubén Martínez Villena and Calle Piro Guinart (A2), ☎ (419) 4315. Open 11am-5pm. This charming colonial-era house is located on the delightful Plaza Real del Jigüe where Trinidad's founding Mass was celebrated in 1514 by Bartolomé de las Casas. Chicken specialities served on the open-air terrace overlooking the square.

Manaca Iznaga, at km 12 on the road to Sancti Spíritus, Valle de los Ingenios, ☎ (419) 7241. Open midday-8pm. Catering mostly to a tour group clientele in surroundings reminiscent of former glories, this restaurant is in the great mansion built by the immensely wealthy Iznaga family. The furniture and fittings are appropriately opulent and there is a fine view over the San Luis valley. A good place to have a drink even if you are not a member of a group.

Grill Caribe, Carretera a Ancón. 8am-11pm. Close to the María Aguilar beach. Seafood served overlooking the sea.

Between US$10 and US$20

Trinidad Colonial, on the corner of Calle António Maceo No. 402 and Calle Colón (B3), ☎ (419) 3873. Open 10am-10pm. As its name suggests, this restaurant is in a fine old colonial-era mansion. The elegant dining room with its antique furniture seems perfectly in tune with the spirit of Trinidad, but the creole cuisine, though more than adequate, doesn't quite match the surroundings. There is also a piano bar.

WHERE TO HAVE A DRINK

Trinidad really wakes up in the evening, and you need to stay here for several nights to appreciate everything that goes on.

Bars – La Canchánchara, on Calle Rubén Martínez Villena between Calle Ciro Redondo and Calle Piro Guinart (A2). Open 9am-midnight. Taberna with rustic decor, in the same block as the Convent of St Francis of Assisi. Attractive shady patio with frequent evening entertainment provided by musicians and dancers. The house speciality is *canchánchara*, a local cocktail made with rum, honey and lemon juice. One of the liveliest bars in Trinidad, very popular with visitors from abroad.

Concerts – Casa de la Cultura, corner of Calle FJ Zerquera and RM Villena. One of the few places in Trinidad with an almost entirely Cuban clientele. Dancing in the spacious but crowded courtyard to salsa and son.

Casa de la Trova, on the corner of Calle Fernando Hernández Echerri and Calle Jesús Menéndez (B2). Open 9am-4pm. Two blocks east of the Plaza Mayor, this 19C residence stages frequent traditional music events in its courtyard, and there are weekend performances 9pm-1am. The **Conjunto Folklórico** has regular rehearsals in the courtyard of its school on Calle Fernando Hernández Echerri No. 21, close to the Plaza Mayor (A2). The beat of a batá drum tends to attract a handful of spectators, but otherwise this is a moment to treasure, as the members of the group practise the rumba or the balo.

Casa Fischer (or Artex), Calle L Pérez between Calle Maceo and Calle Martí. Another fine courtyard house with good music, still not completely over-run by tourists.

Discotheques - Las Cuevas is the night-club of the Motel Las Cuevas (C1), and is one of the town's most popular hang-outs. Open midnight-3am. Fitted into a sort of cave, with salsa and techno making the stalactites rattle.

La Casa de la Música (*See below*) transforms its rear courtyard (off Calle J M Márquez) into a night club, with music by Cuban rock and salsa bands.

OTHER THINGS TO DO

Excursions – As well as the *Cubatur* and *Rumbos* travel agencies, the hotels in Trinidad and Ancón organise day trips by steam train through the San Luis valley. They can also advise on where to walk or ride in the Sierra del Escambray. Horses are available at the Finca María Dolores.

Sports – The two hotels on the Ancón peninsula offer a wide range of watersports including scuba diving. The coral reef close to Cayo Blanco 20km southeast of the peninsula is a superb diving site. Instruction on scuba diving and catamaran lessons at the sports centre of Villa Guajimico.

SHOPPING

Cigars – The **Fábrica de Tabacos** on the corner of Calle António Maceo and Calle Colón (B3) offers guided tours of fairly short duration, after which there is a chance of purchasing the product. There is a **Casa del Tabaco y del Ron** on the corner of Calle Zerquera and Calle Maceo, and the **Casa del Tabaco** on the corner of Calle Martí and Calle Pérez has a bar and smoking room.

Crafts – There is a daily open-air craft market by the Casa de la Trova, a stone's throw from the Plaza Mayor, with a good choice of lacework among other products.

Craft gallery, opposite the Palacio Cantero. **Oscar Santander Rodríguez**, Calle Concordia between Calle Maceo and Calle Nueva. To the east of Trinidad, there is a pottery which has been in the same family for 15 generations.

Casa de la música on the Plaza Mayor and Calle Francisco Javier Zerquera. At the top of the steps to the right of the Church of the Santísima Trinidad, this colonial-era mansion is completely given over to music, with discs, cassettes and drums for sale, and occasional performances in the courtyard.

Art gallery – The work of contemporary Cuban artists can be admired and purchased in the old Ortíz palace on the Plaza Mayor.

Making the most of Trinidad

SANCTI SPÍRITUS ★

Capital of Sancti Spíritus province
Pop 100 000
70km from Trinidad and 348km from Havana

Not to be missed
A stroll through the old colonial quarter.
A speedboat trip on Lake Zaza.

And remember...
The city's museums and restaurants are closed on Monday.
Winter is the best season for trout-fishing.

The road from Trinidad follows the railway line all the way to the station at Sancti Spíritus. Turn right on to Avenida Jesús Menéndez, cross the river and continue for 500m to the Parque Serafín Sánchez.

All roads in Cuba lead to Sancti Spíritus, close to the geographical centre of the island. Its location at the meeting point of the old provinces of Oriente and Occidente means that most travellers pass through here at one time or another. But in spite of its being a provincial capital and a designated national monument, few people make the effort to explore the town. Sancti Spíritus has long been written off as a place of no special interest, not least by the young Winston Churchill, who described it in 1895 as "second rate" and "most unhealthy". Nevertheless, it is an historic town with a labyrinth of colonial-era streets and a number of architectural highlights. And while hardly in the same league as Trinidad, it has something of the atmosphere of an overgrown and undiscovered village, which lends it a certain charm.

Sugar capital
The fourth of the seven *villas* established by the Spaniards, Sancti Spíritus was founded in 1514. The site chosen for the town turned out to be unsuitable and after only eight years it was rebuilt at its present location. Well inland, it nevertheless attracted the attention of pirates, who sacked it several times in the course of the 16C and 17C.

Eventually the raids ceased, and in the 18C the town prospered thanks to the slave-worked sugar plantations all around.

Sancti Spíritus still depends on sugar; the country's biggest sugar refinery, Central Uruguay, is sited nearby, and a cane by-product provides another local industry, the Jatibonico paper mill, with its raw material.

The town
Allow 1hr

Like Trinidad, Sancti Spíritus lacks the clear layout of the typical Cuban colonial-era town, and its maze of streets can tempt visitors to wander at will. But most of the things to see are located between the Parque Serafín Sánchez and the bridge over the Río Yabayo.

The Parque Serafín Sánchez is named after a local hero who fell in the struggle for independence in 1896. The vast square, with its shade trees and its neo-Classical buildings, forms the heart of the town, and by Cuban standards it is bustling with traffic.

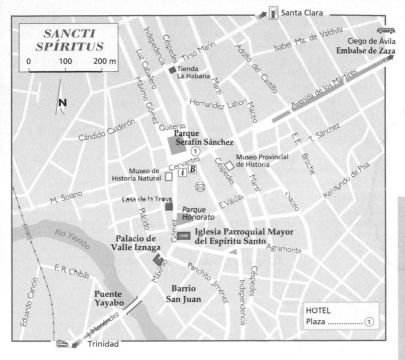

Leave the square by the Hotel Plaza and go along Avenida de las Mártires, then turn first right into Calle Céspedes.

Calle de Céspedes No. 11 is the **Museo Provincial de Historia** *(Open 8.30am-midday and 1pm-5pm; 8.30am- midday Sunday; closed Monday. Admission charge)*. Housed in a particularly fine example of a 19C colonial mansion, the museum traces the history of the town and its surroundings, from pre-Conquest times up to the Revolution.

Return to the Parque Serafín Sánchez.

The little **Museo de Historia Natural** *(Open 8.30am-5pm; 8.30am midday Sunday; closed Monday. Admission charge)*, is just a few steps from the square, at Calle Máximo Gómez No. 2. With its array of stuffed animals and rather dusty displays of minerals, shells, and insects, it is not exactly one of the world's most exciting museums.

Continue along Calle Máximo Gómez for 200m to the Parque Honorato.

The town's principal church, the **Parroquial Mayor del Espíritu Santo** *(Open 9am-11am and 2pm-5.30pm. Admission free)* has a tall yellow tower which dominates the little square, the Parque Honorato. From the very beginning the church shared the fate of Sancti Spíritus. Like the town, it was founded in 1514, then in 1520 it was moved, along with everything else, to the new location. In the 17C it was sacked by pirates, then rebuilt in 1680. The tower was added in the 18C, the cupola in the 19C. The nave ceiling has beautiful **carving**★★.

The corner of Calle Máximo Gómez is graced by the **Palacio de Valle Iznaga★★**, housing the **Museo de Arte Colonial★★** *(Open 8.30am-5pm; 1pm-8pm Saturday; 8.30am-12.30pm Sunday; closed Monday. Admission charge)*. This palatial residence dates from the 18C and was the first two-storey building to be erected in the town. Outside are window grilles and a fine balcony, all in wrought iron, while the aristocratic interiors have fine 19C furniture made locally, as well as stained glass and an array of decorative items. The museum is currently undergoing restoration.

Continue along Calle Máximo Gómez, turning left into Calle Padre Quintero, the final street before the bridge.

The Barrio San Juan★★, the old colonial quarter of Sancti Spíritus, consists of several streets between Calle Panchito Jiménez and the Río Yayabo. The quiet cobbled lanes and the little colour-washed houses with pretty red-tiled roofs are reminiscent of Trinidad, but are mercifully free of tourists.

At the riverside, the scene is dominated by the grey outline of the **Puente Yayabo**, the arched bridge over the river of the same name. It dates from 1825 and is one of the oldest in the country.

Around Sancti Spíritus
See map page 206

Embalse de Zaza★ (Zaza reservoir)
From the Parque Serafín Sánchez go along Avenida de los Mártires and then along the Carretera Central towards Ciego de Ávila. After 3km turn right at the sign pointing to the Hotel Zaza and continue for 5km.

This artificial lake with its capacity of 1 020 million cubic metres is the country's biggest freshwater reservoir. It is well stocked with trout *(See Making the most of Sancti Spíritus)* and the well-wooded surroundings offer good hunting.

Making the most of Sancti Spíritus

COMING AND GOING

By train – The *Estación de Trenes*, ☎ (41) 2-4790, is located at the junction of Avenida Jesús Menéndez and the main road to Trinidad, 300m southwest of the bridge over the Yayabo. One train a day links Sancti Spíritus to Havana (8hr) and there are two trains a day to Cienfuegos (4hr) and Santa Clara (2hr).

By bus – The *Estación de Ómnibus* is on the Carretera Central in the direction of Ciego de Ávila, 1km from the Parque Serafín Sánchez. *Viazul* coaches stop here twice a week on the route between Havana and Santiago (Tuesday and Friday, Monday and Thursday in the reverse direction), and there is a service every other day to Trinidad. Additional, but less reliable services are run by Astro.

GETTING AROUND
Since most of the places of interest to visitors are concentrated in the historic centre of Sancti Spíritus, the best way to explore the town is on foot.

By carriage – An alternative to strolling around the town is to hire one of the many horse-drawn carriages for a peso or two. Small change should be kept for this purpose.

Taxis – Taxis can normally be found outside the Hotel Plaza and the Hotel Zaza

Car hire – The *Transautos* office is in the Hotel Plaza and *Havanautos* shares the *Islazul* office (*See below*).

ADDRESS BOOK

Post office/Telephone – The *correos* is on Calle Independencia 100m south of the Parque Serafín Sánchez. International telephone calls are best made from the Hotel Zaza.

Tourist information – Tourist information is available from *Islazul* on the south side of the square at Calle Cervantes No. 1 (first floor). They can also provide tours of the town.

Banks and money – *Banco Financiero Internacional*, Calle Independencia No. 2.

Health service – 24hr pharmacy on the north side of the square in front of the Caridad church.

Servicupet service stations – *Chambelón*, to the northwest of the town on the road to Santa Clara; *Majagua*, on the road towards Ciego de Ávila.

WHERE TO STAY

Under US$10

Casa de la Amistad, Calle Agramonte No. 108 between Calle Llano and Calle Independencia, ☎ (41) 2-7936 – 4 rm. A fine old colonial-era house with limited accommodation. Closed in August.

Under US$30

Hotel Plaza, on the corner of Calle Independencia and Avenida de los Mártires, ☎ (41) 27124/68 - 27 rooms ⌗ ▤ ℘ TV ✗ This city centre hotel occupies a fine old building in the Parque Serafín Sánchez. Some of the rooms have been refurbished. The best are the ones facing the square. Inexpensive.

Between US$30-50

Hotel Zaza, Finca San José, Lago Zaza, ☎ (41) 28512-6, Fax (41) 28334 – 65 rm. ⌗ ▤ ℘ TV ✗ ⟁ CC Medical services. 10km from Sancti Spíritus, this concrete building on the banks of the Zaza reservoir is patronised by fishermen as well as by tour groups en route from one end of the country to the

other. The natural surroundings are attractive and boat trips and horse riding are available. Rooms are reasonable for the price.

EATING OUT

The food provided in the town's state restaurants is not of a high standard and most are closed by 8.30pm. A better bet is simply to ask around for addresses of paladares. Two of the better ones are close to the church. **El Mesón** is opposite, and **El Conquistador** is in Calle Agramonte. Sino-Cuban cuisine is served in **El Shanghai** at Calle Independencia No. 65.

WHERE TO HAVE A DRINK

Concerts – Night life in Sancti Spíritus is fairly limited, but one place to try is the **Casa de la Trova** at Avenida Máximo Gómez No.26, 150 metres to the south of the Parque Serafín Sánchez, where there is a bar and the chance of hearing local musicians playing traditional music.

OTHER THINGS TO DO

Excursions – Boat trips around the lake and horse riding can be arranged at the Hotel Zaza (*See above*).

Sports – The Hotel Zaza can arrange a variety of activities including fishing trips and hunting expeditions. There is an annual fishing competition in September.

SHOPPING

Tienda La Habana on the corner of Calle Céspedes and Calle Tirso Marín is a well-stocked supermarket, a good place to get a picnic together or to eat in the cafeteria on the first floor.

Market – In Calle E Valdés between Calle Independencia and Calle Céspedes. 8am-4pm except Sunday. Mangoes, avocados, bananas. Excellent *batidos* (milk shakes) are also available (mornings only) for the princely sum of 2 pesos.

Art – Calle Céspedes No. 26, close to the provincial museum.

CIEGO DE ÁVILA

Capital of Ciego de Ávila province
Pop 90 000
425km from Havana and 440km from Santiago de Cuba

Not to be missed
The "pedraplén", the causeway linking the mainland to Cayo Coco.
The beach at Cayo Coco or Cayo Guillermo.

And remember...
The little town of Morón is a better overnight stop than Ciego de Ávila.
Mosquito repellent is a must when exploring the keys and lagoons.

After leaving Sancti Spíritus the Carretera Central skirts Lake Zaza and then runs directly for 74km to Ciego de Ávila.

Since main roads and railways converge on the town and it has its own airport, Ciego de Ávila is an important communications centre which it is almost impossible to avoid when travelling through this part of Cuba. The effects of this strategic location are not always pretty, as local people living in houses shaken by lorries and blackened by diesel fumes might testify. Few tourists stop here, most simply passing through on their way to the necklace of *cayos* strung along the north coast. However, the countryside around the town is attractive, with villages lost among orchards and canefields, and, in pleasant contrast to the rather grim and noisy provincial capital, the small town of Morón makes a good base for anyone wishing to explore the area.

Staging-post between east and west

The origins of Ciego de Ávila go back to 1538, when the Spaniard Jácome de Ávila acquired land-holdings in the area. As his estate prospered, it developed into an important way-station for travellers making the long journey between Havana and Santiago de Cuba. However, the town itself was only founded as recently as 1840. A few years later the area played an important part in the wars of independence. This is one of the narrowest points of Cuba, little more than 70km from Caribbean to Atlantic, and it was here that the Spanish military decided to construct a defensive wall all the way from Morón in the north to Júcaro in the south. Called the *Trocha* (path) it was intended to prevent the rebels in Oriente province from moving westward, but failed in its purpose, being breached on more than one occasion. Much later, it was manned by the Batista army in an attempt to prevent Castro's revolutionaries in east and west from joining forces. Today there are only a few remains of this once impressive line of fences, ditches and forts, mostly around Morón.

Around Ciego de Ávila
See map page 207

The biggest draw in Ciego de Ávila province are the two *cayos* linked by road to the mainland and reserved exclusively for foreign holidaymakers. This is the most tempting excursion for visitors staying in Morón, but the countryside around the town is not without its own low-key attractions.

Morón*
36km, allow 45min. Turn left off the Carretera Central 300m beyond the Ciego de Ávila bus station. 1km further on turn right on to the road leading to Morón.

The entrance to this town of 55 000 inhabitants is guarded by a cockerel, cast in bronze, and programmed to emit a strange call twice a day. Apart from its mechanical rooster, there's little to distinguish Morón from a hundred other Cuban towns, though it is a pleasant enough place to linger for a while, perhaps with a *batido de plátano* (banana milk-shake) beneath the arcades lining the main street, Calle José Martí. Morón's inhabitants are used to visitors; the place was once a spa, and the architecture and faded colours of some of its buildings recall former glories. The railway station is particularly grandiose. But follow any one of the streets leading off José Martí and it is surprising how soon they turn into dirt tracks leading through the fields.

The Museo Municipal *(Open 8.30am-midday and 1pm-5.30pm; closed Sunday afternoon. Admission charge)* is in the town centre on Calle Martí between Calle D Daniel and Calle S Antunás. The museum's collections (currently being re-arranged) include prehistoric items from various Latin American countries such as stone axes, ceramics and *esferolitias* (stones buried with the dead). There are documents and personal effects, evoking local heroes of the struggle for independence and the last rooms are devoted to religious observances influenced by Haitian voodoo.

Around Morón

Go along Calle José Martí as far as the northern side of the Parque Agramonte. Turn right, then left into Calle López. Continue for 5km parallel to the canal.

The Laguna de Leche (Milky Lagoon) gets its name from the suspended sodium carbonate which turns it a milky white when the wind ruffles the surface. With an area of 67sqkm it is the country's largest lagoon. Boats can be hired from near the restaurant.

From Calle José Martí in the town centre, go along Calle Libertad to the new highway leading to the keys.

The **Laguna La Redonda** 16km to the north of Morón offers some of the best trout fishing in Cuba. There is a lakeside restaurant and boats can be hired.

Some 4km further on towards Cayo Coco the road passes close to the **Pueblo Celia Sánchez**, also known as the "Dutch Village". Built by Fidel Castro's secretary and confidante, its half-timbered, high-gabled houses are an incongruous sight in these tropical surroundings.

The road turns right towards Cayo Coco and Cayo Guillermo.

If time is short, the beach at La Tinaja is popular with local people and perfectly reasonable *(Turn right towards San Rafael before joining the new highway, then left after Manatí).*

The Cayos**

From the Pueblo Celia Sánchez continue for 7km as far as the coast. A checkpoint marks the beginning of the road leading to Cayo Coco and Cayo Guillermo, which are off-limits to Cubans. There is a toll of US$2. Allow 2hr for the drive from Morón to Cayo Guillermo.

Anyone immune to the attractions of beach holidays need not linger long on these islands, since there is nothing else to do apart from swimming and sunbathing and the usual watersports. However, the **"pedraplan"***, the causeway linking the mainland to Cayo Coco is a different matter, worth a detour for anyone driving through Ciego de Ávila province. Running ruler-straight into the Bahía de Perros (Bay of Dogs), the road atop the 20km causeway seems to be heading into the wide blue yonder of the Atlantic. The scene here as the sun goes down is unforgettable, but be warned; there are no safety barriers and no lighting.

Ciego de Ávila

G. Alberto Rossi/ALTITUDE

The "pedraplén" to Cayo Coco

Some 17km beyond the checkpoint the road crosses the marshy southern coast of **Cayo Coco★★**. The 370sqkm island is mostly covered in forest, the habitat of numerous bird species, and pink flamingos, pelicans, and ibis can often be seen from the road. The road continues for a further 15km to the north of the cayo. The hotels already built along the glorious 20km of sandy beach of this northern shore are no doubt the predecessors of many more.

From the Hotel Cayo Coco go back towards the causeway and turn right after 5km. Continue west for 35km.

The road runs through a number of mangrove islands before reaching **Cayo Guillermo★★**. Much smaller than its neighbour, with a surface area of only 13sqkm and 5km of beach, this key has a pleasantly intimate atmosphere. It also offers excellent fishing.

The only other cayo accessible to visitors is **Cayo Paredón Grande**, to the north of Cayo Romano, reached via the road running east from the Cayo Coco round-about. It has a lighthouse and a chain of completely unspoiled beaches.

COMING AND GOING

By plane – The **Aeropuerto Internacional Máximo Gómez**, ☎ (33) 2-3475 or 2-5717 is at Ceballos, 24km from Ciego de Ávila. A number of companies operate direct weekly flights from Canadian cities to Ciego de Ávila with transfer by bus to Cayo Coco or Cayo Guillermo, and in season there is a weekly Cubana flight from Paris. **Cubana** also has several flights a week to Havana and the charter company **Aerotaxi** has flights to a number of provincial cities.

By train – The **Terminal de Ferrocarriles**, ☎ (33) 2-3313 is close to the town centre on Calle Van Horne at the end of Calle Agramonte. There are three departures daily to Havana (8hr) and one service daily to Santiago de Cuba (overnight train), Camagüey, Morón and Santa Clara.

By bus – The **Terminal de Ómnibus Nacionales** is on the Carretera Central in the direction of Camagüey on the outskirts of town. There are several services a day to most provincial cities, but the twice-weekly **Viazul** service between Havana and Santiago is the most reliable option

GETTING AROUND

By taxi – A round-the-clock service is offered by **Cubataxi**, ☎ (33) 2-7636, and **Taxi Transtur**, ☎ (33) 2-2997. There are usually taxis to be found in front of the Hotel Ciego de Ávila.

Car hire – **Havanautos, Transautos**, and **Cubacar**, ☎ (33) 2-8013) have a desk in the Hotel Ciego de Ávila. Havanautos are also at the airport.

ADDRESS BOOK

Tourist information – **Rumbos** have an office in the western part of the town in the Edificio Girón No. 1, Rpto Vista Alegre, ☎ (33) 2-8738, and tourist information is available in the hotels.

Banks / Currency exchange – There is a branch of the **Banco Financiero Internacional** on the corner of Calle H Castillo and Calle J de Agüero, and currency and cheques can also be changed at the Hotel Ciego de Ávila.

Post office / Telephone – The **correos** is at the corner of Calle Chicho Valdés and Marcial Gómez, 100m from the Hotel Santiago-Habana. The **centro telefónico internacional** is on Calle Honorato de Castillo on the Parque José Martí.

Health – The town's two hotels both have medical services.

Airline offices – The **Cubana** office, ☎ (33) 2-5316 is right in the middle of town at Calle Chicho Valdés No. 83 between Calle Maceo and Calle Honorato del Castillo. **Aerotaxi** ☎ (33) 2-3937 has a desk at the airport.

Servicupet service stations – **Oro Negro** at the junction of the Carretera Central with Calle Independencia close to the bus station; **Norte** at the junction of the Circunvalación with the road to Morón, on the north side of town; **Florida**, on the road between Ciego de Ávila and Camagüey.

WHERE TO STAY

Under US$30

Hotel Santiago-Habana, at the corner of Calle Chicho Valdés and Calle Honorato del Castillo, ☎ (33) 2-5703 – 72rm. 🛏 🍽 🅿 📺 ✕ 🆑 Medical services. The most central hotel in town is also the noisiest, thanks to its location on the Carretera Central. Basic rooms, moderately well kept.

Hotel Ciego de Ávila, on Carretera de Ceballos at the 2.5km mark, ☎ (33) 2-8013 – 143rm. 🛏 🍽 🅿 📺 ✕ 🏊 💈 🆑 Bureau de change, car hire, medical services. 3km from the town centre, the hotel consists of a series of charmless concrete blocks. The rooms are no more than functional, but the hotel is nevertheless a better choice than the Santiago-Habana.

HAVING A DRINK

Concerts – Traditional music can often be enjoyed at the **Casa de la Trova** on the corner of Calle Libertad and Calle Simón Reyes, two blocks away from the Parque José Martí.

Central Cuba

COMING AND GOING

By train – The **Terminal de Ferro-carriles** is at the beginning of Calle José Martí on the way into town from Ciego de Ávila. There are several services daily to Ciego de Ávila and one service a day to Camagüey and Santa Clara.

By bus – The **Estación de Ómnibus** is located opposite the railway station. Daily departures to Camagüey and Santa Clara and every other day to Havana. Tickets need to be bought well in advance.

HOW TO GET AROUND

Car hire – **Cubacar** ☎ (335) 3901/03 can be contacted at the Hotel Morón, and **Havanautos** are located close to the petrol station.

ADDRESS BOOK

Tourist information – The **Cubanacan** travel agency at Calle Cristóbal Colón No. 49 organises trips to the cayos and to other destinations in Cuba, ☎ (335) 3168.

Banks / Currency exchange – The Hotel Morón will change travellers cheques and currency.

Post office / Telephone – The best place from which to send mail or make an international telephone call is the Hotel Morón.

Servicupet service station – **Morón**, Avenida Tarafa, close to the Hotel Morón. Fuel must be paid for in dollars.

WHERE TO STAY

There is plenty of private accommodation in the town for visitors who do not intend spending the day on the cayos.

Under US$30

Dr Ricardo Castro, Calle Narciso López No. 400 between Calle Céspedes and Calle Varona, ☎ (335) 3251 – 2rm. ⌂ ▤ In the centre of town just north of the station, private rooms of hotel standard plus meals. The friendly proprietor is a medical man, who will help find alternative accommodation if he is fully booked.

Between US$30-50

Hotel Morón, Avenida Tarafa, ☎ (335) 3901/04, Fax (335) 3076 – 144rm. ⌂ ▤ ℱ ▣ ⌕ ㏄ Bureau de change, car hire, medical services. This large modern hotel is located 1.5km from the centre on the way in to town from Ciego de Ávila. The foyer is huge but welcoming, there is an attractive swimming pool, and the rooms are comfortable and well kept.

Casona de Morón (Centro internacional de Caza y Pesca/International Centre for Hunting and Fishing), Calle Cristóbal Colón No. 41, ☎ (335) 4563 – 7rm. ⌂ ▤ TV ✕ ⌕ Spacious well-kept rooms in an elegant classical-style house in rural surroundings to the east of the station. The hunting season lasts from October to March.

WHERE TO EAT

Enquire locally about paladares. The restaurant of the Hotel Morón has a good reputation.

WHERE TO HAVE A DRINK

Concerts – There are occasional performances of traditional music in the courtyard of the **Casa de la Trova**, Calle Libertad between Calle José Martí and Calle Narciso López.

Otherwise the town's nightlife takes place in the discotheques of the Hotel Morón and the Casona Morón.

OTHER THINGS TO DO

Excursions – Morón is a good base for trips to Cayo Coco and Cayo Guillermo. Enquiries should be made at the Fantástico travel agency or at the Hotel Morón.

Sports – Trout fishing can be arranged through the **Centro Internacional de Pesca de la Trucha** at the La Redonda lake, and hunting parties through the **Coto de Caza Aguachales de Falla**. Further details from the tourist office at the Hotel Morón.

Making the most of the Cayos

COMING AND GOING

By plane – Cayo Coco has an aerodrome, ☎ (33) 30-1165, served by the **Aerotaxi** and **Aerocaribbean** charter airlines. All the larger hotels in Havana and Varadero arrange trips to Cayo Coco with a minimum stay of one night. The planes used are small and the number of seats limited so places should be reserved well in advance.

HOW TO GET AROUND

The best way of getting to know the islands and other nearby areas is by taxi or by hiring a car (**Cubacar**, **Havanautos**, or **Transautos**) at your hotel.

Car and motorbike hire – The hire company **Cubacar** has a desk at the Hotel Cayo Coco and the Villa Cojímar on Cayo Guillermo has a **Transautos** desk.

ADDRESS BOOK

Tourist information – Tourist information is available from **Rumbos** at the La Silla viewing point (observation point for flamingoes), at the Cayo Coco end of the pedraplén.

Banks / Currency exchange – **Banco Financiero Internacional** at the Hotel Tryp Cayo Coco.

Health services – There is an international clinic at the Hotel Tryp Cayo Coco.

Servicupet service stations – On the roundabout in the centre of Cayo Coco, and at the **Marina Puertosol** on the way into Cayo Guillermo, ☎ (33) 30-1737.

WHERE TO STAY AND WHERE TO EAT

Spanish and Cuban companies have recently built hotel complexes on the keys. The accommodation is basically all of the same type, and there is usually no alternative to full board. Rates are less if bookings are made through a travel operator.
Under US$30
Campismo Cayo Coco, in the western part of the island towards Cayo Guillermo, ☎ (33) 30-1105 –

62 chalets ⁴⁾ 🍴 ✗ Mostly used by Cuban holidaymakers, these beachside chalets offer the opportunity to live cheaply on these otherwise expensive islands. Some of the chalets are being renovated specifically for the use of visitors from abroad.

• Cayo Coco

New hotels are likely to open soon, but in the meantime the only places to stay are the two establishments run by the Spanish Tryp company.
Over US$100
Hotel and Club Tryp Cayo Coco, Cayo Coco, Morón, ☎ (5) 30-1300, Fax (5) 30-1380, come@club.tryp. cma.net – 458 and 514rm. ⁴⁾ 📺 🐾 TV ✗ 🍴 ♨ CC Car hire, bureau de change, medical services. Every effort has been made to give guests a pleasant stay in what amounts to a fair-sized seaside village in an attractive garden setting. The "club part" is "all-in", and the hotel section is preferable anyway; not only is it possible to make individual arrangements, but the hotel is the oldest establishment of its kind on the islands, built in an attractive colonial style. Rooms offer every comfort, and each has a balcony or a terrace with a view of the beach, the lagoon or the swimming pool. Excellent range of sporting and other activities as well as organised excursions.

Hotel Sol Club and Meliá Cayo Coco, to the east of the above establishment, ☎ (33) 30-1280 (Sol) and 30-1195 (Meliá), Fax (33) 30-1285 and 30-1195, www.solmelia.es

• Cayo Guillermo

More than US$100
Sol club or Meliá Cayo Guillermo, Cayo Guillermo, ☎ (33) 30-1760, Fax (33) 30-1748, internet site as above. Almost at the furthest extremity of the island, with sand dunes and Playa Pilar, one of the finest of all the beaches on the cayos.

Iberostar Daiquirii, ☎ (33) 30-1650, Fax (33) 30-1645 – 312rm. Located just before the above establishment, this is the least expensive of the "all-in" hotels.

WHERE TO EAT

A number of newly-opened beach retaurants make an attractive alternative to the hotel buffets, particularly on Playa Prohibida, Playa Flamingo and Playa Pilar.

Between US$5-15

La Roca, Playa Prohibida, Cayo Coco. In the northern part of the cayo, between a lagoon and a fine beach where building has been prohibited (hence its name). Fresh lobster and other seafood.

HAVING A DRINK

Discotheques – The **Cueva del Jabalí**, not far from Playa Prohibida on Cayo Coco. 10pm-2am. In a cave on the lagoon. Cabaret at 10pm. US$5 including a drink. There are also discotheques in the hotels.

OTHER THINGS TO DO

Excursions – Each of the hotels has a travel bureau. For trips to various points around the cayos or to the mainland, enquire at **Rumbos** at the La Silla viewing point, or **Cubatur** at the Hotel Tryp.

Sports – All kinds of water-based activities are available at the hotels, including windsurfing, sailing, diving and deep-sea fishing. Enquire at the **Marina Puertosol** on the way in to Cayo Guillermo, ☎ (33) 30-1737 or at the diving centre at the **Marina Marlin** at the Tryp.

Walking tours and horse-riding organised by **Sitio la Güira**, on Cayo Coco on the road towards Guillermo (on the left). Accommodation is available too in one of the establishment's 4 rooms, US$20, ☎ (33) 30-1208 or 30-1362.

M. Renaudeau/HOA QUI

Sea breezes at Cayo Coco

CAMAGÜEY★★
Capital of Camagüey Province
Cuba's third largest city – pop 320 000
535km from Havana and 330km from Santiago de Cuba
See map page 207

Not to be missed
Getting pleasantly lost in Camagüey's labyrinth of lanes and twisting streets.
Watching the world go by on Plaza San Juan de Dios.
Lazing on the beach at Playa Los Cococ.

And remember...
Park the car and explore the city centre on foot.
A beach holiday at Santa Lucia is cheaper if booked through a tour operator.

The Carretera Central from Ciego de Ávila skirts the centre of Camagüey to the south. To reach the historic city centre, bear left beyond the service station, cross the Caridad Bridge over the Río Hatibonico and keep straight on.

Visitors to Cuba who have got used to the regular chequerboard layout of most of its towns can easily lose their way in Camagüey's complex web of winding streets. The town seems to have been deliberately laid out in an irregular way in order to confuse raiding pirates, though this can scarcely be the reason why today's road signs seem designed to lead even the most alert drivers astray.

With some 20 places of worship in the city centre, Camagüey is sometimes called the "city of churches". The best way to explore is by simply wandering around without a particular destination in mind. There are lots of little discoveries to be made, among them the **tinajones**, the huge terracotta pots which have become the symbol of the city. There are few natural sources of water in this part of Cuba and the area has always suffered from droughts. As far back as the 16C, the early settlers began to use clay from the Sierra de Cubitas to fashion vessels for storing water. The rain falling on roofs was collected by elaborate systems of guttering and led into these containers. Up to two metres high, they were very much like the traditional Spanish jars used to store olive oil. More than 16 000 of them have been counted in Camagüey. Most tinajones date from the 19C and the majority of them are now ornamental rather than functional, perhaps to be found gracing shady patios behind heavy wooden doors.

A turbulent city
Founded in 1514 by **Diego Velasquez**, Camagüey was the sixth of the Spanish colonial *villas*, but it was some time before the town settled in its final location. Its original name was Santa María del Puerto Principe and it was sited, not where it is now, but on the western shore of the Bay of Nuevitas. In 1516 it was moved to a new site on the banks of the Río Caonao, then, following a fire, it was moved again, to its present location further inland.

This proved to be not much of a deterrent to pirates and buccaneers, and as the town prospered it was subjected to frequent raids. The most dramatic episodes of this kind came in the late 17C. In 1668 Captain Henry Morgan pillaged the place and made off with 500 head of cattle, then a few years later in 1679 it was sacked by the Frenchman François Granmont.

At the end of the 19C Camagüey was deeply involved in the struggle for independence, with a local man, **Ignacio Agramonte**, playing a particularly important role.

Central Cuba

The town
Allow half a day for a leisurely visit

Calle Republica is one of the few straight streets in Camagüey, cutting through the city centre from north to south. It is lined with dozens of small shops, some selling food, some with more or less empty shelves, others undertaking to repair every imaginable kind of article. Most of the main sights are to the west of this busy thoroughfare, a useful reference point in the otherwise chaotic street pattern.

On the way into Camagüey from Ciego de Ávila, cross the Río Hatibonico on the Carretera Central and go along Calle Independencia. Turn first left into Calle Matías Varona and continue for 300m.

Plaza San Juan de Dios★★

This spacious square is a designated national monument, the pride of colonial-era Camagüey. In addition to a number of recently restored and perhaps over-colourful single storey dwellings, the plaza boasts a church with a tower and some pleasantly shaded restaurant courtyards.

The **Church and Hospital of San Juan de Dios★** takes up the whole of one side of the square. Dating from 1728, it is a particularly fine example of this kind of architectural complex. The church has recently been restored, and contains some fine carving. The hospital building was the first establishment of its kind in the city and continued to function in its original role right up to the 1970s. It is now the home of the **Centro Provincial de Patriomonio** *(Open 9am-5pm; closed*

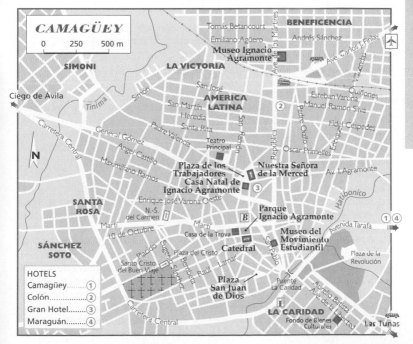

Sunday. Admission charge). The rooms opening off the cloisters have been converted into restaurants, while the first floor is given over to plans and photographs of the city from its earliest days to the present. A second cloister is currently being restored for conversion into a hotel.

Go back to the beginning of Calle Independencia and then turn second left into Calle República.

Calle República No. 69 is the **Museo del Movimiento Estudantil Camagüeyano** *(Open 9am-7pm; closed Sunday. Admission charge)*, housed in the former home of Jesús Suárez Gayol, a comrade of Che Guevara who died alongside him in Bolivia in 1967. The museum traces the career of this local revolutionary as well as dealing generally with the anti-Batista struggle.

Go two blocks up Calle República and turn left into Calle José Martí which leads after 300m to the Parque Agramonte.

Parque Ignacio Agramonte★

In a town with so many squares and churches, it is difficult to decide exactly where the centre of the city is. But the Parque Agramonte is at the heart of the historic district of Camagüey and is a much-favoured spot for locals to relax on a shady bench or maybe enjoy a *batido* (milk-shake) in the Casa del Batido.

The park was the earliest of the city's squares, laid out in 1528 and called Plaza de la Iglesia. The buildings around it were burnt down in 1616, but rebuilt the following year. Renamed Plaza de Armas in 1850, it became an execution ground for many independence fighters condemned to death by the Spaniards. Since 1912 the square has borne the name of Ignacio Agramonte, whose equestrian statue presides over the scene today.

One of the city's main churches, the **Cathedral de Nuestra Senora de la Candelaria**, built in 1864, dominates the plaza. The building has been closed for reconstruction but is due to reopen soon.

Go north along Calle Cisneros for 400m to the Plaza de los Trabajadores.

Plaza de los Trabajadores

"Workers' Square" is more of a huge crossroads than a square, but is lined with a number of interesting buildings.

The **Casa natal de Ignacio Agramonte★** *(Open 10am-6pm; 8am-midday Sunday; closed Monday. Admission charge)* is a superb example of an 18C town mansion. A balcony runs the whole width of the ochre-coloured facade, and in the courtyard there are several fine *tinajones*.

The birthplace of Ignacio Agramonte is now a museum devoted to this local man who became one of the most important figures in the independence struggle and who died in combat in 1873 at the age of 32. The interiors recreate the atmosphere of an upper-class residence of the 19C, though the only original piece of furniture is the piano. There are also a few personal items which recall Agramonte's prominent role in the Ten Years War.

Opposite the museum stands the **Church and Convent of Nuestra Senora de la Merced★** *(9am to 11.30am and 3pm to 6pm. Admission charge)* completed by the Carmelites in 1724 and rebuilt in the middle of the 19C. In the middle of the conventual buildings is a well-kept garden with benches and a number of *tinajones*, while inside the church, to the left of the choir, is a fine **altarpiece★** dating from 1762 and made up of 20 000 pieces of silver.

Steps lead down to the **crypt** where, there are not only human remains and a chaotic array of religious objects, but also a fine tabernacle dating from 1733.

Go east along Avenida Ignacio Agramonte, turn left into Calle República and continue as far as the railway station.

Impossible to miss, the huge structure one block beyond the railway on Avenida de los Mártires is the **Museo provincial Ignacio Agramonte** *(Open 9am-5pm, 11am-8pm Wednesday; 8.30am-midday Sunday; closed Monday. Admission charge)*. The colonnaded neo-Classical building housing the museum was built in 1848 as a military barracks. It is laid out around a spacious courtyard, where big *tinajones* rest at the foot of exotic trees.

Currently under reconstruction, the museum's rooms are filled with an array of stuffed creatures from around the world, plus a 19C decorative arts collection. One room is devoted to the fine arts, with works by Cuban painters from the 18C to the 20C.

Around Camagüey
See map page 207

The city of Camagüey lies in the middle of its province, about 80km from both Atlantic and Caribbean. Some 14 150sqkm in extent, the province is the largest, as well as the flattest, in Cuba. The roads leading from the city to the beaches on the north coast pass through sugar plantations as well as through pasturelands which are important for milk production. The interminable plains continue well into the neighbouring province of Las Tunas.

Revolutionary cows
The dairying country around Camagüey is notable for an unusual breed of cattle, the result of a post-Revolutionary effort to increase milk production. The humped oxen which had been brought in from abroad because of their tolerance of tropical conditions were crossed by artificial insemination with Canadian Holsteins, less hardy but good milkers. Thus was born the F-I, a new breed of dairy cow, a hardy creature easily identified by its hump.

Cayo Sabinal★
90km, allow 1hr30min. Leave Camagüey by Avenida Carlos J Finlay towards the airport and Nuevitas. After 64km, 11km short of the industrial and harbour town of Nuevitas, turn left by a big banana plantation.

Cayo Sabinal is famous for its bird life, in particular for its flocks of pink flamingos. The road leads to a superb beach at the far eastern end of the island, with the highly appropriate name of Playa Bonita. There is a restaurant here, and another one in the centre of the island, on Playa los Pinos.

Playa Santa Lucía★
110km, allow 2hr. Leave Camagüey in the direction of the airport. 16km beyond the village of Minas turn right towards San Miguel de Bagá. Continue along the main road to Playa Santa Lucía.

A number of recently built hotels are the focal point of this rather undistinguished resort. But there is a coral reef, as well as 20km of sandy beach and plenty of people come here to swim, scuba dive or indulge in watersports of all kinds.

Continue north for a further 6km beyond the Santa Lucía hotels. The little watercourse on the far side of the fishing village of La Boca can be forded or crossed by boat.

Playa Los Cocos★★ is a little paradise of a beach, complete with palm trees, and is not reserved for foreigners. Anyone coming here very early in the morning is likely to have the place to themselves. For the time being the only facilities

M. Gotin/SCOPE

Humped oxen or Holsteins? No, F-1s!

consist of a restaurant serving excellent grills, but there are plans for a 5-star hotel so the scene is likely to change fundamentally. There is a ferry across to Cayo Sabinal.

The road to Holguín

After skirting the centre of Camagüey, the *Carretera Central* heads towards the eastern provinces. The provincial capital of Las Tunas, 125km from Camagüey, has little to offer the visitor; the town's colonial-era buildings were destroyed by fire during the 19C, and the main road runs past lines of later buildings in neo-Classical style painted in lurid colours. Beyond Las Tunas the highway runs through an undistinguished countryside of canefields and cattle ranches.

COMING AND GOING

By air – Camagüey's airport, the *Aeropuerto Internacional Ignacio Agramonte*, ☎ (322) 6-1862 or 6-1010, is 9km northeast of the town on the road to Nuevitas. There are weekly flights to and from Canada and Italy, and a daily Cubana flight to and from Havana.

By train – The **Terminal de Ferrocarriles**, corner of Avenida Carlos J Finlay and Calle República, is a few blocks north of the city centre. There are three trains daily to Havana (night trains, journey time 10hr), which stop at Ciego de Ávila, Santa Clara and Matanzas. Two trains daily to Santiago de Cuba (6hr).

By bus – The *Viazul* tourist coach stops in Camagüey on its journey between Havana and Santiago de Cuba on Tuesday and Friday, and in the reverse direction on Monday and Thursday. The stop is at the junction of the Carretera Central with Calle Perú.

The **Terminal de Ómnibus Interprovinciales Álvaro Barba** is 2km from the city centre on the Carretera Central in the direction of Las Tunas. There are daily buses to all major provincial towns, as well as three buses daily to Havana.

Buses to Nuevitas and Santa Cruz del Sur leave from the **Terminal de Ómnibus Intermunicipal** close to the railway station.

GETTING AROUND

The easiest way of getting around the city centre is on foot.

By taxi – *Turistaxi* vehicles can normally be found in front of the Hotel Camagüey. 24-hour service, ☎ (322) 8-7267.

Car hire – **Havanautos**, **Transautos** and **Micar** are all represented at the Hotel Camagüey, ☎ (322) 8-7267, and Transautos at the airport.

ADDRESS BOOK

Tourist information – Tourist information and details of excursions from **Rumbos**, Parador de los Tres Reyes, Plaza de San Juan de Dios, ☎ (322) 9-7995. The Hotel Camagüey is also a useful source of information.

Banks / Currency exchange – The **Banco Financiero Internacional**, Calle Independencia between Calle Hermanos Agüero and Calle Martí. The Hotel Camagüey will also change money.

Post office / Telephone – The main post office is on Plaza de los Trabajadores opposite the Church of la Merced. International calls are most easily made from the Hotel Camagüey.

Airline companies – The **Cubana** office is at Calle República No. 400 at the corner with Calle Correa, four blocks from the railway station, ☎ (322) 9-1338 or 9-2156.

Servicupet service stations – **Florida**, between Ciego de Ávila and Camagüey, **Libertad**, on the Carretera Central to the south of the town near the bridge. Via Blanca, on the corner of the Carretera Central and Via Blanca. On Calle Agramonte in Nuevitas.

WHERE TO STAY

Camagüey has plenty of residents able to offer private accommodation. Parking is difficult in the city centre, but some residents can provide a garage.

Under US$20

Pedro Alcantara, Calle Santa Rita between Calle República and Calle Santa Rosa, ☎ (322) 9-6754. 🍴 🛏 Friendly reception in an ordinary house located between the town's two hotels. Peaceful room. Generous breakfast and garaging nearby.

Manuel Banegas Misa, Calle Independencia No. 251 altos, ☎ (322) 9-4606. 🍴 🛏 Good position to the north of Parque Ignacio Agramonte. Upper floor apartment with rooms with a view of the town.

Under US$30

Hotel Colón, Calle República No. 274, ☎ (322) 8-3368 – 48rm. 🍴 🛏 ✂ ✗ 🆑 This neo-colonial building has a certain kind of charm, with its fine bar and spacious foyer. The standard rooms open on to a gloomy corridor, while for a little more money, the "especial" is much bigger and looks out on to a delightful courtyard. Parking available to the rear of the hotel.

Between 30-50

Gran Hotel, Calle Maceo No. 67 between Calle Ignacio Agramonte and Calle General Gómez, ☎ (322) 9-2093/4, Fax (322) 9-3933 – 72rm. 🍴 📧 ✎ 📺 ✗ 🛁 cc The Grand has always been the city's most prestigious hotel, and its recent renovation justifies the rise in its charges. There is a new swimming pool, and the hotel is very well located in the heart of one of the busiest parts of town. The rooms are quite spacious and well-kept, and there is a fine view over the town from the top floor restaurant.

Between US$30-50

Hotel Camagüey, Avenida Ignacio Agramonte, ☎ (322) 8-7267/70, Fax (322) 8-7180 – 142rm. 🍴 📧 ✎ 📺 ✗ 🛁 cc Car hire, bureau de change, medical services. Forbidding-looking concrete structure 5km from the city centre towards Las Tunas. Functional rooms currently being refurbished. A good range of services, but not very practical for those without their own means of transport.

More than US$50

Hotel Maraguán, Circunvalación Este, ☎ (322) 7-2017 – 35rm. 🍴 📧 ✎ 📺 ✗ 🛁 cc This hotel can be reached by turning left off the Carretera Central 1km beyond the Hotel Camagüey. It is in an attractive and peaceful setting, and though expensive, the rooms are comfortable. Deep in the countryside, it is only suitable for those with cars.

EATING OUT

Camagüey has a number of paladares including several pizzerias lined up along the Carretera Central towards the Hotel Camagüey. Calle República has lots of little stalls selling ices, drinks and various sweetmeats.

Under US$10

La campana de Toledo, Plaza San Juan de Dios. 10am-10pm. A flight of steps leads up to this 18C colonial-era house in one of the town's prettiest squares. Tables are laid out around the shady courtyard with its *tinajones*. The house speciality is "boliche mechado" (stuffed beef). Prices rather high but worth it for the delightful setting.

HAVING A DRINK

Bars – El Cambio, Parque Ignacio Agramonte. This delightful bar from the turn of the last century used to be the place where local people bought their lottery tickets. When gaming houses were closed down it continued to function as a café. As well as drinks there are also light meals.

Concerts – The **Casa de la Trova**, Calle Cisneros No. 171 on Parque Ignacio Agramonte has traditional music sessions every evening, beginning at 8.30pm. Closed Monday.

OTHER THINGS TO DO

Theatre / Dance – Every other year in September, Camagüey is the venue for the country's biggest drama festival. In alternate years there is a dance festival (in June or December).

Outdoor pursuits – The **Hotel Florida**, ☎ (322) 5-3011, 40km northwest of Camagüey on the Carretera Central towards Ciego de Ávila, has facilities for hunting and fishing in the surrounding countryside. The **Rumbos** travel agency can also help organise excursions.

SHOPPING

Market – There is a market on the riverbank to the south of the Plaza San Juan de Dios.

Arts and crafts – The **Fondo de Bienes Culturales**, Avenida de la Libertad between Calle Nolasco Rodríguez and Calle General de la Vega, four blocks south of the river, is a shop with a small selection of craft items, recordings, and musical instruments. Closed at the weekend.

Making the most of Santa Lucía

COMING AND GOING

Playa Santa Lucía is poorly served by public transport, and for visitors who are not part of an organised group, the only really practical way to get in and out of the area is by car.

GETTING AROUND

By taxi – Taxis OK, ☎ (32) 3-6464, usually have vehicles on the stands in front of the hotels.

Car hire – Cubacar and **Transautos** have representatives in most of the hotels.

ADDRESS BOOK

Medical service – Clínica Internacional and **Farmacia**, Residencia No. 14, ☎ (32) 3-6203, on the way into the resort on a road running parallel to the main road.

Servicupet service stations – Policentro, on the roundabout on the way to the hotels.

WHERE TO STAY

Most of the hotels, with one or two exceptions, cater for tour groups and operate on the all-in system with full board.

Under US$50

Hotel Tararaco, Playa Santa Lucía, ☎ (32) 36-5184 – 30rm. 🍴📋 ✏ 📺 ✕ 🐟 This hotel is at the far end of the resort coming from Camagüey, on the busy but beautiful Tarara Beach. Friendly staff and a nearly completed renovation programme. The least expensive of the resort's places to stay (Rates include half-board).

Around US$100

Hotel Cuatro Vientos, Playa Santa Lucía, ☎ (32) 36-5120, Fax (32) 36-5142 – 412rm. 🍴📋 ✏ 📺 ✕ 🐟 🍽 cc Car hire, bureau de change. The first hotel on the road in from Camagüey is a large-scale complex, with thatched buildings disposed around a big swimming pool which is also the focus of the entertainment programme. The rather characterless rooms are clean and comfortable. It is possible to opt out of the all-in rate. **Qualton Club Mayanabo**, Playa Santa Lucía, ☎ (32) 3-6184/85, Fax (32) 365176 – 225rm. 🍴📋 ✏ 📺

✕ 🐟 🍽 ✕ cc Bureau de change. With its long and gloomy corridors, this is not the most welcoming of buildings, and the furniture and fittings from the 1970s now give it a rather kitsch character. It is not worth paying the US$10 supplement for a suite, and in general the establishment does not offer value for money.

Vita Club Caracol, Playa Santa Lucía, ☎ (32) 36-5158, Fax (32) 36-5167 – 150rm. 🍴📋 ✏ 📺 ✕ 🐟 🍽 cc Car hire, bureau de change. This recently built complex consists of chalets in a garden setting. The rooms are comfortable and unusually spacious and all have a small living room. Easily the most attractive accommodation are the chalets right on the beach.

EATING OUT

Eating out can be problematic, and it is probably best to stick to the full board arrangement with your hotel. However, there are a number of beach restaurants offering good grilled fish and lobster.

Playa Tarará, The Italian chef from the restaurant of the Marina Marlin welcomes visitors with his expertly prepared and delicious fish and other seafood. 10am-midnight.

OTHER THINGS TO DO

Excursions – The **Agencia de viajes Cubanacan**, Casa No. 38 Zona Residencial, ☎ (32) 3-6412, will organise excursions in the surrounding area and trips to Camagüey. The various hotels will also help with excursions.

Outdoor pursuits – The **Marina Marlin** on Tarara Beach and its Italian staff offer water-skiing, fishing trips, and fascinating catamaran expeditions to observe a colony of tame sharks and the fish of Cayo Sabinal (US$60). It also runs the diving centre called **Shark's Friends**, ☎ (32) 3-6404, to the rear of the Hotel Cuatro Vientos, which gives diving instruction and operates twice-daily diving trips (US$35).

The "all-in" terms in the hotels usually include use of all watersports equipment, except for fuel which must be paid for separately.

Basilica of Nuestra Senora de la Caridad at El Cobre

P. Hausheer/HOA QUI

EASTERN CUBA

On the far side of the country's highest mountains, this is the region where the Cuban nation was born. From the foundation of the Spaniards' first *villa* right up to Fidel Castro's Revolution, Oriente has been the scene of many of the climactic events in Cuba's history as well as a melting pot of the various cultures that contribute to the country's identity. It is here that Africa's rhythms resound most vigorously, and here that Spain has left some of its finest colonial architecture. Contributions from France include dances and a number of place-names, the *cornetines chinos* of carnival time recall the Asian heritage, and the United States maintains a presence in the form of the great naval base at Guantánamo. And, close to Santiago, the nation's second city, is the most sacred spot in Cuba, the shrine of the Virgin of El Cobre.

HOTELS

Baracoa
Castillo (El) .... ①
Porto Santo........................ ②
Rusa (La) .... ③
Villa Maguana .... ④

Bayamo
Royalton............................ ⑤
Sierra Maestra.................... ⑥
Villa Balcón de la Sierra.... ⑦
Villa Bayamo..................... ⑧
Villa Santo Domingo .... ⑨

Guantánamo
Guantánamo .... ⑩
Villa La Lupe..................... ⑪

Guardalavaca
Atlántico........................... ⑫
Brisas (Las) .... ⑬
Club Río de Luna............... ⑭
Guardalavaca .... ⑮

Melía Río de Oro................ ⑯
Sol Río de Mares................ ⑰
Villa Cayo Saetía .... ⑱

Holguín
Centro turístico Mirador
de Mayabe......................... ⑲

Santiago de Cuba
Bucanero............................ ⑳
Corales (Los) .... ㉑
Costa Morena..................... ㉒
El Colibri............................ ㉓
Gran Piedra........................ ㉔

Manzanillo
Farallón del Caribe .... ㉕
Galeones (Los) .... ㉖
Guacanayabo .... ㉗
Guamá .... ㉘
Marea del Portillo .... ㉙
Sierra Mar .... ㉚
Villa Punta Piedra.......... ㉛

Bahía de
Puerto Padre

Bahía
de
Gibara

Puerto
Padre

Gibara

27

60

Holguín

Mayabe

⑲

Carretera Central

Las Tunas
Camagüey
La Habana

Cacocum

68

E. Cauto del Paso

69

Cauto Cristo

Cauto

Golfo de
Guacanayabo

Río Cauto

Cauto

Guacanayabo

Jiguaní

Manzanillo ㉗

⑤

Bayamo

⑥

Parque Nacional
La Demajagua

20

⑧

Carretera Central

Contramaestre

Yara

37

Media
Luna

60

Cauto

del

Bartolomé Masó

E. Carlos
Manuel de
Céspedes

68

Palma Soriano

Niquero

Llanura

28

M A E S T R A ★

Cauto

SIERRA

⑦

Santo
Domingo

⑨

★★Pico
Turquino

Pico
Bayamesa
▲ 1730

Belic

41

39

▲
1972

41

76

★ N.-S. de
la Caridad
del Cobre

Playa
Las Coloradas

Pilón

㉛ ㉕ ㉙

85

㉖

㉘ ㉚

Cabo
Cruz

Punta
del Inglés

Marea
del Portillo

Las Cuevas

Uvero

Chivirico

Parque Nacional
Desembarco del Granma

M A R

262

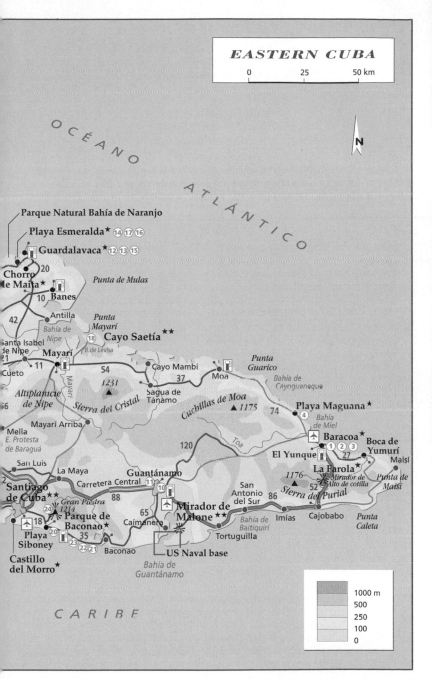

EASTERN CUBA

0   25   50 km

N

OCÉANO

ATLÁNTICO

Parque Natural Bahía de Naranjo
Playa Esmeralda★ ⑭⑰⑯
Guardalavaca★ ⑫⑬⑮
Chorro
de Maita★
20
Banes
10
Punta de Mulas
Antilla
42
Punta
Mayarí
Bahía de
Nipe
Santa Isabel
de Nipe
21
Mayarí
11
Cueto
54
Cayo Mambí
1231
Sagua de
Tánamo
37
Moa
Punta
Guarico
Bahía de
Cayoguaneque
B.de Levisa
⑱ Cayo Saetía★★
Altiplanicie
de Nipe
56
Sierra del Cristal
Cuchillas de Moa
▲1175
74
Playa Maguana★
④
Bahía
de Miel
Mayarí Arriba
120
Toa
Baracoa★
①②③
Boca de
Yumurí
Mella
E. Protesta
de Baraguá
El Yunque★
Malsí
San Luis
La Maya
Guantánamo
⑪
La Farola★
1176
Mirador de
Alto de cotilla
Punta de
Matsí
Santiago
de Cuba★★
Carretera Central
⑩
52
27
Sierra del Purial
24
Gran Piedra
1214
88
65
San
Antonio
del Sur
86
18
Parque de
Baconao★
Caimanera
Mirador de
Malone★★
Bahía de
Baitiquirí
Imías
Cajobabo
Punta
Caleta
Playa
Siboney
20
35
23
22 21
Baconao
US Naval base
Tortuguilla
Castillo
del Morro★
Bahía de
Guantánamo
CARIBE

1000 m
500
250
100
0

263

HOLGUÍN

Capital of Holguín province
Pop 230 000
135km from Santiago de Cuba
See map page 262

Not to be missed
The pre-Conquest cemetery near Guardalavaca.
A photo safari on Cayo Saetia.
And remember...
Sunday is not the best day to visit Holguín as all the town's museums are closed.
A stay in Guardalavaca is better value if booked through a tour operator.
A jeep is the best way of getting around Cayo Saetia in the rainy season.

The Carretera Central from Las Tunas comes into Holguín on the west and leads into Calle Frexes which runs directly to the Parque Calixto García.

Most of the tourists landing at Holguín's international airport ignore this provincial capital and go straight on to the glorious sandy beaches at Guardalavaca on the north coast. It is true that the city shows little trace of its colonial origin, despite having been founded by Captain García Holguín as early as 1525. And it is also true that it shares its grid of streets, swarms of bicycles, decrepit buildings and statues of local heroes with many other Cuban towns.

And yet...it is after all the country's fourth biggest city, a lively and friendly place. Once beyond the apartment blocks of the uninspiring modern suburbs, the city centre is a relaxed and spacious place, with a whole series of fine park-like squares which have led Holguín to be called "the city of plazas". The city is also the home of Mayabe beer, considered by some connoisseurs to be Cuba's best. Holguín deserves better than simply to be bypassed in a hurry.

The town
Allow 2hr

The main axis of the city is formed by its squares: peaceful Parque Céspedes, overlooked by the Church of San Juan, to the south Parque Calixto García and finally the charming Parque de Las Flores with its *bici-taxis*. A ride in one of these pedicabs is one of the best ways of getting to know Holguín.

Parque Calixto García (B3)

Most of Holguín's tourist attractions are located around the city's spacious central square or close by. Local people throng the cafes and shops in the arcades or relax in the shade in the middle of the square. The statue is of General Calixto García, a *Holguínero* who was one of the leading figures in the wars of independence.

The northern side of the square is dominated by the **Periquera**, a handsome blue-shuttered building which is now the **Museo Provincial** (*Open 9am-5pm; 9am-1pm Sunday. Admission charge*). Built by slave labour for a wealthy Spanish businessman between 1860 and 1868, then used as a barracks, the "parrot cage" earned its scornful epithet because of the elaborate and brightly coloured uniforms of its Spanish garrison.

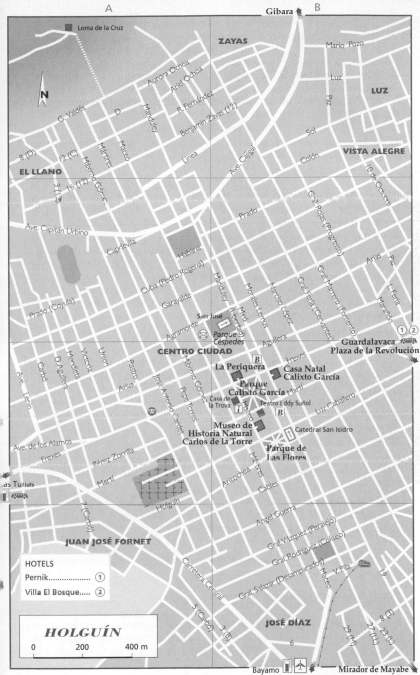

A

B

Loma de la Cruz

Gibara

ZAYAS

Mario Pozo

Luz

LUZ

N

Aurora Ochoa

Ariel Ochoa

R. Fernández

Paz

Sol

VISTA ALEGRE

G. Valdés

D

Manduley

Benjamín Zayas (12)

Martíres

Máximo Gómez

Maceo

Colón

10 de Octubre

8 (D)

2 (C)

3 (E)

16 (12)

Línea

Ave. Cajigal

EL LLANO

Ave. Capitán Urbino

Caprevilla

Habana

Prado

C. J. Rojas (Progreso)

Arias

Paz

L. Feria

L. Maridó

Cuba (Pedro Rogena)

Prado (Coyula)

Garayalde

Manduley

Miró (Libertad)

Morales Lemus

Narciso López

Gral. Marrero (Fomento)

Gral. Peña (Cervantes)

San José

Agramonte

Parque
Céspedes

Aguilera

Guardalavaca
Plaza de la Revolución

① ②

CENTRO CIUDAD

B

Frexes

La Periquera

**Casa Natal
Calixto García**

Ave. Lenin

Carbó

Victoria

D. Aguilera

Mendieta

Unión

Rastro

Arias

José Antonio Cardet

Pepe Torres

Máximo Gómez

**Parque
Calixto García**

Casa de
la Trova

Martí

Teatro Eddy Suñol

B

Luz Caballero

i

Catedral San Isidro

i

**Museo de
Historia Natural
Carlos de la Torre**

**Parque de
Las Flores**

Ave. de los Álamos

Frexes

Pérez Zorrilla

Martí

Holguín

Aricochea

Martíres

Cables

as Tunas

JUAN JOSÉ FORNET

7 (Carbó)

Ángel Guerra

Gral. Vázquez (Peralejo)

Gral. Rodríguez (Coliseo)

HOTELS

Pernik.................. ①

Villa El Bosque..... ②

Carretera Central

Gral. Salazar (Desamparados)

Maceo

V. Pita

3

9

8 (3)

27 (LL)

23 (C)

29 (F)

HOLGUÍN

0   200   400 m

5 (Carbó)

3 (B)

JOSÉ DÍAZ

6

Bayamo

Mirador de Mayabe

The building then served as the headquarters of the provincial government until 1984 and was subsequently converted to house the regional museum. Its spacious interiors now have displays tracing the history of the area from pre-Columbian times to the Revolution. Among the bones and implements of the original inhabitants is the symbol of the town, a pre-Columbian stone **axe** shaped in the likeness of a man. A section of the museum is devoted to the wars of independence, with an fascinating collection of weapons, flags and banners, and the cloth which is supposed to have covered the corpse of José Martí. There are also temporary exhibitions of decorative arts.

At the junction of Calle Frexes and Calle Miró one *block* away from the square is the **Casa Natal de Calixto García** (*Open 9am-4pm; 9am-1pm Saturday; closed Sunday. Admission charge*), devoted to the memory of this local hero, born here in 1839. The house has wooden grilles painted blue, tiled floors, and its original furniture and fittings, as well as weapons and pictures from the War of Independence, and exceptional care has gone into the presentation of the exhibits.

At Calle Maceo No. 129, 100m from the square, there is an endearingly old-fashioned introduction to natural history in the shape of the **Museo de Historia Natural Carlos de la Torre** (*Open 9am-5pm; 1pm-5pm Saturday; closed Friday. Admission charge*). As well as a stunning collection of brightly coloured snail shells and an array of stuffed animals there are Cuba's two national birds: the *zunzuncito*, the hummingbird which can be found all over the country, and the *tocororo*, its plumage echoing the colours of the national flag.

Parque de las Flores (B3)

Not as extensive as Parque Calixto García, this square is at its liveliest when the ice-cream parlour is open and an immensely long queue develops. In the middle is a statue of another local hero, Julio Grave de Peralta, who led the anti-Spanish rising in 1868 and laid siege to the "Periquera" on Parque Callixto García. On one side of the square stands the city's most important church, the **Cathedral of San Isidro**. Built in 1720, but much altered subsequently, the twin-towered church is rarely open, but has a fine facade, recently restored, and an elaborate timber ceiling (open for evening mass and on Sunday).

Return to Parque Calixto García and go north along Calle Maceo to the foot of the hill. To drive to the summit, go up one of the roads to the left. On reaching Avenida Capitán Urbino turn right.

A deep breath is needed before braving the 460 steps leading to the top of **Loma de la Cruz (A1) (Hill of the Cross)** where there is a cross dating from the 18C. It is best to come here early in the morning or late in the afternoon in order to enjoy the view of the town without being blinded by the sun.

Go to the eastern end of Calle Martí and turn left into Avenida de los Libertadores, then left again beyond the stadium.

Plaza de la Revolución (towards B3)

This vast open space 3km east of the city centre commemorates the heroes of the wars of independence. A great concrete frieze is adorned with the features of the military men from Holguín who distinguished themselves in the struggle. Here too is the tomb of General Calixto García whose ashes were brought back from the United States on 11 December 1980.

Around Holguín
See map page 262

Holguín province is one of the country's most important sugar-producing areas and the eastern part of the region has a number of cobalt and copper mines. But the area is not just important in economic terms, since there are several sites of historic importance as well as attractive landscapes within easy reach of the city of Holguín or Guardalavaca on the northern coast.

Mirador de Mayabe
20km from Holguín, allow 15min. From the southern end of Calle Maceo follow the Carretera Central to its junction with the Circunvalación (bypass). Turn left on to the bypass, then turn second right on the road leading to the Mirador.

The various visitor facilities of the Mirador de Mayabe are spread out over this hilltop 10km from the city centre. Apart from the panoramic view over the Mayabe valley, the place's main attraction is the country's most famous donkey. Housed in his own little stable at the end of the bar, "Panchito" has developed an insatiable thirst for the product of the local brewery and will down all the beer tourists can afford to offer him.

Gibara
35km from Holguín, allow 30min. Leave Holguín by going along Calle Manduley (Libertad), taking the right fork into Avenida Cajical and continuing north towards Gibara.

Well off the tourist trail, the little harbour town of Gibara was the most prosperous port on the northern coast in the 19C. But its glory days are over, and it is now a sleepy backwater, dozing in the tropical heat, its colonial-era fortifications in ruins and its venerable houses threatened with collapse.

To the west of the town, the Bay of Bariay may well be where Columbus made his first landfall on Cuba. In his logbook the great navigator described a flat-topped mountain, which could quite possibly be the *Silla de Gibara* (Gibara Saddle). This is of course disputed by the inhabitants of Baracoa, who have an unshakeable belief that the mountain concerned was theirs.

Gibara has a trio of museums close to one another in the Calle Independencia, the town's main street.

The Museo Municipal *(Open 8am-midday and 1pm-5pm; 8am-midday Sunday; closed Monday. Admission charge)* traces the history of the town with plans and photographs and pays tribute to the many local people who lost their lives in the various wars. It is one of the few provincial museums to make any mention of the war in Angola *(See page 30)*. It is now under renovation.

The building used by General Calixto García as his headquarters in 1898 now houses the **Museo de Arte Colonial** *(Open 8am-midday and 1pm-5pm; closed Monday. Admission charge)*. The interior is furnished in the style of an aristocratic residence of the 19C, and a special feature is the stained glass once used in doorways.

On Calle Luz Caballero, between Calle Independencia and Calle J Peralta, is the **Museo de Historia Natural** *(8am-midday and 1pm-5pm; 8am-midday Sunday; closed Monday. Admission charge)*. Besides collections of sea-shells and stuffed birds it has the skeleton of a whale. Beyond the geology room there is a pleasant courtyard.

Guardalavaca★

55km from Holguín, allow 1hr. From Holguín go down Avenida XX Aniversario to the roundabout 1km beyond Plaza de la Revolución and follow signs to Guardalavaca.

Most tourists visiting Holguín province make directly for the area's main attraction, the picture postcard beaches at Guardalavaca. The resort is not a real village but a series of hotel complexes sited along the shore at regular intervals, an international enclave like Varadero where the only Cubans are those brought in to serve the foreign clientele. Some 6km to the west of the main beach is the charming **Playa Esmeralda★** where the luxury hotels seem almost smothered in the luxuriant vegetation.

About 4km to the south of Playa Esmeralda on the road towards Holguín is the **Parque Natural Bahía de Naranjo**. Footpaths lead through the hills of this protected landscape overlooking the sea. In the middle of the bay is an island with an **aquarium** where visitors can swim in the company of dolphins.

Return to Guardalavaca and go east towards Banes. After 6km turn right on to a road lined with bohíos and palm trees which climbs for 2km up to the Chorro de Maita.

The Chorro de Maita★ *(Open 9am-5pm; 9am-1pm Sunday; closed Monday. Admission charge)* is generally considered to be the largest Indian cemetery in the whole of the Caribbean. Discovered in 1930, the remains of 62 people who lived between 1490 and 1530 are now displayed in a building erected over the site. Some skeletons are in the foetal position which was the custom in pre-Conquest times, some are outstretched with their arms folded across the chest showing the influence of the Christianity brought by the Spaniards. On display are grave offerings made of gold, coral and bone, as well as ceramics, pottery, jewellery and everyday objects and photographs taken during the excavation of this fascinating site.

Banes

33km from Guardalavaca, allow 30min. The road between Guardalavaca and Banes runs through an undulating, fertile landscape of banana plantations and *bohíos*, the typical thatched farmsteads of the Cuban countryside. The busy little town of Banes belongs to a world quite different from that of the tourist beaches. This part of Cuba was relatively densely populated in pre-Conquest times, and some local people are obviously descended from Taino forebears. Others are descendants of workers brought in from Jamaica in the early years of the 20C, when Banes was a company town, a luxury residential area for the privileged American and Cuban employees of the United Fruit Company. Fidel Castro was married here on 10 October 1948, to Mirta Díaz-Balart, daughter of a wealthy Banes family.

Little trace of the United States connection remains today. Instead, the town is famous, firstly for its *pan con lechón*, the pork sandwiches sold from stands along the dilapidated main street and secondly, and perhaps more importantly as the "archeological capital of Cuba", with a museum whose collections come from the dozens of pre-Conquest sites in the surrounding area.

The Museo Indocubano Baní★ *(Open 9am-5pm; 8am-midday Sunday; closed Monday. Admission charge)* is on Calle General Marrero between Avenida José Martí and Avenida Carlos Manuel de Céspedes, not far from the town's main street. It is one of the finest of the country's archeological museums, if not the finest, with extensive collections of tools and implements, cooking utensils, jewellery and

Bahía de Naranjo

an array of ceramics. The most striking single item is a reproduction of the **Idol of Banes**, a tiny female figure in gold. Lack of resources means that the presentation of the exhibits is not always to the highest standards.

Cayo Saetía★★

Access by helicopter or along a very poorly maintained road. Go south from Banes to Santa Isabel de Nipe and here turn left on the road towards to Moa. 2km beyond Mayarí turn left. Allow 2hr30min for the return trip from Cayo Saetía to Guardalavaca.

Cayo Saetía is a 42sqkm peninsula protruding into the Bay of Nipe 130km east of Holguín and 40km northeast of Mayarí. It is one of the country's finest *cayos*, with luxuriant vegetation forming a habitat for an extraordinarily varied wildlife, including zebra, buffalo and antelope imported from Africa. Although hunting is allowed at certain times of the year, the main tourist activity organised by the guides at the tourist centre is a photo-safari aboard one of the Cuban army's venerable jeeps.

COMING AND GOING

By air – *Aeropuerto Internacional Frank Pais*, ☎ (24) 46-2512, off the Carretera Central 14km south of Holguín. The city's airport has a new terminal for international flights.

There is at least one Cubana flight a day to Havana.

Reckon on around US$10 taxi fare to the city centre.

By train – The ***Terminal de Ferrocarriles*** (B4) is on Calle V Pita to the south of the city centre, 8 blocks from Parque Calixto García. Tickets can be purchased for dollars at the Ladis counter. There is one train daily to Las Tunas, Camagüey and Santiago de Cuba (4hr) and an overnight train to Havana (13hr).

By bus – The ***Terminal de Ómnibus Nacionales*** (indicated at A3 on city plan) is at the junction of the Carretera Central and Calle 1 de Mayo in the direction of Las Tunas. The ***Viazul*** tourist coach calls at Holguín twice a week on its way from Havana to Santiago de Cuba and twice a week in the reverse direction (Havana US$44 single fare), serving all major towns en route. There are other long-distance services to these towns, but they are liable to delays and cancellation. The other bus station, the ***Terminal de Ómnibus Provinciales*** (indicated at B3 on city plan) is close to the sports stadium on Avenida de los Libertadores in the direction of Mayarí. There is a daily service between Holguín and the beaches at Guardalavaca.

GETTING AROUND

By taxi – *Taxi Transtur*, ☎ (24) 42-4187, and ***Cubataxi***, ☎ (24) 46-8294, have taxis available round the clock. There are taxi stands at the airport and in front of the Hotel Pernik.

Car hire – *Havanautos*, ☎ (24) 48-1012, are represented at the Hotel El Bosque, and ***Transautos***, ☎ (34) 48-1011 at the Hotel Pernik. ***Havanautos*** are also at the airport, ☎ (24) 46-2521.

Pedecab – Bicycle rickshaws are a favourite local means of transport. They can usually be found around the Parque de las Flores or can be flagged down anywhere in town. Reckon on 5 pesos for a town centre journey, and have the exact change ready.

ADDRESS BOOK

Tourist information – *Rumbos* (B3) can supply details of tourist attractions in the area and can organise excursions. The office is in the La Begonia bar, 10am-7pm, closed Sunday, ☎ (24) 46-3434. Hotels can also help with tourist information.

Banks / currency exchange – *Banco Financiero Internacional*, Calle Manduley (Libertad) No. 165, and Cadeca, in the same street at No. 205.

Both the Hotel Pernik and the Hotel El Bosque can change money.

Post office / Telephone – The ***Correos*** (A2) is in a building on the west side of Parque Céspedes. The ***Centro telefónico*** (A3) is on the corner of Calle Frexes and Calle Rastro, 5 blocks west of Parque Calixto García. The hotels can also deal with mail and international telephone calls.

Medical service – Both hotels have medical services.

Airline companies – The ***Cubana*** offices, ☎ (24) 42-5707, are on the second floor of the Edificio Pico de Cristal on the corner of Calle Manduley (Libertad) and Calle Martí (B3).

Specialising in internal flights, ***Aerotaxi*** have an office at the airport, ☎ (24) 46-2512.

Servicupet service stations – *Servicentro Oro Negro*, on the Carretera Central in the direction of Bayamo. ***Ciudad Jardín***, on the Carretera Central in the direction of Las Tunas.

WHERE TO STAY

The conventional hotels are some distance from the city centre, but anyone wishing to stay in the middle of town will find plenty of private accommodation.

• **Holguín**

Under US$20

Sonia Cacer, Calle Miró No. 181 between Calle Martí and Calle Luz Caballero, ☎ (24) 42-3296 – 3rm. 📶 🍴 🗙
Close to the city centre, these first floor

Eastern Cuba

rooms are clean and peaceful. The nicest is the one overlooking the vine trellis. Friendly reception.

Evaristo Bofill, Calle L Caballero No. 78 altos between Calle Miró and Calle M Lemus ⚐📧 Several rooms close to the Parque de Las Flores. The one on the top floor has an attractive view. Peaceful and cheerful.

Mireya Días, Calle Martí No. 137 altos Between Calle Martírez and Calle M Gómez, ☎ (24) 46-1227 ⚐📧 Close to the main square, an upper-floor apartment, well-kept, with attractive rooms. Friendly reception.

Between US$30-50

Villa El Bosque, Avenida Jorge Dimitrov, Reparto Pedro Díaz Coello (3km from the city centre) (indicated at B3 on plan), ☎ (24) 48-1012, Fax (24) 48-1140 – 69rm. ⚐📧 🖊 📺 ✗ ⌇ CC Car hire, bureau de change. Located to the east of the Plaza de la Revolución, this is Holguín's most attractive hotel, in a delightful green setting. It is a favourite with both visitors from abroad and Cuban holidaymakers. The accommodation in chalets scattered around the grounds is comfortable and spacious. It is best to have your own transport for getting to and from the city centre.

Hotel Pernik, Avenida Jorge Dimitrov (2km from the city centre) (indicated at B3 on plan), ☎ (24) 48-1011 or 48-1081 – 204rm. ⚐📧 🖊 📺 ⌇ Car hire, bureau de change, medical services. Close to the Plaza de la Revolución, this concrete monster has little to distinguish it from the many other structures of this type to be found in Cuba. The rooms lack charm, but the size of the place means that visitors will always find a room here in the event of the Hotel Bosque being fully booked.

• Around Holguín
The location of these hotels is shown on the map of Eastern Cuba page 262.

Between US$30-50

Centro turístico Mirador de Mayabe, Alturas de Mayabe, ☎ (24) 42-2160 or 42-3485, Fax (24) 42-5347 – 24rm. ⚐📧 🖊 📺 ✗ ⌇ CC In a rural setting 8km southeast of Holguín atop a hill overlooking the Mayabe valley, this small-scale tourist complex is

a haven of tranquillity once the swimming-pool's sound system has been switched off. The attractive, recently refurbished rooms overlook a little woodland. The centre offers a pleasant countryside stay for anyone with their own transport.

EATING OUT
Holguín has very few restaurants, but there are plenty of paladares in the city centre.

• Holguín
Under US$10

La Magia, Calle L Caballero between Calle Manduley (Libertad) and Calle Miró. This is the best paladar in town, with good fish and seafood dishes (lobster US$12) and attentive service.

El Mirador de Riberón, corner of Calle Mártires and Calle Cuba. In the northern part of town, an open-air establishment with a thatched canopy. The speciality is pork in all its forms, prepared before your eyes. The kebab is particularly good. Every evening except Sunday.

El Polinecio, Avenida Lenin between Calle Garayalde and Calle Agramonte. In the western part of town, a 13th floor establishment which has somehow managed to create a beachside atmosphere. The cuisine is standard Cuban.

• Gibara
Between US$10-20

🍽 ***El Faro***, Plaza del Fuerte, ☎ (24) 3-4596. Spacious, simply decorated restaurant and cafe with a terrace overlooking the sea. Fish and lobster specialities at relatively high prices, but the portions are generous and the quality good. There is swimming in the inlet just in front of the restaurant.

HAVING A DRINK

Bars – *La Begonia*, on Parque Calixto García (**B3**) to the left of the Casa de la Trova. A delightful courtyard café with an arbour about to collapse under its weight of flowers.

La Taberna Pancho, Avenida Jorge Dimitrov, halfway between the Hotel Pernik and the El Bosque. Beer and hamburgers served in a big tavern with wooden furniture, with only the music to remind people that they are in Cuba. Midday-midnight.

Cremería Guamá, corner of Calle Luz Caballero and Calle Manduley (Libertad) on Parque de las Flores (B3). This is the town's biggest and most popular ice-cream parlour.

Concerts – The **Casa de la Trova** (B3), Calle Maceo on Parque Calixto García, has traditional music in a lovely courtyard setting from 9pm every evening except Monday.

Café Cantante, in the northeastern corner of the main square. Traditional Cuban singing weekend evenings.

Fondo de Bienes Culturales, next to the Museo Provincial, stages weekend concerts.

Night life – The **Cabaret Nocturno**, ☎ (24) 42-5185, 6km west of the city centre on the Carretera Central towards Las Tunas. Open-air show every evening at 8pm except Monday.

Discotheques – The El Bosque is the home of **El Pétalo**, the most popular discotheque for local people as well as visitors from abroad. Salsa and techno every evening from 9pm-2am.

OTHER THINGS TO DO

Excursions – The **Rumbos** travel agency will organise trips to Gibara, Guardalavaca and Chorro de Maita.

Horseriding in the Mayabe valley can be arranged through the Hotel Mirador de Mayabe.

Theatre – The **Teatro Eddy Sunol** (B3), Calle Martí between Calle Maceo and Calle Libertad on Parque Calixto García, stages performances of opera and ballet.

Open-air pursuits – There are baseball games at the **Estadio Calixto García**, the city stadium on Avenida de los Libertadores, 500m from the Hotel Pernik.

SHOPPING

Arts and crafts – The **Fondo de Bienes Culturales**, on Parque Calixto García next to the Museo Provincial (B3) has a selection of local craft items. 10am to 5pm, closed Sunday.

Art Galleries – There are exhibitions of contemporary art at the **Centro de Arte**, in the southwestern corner of the main square. 9am-9pm; 9am-1pm Sunday.

Bookshops – Pedro Rogena, Calle Manduley (Libertad) between Calle Martí and Calle Frexes, on Parque Calixto García (B3).

Making the most of Guardalavaca

COMING AND GOING

Guardalavaca is not well served by public transport, and most visitors are here on an organised tour or holiday.

By boat – The **Marina Bahía de Naranjo**, Carretera de Guardalavaca, ☎ (24) 3-0132, is located on a cayo with just a restaurant, a boutique and a natural aquarium.

GETTING AROUND

By taxi – Taxis OK, ☎ (24) 3-1243, have vehicles at most of the hotels.

Car hire – Cubacar, ☎ (24) 3-0389, are between the Hotel Guardalavaca and the Hotel Las Brisas, **Havanautos** are in the shopping centre, and **Via** in the hotels on Playa Esmeralda.

ADDRESS BOOK

Tourist information – The **Cubanacan** travel agency is represented in each of the hotels or can be contacted, ☎ (24) 3-0226.

Medical service – Clínica Internacional, Calle 2, ☎ (24) 3-0291, opposite the Hotel Atlántico.

Servicupet service stations – Guardalavaca, on the way into the resort coming from Holguín.

WHERE TO STAY

Hotels are shown on the map of Eastern Cuba page 262.

The more expensive hotels are better value if booked through a travel agent. The charming El Cayuelo restaurant at the eastern end of Guardalavaca has rooms for US$20, and if these are taken it may be possible to find accommodation of a basic kind with local fishermen. There is some private accommodation in Banes.

• **Playa Guardalavaca**

Between US$50-100

Hotel Atlántico and Bungalows, ☎ (24) 3-0180 or 3-0195, Fax (24) 3-0200 – 234rm. and 136 chalets. 🍴 🗐 🖉 📺 ✕ 🛋 🐾 🆑 Car hire, bureau de change, medical services. Large hotel built on the resort's main beach. The rooms are comfortable and well kept. The best have sea views. The chalets are about 500m from the beach.

Hotel Guardalavaca, ☎ (24) 3-0121 – 225rm. 🍴 🗐 🖉 📺 ✕ 🛋 🐾 🆑 Car hire, bureau de change. This modern hotel is a short distance from the beach. The rooms are similar to those in the Hotel Atlántico. They either face the gardens or the Atlántico.

More than US$100

Hotel Delta Las Brisas, ☎ (24) 3-0218, Fax (24) 3-0018 – 231rm. 🍴 🗐 🖉 📺 ✕ 🛋 🐾 🍸 🆑 car hire, bureau de change, medical facilities, creche. This is the resort's latest hotel, with the widest range of amenities including a 500m stretch of private beach. Superior rooms have king-size beds.

• **Playa Esmeralda**

The Spanish Meliá hotel chain has built three hotels on this lovely well-shaded beach. Each hotel is of a high standard, and they only differ according to whether club-type accommodation is offered and whether full board is taken. Full range of watersports. www. solmelia.es.

Between US$50-100

Sol Río de Mares, ☎ (24) 3-0060, Fax (24) 3-0065 – 232rm. This is the least expensive option and the only one which is not all-in.

Between US$100-300

Sol Club Río de Luna, ☎ (24) 3-0030, Fax (24) 3-0035 – 222rm. Club version mainly for families.

Meliá Río de Oro, ☎ (24) 3-0090, Fax (24) 3-0095 – 294rm. This is the latest addition and the best. The accommodation is in the form of houses built along idyllic water channels and separated by generous planting.

• **Cayo Saetia**

Between US$50-100

Villa Cayo Saetia, ☎ (24) 46-8504, Fax (24) 33-2780 – 11rm. 🍴 🗐 🖉 📺 ✕ 🐾 In a remarkable natural setting, this little establishment consists of 5 bungalows and a single suite. The recently renovated rooms are spacious. Book well in advance.

EATING OUT

Apart from the hotel restaurants, there are restaurants around the beach at Guardalavaca, either by the shopping centre or a little further inland.

El Cayuelo, Playa Guardalavaca, 1km east of the Hotel Las Brisas, a delightful house right by the sea, with a restaurant offering fish and other seafood.

HAVING A DRINK

Discotheques – At the western end of the main beach, **La Roca** is the trendiest disco in Guardalavaca.

Nightlife – Ecos nocturnos, over the shopping centre, puts on a good show 9pm-4am, show at midnight (US$2).

OTHER THINGS TO DO

Most of Guardalavaca's leisure facilities are run by the hotels, which may require day visitors to pay for their use.

Excursions – The aquarium of the Bahía de Naranjo Natural Park can be visited on a boat trip (US$12). There is a supplement of US$25 for swimming with the aquarium's dolphins. The hotels run day trips to Cayo Saetia for around US$100, including helicopter flight, lunch and a guided tour of the island.

Outdoor pursuits – Most of Guardalavaca's hotels organise diving expeditions and a whole range of other watersports. The all-in formula does not include any fuel used. A hunting trip on Cayo Saetia can be organised but fees are expensive.

Making the most of Guardalavaca

THE SIERRA MAESTRA★
FROM BAYAMO TO SANTIAGO DE CUBA

Granma and Santiago de Cuba provinces
Pico Turquino (1 972m), Pico Cuba (1 872m), Pico Bayemesa (1 730m)
See map page 262

Not to be missed
A drive along the coast road to the south of the sierra.

And remember...
Most of the Sierra Maestra National Park is out of bounds to visitors.
Fill up at Manzanillo or Pilón before setting out along the coast road and do the
drive in daylight, preferably in a jeep.

Covering parts of both Granma and Santiago de Cuba provinces, the Sierra
Maestra rises proudly over the island's southernmost coast. Wonderful walking
country and with a scenic road winding along its Caribbean flank, it is Cuba's
highest mountain range, dominating not only the region but also the country's
history. For almost 500 years the sierra and its surroundings have been in the
foreground of the events that have shaped the destiny of Cuba and its people.
It was here that the abolition of slavery was first announced and here that the
independence of the country from Spain was first declared. But more than anything else, the Sierra Maestra became the great symbol of the revolutionary
struggle, when, for almost two years, it harboured Fidel Castro and his guerrilla
warriors before their triumph over the Batista regime.

The Sierra Maestra

B. Brillion/MICHELIN

274

Bayamo
70km from Holguín – Allow 2hr for a tour of the town.

The Carretera Central approaches Bayamo from the west, running into Calle Figueredo. After three blocks this street enters the Plaza de la Revolución on its southern side.

With a population of 130 000, this sleepy provincial capital seems lost in a dream of past glories. When the loudest noise in its streets is the clip-clop of horses' hooves it is difficult to think of the town as the place of destiny implied by the profusion of commemorative plaques on its buildings. But despite the fact that hardly any of its architecture predates the 19C, a visit to Bayamo can be the equivalent of an immersion course in modern Cuban history.

Piracy and poetry
In November 1513 Diego Velázquez founded the villa of San Salvador de Bayamo, only the second (after Baracoa) of the colonial strong points established by the Spanish. Everything possible was done to give the new settlement a good start. The site chosen lay in the middle of a fertile plain, well inland and thus secure from pirate attack. Native resistance was crushed when cacique Hatuey was captured and burnt at the stake.

The town flourished and became rich, less through agriculture or legitimate trade than through smuggling. Dramatic events were few, though one particular episode was immortalised in verse. In 1608, the very first Cuban poem, *Espejo de Paciencia*, was written by **Silvestre de Balboa**. In it the poet describes in mythic terms the kidnapping of a bishop by the French pirate Gilbert Giron, the refusal by the people of Bayamo to pay the ransom demanded, and the subsequent capture and execution of the villain of the piece.

Cradle of Cuban nationhood
On 20 October 1868, 10 days after freeing the slaves on his estate at La Demajagua (*See page 278*), **Carlos Manuel de Céspedes** marched into Bayamo with a small force of rebels and took possession of the town. The town was proclaimed the capital of the Republic in arms, and the rebels celebrated their triumph by singing "To battle, people of Bayamo". Composed by a local man, Pedro "Perucho" Figueredo, this martial air became the national anthem, *La Bayemsa*.

Four months later, on 12 January 1869, Bayamo came under attack by the Spanish colonial army. Rather than see it fall into the hands of the hated enemy, the citizens decided to reduce the town to ashes, a patriotic gesture which was eventually honoured by declaring Bayamo a National Monument.

Plaza de la Revolución
Formerly known as Parque Céspedes and lined with neo-Classical residences, Bayamo's town centre square is human in scale and has little in common with the vast post-Revolutionary parade grounds of other towns. In the centre of the square the bust of Perucho Figueredo, the man who fathered the national anthem, faces the bronze statue of Carlos Manuel de Céspedes, "father of the country". On the north side of the square, the *ayuntamiento* (town hall) has a plaque commemorating the declaration of the abolition of slavery in 1868.

To the west of the square, the **Casa Natal de Carlos Manuel de Céspedes** (*Open 9am-5pm; 9am-1.30pm and 8pm-10pm Saturday; 9am-1pm Sunday; closed Monday. Admission charge*) was spared by the flames which consumed the rest of the town. Céspedes was born here on 18 April 1819. His memory is honoured by an array of documents and objects linked to the struggle for freedom from Spain, among them a copy of *Cubano Libre*, the first periodical advocating independence.

The **Museo Provincial de Granma** *(8am-6pm; 10am-2pm Saturday and Sunday; closed Monday. Admission charge)* is housed in the former home of the conductor Manuel Munoz Cedeno who helped Perucho Figueredo in the orchestration of the national anthem. Among the items from the time of slavery is an extraordinary picture of General Antonio Maceo made by a slave from 13 000 separate pieces of different kinds of rare wood. Even more pieces, 19 109 in total, went into the making of a guitar, complete with case.

Part of the museum is dedicated to the Revolution, in particular to the 1953 attack on the barracks at Bayamo, made at the same time as the more famous attack on the barracks at Santiago de Cuba. For the time being, the museum is under renovation.

Plaza del Himno Nacional

One block away from Plaza de la Revolución, the street widens out to embrace a church surrounded by well-restored little houses. Known as "National Anthem Square", this really is the cradle of the nation, the place where La Bayemsa was first heard. A plaque records that the marching song composed by Perucho Figueredo was played in the church on 2 June 1868 under the direction of conductor Manuel Munoz Cedeno. A few months later, on 8 November, it rang out again when the rebel fighters under Céspedes took control of the town.

La Bayamesa, Cuba's national anthem
Run to combat, men of Bayamo,
May the motherland be proud of you.
Don't fear a glorious death,
For to die for the motherland is to live.
To live in chains is to live
In shame and indignity.
Hear the clarion call,
To your arms, brave ones, run!

Little remains of the **Parroquial Mayor de San Salvador**, the church built in 1613. It was rebuilt in 1740, but the fire which burned the town down in 1869 was started here and only the **Capilla de Dolores** was spared from the flames. The chapel has a particularly fine Baroque altarpiece carved in cedarwood. Opposite the church the little white building called the **Casa de la Nacionalidad** Cubana houses the office of the town historian. The people employed here are usually happy to help with any questions visitors have about the town.

Leave Bayamo on Avenida Amado Estévez on the southwest side of the town and go in the direction of Yara. In Yara turn left towards Bartolomé Masó, then take the road which climbs into the Sierra Maestra.

Sierra Maestra National Park★
59km from Bayamo to Bartolomé Masó
Allow two days to climb Pico Turquino

These glorious mountains are still full of the atmosphere of the time when they were the domain of Fidel Castro's bearded guerrillas. This was the "First Liberated Territory", where the defeats suffered by Batista's forces in the course of 1958 were to lead directly to the triumph of the Revolution. A number of sites in the sierra still evoke the feats of arms of Fidel and his companions.

Access to the mountains has always been strictly controlled, but most of this magnificent National Park has now been closed to ordinary visitors from abroad. Until further notice, foreign tourists are only allowed to go as far as Santo Domingo, and without special permission, the climb to the summit of Pico Turquino is no longer possible and even the lower slopes of Cuba's highest mountain are off-limits.

One reason for restricting access has been an outbreak of disease affecting the coffee plantations around the sierra.

However, visitors are still allowed access to the magnificent **setting*** of the little settlement of Santo Domingo, lost amid luxuriant vegetation. Drivers need to take special care for the whole length of the 22km mountain road up from Bartolomé Masó. The single hotel at **Santo Domingo** is the starting point for a number of guided walks led by the young director of the local museum (Reckon on a fee of US$5 per hour). One walk along the lovely valley between Yara and Providencia crosses the river several times and follows in the footsteps of the guerrillas as they prepared for their final offensive against Batista's forces *(Allow 5hr. Return by car can be arranged)*. Another, more strenuous hike leads to the summit of a local mountain.

The **museo de Santo Domingo** *(8am-midday and 2pm-5pm. Admission charge)* is on the far bank of the river from the village. The museum is housed in a charming little building which was occupied by Mandoza, one of Castro's closest collab orators, and a number of personal effects evoke the deeds of this Revolutionary hero. There is also a fascinating model showing the development of the Sierra Maestra counter-offensive.

In the event of the Sierra being opened up to the public again, the *Alto de Naranjo viewpoint* is 5km further along the road beyond the present barrier. From the viewpoint, a 3km long path leads to the Commandancia de la Plata, Fidel Castro's former headquarters. The encampment includes a field hospital and a museum, with the transmitter of *Radio Rebelde*, the "Voice of the Revolution".

The climb up to **Pico Turquino****, at 1 972m Cuba's highest peak, is a two day trip. The 13km route passes first through a dense tropical forest with tree ferns and orchids which eventually gives way to a cover of conifers.

Before making the final approach to the summit it is usual to spend the night in a mountain hut. The top of the mountain is often shrouded in cloud, but given clear conditions the superb **panorama**** takes in the Caribbean and the whole of the sierra.

It is possible to cross the range and descend by the southern slope to the coast road by Las Cuevas.

Return to Yara by the same road, and turn left in the town towards Manzanillo.

Manzanillo

20km from Yara and 65km from Bayamo
Allow 1hr for a tour of the town

Second city of Granma province, the harbour town of Manzanilla prides itself on its musical traditions. The street organs brought here from France at the end of the 19C helped give much Cuban music its distinctive style, and the town claims to be the birthplace of *nueva trova,* the revived ballad style of the early 1970s. The main square, **Parque Céspedes***, makes its own contribution to the town's musical reputation. At its centre is the **glorieta***, a splendidly elaborate bandstand in Moorish style built in the 1920s and, in comparison with much of Manzanilla's architectural heritage, surprisingly well maintained. Some of the other buildings around the square, like the Edificio Quirch, are in a similar style. Also on the square is the modest **Museo Histórico Municipal** *(Open 9am-6pm; 8am-midday and 8pm-10pm Sunday; closed Monday. Admission charge)* devoted to the local history and culture from the pre-Conquest era to the guerrilla war in the Sierra Maestra.

Manzanillo has had a long history as a port, exporting sugar and importing slaves. Both town and harbour have seen better days, though there are worse ways of spending an hour or two than strolling around the quiet streets. The shabby *malecón* doesn't really bear comparison with Havana's waterfront boulevard although it does give fine views over the Gulf of Guacanayabo.

From the service station to the southwest of the town centre go in the direction of Niquero. After 10km, where a sign points towards La Demajagua, turn right towards the coast.

The Parque Nacional La Demajagua (*Open 8am-5pm. Admission charge*) is the old sugar plantation which once belonged to Carlos Manuel de Céspedes. Now a designated National Monument, this is the place where the Ten Years War broke out when the "father of the country" demonstratively freed his slaves and began his march on Bayamo.

There is a **museum** with some of the great man's personal possessions as well as a number of archeological finds. Outside, the famous bell which was rung to summon the slaves to and from work is now embedded in a stone wall. The last time Céspedes used it was on 10 October 1868, when it rang out to announce that his slaves had been granted their freedom. Among the remains of the plantation and its sugar-mill is a mill-wheel around which a *jagüey* tree has grown.

Return to the main road and continue for 34km to Media Luna. 10km beyond the town the road divides. Take the right fork to Niquero 11km away and then continue for a further 19km to Playa Las Coloradas.

The southern coast★
252km from Cabo Cruz to Santiago de Cuba, allow a whole day.

All the way along this southern shore the Sierra Maestra drops directly into the sea, separated from the Caribbean solely by the coastal highway. This is one of the finest drives in Cuba. The road has recently been improved, but it may be partly blocked by minor landslides, some of it is unsurfaced and there is the occasional pot-hole. Wandering herds of sheep and goats are as likely to be encountered as other vehicles.

The road passes through a series of different landscapes. There are beaches of dark sand and wave-battered cliffs, banana plantations interspersed with tracts of bleached grassland, parched shrubs clinging to walls of rock and little coves ringed with *uvas caletas*. The only settlements to be seen are the rare villages and the odd little hamlet tucked away on the mountainside.

Beyond Belic is the **Parque Nacional Desembarco del Granma**. It was here, at **Playa Las Coloradas**, on 2 December 1956, that Castro and 81 comrades struggled ashore from the launch Granma, after an eventful, week-long voyage from their place of exile in Mexico. The narrow beach bordered by mangrove swamps is one of the most attractive in the area.

A concrete **memorial** 1km in the direction of Cabo Cruz commemorates this fateful day in Cuba's history.

The only place to stay in the vicinity is a camp site on the edge of the beach. Interpretive trails evoke the presence in the area of the native Cubans who inhabited the nearby **caves** (cuevas). One of the caves, **Mollote Fuente** has pictograms and can be explored. The best way of getting to know the area, and its wealth of native trees, is to hire one of the knowlegeable guides (*enquire at the campground or at the tourist information centre at Belic*). Rare birds abound, but so, unfortunately, do mosquitoes.

Cabo Cruz is where the highway ends; the cape is dominated by a **lighthouse** overlooking the mangrove swamps which stretch seaward from the village and merge almost imperceptibly with the sea. A further 6km to the east is **Punta del Inglés,** the southernmost point in Cuba.

Go back 40km to the junction with the main road and turn right towards Pilón, 2km away across the mountains.

13km to the east of Pilón is the resort of **Marea del Portillo**. With the glorious backdrop of the Sierra Maestra on one side and a beach of black sand on the other, it consists of luxury hotel complexes the size of small towns, patronised mostly by Canadians.

Some 78km on from Marea del Portillo, half hidden among the banana plantations between sierra and sea, is the village of **Uvero**. Another 15km further on, the mountains drop abruptly into the 7 000m depths of the Cayman Trench. The final 70km of highway between the village of **Chivirico** and Santiago is in good condition. The beaches along the route are not particularly attractive but at least offer the opportunity to cool off occasionally.

Making the most of Bayamo

COMING AND GOING

By air – The *Aeropuerto Carlos Manuel de Céspedes,* ☎ (23) 42-4502, is off the Carretera Central 4km to the northeast of the town towards Holguín. There are 4 *Cubana* flights a day to Havana as well as flights to Santiago.

By train – The *Estación de Ferrocarriles* is at the end of Calle Saco, several blocks east of the Plaza de la Revolución. There is one train a day to Havana and Camagüey, and two trains a day to Santiago. Facilities for foreign visitors to buy tickets for dollars at the station's Ladis office.

By bus – The *Terminal de Ómnibus* is 1.5km from the town centre on the Carretera Central in the direction of Santiago. The *Viazul* tourist coach calls twice a week on its run from Havana to Santiago, ditto in the reverse direction. There are other, unreliable services to Havana and Santiago as well as to Manzanillo and Santo Domingo (though most passengers have to settle for a place aboard a lorry).

GETTING AROUND

A car is strongly recommended as the best way to explore the Bayamo area.

By taxi – *Cubataxi,* ☎ (23) 42-4313, have a 24-hour service.

By horse-drawn carriage – This is the local means of transport for moving around the town centre. Payment in pesos.

Car hire – *Havanautos* can be found to the rear of the Servicupet petrol station, ☎ (23) 42-7375, and *Transautos* are at the Hotel Sierra Maestra, ☎ (23) 42-7273.

ADDRESS BOOK

Tourist information – The PR manager (Sra Carmen Prieto) at the tourist desk of the Hotel Sierra Maestra will help with advice on exploring the Sierra Maestra and with finding accommodation.

Banks / Currency exchange – *Banco Financiero Internacional,* Carretera Central Km 1 towards Santiago.

Post office / Telephone – The most reliable way of dealing with mail and making international telephone calls is at the Hotel Sierra Maestra.

Airline companies – The *Cubana* office, ☎ (23) 42-3916, is at the corner of Calle José Martí and Calle Parada y Rojas, and there is another at the airport, ☎ (23) 4-3514 or 4-3695.

Servicupet service stations – *El Especial*, junction of the Carretera Central and Calle Hospital to the rear of the bus station in the direction of Santiago.

WHERE TO STAY AND EATING OUT

The hotels in the Bayamo area are inexpensive and there is ample private accommodation.

• Bayamo

Under US$20

Villa Bayamo, main road in the direction of Manzanillo, ☎ (23) 42-3102 – 32rm. 🍴 📋 ✎ 📺 ✗ 🛇 cc To the west of the town, this is a very pleasant, leafy and peaceful place to stay, provided you have your own transport. Friendly reception and reasonable rooms for the price.

Between US20-30

Hotel Royalton, Calle Maceo No. 53 on Parque Céspedes, ☎ (23) 42-2290/68 – 33rm. 🍴 📋 ✎ 📺 ✗ In the middle of the town, a handsome renovated 19C building with attractive rooms. Good value for money.

Hotel Sierra Maestra, Carretera Central Km 7.5, ☎ (23) 48-1013, Fax (23) 48-1798 – 204rm. 🍴 📋 ✎ 📺 ✗ 🛇 cc Bureau de change, tourist agency. On the Carretera Central on the edge of town in the Santiago direction. Despite the off-putting concrete architecture and the surroundings, the hotel

has spacious and well-kept rooms for an establishment in this category.

• Parque Nacional de la Sierra Maestra

Under US$10

Campismo La Sierrita, between Bartolomé Maso and Providencia in the Santo Domingo direction, ☎ (23) 42-4807 – 24 cabins. 🍴 📋 ✗ Riverside setting for a group of cabins popular with local holidaymakers.

Under US$30

Villa Balcón de la Sierra, Avenida Masó, Providencia, ☎ (23) 59-5180 - 20 rms 🍴 📋 📺 ✗ 🛇 Hill-top site at Bartolomé Maso, these chalets have little terraces with a view of the Sierra, plus a sitting room and a pair of fairly basic bedrooms. Mostly used by Cubans on holiday.

Villa Santo Domingo, Santo Domingo – 20rm. 🍴 📋 ✗ Rustic chalets in a lovely valley in the Sierra on the banks of the Río Yara. Starting point for hikes and rides in the Sierra.

OTHER THINGS TO DO

Excursions – Enquire at the Hotel Sierra Maestra about hiking possibilities in the Sierra, individually or with a guide. For any special authorisations, check with Ecotur in Havana, ☎ /Fax (7) 24-7520, Alcona, ☎ (7) 22-2526, Mintur, corner of Paseo and Calle 19, ☎ (7) 33-4323, or Ministerio de la Agricultura, ☎ (7) 81-9731 or 84-5330.

Making the most of Manzanillo

COMING AND GOING

By air – The ***Aeropuerto Sierra Maestra***, ☎ (23) 5-4984, is 8km south of the town on the continuation of Avenida de Céspedes. There are 4 flights a week to Havana operated by ***Cubana***, plus some international flights from Canada, with transfers to Marea del Portillo by hotel bus.

By train – The ***Estación de Ferrocarriles*** is at the end of Calle Merchán, 1km northeast of Parque Céspedes. There are two trains a day to Bayamo,

a daily train to Santiago, and a train every other day to Havana. Reliability not guaranteed.

By bus – The ***Terminal de Ómnibus*** is 2km to the east of the town in the Bayamo direction. In theory there are daily services to Havana, Santiago, Bayamo, Niquero and Pilón, but most passengers are carried by lorry.

GETTING AROUND

Car hire – The ***Havanautos*** office, ☎ (23) 5-4815, is at the Manzanillo

Servicupet petrol station, and **Cubacar** is represented at the two hotels in Marea del Portillo, ☎ (23) 33-5301 (ext 4159).

Moped hire – Mopeds can be hired at the resorts in Marea del Portillo.

ADDRESS BOOK

Tourist information – There are tourist information desks at the hotels in Marea del Portillo.

Banks / Currency exchange – There is a bureau de change at the Hotel Guacanayabo and at the resorts at Marea del Portillo.

Post office / Telephone – Mail and international telephone calls can be dealt with at the hotels.

Airline companies - The **Cubana** office, ☎ (23) 5-2800, is on the corner of Calle Maceo and Calle Merchán y Villuendas on Parque Céspedes.

Medical service – There are medical facilities at the Hotel Guacanayabo and the resorts at Marea del Portillo.

Servicupet service stations – **La Bujía**, at the junction of the bypass and the road to Niquero, 2km south of the town centre, Niquero, on the road out towards Pilón, and Pilón on the main road.

WHERE TO STAY AND EATING OUT

The location of hotels is shown on the map of Eastern Cuba page 262.

● **Manzanillo**

Under US$30

Hotel Guacanayabo, Avenida Camilo Cienfuegos, ☎ (23) 5-4012 – 112rm. ⚐ 🗐 🎧 📺 ✕ ⚘ 🆑 Car hire, bureau de change, medical facilities. On a hilltop overlooking the bypass 2.5km from the town centre. The Gulf of Guacanayabo is visible in the distance, but the hotel's charmless rooms are typical of this kind of dated reinforced concrete structure.

● **Southern coast**

Under US$10

Campismo Playa Las Coloradas, ☎ (23) 42-4807 ⚐ 🗐 ✕ ⚘. By a lovely beach, a group of well-equipped and

well kept chalets. Friendly staff. Anti-mosquito lotion essential for walking in the surrounding area.

Under US$30

Villa Punta Piedra, 6km from Pilón in the Santiago direction, ☎ (23) 59-4421 – 13rm. ⚐ 🗐 ✕ ⚘ 5 minutes from the beach, this simple little hotel has a view of coconut palms and mangroves. The rooms are plainly furnished but comfortable enough, certainly for an overnight stay.

Motel Guamá, 6km to the east of Chivirico, ☎ (23) 2-6124 – 8rm. ⚐ 🗐 📺 ✕ This little hotel is mostly used by Cuban holidaymakers. It has a secluded setting, with rooms overlooking a bay dotted with cayos. Facilities are basic, but it is a useful stopping place on the long road between Pilón and Santiago de Cuba.

Between US$50-100

The luxury hotels along the southern coast cater almost exclusively for Canadian visitors on package holidays, and have all the usual features of a Cuban all-inclusive resort, apart from the quality of the beach, but this is reflected in lower rates.

Hotel Farallón del Caribe, Carretera de Pilón, Marea del Portillo, ☎ (23) 59-7008, Fax (23) 59-70000 – 140rm. ⚐ 🗐 ⚘ 📺 ✕ ⚘ 🆑

Hotel Marea del Portillo, Carretera de Pilón, Marea del Portillo, ☎ (23) 59-7008, Fax (23) 59-7080 – 130rm. ⚐ 🗐 ⚘ 📺 ✕ ⚘ 🆑 Currently undergoing refurbishment.

Hotel Los Galeones, Carretera a Chivirico, ☎ (22) 2-6160 – 34rm. ⚐ 🗐 ⚘ 📺 ✕ ⚘ 🆑

More than US$100

Hotel Sierra Mar, Carretera a Chivirico Km 60, ☎ (22) 2-9110 – 200rm. ⚐ 🗐 ⚘ 📺 ✕ ⚘ 🆑

OTHER THINGS TO DO

Excursions – The tourist information desks in the hotels organise trips to Santiago and Cayo Blanco, as well as jeep safaris and hikes in the Sierra Maestra.

Outdoor pursuits – Wide choice of watersports including scuba diving and deep-sea fishing.

Making the most of Manzanillo

SANTIAGO DE CUBA ★★

Capital of Santiago de Cuba province
Cuba's second city – pop 470 000
865km from Havana
See map page 263

Not to be missed
An evening session at the Casa de la Trova.
A drink on the terrace of the Hotel Casa Grande.
The view from the Castillo del Morro at sunset.

And remember...
Hotel rooms need to be booked well in advance for Carnival.
Except at Carnival time, Santiago is at its most musical at weekends.
Visit the shrine at El Cobre on 8 September, the festival of the Santería deity Ochún.
Despite the heavy police presence,
take special care of handbags and personal possessions.

The city of Santiago has a superb location, at the head of a magnificent bay and overlooked by the foothills of the Sierra Maestra.

From Bayamo, the Carretera Central crosses the sierra and enters Santiago from the north, running into the Plaza de la Revolución.

First capital

Santiago was founded in 1514 by **Diego Velázquez** and became the capital of Cuba one year later. The original location proved unsatisfactory, and after eight years the town was moved to a new site on the far side of the bay. Once its resources began to run out, the conquistadors started to lose interest in the place. With the mineral riches apparently worked out and most of the indigenous labour force dead through disease or maltreatment, Spanish attention turned to Havana, which was chosen as the residence of the Captains-General in the middle of the 16C.

In 1607 Santiago was formally deprived of its title as the country's capital and was downgraded to the "administrative centre of the department of Oriente". In the years that followed, Santiago lived from sugar, ranching, and copper mining. Like other Cuban cities in a similar location, the town suffered repeated pirate attacks, among them a devastating raid in 1554 by the Frenchman Jacques de Sores. In 1633 a degree of security was provided by the construction of fortresses including the formidable Castillo de San Pedro de la Roca (El Morro) which still stands at the entrance to the bay. But even this was not enough to deter Captain Henry Morgan, who succeeded in sacking the city in 1662.

The coming of the French

In 1791 more than 20 000 French colonists fled from Haiti to Cuba because of the slave revolt led by Toussaint-Louverture. The newcomers settled in and around Santiago, bringing with them the cultivation of coffee-beans and more up-to-date methods of sugar production. The city's cultural life was invigorated by this wave of immigration; the language was enriched by an infusion of creole expressions and there was a fusion of French and African influences in music and dance.

Rebel city

Towards the end of the 19C the revolutionary movement in the Sierra Maestra (*See page 275*) took hold in Santiago too, and, hoping to free itself from the domination of far-off Havana, the city threw itself with fervour into the wars of independence.

Born locally, the mulatto rebel leader **Antonio Maceo** became the symbol of this struggle when, at the end of the Ten Years War in 1878, he refused to accept the terms of the Pact of Zanjón. Realising that the truce proposed by the Spanish was not going to bring about either the abolition of slavery, or independence, he called for a resumption of the armed struggle. Known as the *Protesta de Baraguá* (the Baraguá Protest), Maceo's action did not prevent the signature of a peace treaty, which among other things led to his exile. But in 1895 he returned, this time under the inspired leadership of José Martí, to take part in the Second War of Independence.

The renewed struggle for freedom from colonial rule was to involve the United States. The explosion aboard the *USS Maine* in Havana harbour (*See page 25*) led to the sending of an American force which landed in June 1898 at a place called Siboney not far from Santiago. In the weeks that followed the Spanish suffered one reverse after the other. The campaign culminated in the bloody battle of San Juan Hill in which the defenders were finally overcome. One of the leading participants was future US President Theodore Roosevelt, putting into practice his foreign policy dictum "speak softly and carry a big stick".

The Americans were determined to marginalise the Cuban rebels, and despite their contribution to the Spanish defeat, Calixto García and his force of partly Black troops were not allowed into Santiago to join in the victory celebrations. Nor was a Cuban delegation present at the signing of the Treaty of Paris on 10 December 1898 at which Spain formally gave up its colony. The Cuban Revolution just over half a century later is seen by some as belated revenge for these snubs to a proud country.

Birthplace of the Revolution

On 26 July 1953 another event took place in Santiago which became a defining moment in Cuban history. Taking advantage of Carnival time, when most of Batista's soldiery could be relied upon to be dancing or drunk, a group of more than a hundred men led by the young lawyer **Fidel Castro Ruiz** attempted to storm the **Moncada** barracks. But the attack was a disaster; half of the rebels were killed in a hail of bullets or in the repression which ensued and the survivors were put on trial. The proceedings culminated in Castro's *History will absolve me*, the famous speech he made in his own defence. Condemned with several of his comrades to 15 years imprisonment on the Island of Pines (now renamed the Isle of Youth), he was amnestied on 15 May 1955 (*See page 325*). The Moncada attack was to link Santiago more firmly than ever to the course of Cuban history. It was to eastern Cuba that Castro chose to return three years after his release from prison and subsequent exile (*See page 278*), and it was in Santiago itself that a violent diversion took place on the 30 November 1956 in order to cover the landing from the **Granma**. But the uprising, organised by the 26 July Movement (M-26) under the leadership of Frank País, was brutally suppressed. Batista's forces, now on a proper war footing, were aware of the Granma's arrival, which had been delayed by two days. Within three days of landing most of the rebels had been captured or executed and only a small group

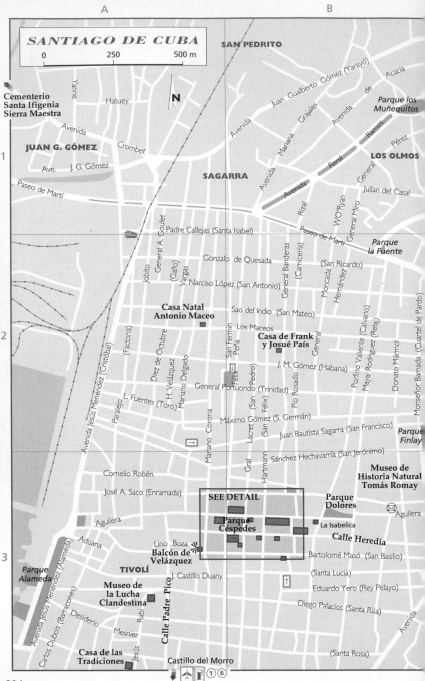

SANTIAGO DE CUBA

0   250   500 m

SAN PEDRITO

Cementerio
Santa Ifigenia
Sierra Maestra

Yanne

Hatuey

N

Avenida

Crombet

JUAN G. GÓMEZ

Ave.   J. G. Gómez

Paseo de Martí

Juan Gualberto Gómez (Yarayó)

Acacia

Avenida   Mariana   Grajales

Avenida

René

Avenida

de

Ramos

*Parque los
Muñequitos*

Pérez

LOS OLMOS

General

Julián del Casal

Rizal

W.O'Ryan

General Miró

SAGARRA

Avenida

Avenida

Paseo de Martí

*Parque
la Fuente*

Padre Callejas (Santa Isabel)

Jobito

General A. Goulet

(Gallo)
Vargas

Gonzalo de Quesada

Narciso López (San Antonio)

General Banderas
(Carnicería)

(San Ricardo)

Moncada

Hernández

**Casa Natal
Antonio Maceo**

Sao del Indio (San Mateo)

Porfirio Valiente (Calvario)

Mayai Rodríguez (Relij)

Donato Mármol

Monseñor Barnada (Cuartel de Pardo)

(Factoría)

Diez de Octubre

H. Velázquez

Mariano Delgado

Los Maceos

San Fermín   Peña

**Casa de Frank
y Josué País**

General

J. M. Gómez (Habana)

Avenida Jesús Menéndez (Cristóbal)

Parajejo

L. Fuentes (Toro)

San   Félix

General Portuondo (Trinidad)

Lacret (San   Pedro)

(San Félix)

Pío Rosado

Máximo Gómez (S. Germán)

Mariano Corona

Juan Bautista Sagarra (San Francisco)

*Parque
Finlay*

Gral
Hartmann

Sánchez Hechavarría (San Jerónimo)

**Museo de
Historia Natural
Tomás Romay**

Cornelio Robén

José A. Saco (Enramada)

Aguilera

SEE DETAIL

**Parque
Dolores**

Aguilera

**Parque
Céspedes**

La Isabelica

Calle Heredia

Lino Boza

**Balcón de
Velázquez**

TIVOLÍ

Aduana

Bartolomé Masó (San Basilio)

(Santa Lucía)

J. Castillo Duany

Eduardo Yero (Rey Pelayo)

*Parque
Alameda*

**Museo de
la Lucha
Clandestina**

Desiderio

Avenida Jesús Menéndez (Alameda)

Carlos Dubois (Barracones)

Rabí

Calle Padre Pico

Diego Palacios (Santa Rita)

Avenida

Mesnier

Jesús

**Casa de las
Tradiciones**

Castillo del Morro

(Santa Rosa)

A   B

1

2

3

284

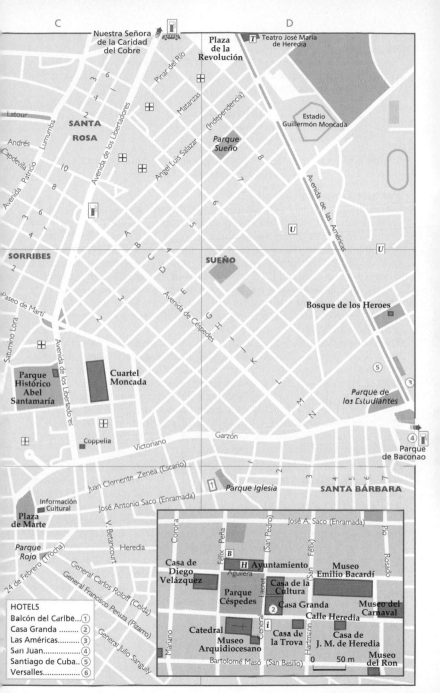

C

Nuestra Señora
de la Caridad
del Cobre

Plaza
de la
Revolución

D

T Teatro José María
de Heredia

Pinar del Río

Matanzas

Latour

SANTA
ROSA

Andrés

Capdevila

Avenida Patricio Lumumba

Avenida de los Libertadores

Ángel Luis Salazar

(Independencia)

Estadio
Guillermón Moncada

Parque
Sueño

SORRIBES

Paseo de Martí

Saturnino Lora

Avenida de los Libertadores

SUEÑO

Avenida de Céspedes

Avenida de las Américas

Bosque de los Heroes

U

U

Parque
Histórico
Abel
Santamaría

Cuartel
Moncada

Coppelia

Victoriano

Garzón

Parque de
los Estudiantes

5

3

4

Parque
de Baconao

Juan Clemente Zenea (Escario)

Información
Cultural

Plaza
de Marte

Parque
Rojo

José Antonio Saco (Enramada)

V. Betancourt

Heredia

Parque Iglesia

SANTA BÁRBARA

24 de Febrero (Trocha)

General Carlos Roloff (Celda)

General Francisco Peraza (Pizarro)

General Julio Sanguily

José A. Saco (Enramada)

Corona

Félix Peña

(San Pedro)

Lacret

(San Félix)

Pío Rosado

Casa de
Diego
Velázquez

B

Aguilera

H Ayuntamiento

Museo
Emilio Bacardí

Parque
Céspedes

Casa de
la Cultura

Casa Granda

2

Casa Granda
Calle Heredia

Museo del
Carnaval

Mariano

Catedral

Museo
Arquidiocesano

i

General

Casa de
la Trova

Casa de
J. M. de Heredia

Hartmann

Bartolomé Masó (San Basilio)

0   50 m

Museo
del Ron

HOTELS

Balcón del Caribe... 1
Casa Granda 2
Las Américas.......... 3
San Juan................ 4
Santiago de Cuba.. 5
Versalles................ 6

285

of survivors managed to find refuge in the Sierra Maestra. But they were the nucleus from which a determined guerrilla campaign developed; two years of fighting in the mountains were brought to a triumphant conclusion on 1 January 1959 when Castro stepped on to the balcony of Santiago's city hall and proclaimed the victory of the Revolution.

Old Santiago

*Allow half a day on foot for the area north of Parque Céspedes
and an additional 2hr for the Tivoli area.*

The core of Santiago consists of a trio of squares, Parque Céspedes, Parque Dolores and Plaza de Martí, and the busy streets between them.

Parque Céspedes (B3, detail D3)

Santiago's central square is small for a city of this size and it helps give the old town an attractive village-like quality. Once called Plaza de Armas and then renamed in honour of the "father of the country" the square is lined with the city's oldest buildings. Busy day and night, this is where Santiago's heart beats most strongly. Most foreign visitors are content to observe the comings and goings from the terrace of the Casa Granda hotel, but anyone wanting to make contact with the *Santiagueros* has only to sit down on one of the benches in the square and conversational partners will soon appear. Some will provide persuasive details of rooms to let or places to eat while others will simply want to practise their English.

The southern side of the square is occupied by the **Cathedral of Nuestra Senora de la Asunción** *(Open for mass daily at 6.30pm and Sunday at 8.30am)*. The cathedral stands on a raised platform occupied by little shops. It was originally built in 1522, the same year the city was moved to its new location. Originally aligned east-west, the cathedral was subjected to a series of earthquakes and fires and was realigned when rebuilding took place. Its last reconstruction dates from 1922. The main facade, neo-Classical in style, is flanked by towers framing an Angel of the Annunciation *(best seen from the terrace of the Casa Granda)*. The relatively plain interior has fine timber ceilings.

At the rear of the building, on the Calle General Lacret side, a flight of steps rises to the **Museo Arquidiocesano** *(9.30am-5.30pm; closed Sunday. Admission charge)*, the country's only museum of religious art, and an institution entirely independent of the state. Its lovely 17C interior with its timber vault contains a series of portraits of bishops from the 16C to the 20C, a crucifix rescued when Bayamo was burnt down, and scores by Esteban Salas, the father of Cuban music. Another room is devoted to paintings by followers of Rivera and Murillo Opposite the Casa Granda on the far side of the square is the **Casa de Diego Velázquez**⋆, the residence of Cuba's first governor, whose name it bears. Built in 1516, it is one of the oldest buildings in Latin America. Behind the sober façade with its Moorish-style wooden grilles is the **Museo de Ambiente Histórico Cubano**⋆ *(Open 9am 5pm; 9am-1pm Sunday. Admission charge)*. The museum's upper floor has a splendid array of furniture illustrating the way in which a distinctively Cuban style emerged from its Spanish origins, best exemplified by fine pieces dating from the end of the 18C when Luis de las Casas was Governor. Unlike the wooden grilles, the wall panelling and other carving is original.

J. F. Galmiche

Santiago's Cathedral
of Nuestra Senora
de la Asunción

On the ground floor are remains of the gold foundry installed here in the early days of Spanish rule, while on the far side of the courtyard is the entrance to a 19C building with furniture of the period as well as the original kitchen.

A clockwise walk around the square leads next to the **Ayuntamiento** (City Hall) with its restored façade. One of the first town halls to be built in the newly-discovered Americas, it was the seat of Santiago's first mayor, Hernan Cortés. It was replaced by a neo-Classical edifice in 1855, which in turn gave way to the present building *(not open to the public)*, erected in the 1950s to plans first drawn up in 1783.

Santiago's **Casa de la Cultura** is housed in the old Club San Carlos on the corner of Calle Aguilera and Calle General Lacret. All kinds of social activities take place in this old town mansion with its faded decor. There are exhibitions of contemporary art on the ground floor, while the upper storey with its splendid marble flooring is used for dances and concerts.

To the left of the exit from the Casa de la Cultura is the **Casa Granda Hotel** with a terrace overlooking Parque Céspedes *(See Making the most of Santiago de Cuba)*. It is open to non-residents and is a pleasant place to stop for a drink and take in the activity going on in the square.

Calle Heredia★ (B3, detail D3)

Running along the southern side of Parque Céspedes, this street is one of the liveliest in Santiago, especially on Saturday evenings. As night falls young people flock here from all over the city and such is the crush that it becomes almost impossible to fight your way through to the Casa de la Trova and the other establishments churning out the music for which Santiago is so famous.

About 50m from the Casa Granda, Calle Herida No. 206 is the home of a city institution with a nationwide reputation, the **Casa de la Trova★**. This is THE place in town to listen to local musicians performing either in the courtyard or in the room lined with pictures of famous faces from the Cuban music scene.

Just beyond Calle Hartmann (San Felix) is the **Casa Natal de José María de Heredia** *(Open 9am-9pm; 9am-1pm and 4pm-8pm Sunday; closed Monday. Admission charge)*. Now used for a range of cultural activities, this 18C mansion was the birthplace on 31 December 1803 of one of Cuba's greatest poets. As well as *Himno del desterrado* (Song of the exile), José María de Heredia was also responsible for *Ode to Niagara* which is considered by some to be the finest poem ever written by a Cuban. Every 7 May a literary festival pays tribute to Heredia and to his fellow-poet and patriot José Martí, both of whom died in May.

The museum is devoted to Heredia's work and to his activities as a seeker after Cuban independence which led to his exile in the United States and then in Mexico, where he died in 1839. His former home has a well-planted **patio**, with jasmine, myrrh, roses, orange trees, and a royal palm.

Santiago's Carnival

Beginning as a religious procession celebrating the feast day of St James (Santiago), Santiago's July Carnival is now more intimately linked with the city's African heritage, 25 July being the only free day of the year for slaves. From the early years of the 20C onwards the festival was organised by "comparsas", neighbourhood associations which replaced the old confraternities of the slaves. Festivities begin with a procession of flower-bedecked floats carrying local beauties. There follow five days of revelry, when the streets packed with people moving to the rhythm of the conga (improvised dances to the sound of drums), paseos (inspired by French orchestral music), and rumbas.

"Cabezones" at Santiago's famous Carnival

At the corner of Calle Pio Rosado (Carnicería) steps lead up to the **Museo del Carnaval**★ *(Open 9am-5pm; closed Monday. Admission charge)*. Visitors to this museum usually come away wishing they had booked their holiday to coincide with Santiago's famous Carnival. The story of Carnival is traced by means of photographs, press cuttings, models, costumes, banners, *cabezones* (giant papier mâché heads) as well as an array of musical instruments used in the procession; these include drums, tumbas (a long cylindrical drum), maracas and a kind of metal wheel used as a percussion instrument.

There are performances of traditional music everyday in the museum courtyard *(Sunday at 11am and from Tuesday to Saturday at 4pm)*.

Go down the museum steps and turn right into Calle Pio Rosado.

The colonnaded neo-Classical structure on the corner with Calle Aguilera is the **Museo Emilio Bacardí**★ (B3 detail D3) *(Open 10am-8pm. Admission charge. English-speaking guides)*. Devoted to the history of the province, this is Cuba's oldest museum, opened in 1899 by Emilio Bacardí Moreau, wealthy son of the rum merchant and the first mayor of Santiago following the end of Spanish rule.

The huge ground-floor hall houses an extraordinary array of objects of every possible kind, crammed together in the display cases without apparent rhyme or reason. There are 19C weapons, amphorae, musical instruments, pieces of pottery, an ancient camera, door knockers, daggers, a boomerang, machetes, pocket watches… Among the collection of cannons, revolvers and rifles are the thigh-pieces worn by General Antonio Maceo and the harness worn by his horse. The first floor is given over to an extensive picture collection. There are works by foreign artists (including works from the Prado) as well as by Cubans, and painters from Oriente are well represented.

The museum's lower ground floor is reached through an entrance on Calle Aguilera. The collections here supposedly represent the pre-Columbian era, but Egyptian statuettes, mummies and sarcophagi compete with items from South America, among them the horrifying shrunken head of a former enemy of the fierce Jivaro tribe.

Around Calle Aguilera (B3, C3)

A short distance along Calle Aguilera is **Parque Dolores*** a long and narrow square with a number of pretty 19C buildings. This is a favourite meeting-place for young people, even though the cafés here are tending more and more to favour a clientele able to pay in dollars. The restored buildings on the north side of the square house a number of new but often empty restaurants, in contrast to the crowds of locals and tourists crammed into the **La Isabelica** café opposite. Calle Aguilera runs into **Plaza de Marte**, the third square in central Santiago. First laid out in 1860 as a parade ground, it was the scene of many public executions during the colonial era. It was restyled in the 1940s.

One block before Plaza de Marte a left turn leads to the **Museo de Historia Natural Tomás Romay** (*Open 8.30am-5.30pm; 9am-midday Sunday; closed Monday. Admission charge*) on the corner of Calle Monsenor Barnarda (Cuartel de Pardo) and Calle JA Saco (Enramada). With sections devoted to world flora and fauna, the museum's collections are really intended for the benefit of students, but have a number of treats for anyone as yet unfamiliar with Cuba's natural history museums. There are fine examples of sponges, corals and *polymitas*, the brightly coloured snails whose habitat is the coffee tree. Among the many stuffed animals is an impressive specimen of a *tinglado*, a giant turtle. On the first floor, next to a lion and a Bengal tiger is a bone from a sperm whale caught off Punta de Maisí (the easternmost point in Cuba) in 1978. The displays of this pleasingly pedantic museum conclude with a herbarium, a selection of mineral specimens, and a section on earthquake prevention.

Go back to Parque Céspedes.

Tivolí** (A3)

From Parque Céspedes go along Calle Felix Pena, the street running along the right side of the cathedral. Turn right at the first junction into Calle Bartolomé Masó.

The French who fled from Haiti at the end of the 18C settled in this hilly area to the southwest of Parque Céspedes. Steep streets and tumbledown little houses make it one of the most picturesque parts of the city, with the laid-back atmosphere of a small town. Life proceeds at a measured pace; women with their hair in curlers climb the streets in stately fashion, past old men playing dominoes on the pavement and future baseball stars practising in the middle of the road.

At the corner of Calle Mariano and Calle Lino Boza the viewpoint known as the **Balcón de Velázquez** gives a superb **panorama**** over part of Tivolí, Santiago Bay and the mountains all around.

Continue along Calle Bartolomé Masó and turn left into Calle Padre Pico.

Calle Padre Pico* is a typical Tivolí street famous for its landmark **steps**. From the top of the stairway there is a fine view over the rooftops.

Turn right at the top of the steps and follow the curving road round as far as Calle Jesús Rabi.

The hilltop is crowned by an exceptionally fine 19C building, the former police headquarters. On 30 November 1956 this was the target of a determined assault by members of the 26 July Movement led by Frank País. It is now the **Museo de la Lucha Clandestina** *(Open 9am-5pm; closed Monday. Admission charge)* with displays telling the story of the anti-Batista struggle. The emphasis is naturally on the attack of 30 November 1956, which was timed to divert attention away from Fidel Castro's landing from the Granma.

At the top of a flight of steps, a short distance along the same street, between Calle José de Diego (Princesa) and Calle C García, is the **Casa de las Tradiciones**, where there are evening performances of good traditional music.

Go back towards the square and the Balcón de Velázquez and turn right into Calle Bartolomé Masó.

Next to the attractive bar-restaurant 1900 *(See Making the Most of Santiago)*, the **Museo del Ron** *(9am-9pm. Admission charge)* not only gives an account of how rum has been and is made, but allows visitors a taste of the product (6-year old Havana Club) at the end of the tour.

North of the city centre
From the Moncada barracks to the Santa Ifigenia cemetery
Allow half a day by car.

This part of Santiago may be less attractive than the old town but it has many mementoes of both the Revolution and the earlier struggle for independence. Rising over the corner of Avenida de los Libertadores and Calle General Portuondo, 500m from the Plaza de Marte, is the **Cuartel Moncada** (C2), the barracks which was the target of the failed attack on 26 July 1953 and which has subsequently become an icon of Revolutionary history. The bullet-holes on the outside were filled in afterwards by the Batista regime and have only been recreated since the Revolution.

Part of the fortress-like structure has been turned into a school, part into the **Museo Histórico del 26 de Julio★** *(Open 9am-5pm; 9am-1pm Sunday. Admission charge)*. The museum's displays of documents, photographs and models deal with the M-26 Movement and the anti-Batista struggle. Among the exhibits are the targets used by the rebels for shooting practice, some of their uniforms, and the vehicle used by Fidel Castro to make his escape.

In poignant contrast to the museum's many images of struggle and violence are the brightly-uniformed children playing happily in the school yard outside.

Part of the action on 30 November 1956 took place in the **Parque Histórico Abel Santamaria** (C2) on the far side of Avenida de los Libertadores, where some of Frank País's men had concealed themselves in the former Saturnino Lora Hospital before launching the attack. This was the very building in which Fidel Castro's trial had taken place on 16 October 1953. In the middle of the park is a fountain with the figure of Abel Santamaria, one of the attackers who was caught and tortured to death by Batista's police. There is also a museum, the **Museo Abel Santamaria** *(Open 9am-5pm; closed Sunday. Admission charge)* with displays evoking life under the Batista dictatorship.

From the northwest corner of the Parque Abel Santamaria drive 8 blocks along Calle Los Maceos to the junction with Calle General Banderas.

A building on Calle General Banderas between Calle Los Maceos and Calle José Miguel Gómez (Habana) is the **Casa Natal de Frank y Josué País** (B2) *(Open 9am-5pm; closed Sunday. Admission charge)*. The house contains some of the personal effects of these two brothers who achieved martyr status under the tyrannical Batista regime. The outstanding figure of the two was Frank, as it was he who led the assault on 30 November 1956 at the age of only 22. He was tried, released, but then murdered on 30 July 1957, a month to the day after his brother, who was also a member of M-26. Among the most impressive images in the museum are the photographs showing the crowds lining the streets as his funeral cortege proceeded from Parque Céspedes to the Santa Ifigenia cemetery.

Return to Calle Los Maceos and go west for 300m.

Calle Los Maceos No. 207 is a fine residence dating from the beginning of the 19C. It was the birthplace in 1845 of Antonio Maceo, who was to become one of the outstanding military commanders of the two wars of independence. The **Casa Natal de Antonio Maceo** (A2) *(Open 9am-5pm; closed Sunday. Admission charge)* pays tribute to the great man, who died in combat on 7 December 1896 at San Pedro de Punta Brava, to the south of Havana.

The museum has numerous mementoes of the wars of independence as well as some of the the personal possessions of the man who came to be called the "bronze Titan". As well as the flag used during Maceo's invasion of western Cuba, there is the printing press used to produce *Cubano Libre*, the paper which earned the epithet "the artillery of the Revolution". The two mango trees in the courtyard were planted to symbolise the spread of the struggle for independence from east to west. One is from Baraguá where Maceo denounced the terms of the peace treaty with Spain in 1878, the other from Mantua (Pinar del Río province) where his troops made their advance in 1896, the year after his return from exile *(See page 24)*.

At the end of Calle Los Maceos turn right and follow the line of the railway for 500m as far as Avenida Crombet. Turn left, then left again beyond the canal as far as the cemetery car park.

The **Santa Ifigenia cemetery**★ (A1) *(Open 8am-6pm. Admission charge)* is a vast necropolis founded in 1868, the resting place of numerous national heroes who died in the course of the wars of independence or during the Revolution. The graves of some of the most important figures, many of them from this part of the country, are decorated with the Cuban flag or the M-26 banner.

The **Emilio Bacardí Moreau mausoleum** is in the form of a pyramid, a reminder that this prominent member of the famous rum-distilling dynasty was also a Freemason. Another tomb is that of the mother of the Maceo brothers, **Mariana Grajales**, who is still referred to as "the mother of the Cuban nation". A **Veterans' Pantheon** in the form of a castle contains the remains of 11 of the 27 generals who died in action during the wars of independence. An eternal flame atop a column marks the **last resting place of Carlos Manuel de Céspedes**, the "father of the country", while a granite obelisk flanked by four palm trees rises above the tomb of **Pedro Figueredo Cisneros**, composer of the Cuban national anthem. There are a number of tombs of the martyrs of M-26, among them those of **Frank** and **Josué País**, draped with the Cuban flag and the banner of their movement.

But the most striking of all the cemetery's monuments is the **Mausoleum of José Martí**★. The "Apostle of Independence" is honoured with a great hexagonal tower pierced by arches which allow the light of the sun to fall on the tomb at all hours of the day. Each face of the tower has a caryatid, which between them represent

The statue of Antonio Maceo on Plaza de la Revolución

Cuba's original six provinces. Every detail of the mausoleum makes reference to an idea of Martí or to an episode from his life, and each of the 26 stone blocks on the outside of the tomb recalls one of his campaigns, including the fatal encounter at Dos Ríos on 19 May 1895 in which he was felled by a Spanish bullet.

Eastern Santiago: Avenida de las Américas (D1-2)

The Hotel Santiago de Cuba stands at the meeting-point of several of the city's neighbourhoods: to the east is the residential area of **Vista Alegre** with its many fine old houses, to the southwest the historic centre with its winding streets, and to the north Avenida de las Américas running ruler-straight to the edge of town. The brightly coloured and asymmetrical **Hotel Santiago de Cuba** was designed by José Antonio Choy, a young local architect. Completed in 1991 and 15 storeys high, it is an important landmark, a useful reference point for anyone exploring Santiago. There is a wonderful panoramic view of Santiago in its setting from the bar on the topmost floor.

The mound on the far side of the avenue from the hotel is known as the **Bosque de los Heroes** (Heroes' Grove). At its centre is a **monument** to Che Guevara and the comrades who died with him in Bolivia in 1967.

Two kilometres further along the avenue is the vast space of the **Plaza de la Revolución★** (D1). Able to hold a crowd of 200 000, the plaza has as its focal point a colossal equestrian **statue of Antonio Maceo★★**, his arm raised to urge his followers into battle. The 23 steel girders representing machetes are intended to evoke 23 March 1878, the date of the *Protesta de Baraguá* (*See page 24*).

The monument is built over the **Museo Holográfico** (*Open 9am-5pm; 9am-1pm Sunday. Admission charge*) which has a series a holograms depicting objects associated with the wars of independence. In 1984 the city of Santiago was granted the title of "Hero City" and awarded the Order of Antonio Maceo, and these decorations can be seen at the entrance to the museum.

Around Santiago de Cuba

Just beyond the city limits of Santiago and within range of a day trip lies one of the most fascinating regions in all of Cuba. The mountains stretch out on both sides of the city, to the west the Sierra Maestra (*See page 274*), to the east the uplands of the Gran Piedra. The beaches along this southern coast are not particularly attractive, but this is more than made up for by the other landscapes experienced along the way.

Castillo del Morro★ (south of A3 on plan)

10km from the city centre. Allow 2hr including a tour of the castle. Go in the direction of the airport for 7km, then follow signs to El Morro.

Originally called the Castillo San Pedro de la Roca, this splendid stronghold crowns the clifftop at the entrance to Santiago Bay and gives spectacular **views**★★ over the harbour, the Caribbean and the Sierra Maestra.

Built in the first half of the 17C, the fortress was ideally sited to ward off the frequent raids made by pirates, though in 1662 it was stormed and partly destroyed by the English adventurer Captain Henry Morgan. In the 18C it was rebuilt, and then, as the pirate threat subsided, converted into a prison. During the wars of independence it was here that many of the *mambises* captured by the Spaniards were incarcerated.

The fortress is now a World Heritage Site, and after half a century of neglect has finally been restored. Its labyrinthine interiors now house the **Museo de la Piratería** (*Open 9am-5pm; 8am-4pm Saturday and Sunday. Admission charge*), and its massive walls now guard displays of documents, pictures and weapons evoking the days when pirates sailed the Spanish Main. One room is devoted to the naval battle which took place when the Spanish fleet attempted to break out of Santiago harbour during the Spanish-American War.

Go back the way you came and after 3km take the left turn (the road sign for vehicles coming from Santiago points left to El Morro and right to Cayo Granma). Follow the road along the coast for 2km to the landing stage for the ferry to Cayo Granma. 20min trip with several intermediate stops. 10 pesos charge for ferry.

A few hundred metres away, the fishing village of **Cayo Granma** on its island in the middle of the bay could be a little paradise on earth. Unfortunately, spillage from nearby industries means that the waves that lap its shore are black rather than blue.

Basilica of Nuestra Senora de la Caridad del Cobre★

20km from Santiago, 2hr return including a tour of the church. Go along the Avenida de los Libertadores which joins the Carretera Central just beyond the Plaza de la Revolución (C1). After 16km turn left at the sign to "El Cobre" and continue for a further 4km.

The basilica is open from 6.30am-6pm. Daily mass at 8am, and additional services at 10am and 4.30pm on Sunday.

Every Sunday, the winding mountain road running west from Santiago is crowded with a procession of vehicles carrying worshippers to Mass; there are lorries sagging beneath the weight of hitch-hikers and extended families crammed into gas-guzzling limousines. Some of the vehicles barely make it up the steep grades, but eventually a miraculous apparition comes into view. This is the great Basilica of El Cobre, its three towers dramatically framed by the deep green of the luxuriantly forested slopes *(See illustration page 260).* The approach to the mining village of El Cobre (copper in Spanish) is lined with flower-sellers and children hawking chunks of fool's gold (iron pyrites), and the car park is full of souvenir merchants and would-be car washers. The basilica's great treasure is the statue of the **Virgen de la Caridad del Cobre** (Our Lady of Charity of El Cobre), who was declared patron saint of Cuba in 1916. The figure has long been the object of a passionate cult, not least because she was also identified with the *santería* goddess **Ochún** who presides over love, fresh water, and femininity.

The first sanctuary housing the statue was built between 1683 and 1710, close to the local copper mines. It was replaced by the present basilica in 1927 On the ground floor of the basilica is a chapel full of votive offerings brought here by pilgrims. There are crutches left here after miraculous cures, clothes, lockets of hair, letters addressed to Our Lady, photographs, baseballs and

S. Caron–Icone/HOA QUI

Our Lady of Charity of El Cobre
The cult's origin goes back to 1606, when three miners out fishing found the figurine of Our Lady floating in Nipe Bay on the north coast of Oriente Province. At the base of the figure was the inscription "Yo soy la Virgen de la Caridad" (I am the Virgin of Charity). The little statue was carried in procession across the island from north to south as far as the village of El Cobre, where it was placed in a hermitage.

footballs. Ernest Hemingway left his Nobel Prize medal here, but after being stolen and recovered, it is no longer on show. A stairway leads up to the *camarín*, a first floor chapel where pilgrims leave bouquets at the foot of the **statue of Our Lady of Charity** *(no photography).* The little figure is dressed in an elaborate yellow robe (the colour associated with Ochún) and wears a crown. When mass is celebrated she is turned to face the congregation assembled in the nave.

Parque de Baconao★ (Bacanao nature park)
90km, allow half a day.

This vast nature park covering an area of 800sqkm extends east of Santiago to the mouth of the Río Baconao. A designated UNESCO Biosphere Reserve, it takes in the mountains of the Gran Piedra range – part of the Sierra Maestra – as well as an attractive stretch of coastline. The park was provided with an array of visitor attractions at a time when the government was intent on developing domestic tourism, but most of these are likely to be of less appeal to the foreign visitor than the landscapes in which they are set.

Drive east from Santiago via the Hotel Las Américas roundabout and Avenida Raul Pujol towards Baconao (D2). 3km beyond the village of Sevilla (and 12km from Santiago) turn left at the Las Guásimas junction where a not very legible sign points to La Gran Piedra.

Five hundred metres beyond the turning, on the left-hand side of the road is the **Prado de los Esculturas** *(Open 8am-4pm. Admission charge)*. The "field of sculptures" extends over an area of 40ha, so it is just as well that it can be driven around as well as inspected more closely on foot. Scattered around are some 20 monumental sculptures in timber, metal, concrete and stone, the work of contemporary artists from Cuba and abroad. The "field" is grazed by cattle who pay as little attention to the artworks as they do to the egrets pecking away at their hide.

As the road begins to climb it is bordered by mango trees, *yagrumas*, and coffee bushes, which eventually give way to bamboo and pines as the temperature falls. Some 14km beyond the field of sculptures, the road arrives at the hotel at the foot of the **Gran Piedra**★. The 1 234m high mountain owes its name to the immense boulder perched on its summit, reached by 425 steep steps (US$1). From the **viewpoint**★ the panorama stretches over a vast area which extends – so it is said – as far as Jamaica and Haiti when conditions are right *(Often they are not. Clouds tend to form during the day, so it is best to make the ascent as early as possible)*.

Driving is difficult on the road beyond the Gran Piedra, especially after rain. After fleeing from Haiti in the early years of the 19C, a number of French coffee-growers settled in this area, and after 2km the road reaches the **Cafetal La Isabelica** *(Open 8am-4pm; closed when it rains. Admission charge)*, a former coffee plantation established by one of these exiled Frenchmen, and now a museum. The flat areas in front of the austere-looking house were used to dry the coffee. The ground floor of the building has displays on coffee-growing as well as the instruments of torture used to keep the slaves in order. Pregnant female slaves were given their punishment lying on a floor where a special hole had been made to accommodate them. There is also a photograph of Cuba's very last slave, who is supposed to have died in 1972 at the age of 132.

The panelled rooms on the first floor are where the owner and his family lived and still contain some original furniture.

Return to the hotel, and just beyond it turn right.

Anyone with the slightest interest in botany should go along the track leading round to the other side of the mountain and the **Jardin Botánico** (7am-4pm. Admission charge). This is a real garden of paradise, with not only Cuba's national flower, the mariposa, but exotic blooms creating a colourful pattern throughout the year.

Go back to the Las Guásimas junction and turn left towards the sea in the direction of Siboney.

For a couple of kilometres the road towards Siboney is lined with memorials commemorating the 26 rebels who lost their lives during or after the attack on the Moncada barracks on 26 July 1953. The **Granjita Siboney** *(Open 9am-5pm. Admission charge)* is the farmhouse where Fidel Castro and his comrades assembled before launching the attack. It is now a museum, with a number of

J.-F. Galmiche

Cayo Granma

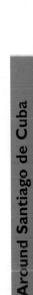
personal effects and full explanations of how the assault was prepared. As the invoice for their last meal reveals, the attackers stayed sober before setting out, consuming much mineral water but only three beers between them.

On the same road is a building housing the **Museo de la Guerra Hispano-cubano-norteamericana** *(9am-5pm. Admission charge)*. The museum was opened in 1998 to mark the centenary of Cuban independence and the end of Spanish colonial rule.

Two kilometres beyond the farmhouse is **Playa Siboney**. Lined with palms and backed by hills, it is a pretty spot, but the beach itself is nothing special. Nevertheless it is popular with local people, especially at weekends, and it is a convenient place to stop for lunch and enjoy sea views *(See Making the most of Santiago de Cuba)*.

The road continues southeastwards and, some 9km beyond the Las Guásimas junction, runs through the **Valle de la Prehistoria** (Valley of Prehistory) *(Open 8am-7pm. Admission charge)*. A huge artificial stone arch marks the entrance to Cuba's answer to Jurassic Park, with some 40 life-size concrete replicas of dinosaurs and other giant creatures from the prehistoric past. Frozen in fierce postures, they are ignored by the goats grazing at their feet, and will delight children (and most adults) of any age.

Two kilometres further on, the **Museo Nacional del Transporte** *(Open 8am-5pm. Admission charge)* has a collection of venerable Oldsmobiles, Lincolns and Cadillacs, as well as a stupendous array of hundreds upon hundreds of model cars.

On the right, 300m beyond the museums is the turning which leads to **Playa Daiquirí**, a sandy beach nestling between two hills, at the end of a hotel complex, and mostly patronised by foreign tourists. US troops landed here in 1898 in the course of the Second War of Independence. They seem to have taken to a drink much in favour among the local miners, a mixture of rum, sugar and water, and subsequently spread the name of Daiquirí wherever they went.

About 25km further on, just before the road reaches the Hotel Carisol, there is an **Aquarium** (*Open 9am-5pm; closed Monday. Admission charge*), where visitors are invited to take to the water with the resident dolphins. The paved road continues as far as the **Laguna Baconao**. The lake's attractions include boat rides or a visit to a small **crocodile farm** with its pleasant restaurant. The road deteriorates rapidly beyond the lagoon making further progress something of an adventure.

Making the most of Santiago de Cuba

COMING AND GOING

By air – The **Aeropuerto Internacional Antonio Maceo**, ☎ (226) 9-1014, is 8km south of the city centre, off the Carretera del Morro. In season there are flights to and from a number of European airports. Luggage and customs clearance can take some time. US$20 airport tax payable on departure.

There are several flights a day between Santiago and Havana and a flight most days to Baracoa and to Varadero. Transfer downtown by hotel bus (US$4) or taxi (around US$5 to Parque Céspedes).

By train – The **Terminal de Ferrocarriles** (A2) is close to the bay at the end of Avenida Jesús Menéndez. There are daily trains to most major provincial towns, and an overnight, air-conditioned train to Havana (journey time 16hr). There is an information service and a Ladis office where tickets can be purchased in dollars. Book the day before travelling or at the latest the morning before.

By bus – The **Terminal de Ómnibus Interprovinciales** (C1) is on Avenida de los Libertadores, close to Plaza de la Revolución. The **Viazul** tourist coach, ☎ (226) 2-8484, goes three times a week (overnight) to Havana, calling at major towns en route (single fare US$51, journey time 16hr). The other bus services are less reliable.

By boat – Sailors can tie up at the **Marina Marlin**, Carretera Turística, ☎ (226) 9-1446, Fax (226) 8-6108. 8km southwest of the city centre, opposite Cayo Granma, 30 berths, with drinking water, electricity, fuel, maintenance and repair facilities.

GETTING AROUND

By taxi – A 24-hr service is operated by several taxi companies, including **Transtur**, ☎ (226) 8-7000, **Cubataxi**, ☎ (226) 5-1038, **Taxi-OK**, ☎ (226) 5-2323, and **Pantaxi**, ☎ (226) 81-0153, and there are taxi stands in front of the hotels and on Parque Céspedes.

Owners of Ladas and ancient American saloons cars operate as clandestine taxis. There is of course no taximeter. Fares are payable in dollars. Reckon on US$2 between Parque Céspedes and the Hotel Santiago and US$15 for a day driving around the city and its surroundings.

Car hire – Despite the number of rental firms, vehicles are often in short supply and it is essential to book a car well in advance during the season.

Havanautos are represented at the Hotel Las Américas (D2), ☎ (226) 4-1388, and at the airport, ☎ (226) #9-1014.

Transautos can be found beneath the Hotel Casa Granda (B3, detail D3), ☎ (226) 8-6107, at the Hotel Santiago de Cuba, ☎ (226) 4-1121, at the Hotel Las Américas, ☎ (226) 8-7290, at the Hotel San Juan, ☎ (226) 8-7206, and at the airport, ☎ (226) 9-2245.

Micar are at the Oro Negro service station, at the corner of La Trocha (Avenida 24 de febrero) and the Carretera al Morro, ☎ (226) 2-2995.

Cubacar are represented at the Hotel Santiago de Cuba, ☎ (226) 8-7070, and at the Hotel Versalles, ☎ (226) 9-1123.

ADDRESS BOOK

Tourist information – The **Rumbos** travel agency is located opposite the Hotel Casa Granda on the corner of Calle Heredia and Calle General Lacret (San Pedro) (B3, detail D3). Their staff will provide information of all kinds about Santiago, and can book excursions to attractions in the surrounding area or to destinations further afield. The main hotels can also supply tourist information.

There is a **Cultural Information Bureau** at Calle Francisco Pérez Carbo No. 5 on the Plaza de Marte (C3). Open round the clock as a bar, it hosts music sessions and also provides information (including a weekly bulletin) about cultural activities in the city. This section is open 8am-midday and 1pm-5pm; 8am-midday Saturday; closed Sunday.

Banks / currency exchange – Money can be changed at the **Banco Financiero Internacional** (B3, detail D3), Calle Felix Pena No. 565 close to Parque Céspedes, 8am-3pm, closed at the weekend. The main hotels have a bureau de change.

Post office / Telephone – The **Correos** is on Calle Aguilera between Parque Dolores and Plaza de Marte. The **Centro telefónico** is by the Cathedral on the corner of Calle Heredia and Calle Felix Pena (B3, detail D3). All the main hotels have postal, fax and telephone facilities.

Medical service – The **Clinica Internacional** is situated close to the Hotel San Juan, at the corner of Calle 13 and Calle 14, Reparto Vista Alegre, ☎ (226) 8-7001. Consultations and treatment payable in dollars.

Immigration – The US$25 stamps necessary to extend your tourist card can be purchased at **Bandec** on Parque Céspedes at the corner of Calle Aguilera and Calle Lacret (8am-5pm except at the weekend). The **immigration office** is on the corner of Avenida Raúl Pujol and Calle 1.

Airline companies – The **Cubana** offices, ☎ (226) 2-4156, are on the corner of Calle J Saco and Calle Lacret (B3, detail D3)

Servicupet service stations – **Oro Negro**, on the Carretera Central 2.5km north of the Plaza de la Revolución. **La Bujía** (C1), corner of Avenida de los Libertadores and Avenida Céspedes in the direction of Plaza de la Revolución, **Trocha**, corner of Avenida 24 de Febrero and Carretera del Morro, south side. **La Punta**, Carretera de Baconao Km 25, close to the Museo del Transporte.

Other – The **Asitur** organisation, ☎ (226) 8-6128, by the Hotel Casa Granda, can help visitors from abroad with legal, insurance or medical problems.

WHERE TO STAY

Santiago's numerous hotels are relatively expensive. Visitors on a budget may find it preferable to look for accommodation among the growing number of private individuals offering bed and breakfast, particularly in the Céspedes area.

Under US$20

Sorangel Schmidt, Calle Corona No. 656, between Calle Heredia and Calle Bartolomé Maso, ☎ (226) 2-3182 – 4rm. ⌨ ▤ Close to the Balcón de Velázquez, this lovely colonial-era dwelling is owned by a genial young couple and has well-kept rooms, a patio and a terrace with a view over the bay.

Geovanni Villalón, Calle Heredia No. 353 between Calle Relaj and Calle Calvario, ☎ (226) 5-1972. Another fine house, with a spacious bedroom overlooking a verdant courtyard. Friendly reception. Additional guests can be accommodated nearby.

El Holandés, Calle Heredia No. 252 at the corner with Calle Hartmann, ☎ (226) 2-4878 – 2rm. ⌨ ▤ Close to the Casa de la Trova, these rooms are sufficiently high up to remain peaceful. There is a terrace, courtyard, and good cooking.

El Mirador, Calle Corona No. 603 altos between Calle Heredia and Calle Aguilera – 2rm. ⌨ ▤ The view from here equals that from the Casa Granda, the food likewise. Plainly furnished but comfortable. The family are convivial and are happy to act as guides.

Under US$50

Hotel Balcón del Caribe, Carretera del Morro Km 7.5, ☎ (226) 9-1011, Fax (226) 9-2398 – 96rm. ⌨▤ ✆ TV ⌣ 7km from the city centre, this hotel is located between the airport and the Castillo del Morro. It lacks charm, as do its rooms, but the setting is pleasant. Some of the bedrooms overlook the bay. Own transport advantageous.

Between US$40-70

Hotel Las Américas, corner of Avenida de las Américas and Avenida General Cebreco, ☎ (266) 4-2011, Fax (226) 8-7075 – 70rm. ⌨▤ ✆ TV ⌣ CC Car hire, bureau de change, tourist agency. This 1970s building is opposite the Hotel Santiago de Cuba close to the main residential area. The pleasant reception, the variety of facilities and the attractively refurbished rooms justify the recent rise in charges, and the hotel is still the least expensive in the city centre.

Hotel San Juan, Carretera Siboney Km 1.5, ☎ (226) 8-7200, Fax (226) 8-7017 – 112rm. ⁊ 🖃 𝒫 TV ✗ ⌇ CC Car hire, tourist agency. On the way towards the Parque Baconao, 500m beyond the zoo, a century-old building converted into a restaurant dominates a densely planted garden. Beyond are chalets with spacious and attractive rooms. This hotel is a good choice for anyone hoping for peace and quiet at a certain distance from town.

Hotel Versalles, Carretera del Morro Km 1, ☎ (226) 9-1016 or 9-1504, Fax (226) 8-6145 – 61rm. ⁊ 🖃 𝒫 TV ✗ ⌇ ⚬ CC Car hire, tourist agency. Hill-top location overlooking the road to the Castillo del Morro and the city. Spacious and comfortable rooms. Quiet, attractive surroundings. Prices reflect the range of facilities and amenities.

Around US$100

☺ **Hotel Casa Granda**, Calle Heredia between Calle San Pedro and Calle San Felix, ☎ (226) 8-6600, Fax (226) 8-6035 – 58rm. ⁊ 🖃 𝒫 TV ✗ CC Car hire, bureau de change. On Parque Céspedes, this fine neo-Classical building is the most centrally situated and the most charming hotel in Santiago. Some of the rooms are not quite what they might be; the best, with high ceilings and a view over the square, are on the upper floors. Breakfast is included, and is in the form of a well-stocked buffet. Because the hotel's accommodation is limited it is advisable to book well in advance.

More than US$100

Hotel Santiago de Cuba, Avenida de Las Américas between Calle 4 and Avenida Manduley, ☎ (226) 8-7070, Fax (226) 8-7170 – 302rm. ⁊ 🖃 𝒫 TV ✗ ⌇ CC Car hire, bureau de change tourist agency medical facilities. The tallest and most modern hotel in Santiago. The bedrooms are less striking than the building itself, but have all the comforts expected of this kind of international hotel. The best views are from the top floor. Largely business clientele. Several restaurants.

• **Parque Baconao**

The location of the hotels is shown on the map of Eastern Cuba page 263.

Because the beaches are within reach of a day trip from Santiago (between 25 and 50km away), these hotels cater more for tour groups than individual travellers.

Under US$20

Ovidio Gonzalez, Avenida Serrano alto, Playa Siboney, ☎ (22) 3-9340 ⁊ 🖃 Just a few steps away from the lively beach by a pharmacy, accommodation in nicely kept rooms or in a separate little house. Good food served in what used to be a paladar. Warm reception and jolly holiday atmosphere.

Under US$50

Hotel Costa Morena, Carretera Baconao Km 38.5, ☎ (226) 35-6126, Fax (226) 35-6155 – 115rm. ⁊ 🖃 𝒫 TV ✗ ⌇ CC Bureau de change. 45km from Santiago before getting to Sigua, this is an international complex with a saltwater pool compensating for the lack of a real beach. Full board not compulsory. The least expensive establishment at Parque Baconao.

Hotel El Colibri, Carretera de Baconao Km 9.5, ☎ /Fax (226) 8-6213 – 40rm. ⁊ 🖃 𝒫 TV ✗ ⌇ ⚬ CC A short distance beyond the Valley of Prehistory by the El Indio sign on the right, a road leads to an inlet with a sandy beach among rugged hills. The accommodation is in pretty chalets scattered throughout a well-wooded park. The mostly Canadian clientele seem to appreciate the nature trails in the surrounding area.

Motel Gran Piedra, Carretera Gran Piedra Km 14, ☎ (226) 5-1206 – 22rm. ⁊ TV ✗ The accommodation is in well-equipped little buildings overlooking the sea from the heights of the sierra. The air is fresh and the view superb. An ideal place for walkers (guides available for US$5 per day).

Around US$100

Hotel Los Corales-Carisol, Carretera de Baconao, Playa Cazonal, ☎ (226) 35-6122/15, Fax (226) 35-6116/06 – 166 and 144rm. ⁊ 🖃 𝒫 TV ✗ ⌇ ⚬ CC Bureau de change. 50km from Santiago, close to the Baconao lagoon, two hotels share the same beach of white sand. Arrangements are all-inclusive, with plenty of facilities and activities. The comfortable rooms all look out over the Caribbean.

Hotel Bucanero, Carretera de Baconao Km 4, Arroya La Costa, ☎ (226) 8-6363, Fax (226) 8-6070 – 193rm. ⁊ 🖃 𝒫 TV

✕ ⌁ ⚡ cc Bureau de change. 25km from Santiago, this tourist complex is on a little cliff-girt beach. Arrangements are all-inclusive, with a full range of recreational facilities. Currently undergoing renovation.

EATING OUT

Under US$10

Las Gallegas, Calle B Masó altos between Calle General Lacret and Calle Hartmann (B3). To the south of the square, a fine old interior lit by chandeliers makes an appropriate setting for savoury meat dishes.

Dona Nelly, Calle Pio Rosado between Calle S Hechavarría and Calle J B Sagarra (B2), ☎ (226) 5-2195. To the north of the Museo Bacardí, good meat dishes including rabbit in a particularly delicious sauce. The small room at the lower end of the terrace has a superb view. The lovely room above it can be rented.

Paladar Gilda, San Basilio No. 116 between Calle Padre Pico and Calle Teniente Rey (A3). A handful of tables set out along a corridor with walls covered in graffiti recall Havana's Bodeguita del Medio. Apart from this the setting is nothing special, but the food is perfectly acceptable and the portions generous.

1900, Calle San Basilio No. 354 between Calle Pio Rosado and Calle Hartmann (B3, detail D3), ☎ (226) 2-3507. Two blocks away from Parque Céspedes, the old home of the Bacardí family is now the best-known restaurant in Santiago. Some of the prestige of yesteryear has faded, and the main dining room is now rather forlorn, but the terrace is usually lively and has a fine view. It is at the very least a good place to enjoy a beer. The menu may be labelled in pesos but payment is in dollars and is still good value. The best dishes are probably those based on chicken.

Don Antonio, Parque Dolores (B3). Catering primarily for tour groups but often empty, this state restaurant is the most agreeable of the trio on the square. Fine fish dishes and an attractive courtyard.

Between US$10-20

🍴 **El Morro**, Carretera del Morro, ☎ (226) 9-1576. Midday-9pm. Clifftop location close to the Morro fortress, this terrace restaurant has a superb view over the Caribbean. The menu features creole dishes, and the establishment caters mostly for tour groups on their way from the fortress. Good food and generous portions. This is a good place for lunch or for a sundowner.

Casa Granda (B3, detail D3), ☎ (226) 8-6600. 11am-10pm. In the hotel of the same name, this chic restaurant is a reliable port of call in the city centre. The atmosphere is a bit starchy, but the cuisine is considerably more refined than in any of the other restaurants, whether state or private.

Zun Zún, Avenida Manduley between Calle 5 and Calle 7, ☎ (226) 4-1528. In the Vista Alegre area which is the equivalent of Havana's Vedado, high standard of international cuisine served in a series of intimate spaces. A good prelude to an evening spent at La Maison (*See "Nightlife" below*).

Kiam Sand, Carretera Punta Gorda, ☎ (226) 9-1889. Midday-9pm. A few steps from the Morro, chop suey with a Cuban flavour, in a carefully crafted Chinese setting or on a verdant terrace. Convenient for those staying in the southern part of the city.

• **Playa Siboney**

La Rueda, Playa Siboney, ☎ (226) 3-9325. 9am-9pm. High above the beach, fish dishes, prawns, and lobster (US$19).

HAVING A DRINK

Bars – The **Hotel Casa Granda** has a pair of good bars. On the ground floor, the tables set out on a terrace overlooking Parque de Céspedes are patronised almost entirely by an international clientele. The open-air top floor has a bar (to which a restaurant is to be added), with a fine view of the bay and the sierra.

On the top floor of the **Hotel Santiago de Cuba** (D2), the big windows of the **Pico Real** offer the very best view over the city in daytime, and there is an evening floor-show (10.30pm-2am). But the atmosphere is not particularly Cuban.

La Isabelica (B3), Parque Dolores. This bar occupies a fine colonial-era building on the square. It has a friendly atmosphere and is a good meeting place for both foreign visitors and local people. Open round the clock.

The Santiago branch of **La Coppelia** (C2), the ice-cream parlour which is a Cuban institution, is sited on rising ground close to the famous Moncada Barracks, at the meeting point of Avenida de los Libertadores and Avenida Victoriano Garzón. A 1970s setting for excellent ice-cream. Foreigners pay in dollars. Closed Monday.

Concerts – Music is king in Santiago, and sometimes it is enough simply to wander around and come across people making music spontaneously. However, no-one should leave the city without having spent time at the **Casa de la Trova** (B3, detail D3), Calle Heredia No. 206. Well-known and not so well-known groups make music here, beneath the portraits of august predecessors who have made the walls shake. Unlike similar establishments elsewhere in Cuba, this one is used to catering for tourists. In fine weather, performances are in the courtyard. There are concerts several times a day, from 10am-1pm, 3pm-5pm, 8pm-midnight, and the bar is open from 10am.

More intimate and still quite authentic is the **Casa de las Tradiciones**, Calle Jésus Rabí, between Calle José de Diego and Calle C García (A3). At some distance from the centre in the Tivoli area, it is worth coming here for the wonderful quality of the singers of *son*. Some tourists find their way here, but the clientele is mostly Cuban, a cross-section of society, and the atmosphere is lively, with plenty of incentive to take to the floor.

One way of ending an evening would be to seek out **Artex**, Calle Heredia, opposite the Museo del Carnaval (B3), where fine musicians fill the courtyard with good sounds. 10pm-late.

Much more touristy is the courtyard of **Los Dos Abuelos**, at the same location as the Bureau of Cultural Information (C3) on Plaza de Marte, Calle Francisco Pérez Carbo. Music from 10pm.

Night life – The **Tropicana**, autopista nacional km 1.5, exit 5, ☎ (226) 4-3036. Shows at 10pm and 1am, closed Monday and Tuesday. Admission between US$30 and US$45 according to where you sit. 2km north of Plaza de la Revolución, a lavish cabaret along the lines of its more famous namesake in Havana. The **Cabaret San Pedro del Mar**, Carretera del Morro Km 8, ☎ (226) 9-1287, adjacent to the Hotel Balcón del Caribe.

Similar show to the Tropicana but on a smaller scale and less expensive. Every evening except Tuesday at 10pm. Admission US$5.

La Maison, at the corner of Avenida Manduley and Avenida 1, is a branch of the Havana institution of the same name. It is housed in a fine mansion in the Vista Alegre residential area, ☎ (226) 4-2011. A few steps from the Hotel Las Américas, it stages a fashion show every evening at 9pm. On the whole, the models steal the show from the clothes.

One way of getting a closer feeling for the African and Haitian roots of Cuban music is to pay a visit to the **Casa del Caribe**, in the Vista Alegre area, at the corner of Calle 13 and Calle 8. The Casa organises the annual Caribbean Festival at the beginning of July. A little further along the same road is the **Casa de las Religiones Populares Cubanas**, a magical place in which to experience something of voodoo, santería, crusado, conga. 9am-5pm except at weekends.

Santiago has any number of cultural organisations, most of which devote their time to preparing for carnival. Some of their rehearsals are open to the public. The most famous association of this kind is the **Conjunto Folklórico Cutumba**, the headquarters of which is in Calle José A Saco between Calle Padre Pico and Calle Corona. Dance routines can be enjoyed on Saturday at 9pm and Sunday at 11am.

Discotheques – The hotel night-clubs have given way to more straightforward places. **La Claqueta**, on Calle Felix Pena opposite the Cathedral, which functions as a night-spot or puts on music in the open-air, and is much appreciated by local people. 10pm-2am. **La Iris**, on the corner of Calle Aguilera and Plaza de Marte, has opened up to visitors from abroad and puts on both Latin sounds and techno. 10pm-3am.

OTHER THINGS TO DO

Excursions – The various travel agencies like **Rumbos** opposite the Hotel Casa Granda, **Havanatur** nearby, **Cubanacan** opposite the Hotel Santiago, or **Cubatur**, behind the hotel, offer the same kinds of tours at more or less the same price. Cubanacan have a helicopter trip over the Sierra Maestra or to Baracoa.

Art / Culture – The *Casa de la Cultura* (B3, detail D3) or the *Galeria Oriente* next door, on Parque Céspedes, close to the Casa Granda (B3), stage exhibitions of the work of contemporary artists.

The *Galeria de Arte Universal*, Avenida de las Américas, to the rear of the Bosque de los Heroes (D2), has an interesting selection of works of art. 9am-5pm except Monday.

The *Uneac*, Calle Heredia No. 268 (B3), has exhibitions of work done by members of the association. 10am-6pm; 10am-2pm Saturday; closed Sunday.

The *Alliance Francaise*, at the corner of Calle 6 and Calle 11 (Vista Alegre) has views and classical music concerts every Friday at 6pm.

Theatres – The *Teatro José María de Heredia* (D1), founded in 1992, is located on Plaza de la Revolución, on the corner of Avenida de las Américas and Avenida de los Desfiles.

Cinemas – *Rialto*, Calle F Pena, close to the Cathedral; *Cuba*, Calle J Saco between Calle Lacret and Calle Hartmann.

Outdoor pursuits – There are baseball games at the *Estadio Guillermo Moncada* (D1), Avenida de las Américas halfway between the Hotel Santiago de Cuba and Plaza de la Revolución, ☎ (226) 4-1090.

Market – There is a little *agromercado* with fruit and vegetables at the end of Calle Heredia, to the west, and another, larger market at the end of Avenida 24 de Febrero, to the west.

Rum and cigars – The shop in the Museo del Ron, corner of Calle B Masó and Calle Pio Rosado (B3), sells good quality rum. 9am-9pm.

The *Fábrica de tabacos Cesar Escalante*, Avenida Jesús Menéndez No. 703 (A3) can be visited in the course of a tour organised by Rumbos, and cigars can be purchased.

Arts and crafts – The *Galería Santiago (Fundo de Bienes Culturales)*, to the left of the Cathedral (B3), has a selection of arts and crafts. 10am-6pm except Sunday.

The nearby *Calle Heredia* has a number of places selling wooden or papier-mâché items including fine carnival masks.

Bookshops – The *Librería Internacional* by the Cathedral (B3, detail D3) has the biggest choice of books, including books in languages other than Spanish. City plans. 8am-8pm.

Music – The *Tienda de la Música* (B3), Calle J Saco between Calle Lacret and Calle Hartmann, has CDs and cassettes of Cuban music. 9am-6pm; 9am-1pm Sunday.

Making the most of Santiago de Cuba

GUANTÁNAMO
Capital of Guantánamo Province
Pop 200 000 – 92km from Santiago
See map page 263

And remember...
Allow half a day for a visit to the US naval base.
Make arrangements in advance if visiting the naval base en route to Baracoa since
you must be accompanied by a guide (See Making the most of Guantánamo).

Leave Santiago on Avenida General Cebreco which leads to the A1 autopista. After 13km turn right off the motorway towards El Cristo and continue on the Carretera Central, following signs to Guantánamo. The Carretera Central turns into a motorway which enters the town from the north, 1km west of Plaza de la Revolución.

When not being serenaded, filmed or invaded by hordes of journalists, Guantánamo gets on without fuss with its own life as a provincial capital. It is a relative late-comer among Cuban cities, having only been founded at the beginning of the 19C, and its lack of conventional historical monuments has kept it off the normal tourist trail. But its name is known all over the world, not only because of the huge American base straddling the entrance to the bay, but because of the international hit *Guantanamera*, composed in the 1930s by Joseíto Fernández. Guantánamo itself is a workaday place, with little of the allure of the lady in the song. However, with horse-drawn traffic clip-clopping along the arcaded main street, recently renovated, and a virtual absence of tourists, the town has an air of authenticity not always found in more popular places. The days have long since gone when US servicemen flocked here from the confines of the naval base in search of rest and recreation in a characteristic Cuban environment.

The town
Allow 1hr30min

Guantánamo's handful of sights are in or close to the charming main square, **Parque José Martí**. In the centre of the square, near the late 19C **Church of Santa Catalina**, stands a statue in honour of General Pedro A Pérez, a local patriot. Facing the church is **La Indiana**, as good a place as any to down a *café cubano* while observing the comings and goings of the *Guantanameros*.

Calle Pedro A Pérez is Guantánamo's main street, usually thronged with people and with vehicles of one kind or another. There are a few shops opening off the arcades, together with the stalls set up by bookdealers. The **Palacio Salcines★** is one block north of Parque José Martí by the junction with the Prado. It is a striking structure from the 1920s, its dome topped by the figure of a female trumpeter. Her name is *La Fama*, and she is as much a symbol of Guantánamo as the *Giraldilla* is of Havana. The palace is now the home of the Centro Provincial de Artes Visuales, which puts on shows of contemporary art.

Turn left and walk one block along the Prado.

On the corner of the Prado and Calle José Martí, the **Museo Provincial** (*Open 8am-midday and 2pm-6pm; 2pm-6pm Monday; closed Sunday. Admission charge*) is housed in what used to be the town prison. Its displays tracing the history of the area from pre-Conquest times to the Revolution differ little from those in similar museums elsewhere in Cuba.

Eastern Cuba

Continue along the Prado for two blocks and turn right into Calle Ahogados which leads directly to Plaza de la Revolución. Allow half an hour on foot.

The view from the La Indiana café

J. F. Galmiche

The Soviet-style housing area 2.5km north of Parque José Martí is also the location of the town's only hotel and the **Plaza de la Revolución Mariana Grajales**. Dotted with memorials commemorating the heroes of Cuban independence, this vast space laid out in 1985 owes its name to the mother of Antonio Maceo. A concrete sculpture celebrates the woman sometimes called "mother of the nation" who numbered among her 17 offspring two national heroes, Antonio and José Maceo.

Guantánamo US naval base
40km to the lookout point – Allow 3hr
This visit can be combined with a trip to Baracoa

To leave Guantánamo go east along Calle Aguilera from Parque José Martí. Cross the railway and the Río Guaso. At the roundabout beyond the Servicupet service station turn right on to the Carretera Central towards Baracoa. After 23km a checkpoint on the right marks the beginning of the Cuban military zone of Boquerón from which the US base can be observed.

A rough road leads to the Malone observation post, 15km beyond the checkpoint.

Sited on both shores of the splendid natural harbour of Guantánamo Bay, the US naval base is off limits, but the **Malone observation post** gives visitors the chance to view the facility from a distance with the aid of powerful binoculars (*a morning visit is recommended to avoid looking into the sun*). A large model in the observation post allows the various parts of the base to be identified.

Before the Revolution more than 1 000 Cuban workers used to commute into the base. Nowadays a mere 20 or so make the daily crossing, veterans who started work at the base before 1959. Paid in dollars, they are rich by Cuban standards.

The Stars and Stripes have flown over the area since 1903, when the Platt Amendment gave the United States the right to intervene in Cuban affairs (*See page 25*). The Guantánamo naval base allowed America to control the approaches to the Panama Canal and to keep a foothold in Cuba itself. When the Amendment was abrogated in 1934, what had been a lease in perpetuity was changed to one of 99 years, expiring in 2033. This is far from soon enough for Fidel Castro, who frequently denounces the presence of US forces on Cuban soil as a flagrant and continuing example of American interventionism.

Stateside in the tropics
The American base at Guantánamo Bay covers an area of 117sqkm and includes training camps, two airstrips, and a town with a population of more than 7 000. The military personnel and their families live in a residential area complete with churches, supermarkets, cinemas, nightclubs…and the only McDonald's in Cuba.

While many Cubans undoubtedly see the base as an irritant, for others it represents a foretaste of the American dream. Regular attempts were made to cross into the base from the heavily guarded frontier area, and at the time of the mass exodus from Havana in 1994, Guantánamo Bay was transformed into a vast holding centre for refugees. The Clinton administration having abandoned its long-standing policy of admitting all Cuban asylum-seekers, some 20 000 *balseros* were detained at the base pending a solution to the crisis. Some of the escapees tired of conditions in the camp, and wished to return to Cuba, but ironically were prevented from doing so by the totally inflexible nature of the border. It was only in May 1995 that the two countries finally reached an agreement which permitted some three-quarters of the refugees to enter the United States.

Making the most of Guantánamo

COMING AND GOING

By plane – The *Aeropuerto Mariana Grajales*, ☎ (21) 32-4897, is 18km to the southeast of the city centre on the road to Baracoa. Cubana operates a daily flight between Guantánamo and Havana.

By train – The railway line between Guantánamo and Santiago has been cut and is likely to remain closed for some time. There is a replacement bus service.

By bus – The *Terminal de Ómnibus* is 5km from the centre of Guantánamo on the Carretera Central in the direction of Santiago. Daily bus services to and from Santiago, Baracoa and Havana. *Viazul* run a reliable mini-bus service which calls at Guantánamo on its way between Santiago and Baracoa.

HOW TO GET AROUND

The only hotel open to foreign visitors is 2km from the city centre. The easiest way to get into town is to use your own car and then explore on foot.

Car hire – The local *Havanautos* office is at the Servicupet service station, ☎ (21) 35-5405 *(See below)*.

Horse and carriage – This is the most popular way of getting around town. Fares are payable in pesos so have some small change ready.

ADDRESS BOOK

Tourist information – The Hotel Guantánamo has a tourist office.

Banks / Currency exchange – There is a branch of the *Banco Financiero Internacional* at the junction of the Carretera Central with Calle Calixto García, and a *Cadeca* branch on the corner of the Prado and Calle Calixto García.

Post office / Telephone – Postal services and international phone calls available at the Hotel Guantánamo. Post office on Plaza Martí.

Airline offices – The *Cubana* office, ☎ (21) 32-4533, is close to Parque José Martí at Calle Calixto Garcia No. 817 between Calle Aguilera and the Prado.

Servicupet service stations – *Via Azul* on the corner of the Prado and Avenida 6 Este to the east of Parque José Martí on the far side of the Río Guaso, on the road to Baracoa.

WHERE TO STAY

Under US$20
Osmaida Blanco Castillo, Calle Pedro Pérez No. 664 between Paseo and Calle N López, ☎ (32-5193) – 3rm. ⚫ 📺 Clean accommodation in an arcaded building on the main street.

Under US$30

Hotel Guantánamo, Calle Ahogados at the junction with Calle 13 Norte in Reparto Caribe 2km north of the city centre, ☎ (21) 32-6015 - 124 rooms ⏚⏛ ▤ ♬ 🖵 ✗ ⚊ Close to Plaza de la Revolución in an area dominated by 1970s apartment housing. The accommodation is functional and not particularly attractive but the hotel is useful as an overnight stop en route for Baracoa. A rather more cheerful alternative is the **Casa de los Ensueños**, a restaurant run by the hotel, which also has accommodation, in the form of three attractive rooms.

Villa La Lupe, Carretera del Salvador Km 2, ☎ (21) 38-2680 – 30rm. ⏚⏛ ▤ ☎ 🖵 ✗ ⚊ ☕ In a countryside setting to the northwest of the town, attractive chalet accommodation on the banks of a stream. Friendly reception, and the person in charge of PR speaks some English and is very helpful. This is the best place to stay in the area for anyone wanting peace and quiet and who has their own transport.

EATING OUT

Guantánamo's restaurants and paladares all have the same main dish, always at the same reasonable price (around 40 pesos or US$2).

La Cubana, corner of Calle Martí and Calle Flor Crombet.

1870, corner of Calle Pedro Pérez and Calle Flor Crombet.

HAVING A DRINK

Cafe La Inidiana has an attractive interior with wooden tables scattered around. The coffees on offer include "rocio de gallo" laced with rum, which can be sampled while watching a cigarmaker at work or looking through the wrought-iron grilles at Parque José Martí and the church.

OTHER THINGS TO DO

Excursions – A trip to the Malone observation post with its view over the **US naval base** can only be made in the company of a guide. Ask for Peter Hope, in charge of PR at the Hotel Guantánamo. He is normally available between 8am and 4pm and charges US$5 plus US$5 admission per person.

The **Tumba Francesa** stages Franco-Haitian shows, and 25km to the northeast is the **Zoológico de Piedra**, with a marvellous sculpture collection in a natural setting.

SHOPPING

Arts and crafts – The **Fundo de Bienes Culturales**, on the corner of Calle Aguilera and Pedro Pérez, has exhibitions of contemporary painting, as well as ceramics and items made from papier-mâché, wood and leather.

Making the most of Guantánamo

EASTERNMOST CUBA★
FROM GUANTÁNAMO TO BARACOA
Guantánamo Province
160km – 3 hours drive
See map page 263

Remember...
Check the brakes on your car before driving across the sierra.

More than any other part of Cuba, this easternmost extremity of the island has an extraordinary diversity in terms of both climate and landscape. After leaving Guantánamo, the road passes through banana groves which soon give way to grassland and sugar plantations. Then come the coastal foothills, their slopes scorched by the sun and swept by hot, dry winds, an arid scene made all the stranger by an abundance of cactuses. The road now turns inland to link the south of Guantánamo Province to the north. This section of highway over the conifer-clad Sierra del Purial is called **La Farola ("The Beacon")**; consisting almost entirely of hairpin bends, and often cantilevered out over the mountainside, it was only opened in the 1960s. The number of hitch-hikers encountered along the way are an indication of the inadequacy of public transport in the province. Other road-users include coffee-growers trudging along the edge of the highway, people riding donkeys, lorries grinding up the grades, and improvised vehicles of one kind or another coasting downhill wherever possible. Once over the summit, the road descends the northern slopes of the sierra through luxuriant tropical vegetation, in total contrast to the near-desert of the south coast. Finally the little town of Baracoa is reached, nestling among its coconut trees.

Follow signs towards the Guantánamo naval base. After passing through the military zone, continue eastwards on the Carretera Central.

About three kilometres past the entrance to the military zone, the farmland gives way to hilly countryside. The road is generally well-maintained, but caution is still needed because of the occasional pothole. Individual *bohíos* stand by the roadside, and after 13km the dwellings of **Yateritas** appear, albeit half-hidden among the banana groves.

About 5km beyond Yateritas the road becomes a true **coastal highway★★**, following a curving alignment at the foot of the mountains. The vegetation thins out and within a short distance the landscape has changed to one of semi-desert. The first of several fishing villages is **Tortuguilla**, its simple houses thatched with palm-leaves. Beyond the village stretches a splendid coastline with countless little inlets.

The most important settlement along the coast is **San Antonio del Sur**, about 19km from Tortuguilla, its main street bustling with all kinds of activity. Twelve kilometers further on, just beyond **Yacabo Abajo**, is the start of the most unusual section of the route; as far as the **Río Cajobabo**, a distance of about 30km, the slopes are studded with cactus. Not far from the mouth of the Cajobabo is **Playita de Cajobabo**, the beach where José Martí and Máximo Gómez made their historic landing in 1895 *(See page 24)*.

Coastline between Guantánamo and Baracoa

Five hundred metres on the far side of the river, the road turns inland towards the **Sierra del Purial**. Completed in 1964, and with parts of it carried along the mountainside on columns, this section of the highway goes under the name of the **Viaducto de la Farola** (Beacon Viaduct). The tale is told of the project manager being given permission to emigrate provided the road was finished successfully. It was certainly a demanding piece of engineering work, involving clearing the forest, cutting into the mountainside and running the carriageway on reinforced concrete supports for a distance of about 40km. Its completion meant that the town of Baracoa was at last linked to the rest of Cuba by land. Previously, all communication had been by sea. Beyond **Veguita del Sur**, 18km after crossing the Río Cajobabo, there are repeated signs warning motorists of the dangers that confront them when braving the endless bends through the sierra. But given a vehicle in reasonable condition, the Farola is no more dangerous than any other mountain road, and in fact its surface is in a better state than many of the island's highways.

Twelve kilometers of hairpin bends lead up to the **Mirador de Alto de Cotilla★★**, from where the panorama extends over the summits of the Sierra del Purial as far as the eye can see. From here it is downhill all the way to Baracoa, 30km away.

BARACOA*

Guantánamo Province
Pop 50 000
252km from Santiago de Cuba – 160km from Guantánamo
See map page 263

Not to be missed

Lingering over a cup of hot chocolate at the Casa del Chocolate.
Enjoying a musical evening at the Casa de la Trova.
Playa Maguana.
The coast road between Baracoa and Boca de Yumurí.

And remember…

Stay for two days to enjoy the surroundings of Baracoa.
Come equipped for the area's plentiful rainfall.

The La Farola highway enters Baracoa from the southeast and beyond Fort Matachin leads into Calle José Martí, the town's main street.

The luxuriant growth of its palm trees, the roofscape of rusty corrugated iron and the faded paintwork of every façade are eloquent testimony to Baracoa's abundant tropical rainfall. The elements have not been kind to Cuba's eastern-most town of any size and there is hardly anything left of the heritage of colonial times. With no overland link to the rest of the island for more than four centuries, Baracoa had to deal with its problems on its own. Hardly surprising, then, that it is utterly distinct from other Cuban towns of similar size.

Baracoa's isolation seems to have left its inhabitants prey to myths, legends, exaggerated claims, and the invention of fantastical characters. One of the latter is "Pelú", a hairy vagabond who appeared from nowhere at the end of the 19C and has been held responsible for everything unpleasant that has befallen the place since. Pelú still seems a living presence among surroundings which have something of the supernatural about them; the flat-topped mountain overlooking the town has metamorphosed into an anvil (*El Yunque*), while a curvaceous hill has become the Sleeping Beauty. And there is a river (Río Miel) flowing with honey (*miel* in Spanish), immersion in which guarantees a happy return to Baracoa.

"Small but First"

Local people firmly believe that Columbus made his first landfall here, at the Bay of Porto Santo just to the north of the town. However, while it is true that *El Yunque* has the same shape as the table mountain described in the great navigator's logbook, most authorities are inclined to identify it with the *Silla de Gibara* to the north of Holguín (*See p. 267*). The town's foundation has not generated the same amount of controversy. Established in August 1511, Baracoa was the first of Cuba's Spanish *villas*, just as claimed in the municipal motto: "I am the smallest but I will always be first in time".

The town

Allow 2hr including a visit to the museum

The simple plan of Baracoa on the back of the "tarjeta de huesped" (hotel guest card) will help you find your way around.

Baracoa can easily be explored on foot. The streets are laid out on a slightly bent grid pattern, with the main roads running northwest-southeast parallel to the waterfront. The majority of the tourist sights are on either **Calle José Martí** or

Baracoa

Calle Antonio Maceo. Baracoa is not a place where the foreign visitor can stroll undisturbed; even more than elsewhere in Cuba, sightseeing is liable to be interrupted by friendly hissing and invitations to take up lodgings or consume a contraband lobster in a *paladar*.

A trio of old forts have been converted into tourist attractions, and make useful landmarks as you move around the town. On a hilltop to the west, the **Fuerte de Seboruco** is now the El Castillo hotel, while to the northwest the restaurant in the **Fuerte de la Punta** marks the beginning of the 2.5km long **Malecón**. Hardly the equal of Havana's waterfront promenade of the same name, the Malecón is lined with buildings aged by over-exposure to salt spray. It runs for 2.5km before ending at the southeastern end of the town close to the **Fuerte Matachín**. This fort is now the home of the **Mueso Municipal**★ *(Open 8am-midday and 2pm-6pm. Admission charge)*, staffed by enthusiasts who are more than happy to share their encyclopaedic knowledge of Baracoa and its myths and legends with visitors.

The museum itself is also a fascinating source of information about the natural history of the region and its special features like the *Yunque*, a designated national monument, and the *Río Toa*, a UNESCO Biosphere Reserve. The area around Baracoa harbours Cuba's greatest variety of animals and plants; the museum has a display of samples taken from 98 of the 130 tree species which have been identified locally. There are also items evoking the way of life of the Taino people, a few of whose descendants still live in the region. In the 18C, a hundred or so French families came here from Haiti, bringing with them the expertise involved in coffee-growing, as well as more advanced techniques of sugar production. On show in the room devoted to the sugar dynasties they established, is the town's coat of arms, featuring the crown of Castile, a dog, the *Yunque*, a coconut tree and the Bay of Porto Santo. The final section of the museum celebrates local figures such as "Pelú", represented by the only portrait ever painted of him, and "Mima la Rusa" (Mima the Russian), daughter of a Tsarist general who came here in 1929 and in 1953 opened a hotel which is still in operation *(See Making the most of Baracoa)*.

Go along Calle José Martí towards the town centre, turn right after the Cubana office into Calle Ciro Frías, then right again into Calle Antonio Maceo.

Calle Antonio Maceo runs along one side of the **Parque Central**, the little triangular square dominated by the **Cathedral of Nuestra Senora de la Asunción**. Completely rebuilt at the beginning of the 19C, the cathedral's principal treasure is the famous cross known as the **Cruz de la Parra**★. This is thought to date from the 15C, the sole survivor of 29 crosses planted around the island by Columbus in the course of his four trips to America.

In front of the church is a bust of the native chieftan **Hatuey**, who preferred to be burnt at the stake and suffer eternal torment rather than convert to Christianity and go to Heaven where he would have to associate with Spaniards *(See p. 21)*.

About 200m further north, among the porticoed houses and shops of Calle Antonio Maceo, the **Casa del chocolate** is impossible to miss, if only because of the noise coming out and the crowds inside. This is the place to escape to when Baracoa suffers one of its frequent downpours, to try a cup of hot chocolate thick enough for the spoon to stand up in.

Excursions
See map page 263

West of Baracoa
Drive northwest on Calle Primera de Abril towards the Hotel Porto Santo and the airport and continue towards Moa.

The luxuriance of the vegetation around Baracoa is a reminder that the area has some of the highest rainfall in Cuba. Forest roads and unsurfaced sections of the main highway can cause difficulties during the rainy season, when use of a four-wheel drive vehicle is recommended.

About 2km after leaving Baracoa a sign points down a side road towards Finca Duaba. After 400m the track divides, the left turn leading to the foot of **El Yunque** (The Anvil), the flat-topped mountain overlooking Baracoa. Anyone wanting to make the whole-day climb to the summit should arrange for a guide at one of the hotels in town. The reward is a wonderful splash in the crystal waters of a mountain stream.

The right turn leads to **Finca Duaba**, a farmstead now mainly devoted to the sale of souvenirs to passing coach parties, though a guided walk around the grounds is worthwhile for anyone interested in native trees or in finding out more about how cocoa beans are grown and harvested.

Continue along the coast road towards Moa. After 1.5km the road crosses the Río Duaba then after a further 3.5km the much wider Río Toa. On the far side of the Toa the road is unsurfaced for about 10km.

Hidden away about 22km from Baracoa is the pretty little sandy beach of **Playa Maguana***, protected by a belt of coconut palms, the most beautiful of the area. The beach seems more or less deserted, apart from children trying to sell coconuts.

The beach at Maguana

B. Brillion/MICHELIN

Baracoa

There is a small restaurant helping to make a day's outing more feasible, while the charming hotel nearby (*See Making the most of Baracoa*) is an ideal place to retreat to for a day or two.

The road continues westward towards **Moa**, about 67km from Baracoa. Moa is a mining town, founded on the extensive nickel deposits in the area, and the smelter here bears the name of Che Guevara. One of Cuba's big dollar earners, it is definitely not a place that sets out to attract tourists.

Tibaracón
This is the name given to a natural phenomenon which occurs in the area around Baracoa and which is unique to Cuba. Sandbanks build up at the mouth of a river where it enters the sea, and divert its flow parallel to the shore to an outlet some distance away. Over time these sandbanks can become as hard as rock, but this does not stop them being swept away when the river is in flood. Once the flood is over, the sandbanks begin to form again.

East of Baracoa

Drive southeast out of town along Calle José Martí in the direction of the La Farola highway.

The excellent coast road running east from Baracoa passes through fine scenery, with the blue Atlantic on one side and the brilliant green of the tropical forest on the other. Extra splashes of bright colour are provided by the occasional little wooden dwelling among the palms and coconut trees. This easternmost extremity of the island is one of the remotest parts of Cuba, a real lands end, but there are still little touches like the red uniforms worn by schoolchildren to remind travellers of where they really are.

The beaches along this stretch of coast consist of grey sand. This does not stop local people thronging **Playa de Miel** just to the east of the town, or going a little further east to swim in the mouth of the **Río Miel**. Further on, the Río Yumurí offers a whole series of natural swimming pools, while beyond it are a number of fine beaches.

Turn left towards Punta de Maisí 2km beyond the Río Miel, continue for 7km to Jamal and turn left. The road rejoins the coast at Barrancadero.

Twenty-nine kilometers from Baracoa is **Boca de Yumurí**, a small fishing village stretching as far as the banks of the **Río Yumurí**.

Leave your car under the bridge or join a group from the Hotel El Castillo.

From here you are likely to be accompanied to the river by local folk eager to sell *polymitas* (prettily coloured snails) or just to talk. For US$1 a boatman will deposit visitors on the sandbanks in the middle of the river. It is possible to paddle (and even walk dryshod) along the bed of the river, which leads upstream for about 5km through a series of superb canyons. It is a delight to swim in one of the deep pools formed by the river.

On the far bank of the river the well-maintained road leads to Sabana, then deteriorates into an unsurfaced track which eventually arrives at La Punta.

COMING AND GOING

By air – This is probably the best way to get to and from Baracoa and is not particularly expensive. The view over the area from the plane is also something worth experiencing. The **Aeropuerto Gustavo Rizo**, ☎ (21) 4265280 is close to the Hotel Porto Santo, on the western shore of the Bay of Baracoa. There are three **Cubana** flights a week to Havana (around US$100), and one to Santiago (on Sunday, around US$20). In the high season, there are daily **Aerotaxi** flights to Bayamo and Santiago, except on Monday (at 7am).

By bus – The **Terminal de Ómnibus** is at the end of Calle Martí close to the La Punta fort. One bus every other day to Santiago and Havana. Since Baracoa has no rail link, the bus station is even more under siege than in other Cuban towns. There is also a **Viazul** service to Santiago, though bear in mind that it is a minibus with limited capacity. Book in advance.

GETTING AROUND

Car hire – The **Havanautos** office, ☎ (21) 4-3606, is situated between the airport and the Hotel Porto Santo.
By taxi – **Cubataxi**, ☎ (21) 4-3207. Taxis can usually be found outside the hotels.

ADDRESS BOOK

Tourist information – The Hotel El Castillo will provide information about the town and its surroundings.

Banks / Currency exchange – Both hotels have a bureau de change. Black market pesos are on offer from street dealers.

Post office / Telephone – Posting letters and cards and making international phone calls is best done at one of the hotels.

Airline office – The **Cubana** office, ☎ (21) 4-2171, is at Calle José Martí No. 181 between Calle Ciro Frías and Calle Céspedes close to the cathedral.

Servicupet sevice stations – **Cubacu** on the way into Baracoa.

WHERE TO STAY

See the map on page 263 for the location of the hotels.

• Baracoa
Between US$10-20
El Mirador, Calle Maceo No. 84 altos betxeen Calle 10 de octubre and Calle 24 de Febrero, ☎ (21) 4-2111 – 2rm. Living up to its name, this house has a view over the town from the western side of the square. Peaceful and well-kept rooms. Friendly reception.
Nancy, corner of Calle Frías and Calle Flor Crombet – 1rm. Next to the Hotel La Rusa, and with reason, since Nancy is married to the Russian lady's son. A sophisticated establishment.
Nelsy, Calle Calixto García No. 104 between Calle Rafael Trejo and Calle Frank Pais, ☎ (21) 4-3367 – 2rm. Close to the Hotel El Castillo and in a pleasant green setting, this is a quiet and peaceful place to stay. Acceptable rooms and friendly reception.
Lucy, Calle Céspedes No. 29 between Calle López and Calle Maceo, ☎ (21) 4-3548 – 4rm. To the east of the square, a substantial colonial-era house with a top-floor terrace for dining. Basic rooms.
Under US$30
Hotel La Rusa, Calle Máximo Gómez No. 161 at the junction with Calle Ciro Frías, ☎ (21) 4-3011 – 12rm. In a prominent seafront position on Baracoa's Malecón, the hotel was built in the 1950s by the daughter of a Tsarist general. "La Rusa" counted Castro and Che Guevara among her guests and the foyer is decorated with photographs taken by her. The rooms are simply furnished. Advance reservation necessary as the hotel is often fully booked.
Between US$30-50
Hotel Porto Santo, Carretera del Aeropuerto, ☎ (21) 4-3546 or 4-3590 – 63rm. Bureau de change, medical facilities. In a charming

park-like setting directly on the bay, the hotel consists of a number of separate buildings with good-sized rooms facing on to a terrace or tiny garden. The most attractive ones are those facing the sea. The hotel is close to the airport some 4km from the town on the far side of the bay, but given the frequency of flights into and out of Baracoa there is little likelihood of disturbance from aircraft.

&**Hotel El Castillo**, Calle Calixto García, loma del Paraiso, ☎ (21) 4-2125/47, Fax (226) 86-074 – 35rm. ⌂ ▤ ☞ TV ✗ ⚓ cc Bureau de change, medical facilities. This old fort on its hilltop site enjoys fine views over Baracoa and its surroundings. Rooms are comfortable and well kept; the best are Nos. 101 and 201 which overlook both the town and the bay. Within easy reach of the town centre, this hotel is the best choice for anyone without their own transport. Advance booking recommended.

• **Around Baracoa**
Between US$30-50
Villa Maguana, Carretera Baracoa-Moa, 22km from Baracoa, access difficult during the rainy season – 4rm. ⌂ ▤ ✗ ⚓. This little establishment on its inlet close to a sandy beach is an ideal place to stay for anyone wanting to get away from it all. The setting is compensation enough for the rather basic character of the accommodation. Book in advance at the Hotel El Castillo.

WHERE TO EAT

Baracoa has a somewhat different cuisine from the rest of Cuba, with a number of specialities which come as a welcome relief after the monotony of much of the country's food. One dish worth trying is the "ajiaco" (vegetable soup with meat and bacon) served in the Hotel El Castillo. Meals in private homes are also acceptable.

• **Baracoa**
Under US$10
&**La Colonial**, Calle Martí No. 123. An appropriately named establishment with tasteful decor. A pleasant setting for a full meal with generous portions. The fish is especially good.

Walter's Restaurant, Calle Rubert López No. 47, between Calle Céspedes and Calle C Galano. Small dining room plus outdoor terrace. Tasty food.
La Punta, Avenida de los Mártires, ☎ (21) 4-3335. Open 7am-10pm. Tasty creole cuisine can be enjoyed beneath a canopy in La Punta fortress at the end of Calle José Martí. The welcome is warm and friendly and weekend evenings are lively.

• **Around Baracoa**
Between US$10-20
Finca Duaba, Carretera Mabujabo Km 2, from midday-4pm. 6km from Baracoa, this farmstead has been converted into a visitor attraction for tour groups with meals served beneath a vast thatched roof. But individual travellers are also allowed to enjoy the carefully prepared beef country-style, with vegetables, fruit, and a hot chocolate to follow. There is an all-inclusive menu for around US$8.

WHERE TO HAVE A DRINK

Bar – The **Casa de Chocolate**, Calle Antonio Maceo between Calle Maraví and Calle Frank País. This big café is a social centre for local people and is almost always full. The speciality is a drink of hot chocolate accompanied by cakes. Check whether payment can be made in dollars.

Concerts – The **Casa de la Trova** is on the corner of Calle José Martí and Calle Ciro Frías close to the cathedral. Traditional music played by local musicians, mostly to an audience of local people, though any foreign visitor is made welcome. Traditional music can also be heard occasionally at the **Casa de la Cultura**, Calle Maceo No. 122.

Discotheques – **Las Terrazas**, Calle Maceo between Calle Frank Pais and Calle Maraví. A magical open-air venue for the youth of Baracoa to dance the night away to house or techno. **Las Noches de Prada**, on Parque Central next to the bar/restaurant at No. 485, has salsa as well.

OTHER THINGS TO DO

Excursions – *Gaviota Tours*, at the Hotel El Castillo, organise excursions to Yumurí, to the beach at Maguana and climbs up El Yunque. Individual travellers are advised to hire a four-wheel drive vehicle because the earth roads are often in a poor condition.

SHOPPING

Art Gallery – Opposite the Casa del Chocolate at Calle Antonio Maceo No. 120, the ***Casa Yara*** (Fundo de Bienes culturales) shows painting and sculpture by local artists as well as basketwork and other crafts. 8am-8pm, closed Sunday.

Coconuts

B. Brillon/MICHELIN

CUBA'S KEYS AND ISLANDS

Cuba has more than 1 600 keys and islands, strung out along its long coastline like a coral necklace. They are grouped in a series of archipelagos with evocative names like the Colorados, Jardines de la Reina, Canarreos... A rich wildlife has found a refuge on this constellation of keys, where mangrove swamps alternate with beaches of whitest sand. These are places where the modern world can be left behind, where relaxation rules, and there is nothing more demanding to do than to swim out through shoals of tropical fish to a coral reef.

THE ISLE OF YOUTH★
(ISLA DE LA JUVENTUD)

Municipio Especial (Special Municipality) Isla de la Juventud
Canarreos archipelago – Caribbean Sea
Area 2 200sqkm – pop 80 000
45min by air from Havana

Not to be missed
Sampling grapefruit wine in the Casa de los Vinos.
Exploring the deserted beaches of the southern coast.
Scuba-diving off the "Pirate Coast".

And remember...
Foreign visitors to the Island of Youth must have a valid passport.
For a short visit, it's better to hire a car on the island.
A diving mask will help you avoid the jellyfish!

Cuba's largest island, shaped like a comma, is part of the Canarreos archipelago which separates the Caribbean from the Gulf of Batabanó and the mainland. The Isle of Youth is largely flat, though in the north there are hills whose highest point is La Canada (303m). In this part of the island there are cattle pastures, citrus fruit orchards, as well as the extensive pine forests responsible for the island's earlier name – Isla de los Pinos (Isle of Pines). Cuba's most important marble quarry is here, and tungsten is extracted too. To the south, beyond the Ciénaga de Lanier (Lanier Swamp) with its numerous crocodiles, there are limestone plains bordered by mangrove swamps and fine beaches. This is a protected landscape, its coastline inhabited mainly by fishermen who catch lobster and collect sponges. Just offshore is a coral reef which stretches eastward to the Bay of Pigs, but the Isle of Youth's most spectacular reefs are to the west, in the Bay of La Siguanea. Here, an underwater world of amazingly varied flora and fauna makes for the best diving Cuba can offer.

The distance between Havana and Nueva Gerona, the island's capital, is only 140km, but tourism here is far less developed than on some of the smaller *keys*. Despite striking similarities to parts of the mainland, the Isle of Youth has an atmosphere which sets it apart, not least because of its own quite distinct and eventful history. The indigenous Siboney left sparse but highly significant traces of their presence here, while the pirates who used the island as a base left buried treasure and many a tall tale. After a long spell as Cuba's Siberia, a place of imprisonment or exile, the Isle of Youth was turned into a laboratory, where Revolutionary theory could be tested. All in all, the island's past is one of the main attractions for anyone who has begun to succumb to the fascination of Cuban history. But most visitors come here, less out of historical curiosity, than to enjoy the island's superlative diving and fishing.

Treasure island
At the beginning of the 20C cave paintings were discovered in the southeast of the island, evidence that the Siboney had lived here. But, two centuries before Columbus landed here in 1494, these hunter-gatherers had already left the island to settle elsewhere. The Spanish authorities failed to follow up Columbus's discovery, and neglected the island, which for two hundred years

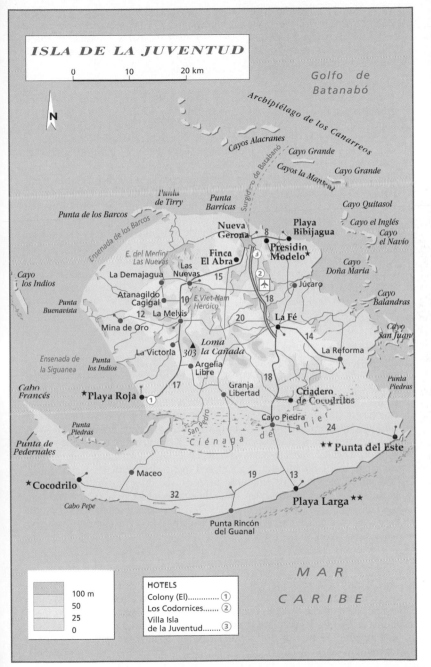

ISLA DE LA JUVENTUD

0   10   20 km

N

Golfo de Batanabó

Archipiélago de los Canarreos

Surgidero de Batabanó

Cayos Alacranes

Cayo Grande

Cayos la Manzana

Cayo Grande

Punta de Tirry

Punta Barricas

Punta de los Barcos

Cayo Quitasol

Cayo el Inglés

Ensenada de los Barcos

Nueva Gerona

8

Playa Bibijagua

Cayo el Navío

E. del Medio Las Nuevas

Finca El Abra

3

Presidio Modelo ★

Cayo Doña María

Cayo los Indios

La Demajagua

Las Nuevas

15

2

✈

Júcaro

Punta Buenavista

Atanagildo Cagigal

10

E. Viet-Nam Heróico

18

Cayo Balandras

Mina de Oro

12

La Melvis

20

La Fé

14

Cayo San Juan

Ensenada de la Siguanea

Punta los Indios

La Victoria

303 ▲ Loma la Cañada

La Reforma

Cabo Francés

★ Playa Roja

1

Argelia Libre

17

Granja Libertad

18

Criadero de Cocodrilos

Punta Piedras

Punta Piedras

San Pedro

Ciénaga de Lanier

Cayo Piedra

24

Punta de Pedernales

Maceo

19

13

★★ Punta del Este

★ Cocodrilo

32

Playa Larga ★★

Cabo Pepe

Punta Rincón del Guanal

MAR CARIBE

HOTELS	
Colony (El)	①
Los Codornices	②
Villa Isla de la Juventud	③

100 m
50
25
0

was a nest of pirates and buccaneers, well placed to intercept the heavily loaded Spanish treasure ships heading for home. A number of place names recall the days when the Jolly Roger flew over the island's Caribbean shore, and the Isle of Pines may well have served Robert Louis Stevenson as the inspiration for *Treasure Island* (1883).

Devil's island

The foundation of Nueva Gerona, the island's first town, marked a new and grim chapter in its history, this time as Cuba's principal prison. Many opponents of the Spanish colonial regime spent time on the Isle of Pines, among them the teenage José Martí, who was exiled here in 1870 for writing a note to a schoolfriend in support of the uprising which led to the outbreak of the Ten Years War.

The ending of Spanish rule did not lead automatically to the incorporation of the Isle of Pines into the new Republic of Cuba. For the first quarter of the 20C its status was in doubt; immigration of American farmers and pleasure-seekers was on a substantial scale and the island might well have become a dependency of the United States. But in 1925 it was formally recognised as part of Cuba, and a year later resumed its role as the national prison. The construction of a huge model penitentiary was ordered by president Machado, designed in line with the latest US thinking on modern methods of incarceration. The new establishment soon began to fill up with victims of the increasingly brutal and dictatorial Machado, but its most famous prisoners were the survivors of the attack on the Moncada barracks in Santiago on 26 July 1953 *(see page 283)*, including Fidel Castro.

Island of the young

By the time of the Revolution, the Isle of Pines had fallen well behind the rest of Cuba in economic terms. Castro's answer to the island's problems of under-population and underdevelopment was to recruit thousands upon thousands of young Cubans and foreigners and send them here in "brigades", in an ambitious experiment in communal endeavour and international solidarity. The country-side was transformed by new plantations, dozens of agricultural schools were founded, and clinics and hospitals were built. The intention was for the state to provide essential services without payment, until the island became self-sufficient. In 1978 the island was renamed the Isle of Youth.

This attempt to create a Communist utopia based on a new morality and the abolition of money is now over. But although numbers have diminished considerably since the glory days of the 1970s, students still come here from the countries of the developing world, particularly Africa, to combine academic studies with work in the fields.

Nueva Gerona

Spread out between two ranges of low hills, the Sierra de Casas and the Sierra de Caballos, and with only 40 000 inhabitants, Nueva Gerona seems less like a capital city than the suburb of some provincial town. There are not very many tourist attractions as such, but the place has a special atmosphere all of its own, an intriguing mixture of rusticity and cosmopolitanism, to which few visitors remain immune.

The town

Nueva Gerona is laid out on the same grid pattern as many another Cuban towns. The streets running south from the coast towards the interior of the island have odd numbers, the east-west streets even numbers. Activity centres on the main square, Parque Central, and the section of Calle 39 between Calle 20 and 28.

Parque Central is the heart of the town, the favourite hang-out of the town's youth. Anyone staying for more than a day or two in town will soon begin to recognise familiar faces.

On the north side of Parque Central the little **Church of Nuestra Senora de los Dolores** seems out of scale with the vast expanse of the square. The present building, in Spanish colonial style, was built in 1929 as a replacement for its predecessor, a 19C edifice destroyed by a hurricane.

On the opposite side of the square, the town hall houses the **Museo Municipal** (*Open 9am-5pm; 9am-1pm Sunday; closed Monday. Admission charge. Under renovation*). There are mildly interesting displays on the history of the island, but this cannot be said to be the most fascinating of the town's museums.

The section of **Calle 39** running north from the square seems permanently thronged with people and vehicles. Its arcades form the town's shopping centre; there are shoe-shine boys and little stalls dispensing Cuban fast food of various kinds, as well as restaurants with terraces which are a good place to sit and have a drink at the end of the day in the company of some of Nueva Gerona's numerous students.

Turn left into Calle 24.

On Calle 24 between Calles 43 and 45, the **Museo de la Lucha Clandestina** (*Open 9am-5pm; 9am-midday Sunday; closed Monday. Admission free*) has an array of documents, photos and other items relating to the guerrilla war leading up to the Revolution.

Return to Parque Central and go three blocks east along Calle 28 as far as the river.

Installed on the riverbank, and complementing a visit to the Museum of the Clandestine Struggle and the Model Prison, is **El Pinero**, the vessel which ferried Castro and his comrades back to the mainland after they had been amnestied and released from prison on 15 May 1955.

Go back the way you came and one block beyond Parque Central turn left into Calle 41 and go along it for 1km.

On the corner of Calle 41 and Calle 52 is the **Museo de Historia Natural** (*Open 9am-5pm; 9am-1pm Sunday; closed Monday. Admission charge*). Like most of Cuba's natural history museums, this establishment's collections consist mostly of stuffed animals and mineral specimens. But there are also reproductions of the cave paintings at Punta del Este in the south of the island, as well as a plane-tarium showing the night sky over the Caribbean.

East of Nueva Gerona

The road running east from Nueva Gerona leads to two of the island's most famous sights, the great model prison with its Revolutionary associations, and the beach of black sand of which local people are inordinately proud.

Drive east along Calle 32 towards Playa Bibijagua.

Four kilometers east of the town the Reparto Chacón road leads to the **Presidio modelo*** (Model Prison), one of the first high security prisons to be built in Latin America. Completed in 1931 during the Machado regime, the jail owes its fame both to its impressive architecture and to the imprisonment here of some of the future leaders of the country.

Rising from the flat grassy surface like great beehives, the prison's five circular buildings create an uncanny, almost surreal atmosphere. The central structure housed the administration while the other four contained cells capable of holding up to 5 000 prisoners. Parts of the prison are now used for storage *(and are officially closed to the public)*. The staff are usually able to show visitors the murals painted by prisoners on the walls of their cells – they include a planisphere and a portrait of St Barbara.

History Will Absolve Me

Tried for his part in the attack on the Moncada barracks in September 1953, Fidel Castro was allowed, as a qualified lawyer, to conduct his own defence. In a long statement made before the court on 16 October, he outlined the reasons for the failure of the attack, but above all used the occasion to expound his revolutionary programme. His speech concluded with the famous words: "Condemn me if you will. History will absolve me!" Castro worked on his manuscript during his enforced stay on the Isle of Pines; it was delivered, fragment by fragment, to fellow-revolutionaries on the outside, who were able to publish it in 1954. But it was only in 1958 that it really became the manifesto of the coming Revolution.

The administration building now houses a **museum** *(Open 8am-4pm; 8am-midday Sunday; closed Monday. Admission charge)*. Photographs and other documentary material trace the history of the prison from its construction along the lines of the State Penitentiary at Joliet, Illinois. Due mention is made of the many political prisoners who spent time here, as well as of the Japanese, Germans and Italians interned here during the Second World War.

The Presidio modelo on the Island of Youth

The second part of the museum deals with the Revolutionary struggle. To stop them influencing other prisoners, some of the men who had carried out the attack on the Moncada barracks were housed in the infirmary. Their names, notably those of Fidel and Raúl Castro, appear above their beds. Fidel had been sentenced to a term of 15 years, which he began on 17 October 1953. As Prisoner No.3859, it was here that he rewrote his famous declaration *History Will Absolve Me*. By the time he was amnestied on 15 May 1955, along with some 20 comrades, he had served 19 months of his sentence.

From the model prison it is a further 4km along the same road to **Playa Bibijagua**, a black sand beach named after the species of ant which plagues tobacco plantations. It is quite popular with local people but does not bear comparison with the lovely beaches elsewhere on the island.

Southwest of Nueva Gerona

Go south along Calle 41 towards La Demajagua. After 3km there is a sign on the right to Finca El Abra

A track leads through an attractive estate to **Finca El Abra** (*Open 9am-5pm; 9am-1pm Sunday; closed Monday. Admission charge*). This is the country residence where the exiled **José Martí** spent two months towards the end of 1870, before being deported to Spain because of his support for Cuban independence. The house is now a museum devoted to the memory of the "apostle of independence", though most of what is on show belonged to his hosts, the Sardá family. The huge *ceiba* tree in front of the house was planted subsequently, to mark Martí's departure from the island.

The southern part of the Isle of Youth

Allow a whole day
Take your own provisions and fill up with petrol in Nueva Gerona

Fantasies of spending a day on a desert island can be turned into reality by driving across the Isle of Youth to its southern shore. Here are superb beaches, in an area which, despite its short distance from Nueva Gerona, remains almost entirely unknown and is without visitor facilities of any kind.

Go east along Calle 32 and turn right on the far side of the river towards La Fé, then right again in 2km on to the motorway. After 14km turn left by a 1970s apartment block and continue for 2km into La Fé.

La Fé

With a population of 10 000, La Fé is the island's second largest town. There is not a lot to see here, but the town hopes eventually to recover its former reputation as a spa by building new facilities. To the south of the town centre is a park with the **Fuente de la Cotorra** (Parrot Spring). The island used to abound in parrots – one of its earlier names was Isla de las Cotorras – Parrot Island – but nowadays the only survivors seem to consist of a couple of caged specimens by the park-keeper's house.

Drive out of La Fé towards Cayo Piedra and in 12km turn left after crossing a bridge. Continue for 7km to the crocodile farm.

For anyone who has not had the opportunity of visiting a crocodile farm on the mainland, it may be worth making the detour to the **Criadero de cocodrilos** (8am-4pm. Admission charge). A guide shows visitors around the establishment, whose denizens (Crocodilus rhombifer – Cuban crocodiles) are kept in enclosures according to their age and size. Visitors should not wander around on their own, as some of the enclosures are not entirely crocodile-proof, and residents have been known to outwit the efforts of the keepers to keep them safely inside.

Go back to the main road and turn south. After 4.5km a check-point marks the entrance to the nature reserve.

The southern coastlands nature reserve*

Entry to the reserve is by permit only *(See Making the most of the Isle of Youth)*. Any complications in obtaining one are soon forgotten, once one is on the road through the mangrove swamps leading to the southern shore.

Twenty-four kilometers beyond the check-point, the pot-holed road terminates at **Punta del Este**** and its long and splendid **beach**** of white sand. For the time being this little bit of paradise is utterly unspoilt, but, inevitably, there are plans for luxury hotel developments.

Inland from the beach is the **cueva***, a cave also known somewhat extravagantly as the "Sistine Chapel of the Caribbean". The cave-paintings here are the work of the Siboney natives. They were discovered in 1910 when a ship was wrecked nearby, and were later studied by the famous Cuban anthropologist Fernando Ortíz. The pictograms in the main cave are in the form of red and black concentric circles. They may well have served as some kind of lunar calendar.

Return to the check-point and turn left.

In much better condition than the road to Punta del Este, this road leads directly to **Playa Larga**** (Long Beach), 12.5km from the entrance to the nature reserve. Just as deserted as the beach at Punta del Este, the glorious sands stretch out along the Caribbean shore for more than 15km.

From Playa Larga, go back the way you came for 4km and turn left on to the main road. In 12.5km there is a turning to the left for Punta del Guanal at the western end of Playa Larga. Stay on the main road, which continues for a further 31.5km to Cocodrilo.

The village of **Cocodrilo*** was founded in the 19C by fishermen who came here from the British colony of the Cayman Islands. They gave the place its name – Crocodile – in memory of where they had come from, rather than because of any crocodiles in the area. Some of the people living here are descendants of these *Caimaneros* and some of them still speak English.

The coastline here with its numerous inlets is magnificent, but the road west beyond the village is closed, and the only access to Cabo Francés is by boat from the El Colony hotel.

The southwest coast*

Allow a whole day for a diving trip

The seabed off the southwestern coast of the Isle of Youth is rich in brilliantly coloured coral, giant sponges and tropical fish. Many visitors to the island ignore Nueva Gerona altogether, and head straight for the Hotel Colony, 41km away.

From Nueva Gerona go south along Calle 41 towards La Demajagua. At the junction for La Demajagua after 15km, continue left on the main road, and follow signs to the Hotel Colony. Watch out for lots of potholes.

Intended as an exclusive retreat for wealthy Americans, the **Hotel Colony** on **Playa roja*** was completed in 1958, just in time to be nationalised in the aftermath of the Revolution. With its own palm-lined beach, it was for many years the only place on the Isle of Youth where visitors from abroad could stay. Still the only hotel on the Bay of La Siguanea, it has a well-equipped diving centre and is the starting point for all boat trips.

It takes two hours by boat from the Colony to reach the **"Pirate Coast"**★★ stretching between **Cabo Francés** and **Punta de Pedernales**, with its total of 56 named diving sites. One of its features is the *pared de coral negro* (wall of black coral), built up of dead coral.

COMING AND GOING

By air – The *Aeropuerto Rafael Cabrera*, ☎ (61) 2-2690, is 5km south of Nueva Gerona on the La Fé road. Cubana has three flights a day between Havana and the Isle of Youth (45min, around US$20). Seats (payable in dollars) are available on each flight for visitors from abroad but it is still advisable to book in advance. Allow US$5 for the taxi between the airport and the town centre and US$30 to the Hotel Colony. Weekly charter flights are operated by *Aerotaxi* between the island and Havana, Pinar del Río and Varadero. For the time being there are no flights to the *Aeropuerto Siguanea*, ☎ (61) 9-8282, close to the Hotel Colony.

By sea – There are several daily sailings between Surgidero de Batabanó on the south coast of Havana Province and Nueva Gerona. The ferry terminal is close to the town centre by the junction of Calle 31 and 22. Tickets (including crossing and transfer from Havana by bus) are available at the bus station near the Plaza de la Revolución in Havana, or at the ferry terminals at Surgidero de Batabanó, ☎ (61) 8-5355 and Nueva Gerona. The ferries have a number of seats reserved for travellers from abroad but it is advisable to book a place well in advance.

The *Kometa hydrofoil* makes two crossings a day. The trip lasts 2hr. The hydrofoil leaves Batabanó at 10am and 4pm, Nueva Gerona at 7am and 1pm (add an hour for winter sailings). US$11 one way.

On Wednesdays, Fridays and Saturdays, the *barco de pasaje* (ferry) leaves Nueva Gerona at 10am and Batabanó at 5.30pm (the crossing takes 5.5hr). US$7 one way.

Vehicles (US$20 one way) are carried on a special ferry arriving the following morning at Nueva Gerona. On the return trip, vehicles must be left at the terminal the day before your own crossing in order to avoid waiting the whole day at Batabanó. If you are only making a short trip to the Isle of Youth it makes sense to leave your vehicle on the mainland and hire a car on the island.

GETTING AROUND

By taxi – There are taxi stands for *Turistaxi* vehicles at the Villa Isla de la Juventud and the Hotel Colony. Visitors from abroad are only allowed into the nature reserve in the southern part of the island in a hire car or official taxi. The best way of travelling around the rest of the island is by private taxi, though this of course carries the risk of a fine for the driver.

Car hire – There is a *Havanautos* office, ☎ (61) 2-4432, in the centre of Nueva Gerona at the corner of Calle 32 and Calle 39, and a *Transautos* desk at the Hotel Colony, ☎ (61) 9-8281. Neither company has many cars, so book well in advance.

ADDRESS BOOK

Tourist information – The island's trio of hotels will help with ideas about what to do on the island, as will *Orosur*, Calle 37 between Calle 22 and Calle 24. 8am-midday and 1pm-5pm; 8am-midday Saturday; closed Sunday.

Banks / Currency exchange – Money can be changed at Cadeca, at the corner of Calle 39 and 20, and at the **Banco Nacional de Cuba** at the corner of Calle 39 and 18 in Nueva Gerona. There is also a bureau de change at the Hotel Colony.

Post Office / Telephone – It is better to take any mail back to the mainland and post it there. International telephone calls can be made from the hotels.

Airline companies – There is a **Cubana** office in Nueva Gerona, ☎ (61) 2-2531, at Calle 39 No. 1415, between Calle 16 and Calle 18. The **Aerotaxi** charter company is located at the Rafael Cabrera Airport, ☎ (61) 2-2690, and at the Siguanea airport, ☎ (61) 9-8282.

Servicupet-service station – Isla de la Juventud on Parque Central in Nueva Gerona at the corner of Calle 30 and 39. Fuel must be paid for in dollars.

WHERE TO STAY

A private room is the best option for anyone wanting to stay in Nueva Gerona. Reckon on a maximum of US$15 for a double room.

• **Nueva Gerona**
Under US$20
Marina Troncoso, Calle 35 between Calle 24 and Calle 22, ☎ (61) 2-4379 📶 📧 The best address in town, a handsome town centre house surrounded by a garden, with a well-kept interior, large guest bedroom, warm welcome.
Andras y Idalmis, Calle 24 No. 5305 altos between Calle 53 and Calle 55, ☎ (61) 2-4437 (next door). 📶📧 Well-kept, quiet rooms just to the west of the town. Idalmis is a qualified nurse. If the rooms are fully-booked, try next door at Marlen's.

• **Around Nueva Gerona**
Under US$10
Campismo Arenas Negras, Playa Bibijagua, ☎ (61) 2-5266 – 24 cabins 📶📧🍴 Surrounded by trees and close to the water, basic accommodation with cooking facilities convenient for the beach 6km to the east of the town.

Between US$20-30
Villa Isla de la Juventud, autopista Nueva Girona-La Fé Km 1, ☎ (61) 2-3290 - 20rm. 📶📧🅿️📺🍴🏊 In quiet surroundings 3km outside town, this is a small-scale establishment with a family atmosphere. The accommodation consists of chalets laid out around a large swimming pool which is the centrepiece of evening activities (discotheque during the week-end). Rooms are simply furnished but comfortable and each has a terrace.
Hotel Los Codornices, autopista Nueva Gerona Km 7, ☎ (61) 2-4981 – 40rm 📶📧📺🍴🏊 Close to the airport and to the hills, this is the same kind of establishment as the one above, though marginally inferior. Lively poolside atmosphere.

• **Playa Roja**
Between US$30-50
Hotel Colony, Carretera de Siguanea Km 46, ☎ (61) 9-8282, Fax (7) 66-6915 – 77rms. 📶📧🅿️📺🍴🏊🏊🆑 Car hire. In a remote spot on the island's southwestern coast, the Colony is known to scuba divers all around the world. The building dates from the late 1950s and is beginning to show signs of its age, but the rooms are quite acceptable and until more hotels are built this remains the best place to stay on the island. Wide range of sporting and recreational activities.

WHERE TO EAT

State-run restaurants are not the Isle of Youth's strong point, and visitors should take advantage of the island's paladares. The main item on the menu is likely to be the local speciality, lobster.

• **Nueva Gerona**
Under US$10
El Conchito, corner of Calle 39 and Calle 24, ☎ (61) 2-2809. From 2pm-midnight. Creole cuisine served in a spacious dining room. Most dishes feature that Cuban favourite, pork. The portico is a good place to enjoy a drink while observing the goings-on on Nueva Gerona's main street. Up above, there is a discotheque starting at 9pm.

Taberna Gerona (formerly the Corderito), corner of Calle 39 and Calle 22. From midday to 9pm. When the Corderito changed its name it also gave up its tasty mutton specialities for a much less varied and interesting menu. But its crowded terrace is still one of the liveliest places in town.

HAVING A DRINK

Bars – The most attractive bar in Nueva Gerona is the boat-shaped *Casa de los vinos*, a short distance from the main street on the corner of Calle 41 and Calle 20. This is the place to sample the orange or grapefruit wine, the speciality of the Isle of Youth. Open 2pm-10pm except Thursday.

Like other provincial towns Nueva Gerona has a *Coppelia* ice-cream parlour, on Calle 37 between Calle 30 and 32.

Concerts – The *Casa de la Cultura* on the corner of Calle 37 and 24 puts on occasional concerts, posted at the entrance.

Night-clubs – Two discotheques have a floor show before dancing starts: *El Patio*, Calle 24 between Calle 39 and Calle 37, 11pm onwards, admission US$3, has a better reputation than *El Chino*, Calle 26 between Calle 39 and 37, from 10pm, admission US$3.

OTHER THINGS TO DO

Excursions – There is restricted access to the nature reserve which covers part of the southern half of the Isle of Youth, and anyone wanting to visit the south coast must obtain an official permit from the hotels or *Havanautos*. Whole day hire of a guide to accompany you will cost around US$15. When applying for the permit make sure that all parts of the route are covered in order to avoid any delays at the various check-points.

Recreational activities – The Isle of Youth boasts superb scuba-diving, with more than 50 underwater sites off its southwestern coast. Equipment can be hired from the Hotel Colony which also offers diving lessons. There are boat trips every morning from the diving club to the offshore sites (US$15 for just the trip, US$90 for two dives with all equipment).

SHOPPING

Crafts – Nueva Gerona has a number of low-key craft offerings on Calle 39 between Calle 24 and Calle 26.

Art Gallery – The *Galería de Arte Gerona*, on the corner of Calle 39 and Calle 26 puts on shows of contemporary painting and sculpture. Closed Monday.

CAYO LARGO★★
Isle of Youth Province
Canarreos archipelago – total area 35sqkm
177km southeast of Havana – 45min by air

And remember...
Arrange accommodation in advance through a travel agency.
Take along your favourite mosquito repellent.

The last in the chain of keys spreading eastwards from the Isle of Youth, Cayo Largo ranks first among all the islands in the Canarreos archipelago for the quality of its beaches. With sand so fine and so white that it has been compared to talcum powder, the beaches extend for 25km beside the turquoise waters of the Caribbean. A further plus is that Cayo Largo has one of the best sunshine records in Cuba. The north shore of the island is bordered by mangrove swamps, a habitat for lizards, iguanas, and *jutías*, large rodents which are native to Cuba. And the rich birdlife includes flamingos, pelicans, and *zunzuncitos* (hummingbirds).

Long and narrow – *largo* in Spanish means long - Cayo Largo is almost too picture-postcard perfect. A wonderful hideaway for anyone hoping to find their own spot in the sun, its only disadvantage is the fact that a stay here gives very little of the flavour of the rest of Cuba.

The beaches★★
A two-wheeler is the best way of getting around Cayo Largo. Hotels will arrange hire.

Tucked away at the far western end of the island, **Playa Sirena** is well sheltered from wind and waves. Its proximity to the airport makes it the most popular destination on Cayo Largo for day visitors from Havana or Varadero.

To the east is **Playa Lindamar**, then **Playa Blanca**, Cayo Largo's longest beach with the majority of the island's hotels.

Cayo Largo

G. Alberto Rossi/ALTITUDE

Cuba's Keys and Islands

About 7km from the Villa Capricho, the last hotel on Playa Blanca, **Playa Los Cocos** owes its name to the coconut palms bordering the beach. The sea is shallow here, and the coral formations can be easily explored just using a mask and snorkel.

Cayo Largo's easternmost beach, **Playa Tortugas**, is where turtles come in winter to lay their eggs.

Making the most of Cayo Largo

COMING AND GOING

By air – Cayo Largo has an **International Airport**, ☎ (5) 79-3255, with direct charter flights from Canada and Italy. **Aerotaxi** and **Aerocaribbean** have daily flights from Havana and Varadero. Travel agents and hotel tourist information desks on the mainland can advise on day trips and short breaks to Cayo Largo.

By sea – The **Marina Cayo Largo del Sur** at the northwestern end of the island has 50 berths with full link-up.

GETTING AROUND

Car and bicycle hire - Transautos. ☎ (5) 33-3156 or 4-8172, can be contacted at the Hotel Isla del Sur.

WHERE TO STAY

AND WHERE TO EAT

Cayo Largo's hotels are grouped close to one another between Playa Lindamar and Playa Blanca. The advertised rates are expensive (more than US$100 per day for a double room with full board) and most stays here are made as part of a prepaid package. Italian visitors are in the majority, but a number of UK-based operators offer holidays on the island, including The Cuba Experience, 240 West End Lane, London NW6 1LG, ☎ (020) 7431 0670, and Captivating Cuba, 1st floor, Fraser House, 15 London Road, Twickenham, Middlesex, TW1 3ST, ☎ (020) 8891 2222. The first four hotels listed below are part of the same complex with a central reservations system, ☎ (5) 79-4215 or 4-8111, Fax 33-2108 or 4-

8201. They also have some shared facilities and activities like horse-riding, tennis, and watersports.

Villa Capricho – 60rm. 🛏️📺 ♦ TV ✕ ♨ CC With its little thatched cabins, this establishment is less luxurious than the other hotels but has a certain rustic charm. Guests have use of the pool belonging to the other hotels.

Villa Iguana – 114rm. 🛏️📺 ♦ TV ✕ ♨ CC

Hotel Isla del Sur – 62rm. 🛏️📺 ♦ TV ✕ ♨ CC Car hire.

Villa Coral – 60rm. 🛏️📺 ♦ TV ✕ ♨ CC These three establishments are typical resort hotels built around a swimming pool which is the focal point of the daily programme of events and entertainments.

Hotel Pelicano – ☎ (5) 119-5395 2105 to 07 or 4-8333, Fax (5) 119-5395-2109 or 4-8166 – 144rm. 🛏️📺 ♦ TV ✕ ♨ CC This is the most recent addition to Cayo Largo's stock of accommodation and the most luxurious, with all the facilities expected of a hotel in this category.

THINGS TO DO

Excursions – Trips to some of the other unspoiled keys and islands of the archipelago are organised by the hotels and there are also day excursions to Havana and Trinidad.

Outdoor pursuits – The hotels can provide mounts for riding along the beach as well as equipment for a whole range of waterbased activities including surfboarding, sailing, deep-sea fishing and scuba diving.

NOTES

NOTES

INDEX

Baracoa: place or attraction described in the text
Agramonte (Ignacio): individual
Balseros (crisis): term explained in the text
Glossary: practical information

Maps and plans

Manufacture Française des Pneumatiques Michelin
Société en commandite par actions au capital de 2 000 000 000 de francs
Place des Carmes-Déchaux – 63000 Clermont-Ferrand (France)
R.C.S. Clermont-Fd B 855 200 507

© Michelin et Cie, Propriétaires-éditeurs, 2000
Dépôt légal avril 2000 – ISBN 2-06-855201-9 – ISSN 0763-1383
No part of this publication may be reproduced in any form without
the prior permission of the publisher.

Printed in the EU 04-00/1
Compograveur: Nord Compo – Villeneuve d'Ascq
Imprimeur: IME – Baume-les-Dames

Cover photography:
Working in the "vegas". Ph. Beuren/SCOPE
Man on his balcony. J. Derei/VISA
Public telephone. P. F. Bentley - Time Magazine/RAPHO

Your opinion matters!

In order to make sure that this collection satisfies the needs of our readers, please help us by completing the following questionnaire with your comments and suggestions and return to:

Michelin Travel Publications   or   **Michelin Travel Publications**
The Edward Hyde Building   P.O. Box 19008
38 Clarendon Road   Greenville, SC 29602-9008
Watford, UK   USA

■ YOUR HOLIDAYS/VACATIONS:

1. In general, when you go on holiday or vacation, do you tend to travel...
(Choose one)

☐ Independently, on your own   ☐ With your family
☐ Independently, as a couple   ☐ With a group of friends
☐ With 1 or 2 friends   ☐ On organised trips

2. How many international holidays or vacations of I week or more have you taken in the last 3 years? _____

Last 3 destinations: Month/Year:

_____   _____
_____   _____
_____   _____

3. What do you look for most when planning a holiday or vacation?

	Not at all	Sometimes	Essential
Somewhere new and exotic	☐	☐	☐
Real experience/meeting people	☐	☐	☐
Experiencing the wildlife/scenery	☐	☐	☐
Cultural insight	☐	☐	☐
Rest & relaxation	☐	☐	☐
Comfort & well-being	☐	☐	☐
Adventure & the unexpected	☐	☐	☐

4. When travelling, do you take a travel guide with you?
☐ Always   ☐ Usually   ☐ Sometimes   ☐ Never

■ You and the Michelin NEOS guides

5. About your purchase of a NEOS Guide
How long was your holiday where you used the NEOS guide?
How many days? _____
For which country or countries? _____
How long before your departure did you buy it? How many days? _____

6. What made you choose a NEOS Guide?
Highlight everything that applies.

☐ Something new and interesting   ☐ Quality of the text
☐ The layout   ☐ Quality of the mapping
☐ Easy to read format   ☐ Practical Information
☐ Cultural details   ☐ Michelin quality

7. Which sections did you use most during your holiday or vacation?

Score 1-4   *(1 = least used)*   *(4 = most used)*

	1	2	3	4
"Setting the Scene"	☐ 1	☐ 2	☐ 3	☐ 4
"Meeting the People"	☐ 1	☐ 2	☐ 3	☐ 4
"Practical Information"	☐ 1	☐ 2	☐ 3	☐ 4
"Exploring ..."	☐ 1	☐ 2	☐ 3	☐ 4

8. How would you rate the following aspects of your NEOS guide?

Score 1-4   *(1 = Poor)*   *(4 = Excellent)*

	1	2	3	4
Cover design	☐ 1	☐ 2	☐ 3	☐ 4
Chapter Order	☐ 1	☐ 2	☐ 3	☐ 4
Layout (photos, diagrams)	☐ 1	☐ 2	☐ 3	☐ 4
Ease of reading (typeface)	☐ 1	☐ 2	☐ 3	☐ 4
Style of writing	☐ 1	☐ 2	☐ 3	☐ 4
Text boxes and stories	☐ 1	☐ 2	☐ 3	☐ 4
Plans & Maps	☐ 1	☐ 2	☐ 3	☐ 4
Star ratings system	☐ 1	☐ 2	☐ 3	☐ 4
Format	☐ 1	☐ 2	☐ 3	☐ 4
Weight	☐ 1	☐ 2	☐ 3	☐ 4
Durability	☐ 1	☐ 2	☐ 3	☐ 4
Price	☐ 1	☐ 2	☐ 3	☐ 4

9. Did you use other travel guides during your trip?   ☐ Yes   ☐ No

If yes, which ones? _____

10. Please give your NEOS guide a rating out of 20: ____/20 (with 20 as top rating)

Would you use a NEOS guide for your next trip?   ☐ Yes   ☐ No

If no, why not? _____

Which other destinations would you like NEOS to cover? _____

11. Any other comments or suggestions: _____

_____

_____

_____

_____

_____

_____

Surname/Last Name: _____ First Name: _____

Address: _____

Age: _____ Sex: ☐ M ☐ F

Profession: _____

Where did you purchase your NEOS Guide: What type of store?
                                             Which country?